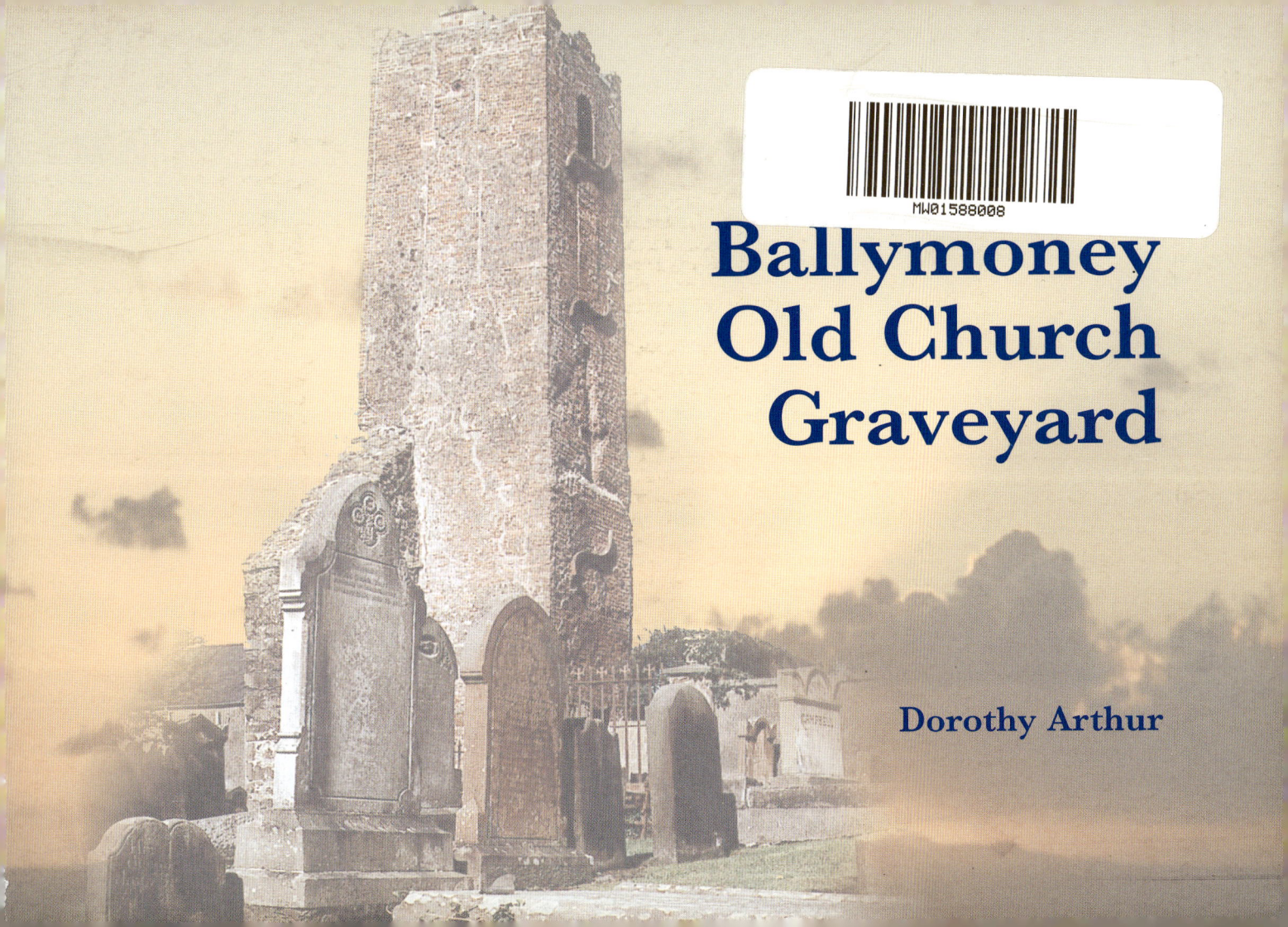

Ballymoney Old Church Graveyard

Dorothy Arthur

© Dorothy Arthur 2008

www.ballymoneygraveyard.com
dorothy@ballymoneygraveyard.com

A copy of the graveyard map is available on request from the author.

Designed & Printed by
Impact Printing, Ballycastle
Tel: 028 2076 2469

ISBN: 978 1 906689 08 7

Introduction

I grew up just outside Ballymoney and from an early age was always interested in family history. I kept notes of some of my conversations with my great aunts. My ancestors are buried in the Old Churchyard in Ballymoney and I have spent many hours reading the graves. When I got as far as I could with my own family tree I started helping others with theirs as I had accumulated a considerable amount of information on the families around Ballymoney. A few years ago, I thought it would be a good idea to publish my research and try to help other people looking for their Ballymoney ancestors.

Researching family history in Ballymoney

The Old Churchyard is cared for by Ballymoney Borough Council. Among their records is a map and headstone listing which has been of great benefit to my work. For consistency, I have adapted this map for the purposes of this book. Irish records tend to be poor due to the loss of so many in Dublin at the time of the troubles in the twenties. However, we are lucky in the Ballymoney area as some of the church records go back to the 1700s. In addition, we have the 1901 census, an 1803 agricultural census, 1825 Tithe Applotment records, 1859 Griffith valuation and street directories of 1824, 1846, 1856, 1864, 1905, and 1952. All these archive documents give valuable information for researchers.

Church Records

1st Ballymoney Presbyterian Church has part of an old Baptismal register from the mid 18th century. The records of this church were held in the house of Hugh Orr and the majority of them were destroyed in a fire. Rev. Robert Park kept very accurate records of baptisms and marriages of this church during the time of his ministry. He also carried out a census of his Congregation at the start of his ministry in 1817. It lists all the families with their children in order of birth, and where they lived.

    The records of St. Patrick's Parish Church are relatively complete and go back to the early 19th century. They include a book which list both the Presbyterian and Established Church (or Church of Ireland) burials from 1807 - 1825 in the Old Churchyard. From 1825 to present day, the Presbyterian burials are no longer noted. Baptisms and marriages are recorded also from 1807. There is also a census of the congregation taken in 1871. St. James Presbyterian Church has baptismal and marriage records from 1835 with a census of the congregation in 1837.

Unfortunately early records from Trinity Presbyterian Church are missing with only marriages from 1845 and baptisms from 1869. A fortunate discovery was records from the Unitarian Church in Ballymoney. This church no longer exists. As well as baptisms and marriages, there are several censuses of this small congregation and notes of members deaths and emigration.

George Millars's list
George Millar, who was born in Ballymoney in 1797, and lived there until 1837 when he moved to Belfast, compiled a list from memory in 1871 of the inhabitants of Ballymoney between 1804 and 1811. This is referred to Millar's list throughout the book.

The Graves
It is interesting that not all the graves in the Old Churchyard belong to people who lived in Ballymoney. There are Hunter and Moore families from Dunluce, with more of these Moore families also found in Kilraughts Old Graveyard. McKighan is another Kilraughts family. There is a Craig from Islandbuoy which is closer to Ballycastle, with no known links in the town.

There are over four hundred graves in the churchyard, many of them completely illegible and some partly readable. I have used different approaches and techniques to try and transcribe them. Many of the gravestones have been vandalised in the last few years. A 1960s survey of the Old Churchyard is included in the McClay collection, which is held in the Public Record Office of Northern Ireland (PRONI). The survey has been very useful although parts of it are missing. I have used church records to try and piece together a small history of each family as reading a list of inscriptions doesn't really tell much about the families, their lives and occupations. Some of the graves have only a name and no other details. This seems to be a trend of the trades families in the town. Not all graves were of wealthy people. It seems that some of these have been erected by their children who have emigrated and achieved success in their new lives overseas. There was an attempt to close the graveyard for any further burials in 1938, but this created some dispute and the last known burial was in 1975.

Sources used for local research
1660 Hearth Money Rolls
1740 Protestant Householders' Returns
1766 Religious Census
1803 Agricultural Census
1804-1810 Millers list
1825 Tithe Applotments
1859 Griffith Valuation
Old Graveyard Internment Register 1882- 1932
Street Directories
1901 Census

I can only apologise for any mistakes I may have made and welcome any additions and corrections. Most of my research has been done from records rather than hearsay from families. I have added as many family trees as possible. However many of them have been shortened due to limited space. There are variations of the spelling of surnames and townlands and spelling errors on the gravestones themselves. The name index states the names of the people mentioned in the text, but not in the family trees. I have more extensive research on many of the families and I am happy for people to contact me. The family trees are laid out in outline descendant form, with each number representing a generation. Marriages are indicated by + and a second marriage by *.

    I would like to thank my right hand helper Kathleen Connolly who has given me unbelievable help and assistance with this project. Thanks go to the Ballymoney Borough Council who have cleared many of the overgrown areas in the graveyard and allowed me access to their burial records, Keith Beattie at Ballymoney Museum for access to museum records, and Janet McCaughey, the Council registrar in Ballymoney for the cups of coffee while I have ploughed through marriage records. Finally, I am very grateful to all the ministers in Ballymoney and district for allowing me access to their records.

Ballymoney Old Church Graveyard
by Keith Beattie

Ballymoney, County Antrim, is a place that many travelers inadvertently overlook. Driving along the bypass, tourists could be forgiven for seeing no further than the pleasant bungalows which mark the edge of this expanding market town.

However, with a simple detour into Ballymoney, visitors will discover a town full of remarkable history. There are the majestic Assembly Rooms, now bank offices, built c.1760 by the Earl of Antrim to hold his grand balls during the Antrim Hunt. Or the old Town Hall, now the Masonic Hall, built in 1775 and most notably marked with a plaque to commemorate the clock tower from which two rebels of the United Irish Rebellion were hanged. A glance down Charlotte Street will reveal two rows of Georgian terrace houses that still retain much of their period character. In Townhead Street the busy Town Hall is the venue of Ballymoney Museum, the perfect place to begin your tour of the town. And, of course, there are the meeting houses, chapels and churches that testify to the faith and devotion of the congregations of Ballymoney in recent centuries.

Perhaps the most beautiful and historic place in Ballymoney is the Old Church Graveyard, opposite St. Patrick's Church of Ireland, at the top of Church Street. This graveyard is in the heart of the town and a busy road skirts the perimeter stone wall. Yet, within a few steps of the gate, visitors are instantly aware of the peace and tranquility of this ecclesiastical site. It is dominated by the ruins of the ancient parish church and benches are available for anyone who wishes to sit in contemplation. For those who wish to explore, there is plenty to fascinate the eager historian.

A place of worship
The landscape surrounding Ballymoney is rich with the evidence of centuries of human settlement in this area. Stone Age people populated the fertile land on the banks of the nearby River Bann, while early Christian raths and Norman mottes are scattered thoughout the ancient townlands.

The earliest mention of a church at Ballymoney is found in the records of the taxation of Pope Nicholas in 1306. In 1414, the church was dedicated to St. Mary and later this was changed to St. Patrick. The Ulster Visitation Book of 1622 stated that there was a ruined church in the parish. At this point in history, the population of the area was expanding fast with Scottish settlers establishing the new town which became the Ballymoney of today. In 1637, Sir Randall MacDonnell, Earl of Antrim, paid for the construction of the much needed church, and the red brick tower that can be seen today in the Old Church Graveyard is all that remains of this building. Within its ageing walls is a slab that reads "THIS CHVRCH VAS BYLDED TO THE GLORYE OF GOD 1637."

Tragically, early in 1642, soon after being completed, the church was burned by rebel armies along with much of the town during the Irish Rebellion. The church was rebuilt and survived as the parish church of Ballymoney until 1782.

Nevertheless, confusion surrounds some aspects of the church's history before 1637. According to the Ordnance Survey Memoirs for the Parish of Ballymoney, written in 1835:
"The graveyard contains no stone older than 1700. There is a very old one, however, in the wall...all the letters have been obliterated by the weather and storms. The graveyard was established a few years before the foundation of the church and has been used ever since by the Scotch settlers of the district. Previous to 1637 no ecclesiastical building of any kind stood at the site or near it."[1]

These statements are perplexing - the oldest headstone in the churchyard is, indeed, set into a wall, but it is a wall that was built a decade after the Memoirs were written. The headstone in question very clearly reads "Camac 1610". It strongly suggests a burial ground, and it may be argued a church, much longer than "a few years" before 1637.

Despite being a parish church, i.e. the Anglican Church or Church of Ireland, the majority of the early congregation were Presbyterian settlers from Scotland. They successfully secured the appointment of a Scottish Presbyterian clergyman, Reverend James Ker, described at the time as 'not young in years' but with a great reputation for 'honesty and zeal' though of 'little learning and no great judgement'. Ker was a controversial figure who refused to condemn the execution of Charles I in 1649 and who we can assume supported Oliver Cromwell's regime.

Despite his Presbyterian allegiance, Reverend Ker received a portion of the tithe, payable by all tenant farmers to the Church of Ireland clergyman responsible for the parish. In 1656, he is recorded as receiving an allowance from the Cromwellian Government of £120 per year. A few years later in 1661, after the monarchy was restored and King Charles II was crowned, Ker refused to conform to the strict new laws which enforced the Church of Ireland and the English Book of Common Prayer. In consequence, he was ejected and left for Scotland where he died shortly afterwards.[2]

The Church of Ireland clergyman who followed was Reverend James Watson and he was succeeded by John Dunbar (1673), Alexander Moore (1687), William Armar (1691), Philip Matthews (1694), Henry Reynell (1740) and Arthur Mahon (1752). Few of these clergymen would have actually led the worship at the church, as they were most likely absentees with a curate to adopt the duties required by a congregation. These included Reverend M. Cole (1693), James Bashon (1694), William Fletcher (1746), Laurence Grace (1768) and Lindsay Hall (1777).[3]

The road to an unholy row

For several decades, this was the only church in the town. Then, in 1690, the first Presbyterian meeting house was built and many of the families left to join the new congregation. St. Patrick's soon recovered and quickly began to prosper. In 1782, a new parish church was constructed nearby. The old church was vacated and passed into ruins, much as we see it today, although burials continued in the surrounding graveyard. The Ordnance Survey Memoirs record that in 1835 the tower still had "a steeple with a castellated top and a slated, conical roof resembling a spire". Nothing remains of this spire[4].

In the 1840s, with the old church derelict and in ruins, the graveyard itself came under threat. A new road was needed to connect Coleraine and Ballymena. The chosen route for this highway was straight through the churchyard, separating the crumbling church from its newer counterpart and cutting over the graves of many local families. Despite the outrage, the wishes of the townsfolk were over ruled and the proposed road was built. Those graves which rested in the path of the road were lifted, the bodies exhumed and re-intered.

The architect of this unholy act was a young engineer called Sir Charles Lanyon, destined to become famous throughout Ireland for such beautiful buildings as Queen's University in Belfast. Lanyon was a lay preacher in the Church of Ireland and it appears he used his influence and office to succeed where others would have failed.

Within 30 years, this road had further implications for the fate of the churchyard. In 1869, the Church of Ireland was disestablished and lost much of its influence and property. One consequence of this was that graveyards separated from their place of worship by a 'carriage highway' became the responsibility of the Board of Guardians, today's equivalent of a Local Government Authority or Council. For this reason, Ballymoney Borough Council carefully maintains this graveyard and the tower. It was through the Council's efforts that the Church Tower was restored with grant aid from the Heritage Lottery Fund in 1997.[5]

A tunnel under the town

It has always been assumed that there was an extensive tunnel that ran beneath the town of Ballymoney. It was purported to have served as a sanctuary if the town was attacked; or a passage which lead from a long forgotten castle to the church. Reports claimed that it ran from the Old Church Graveyard through to Main Street, and probably beyond. Local people talked of actually being down the tunnel as children and remarked on the considerable distance it seemed to travel in each direction. Yet such a tunnel had never been recorded on any map or historical archive.

An old report states that in 1845, the sexton was opening a grave near the old church when he fell into an underground chamber 'bearing the appearance of an old vault covered with a strong arch'. There he found a silver chalice, an earthen pitcher, a curious shaped hammer and a human skull. The human remains were reburied and the other items have since been lost.[6]

The Ordnance Survey Memoirs recorded the following:
"In the town of Ballymoney, and close to the old churchyard, it is said that a castle formerly stood. No information, however, can be gleaned as to the exact period of the destruction. It appears probable, however, that it took place long before the rebellion of 1641. The situation of the building was at the eastern side of the graveyard. One of the vaults is said to be still in existence, but covered over and concealed by graves and bones...."[7]

Perhaps the tunnel was a secret access to this castle or fortified building. There is other intriguing evidence in the "Jorney made by the Earle of Sussex, Lord Deputye [sic]". In July 1556, as the party traveled to Coleraine the following report is recorded:

"...also this day wee came to a Bishop's house, which was with a castle and a church joyned together in one, called Ballymonin, ye Bishopp McGenusi's house beeing Bpp. of Down and Conner [sic]"[8]

If it is assumed that this building was on the site of the current ruined church (although, as discussed earlier, this cannot be confirmed) it may also support the theory of an access tunnel.

Fortunately, confirmation of a tunnel's existence has been established. In c.1970, road engineers were working adjacent to the churchyard, building a new car park. As they were digging, they encountered a remarkable arched passage, three feet below the surface. The Clerk of Works at the time, Samuel Platt, surveyed the structure of the passage, photographed it and recorded his observations. These details were filed in County Hall, Ballymena, where, frustratingly, they have since been disposed of.

Mr. Platt described the passage, as can be seen in the illustration. It is unclear what function the gate served, if only to hinder pursuit through the tunnel. Due to the years of development and construction in the town, the tunnel had been blocked and filled in, preventing access for any great distance in either direction.

At about the same time, a similar structure was also briefly unearthed in Main Street. Wallace McNaul, then an employee of the Urban District Council, recalls coming across a passage or tunnel with a brick arched ceiling. It was assumed to be a sewer, and therefore not fully excavated, although Mr. McNaul believes it may possibly have been the tunnel. Further excavation throughout the town will probably be the only opportunity to explore this intriguing underground feature. Hopefully when it is next unearthed it will be possible to accurately survey, film and photograph the tunnel.

Burial records 1883-1932

One very valuable historical resource relating to the Old Church Graveyard is a ledger that records all the burials carried out between February 1883 and November 1932. The 1430 burials that took place in the graveyard over this period are listed with details including the individual's date of death, date of funeral, age, religion, occupation, where they lived, if they were married or single and, in some cases, the cause of death. Thanks to the voluntary efforts of my colleague Robert Thompson, all the information in this ledger has been recorded on computer database.

The book of burials provides us with some interesting statistical details. For example, the religious breakdown of the 1430 burials is as follows:

Religion Burials 1882-1932
Baptist 3 Church of Ireland 36 Covenanter [or Reformed Presbyterian] 9 Unitarian 29 Methodist 1 Protestant 182 Presbyterian 1106 Unrecorded 64

These figures must be considered in context with the fact that many local churches also had their own burial grounds by this period. Previous to the disestablishment of the Church of Ireland, tenant farmers paid a tithe to the local Church of Ireland clergyman and could chose to be buried in the parish churchyard. The vast proportion of the local population were Presbyterian and they still chose to inter their deceased family in a churchyard associated with the Church of Ireland, even at a time when other burial grounds were available.

The cause of death is also recorded for 552 of the burials. Of these, 248 died of debility [or old age]; 63 of consumption [or tuberculosis]; 14 were diagnosed as dying of cancer; others were diagnosed as dying of diseases of the head, brain, heart, chest, kidney, liver or leg; the records also include deaths by bronchitis, asthma, blood poisoning, brain fever, concussion, congestion of the brain or lungs, diarrhoea, dropsey, suffocation, and whooping cough; a few died of apoplexy [a haemorrhage]; only one of measles; one drowned, another died of indigestion, another of an overdose of laudanum; interestingly, between 1892-1893, there are also three victims of suicide buried in the graveyard. 73 individuals are listed as cause of death 'unknown'. The ages of the interred range from one day, to two people who lived to 104.

(Keith Beattie is curator of Ballymoney Museum and has been responsible for the Ballymoney Ancestry website).

"*Ordnance Survey Memoirs, Parishes of County Antrim V, 1830-5, 1837-8: Giant's Causeway and Ballymoney Volume 16*" Edited by Angélique Day & Patrick McWilliams, Institute of Irish Studies, Queens University of Belfast.

"*A short history of the Presbyterian Churches of Ballymoney, County Antrim*" A.H. Dill, J. B. Armour, D. D. Boyle, and J. Ramsay, Percy Lund, Humphries & Co. Ltd, Bradford and London 1898.

The Coleraine Tribune, 2 May 1984, "*My Ballymoney: The church which grew out of a bald spot*" by S. A. Blair.

"*Ordnance Survey Memoirs, Parishes of County Antrim V, 1830-5, 1837-8: Giant's Causeway and Ballymoney Volume 16*" Edited by Angélique Day & Patrick McWilliams, Institute of Irish Studies, Queens University of Belfast.

The Coleraine Tribune, 2 May 1984, "*My Ballymoney: The church which grew out of a bald spot*" by S. A. Blair.

Ulster Journal of Archaeology, Vol. 3, "*Antiquarian notes on Ballymoney, Co. Antrim*", James Bell, 1897.

"*Ordnance Survey Memoirs, Parishes of County Antrim V, 1830-5, 1837-8: Giant's Causeway and Ballymoney Volume 16*" Edited by Angélique Day & Patrick McWilliams, Institute of Irish Studies, Queens University of Belfast.

Quoted in "*An historical account of the Diocese of Down and Connor, Ancient and Modern, Volume IV*" Reverend James O'Laverty, 1887.

DRAIN

GRAVE no. 1

BURYING GROUND OF R. DRAIN

1 Drain
.... 2 James Drain 1778 - 1823
.... 2 Hugh Drain 1783 - 1853
.... +Anne Wilson 1800 - 1823
.... 3 Rebecca Drain 1820 -
.... 3 William Drain 1823 -
.... *2nd Wife of Hugh Drain:
.... +Nancy Donaghy
.... 3 Robert Drain 1827 - 1893
.... 3 John Drain 1829 -
.... 3 Jane Drain 1831 - 1884
.... 3 Martha Drain 1833 - 1848
.... 3 Joseph Drain 1841 -
.... 3 Hugh Drain 1835 - 1899
.... 3 Mary Drain 1842 - 1913
.... +James McKeag 1853 - 1933
.... 3 William Drain 1844 - 1892
.... 3 Henry McCay Drain 1849 -
.... 2 Robert Drain 1793 - 1858
.... 2 Martha Drain 1794 - 1871
.... 2 William Drain 1795 - 1886

    This is possibly the grave of Robert Drain who was buried on 16th September 1858 aged 65 years. He was a pensioner and a member of St. Patrick's Parish Church, Ballymoney. He lived in Roddenfoot, Ballymoney where his brother William was a farmer.
    His brother Hugh was a labourer and lived at Meetinghouse Street. He had married twice and had a large family. Other members of his family are buried in grave 417.

FLANIGAN GRAVE no. 2

In Memory
of
Samuel Flanigan
who died
The 17th February
1838
Aged 13 years
The tribute of a mothers affection
to the memory
of a beloved child
In the same grave with the son she loved
here lies Hannah Flanigan who died
June 17th 1868 aged 76 years

1 John Flanagan
.. +Hannah Culbertson 1792 - 1868
.... 2 Samuel Flanagan 1825 - 1838

The Flanigan (or Flanagan) family were farmers at Prospect. John Flanagan married Hannah Culbertson of Ballywattick in 1st Ballymoney Presbyterian Church in 1823 and he appeared to have only one child Samuel.

Hannah was the daughter of James Culbertson who had died before 1817. She had other children Martha and Hugh.

FLANAGAN

GRAVE no. 3

Here
Lieth the body of
Jane Flanagan
Who departed this life
17 Feb 1818 Aged 48
years. Also
John Flanagan
Late of Prospect
Who departed this
Life 16 January
1833 Aged 71 years

1 John Flanagan 1761 – 1833
.. +Jane 1769 - 1818
...... 2 Martha Flanagan
.... +William Robinson
.... 3 Thomas Robinson 1820 -
.... 3 Jean Robinson 1821 -
.... 3 William Robinson 1824 -
...... 2 John Flanagan
.... +see grave 2
...... 2 James Flanagan
...... 2 William Flanagan 1803 -
...... 2 Adam Flanagan 1807 -
...... 2 Ann Flanagan
...... 2 Nancy Flanagan
.... +Daniel Esdale

John and Jane Flanagan had at least seven children. Martha married William Robinson of Ballymoney. Nancy married Daniel Esdale of Booton in 1821 in 1st Ballymoney Presbyterian Church.

HENRY

GRAVE no. 4

In Memory of
John Henry, of Laney
Died 26th June 1924, aged 64 years
His son Robert
Died 11th August 1901, aged 3 years
His wife Mary E.
Died 1st March 1960, aged 86 years

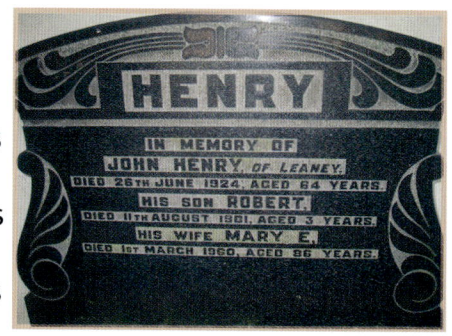

1 John Kennedy Henry 1860 - 1924
.. +Mary Eliza Michael 1873 - 1960
...... 2 William Kennedy Henry 1896 -
...... 2 Robert Henry 1898 - 1901
...... 2 Margaret Henry 1903 -
.... +John Townsend Woodrow 1905 -
.... 3 John Henry Woodrow 1935 -
.... +Isobel Florence Richmond
...... 2 Mary Eliza Henry 1905 - 1950
.... +Alexander Morrison 1903 - 1938
.... 3 Elizabeth Morrison
.... 3 Alexander John Evan Morrison

    John Kennedy Henry, a builder at Leaney, son of Matthew, married Mary Eliza, daughter of Robert and Mary (Townsend) Michael of Culduff, in 1895 in Garryduff Presbyterian Church.
    Their daughter Margaret married John, son of John Henry and Jane (Townsend) Woodrow.
    Their daughter Mary Eliza married Alexander Morrison of Ballymoney in 1935 in Trinity Presbyterian Church.

KENNEDY

GRAVE no. 5

Erected
To the Memory of
William Kennedy
Laney
who died 7th Jany 1879, aged 88 years
Also his wife
Mary
who died 2nd Sept 1879, aged 86 years
Also their son
James
who died 30th Jan 1893, aged 63 years
And their daughter
Margaret
who died 17th Octr 1896, aged 63 years
and their daughter
Jane
who died 25th December 1913
aged 76 years

William Kennedy had at least three children. James and Margaret did not marry. William married Jane, daughter of Matthew Smiley of Drumabest in 1864 in St. James Presbyterian Church.

John Henry of Leaney was witness to the deaths (see grave 4).

WILEY

GRAVE no. 6

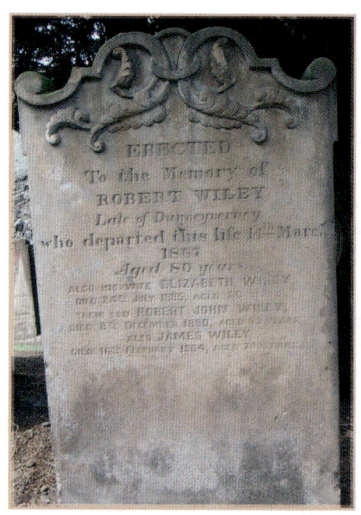

Erected
To the memory of
Robert Wiley
Late of Dunneyverney
who departed this life the 14th March
1867
aged 80 years
Also his wife Elizabeth Wiley
Died 24th July 1885 aged 80 years
Their son Robert John Wiley
Died 8th December 1890 aged 49 years
Also James Wiley
Died 18th February 1904 aged 74 years

 This Wiley (sometimes spelt Willey or Wylie) family were farmers in Dunaverney from the mid 1700s to 1904 when James Wiley left his farm to his sister, Maria Erskine, who passed it to her son Alexander. Robert was the son of John Wiley and had brothers and sisters, Sarah who married a McCurdy, Jean (b. ca. 1786 who married Joseph Wilson in 1806), Margaret (who married Malcolm McIlhargy in 1827), William (b. ca. 1800 who married Agnes McCurdy) and John (b. ca. 1803) who married Nancy Curry of Knockanavery in 1832.

 Robert was the only Wiley to remain at Dunaverney and married Elizabeth Stewart about 1826. They had family of James, a bachelor, who farmed at Dunaverney, Elizabeth who married John, son of William and Mary Cooper of Kilmoyle in 1862, Catherine who married John Shiels of Derrykeighan and Kilmoyle in 1852, Sarah Jane who married Robert, son of William and Rose Ann (Orr) Robinson of Tamlaght, Rasharkin in 1858, Robert John who farmed at Ballaghmore, Maria who married Adam, son of Alexander and Martha (Cameron) Erskine of Dunaverney in 1876 and Matilda who married Marshall Smyth, son of Charles and Ellen McMaster of Movenis, Garvagh in 1867. They all married in 1st Ballymoney Presbyterian Church.

WILEY

GRAVE no. 6

1 Robert Wylie 1788 - 1867
.. +Elizabeth Stewart 1805 - 1885
...... 2 James Wylie 1828 - 1904
...... 2 Elizabeth Wylie 1830 - 1917
.... +John Cooper 1804 - 1887
...............see grave 173
...... 2 Catherine Wylie 1832 - 1917
.... +John Shiels 1814 - 1894
.... 3 John Shiels 1854 - 1932
.... 3 Elisa Shiels 1856 - 1940
.... +Matthew McAfee 1826 -
.... 3 Margaret Shiels 1860 -
.... 3 Maria Shiels 1863 - 1889
.... 3 Catherine Shiels 1865 - 1916
.... 3 Robert Shiels 1868 - 1904
.... 3 Mary Shiels 1870 - 1914
.... 3 Matilda Shiels 1873 -
.... 3 James Shiels 1875 - 1887
...... 2 Sarah Jane Wylie 1834 - 1913
.... +Robert Robinson 1825 - 1875
.... 3 Robert John Robinson 1859 - 1906
.... +Nancy Crawford
.... 3 [1] William Orr Robinson 1860 - 1950
.... +[2] Maria Cooper 1865 - 1942
.... 3 Male Robinson 1864 -
.... 3 Elizabeth A. Robinson 1865 -
.... +John Speers
.... 3 Sarah Matilda Robinson 1867 - 1904
.... +Benjamin Brown 1864 -
.... 3 Maria S. Robinson 1871 -
.... 3 Rosetta Robinson 1872 - 1873
...... 2 Robert John Wylie 1837 - 1890
...... 2 Maria Wylie 1841 - 1932
.... +Adam Erskine 1826 - 1886
...............see graves 236, 237
...... 2 Matilda Wylie 1845 - 1873
.... +Marshall Smyth McMaster 1847 - 1923
.... 3 Mary Ann McMaster 1869 -
.... +Robert Elder
.... 3 Robert Wylie McMaster 1871 -

LILLEY

GRAVE no. 7

In memory
of
James Lilley
Late of Ballymoney
Died 10th Jul 1878
Aged 66 Years
Margaret, his daughter
Died 3rd Nov. 1844
Aged 7 years
Also his wife Margaret
Died 28th March 1885
Aged 74 years
Ellen Lilley
Died 21st January 1930
Aged 80 years

1 James Lilley
.. +Hanna Patton
...... 2 John Lilley 1805 -
.... +Jane Steen
...... 2 Samuel Lilley 1807 -
...... 2 James Lilley 1812 - 1878
.... +Margaret Cameron 1811 - 1885
.... 3 Margaret Lilley 1837 -
.... 3 Archibald Lilley 1839 -
.... 3 John Lilley 1843 -
.... 3 Ellen Lilley 1849 - 1930
.... 3 Alexander Lilley 1852 -
.... 3 Malcolm Lilley 1852 -
...... 2 Alexander Lilley 1814 -
...... 2 Ellen Lilley 1822 -
.... +James Gray
.... 3 Hannah Gray 1854 -
.... 3 Samuel Gray 1857 -

Most of the Lilley families in the area came from Drumaheglis, Drumahiskey and Eden townlands. In 1817, James and Hannah (Patton) Lilley were living at Gate end, in Ballymoney town. In 1817 there was a John Lilley in Ballymoney living with a daughter Jane whom I suspect were James's father and sister. James and his family were members of 1st Ballymoney Church but had moved to St. James Church by 1837.

John, James's eldest son married Jane Steen in 1836. Samuel was born ca. 1807, Alexander in 1814 and Ellen in 1822. James jun. married Margaret Cameron of Ballymoney in 1835 and had family of Margaret, Archibald, John, Ellen, Alexander and Malcolm. She was the daughter of Archibald and Margaret Cameron of Ballymoney (see graves 8, 9). All the family seem to have left the area apart from Ellen who died in Ballycastle in 1930. James was recorded as a spirit merchant in 1846 in Cameron Place, Ballymoney.

CAMERON

GRAVE no. 8

Underneath lie the remains of
Archibald Cameron
late of Ballymoney
who departed this life 27th April
1810 aged 36 years
Also
The remains of
Margaret Cameron
His wife who departed this life
9th March 1855 aged 77 years
Their grandson
James Cameron
of Fassifern
Born 21st April 1840 died 21st Aug 1922

Malcolm Cameron
.. +Jane 1727 - 1822
...... 2 Archibald Cameron 1774 - 1810
.... +Margaret 1778 - 1855
.... 3 Esther Cameron
.... 3 Flora Cameron 1800 -
.... 3 Malcolm Cameron 1802 -
.... 3 Jean Cameron 1804 -
.... 3 James Cameron 1808 - 1886
.... +Ellen Cameron 1812 - 1850
.... see grave 8
.... 3 Margaret Cameron 1811 - 1885
.... +James Lilley 1812 - 1878
.... see grave 6
...... 2 Nelly Cameron 1759 -
...... 2 Charles Cameron
...... 2 Malcolm Cameron 1789 - 1840
.... +Jane Speers 1787 -
.... 3 John Cameron 1807 -
.... 3 Malcolm Cameron 1808 -
.... 3 Archibald Cameron 1809 - 1890
.... 3 Jane Cameron 1811 - 1867
.... 3 Mary Cameron 1814 - 1892
.... 3 Daniel Cameron 1817 -
.... 3 Anna Bell Cameron 1819 -
.... 3 Charles Cameron 1821 - 1902
.... 3 Rachael Cameron 1824 - 1901
.... 3 Elizabeth Cameron 1827 -
...... 2 James Cameron 1776 - 1866
.... +Margaret 1778 - 1836

Archibald Cameron was a carpenter in Church Street, Ballymoney and two of his children are known to have married (see graves 6, 8).

His brother Malcolm married Jane Speers of Ballymoney in Scotland and emigrated to Ohio, where another brother James was already a farmer.

CAMERON

GRAVE no. 9

Sacred to the memory of
Ellen
Wife of James Cameron of Ballymoney
who departed this life 24th September 1856
Aged 38 years
Their son Daniel Cameron
Died 9th December 1864 aged 26 years
Their daughter Margaret Cameron
died 17th October 1869 aged 24 years
Also their son Archibald Cameron
Died 12 November 1878 aged 41 years
The above named Archibald Cameron
Died 6th August 1886 aged 78 years
Also their daughter Ellen
wife of Rev. William Wallace
Died Jul 1890 aged 46 years

Daniel and Malcolm Cameron, members of a Scottish clan were driven from their Highland homes after taking part in the 1715 Rebellion. The two brothers arrived and started a carpentry business in Ballymoney. They soon prospered and became builders and merchants. Cameron Place (now Victoria Street) was built by them. This Cameron family had all left Ballymoney by the early 1900s (see also graves 6, 9, 237, 313, 372, 374).

James, son of Archibald and Margaret Cameron, married Ellen, daughter of Daniel and Grace (Scott) Cameron of Church Street, in 1836 in 1st Ballymoney Presbyterian Church. Their son Daniel was also a merchant and died of

CAMERON

GRAVE no. 9

tuberculosis. James was a linen merchant and moved to Fassifern, Holywood, where he died.

Ellen married Rev. William, son of William and Mary (Moon) Wallace of The Mill, Kilraughts in 1868 in 1st Ballymoney Presbyterian Church. He was the Presbyterian Missionary to the Jews in Italy, based in Turin. He had to give this up in 1877 due to ill health, he returned home in 1877, living between Portrush and Belfast.

Malcolm John was a solicitor in Ballymoney and married Margaret Matchett of Bushmills in 1879 in 1st Ballymoney Presbyterian Church. He died of tuberculosis at Blake House, Ballymoney and is buried in Knock Road Cemetery.

```
1 James Cameron 1808 - 1886
.. +Ellen Cameron 1812 - 1850
...... 2 Archibald Cameron 1836 - 1878
...... 2 Daniel Cameron 1838 - 1864
...... 2 James Cameron 1840 - 1922
.......... +Blanche Brice Killen 1857 - 1951
...... 2 Sara Anne Cameron 1841 - 1915
...... 2 Ellen Cameron 1843 - 1890
.......... +William Wallace 1844 - 1919
............... 3 Donald Cameron Wallace
.................... +Clementine Dickson
............... 3 Eleanor Mary Wallace
...... 2 Margaret Cameron 1845 - 1869
...... 2 William John Cameron 1847 -
...... 2 Malcolm John Cameron 1848 - 1883
.......... +Margaret Matchett
```

DOUGLASS

GRAVE no. 10

Here
Lieth interred
The remains of
Hannah Douglass
wife to
Patrick Douglass
of Balnacree who
Departed this life
October the 2nd 1788
aged 68 years

Patrick and Hannah Douglass had sons James and Alexander who were baptised in 1st Ballymoney Presbyterian Church in 1753 and 1758.

CRAIG　　　　　　　　　　　　　　　　　　　　GRAVE no. 11

Here lieth the body of
Nehemiah Craig late of
Islandboy who died the
7th Febr 1822 aged 83 years
Also the remains of his
wife Jeney Craig alis
Hodges who died the 24th
Decbr 1813 aged 76 years

```
1 Nehemiah Craig 1738 - 1822
.. +Jeney Hodges 1737 - 1813
........ 2 Jane Craig
............ +Charles McCaughan
.................... 3 John McCaughan 1788 - 1867
........................ +Mary Taggart - 1867
............................ 4 John McCaughan 1825 -
................................ +Hannah Getty 1828 -
............................ 4 William James McCahan 1832 -
............................ 4 Charles McCaughan 1822 - 1919
............................ 4 Jane McCaughan
............................ 4 Margaret McCaughan
............................ 4 Fanny McCaughan
............................ 4 Nehemiah McCaughan
.................... 3 Patrick McCaughan
........................ +Mary Hill
............................ 4 Jane McCaughan
............................ 4 Hector McCaughan
.................... 3 Nehemiah McCaughan
........................ +Jane Scott
.................... *2nd Wife of Nehemiah McCaughan:
........................ +Mary McIlfatrick
.................... *3rd Wife of Nehemiah McCaughan:
........................ +Jane Taggart
.................... 3 Jean McCaughan
.................... 3 Alexander McCaughan
........................ +Jane Weir
.................... 3 Manus McCaughan
.................... 3 Charles McCaughan
.................... 3 Samuel McCaughan
........................ +Isabella Gilmour
.................... 3 William McCaughan
........................ +Catherine Simpson
```

Nehemiah and Jeney Craig had one known daughter Jane who married Charles, son of Patrick and Rose (Stuart) McCaughan (of Kilmahamogue, Ballintoy).

GALLOWAY

GRAVE no. 12

Here lieth the body
of James Galloway
late of Ballymoney
who departed this life
2nd September 1839 aged 80 years

James Galloway was possibly the brother of Neal Galloway. According to Miller's list of inhabitants of Ballymoney he was an Innkeeper in Main Street, Ballymoney (see graves 338, 339, 391).

MCKIGHAN

GRAVE no. 13

Here
Lieth the body of
Mary McKighan
who departed this
Life the 9th of June
1798 aged 56 years
wife of
James McKighan of
Inchinaugh

Baptisms were registered in the 1750s for the children of John and Alexander McKighan in 1st Ballymoney Presbyterian Church.

There was a James McKighan, farmer of Garryduff, in the Tithe applotments of 1825.

MALLETT

GRAVE no. 14

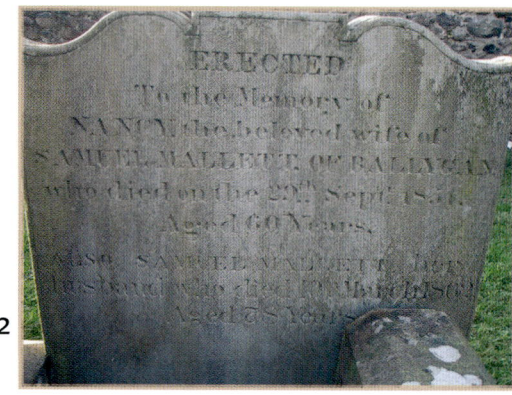

Erected
To the memory of
Nancy the beloved wife of
Samuel Mallett of Ballygan
who died on the 29th Sept 1851
Aged 60 years
Also Samuel Mallett her
husband who died 10th March 1862
Aged 78 years

1 James Mallett - 1817
.... 2 Samuel Mallett 1783 - 1862
.... +Nancy Lamont 1791 - 1851
.... 3 Mary Ann Mallett 1819 -
.... +Henry Johnston
.... 3 James Mallett 1821 - 1910
.... +Isabella Huey 1829 - 1896
.... 3 Robert Lamont Mallett 1825 -
.... 3 Jean Mallett 1828 -
.... +James Kennedy
.... 3 John Mallett 1830 -
.... 3 Nancy Mallett 1833 -
.... +William White
.... 4 Robert White 1864 -
.... 2 Mary Mallett 1791 - 1865
.... +Thomas Patton 1783 - 1861
.... 2 Robert Mallett
.... +Jennett Hackett
.... 3 William Mallett 1824 -
.... 3 Eliza Mallett 1826 -
.... 3 Peggy Ann Mallett 1830 -
.... 2 John Mallett

Samuel, the son of James Mallett, had brothers Robert and John and a sister Mary. He married Nancy (or Ann), daughter of Robert and Jennett Lamont of Ballygan.

His sister Mary married Thomas, son of Robert and Jean Patton of Drumaheglis, in 1822 in 1st Ballymoney Presbyterian Church.

His brother Robert married Jennett, daughter of John and Margaret (Lyons) Hackett of Drumaheglis in 1823 in 1st Ballymoney Presbyterian Church. The Hackett family belonged to the Unitarian Church and is buried in St. Patrick's Parish Churchyard.

MALLETT

GRAVE no. 15

Erected
by
James Mallett
in
memory of
John Huey
his brother in law
who died 7th Feby 1886
aged 86 years
Isabella Huey wife of
James Mallett
died 23rd April 1896
aged
67 years
The above
James Mallett
died 17th October 1910
aged 89 years

James Mallett, son of Samuel and Nancy (Lamont), married Isabella, daughter of Robert Huey of Knockahollet, Kilraughts in 1854 in 1st Kilraughts Presbyterian Church. John Huey who was buried with them, was Isabella's brother. He was a bachelor and living with them in Ballygan at the time of his death. James died at Desert Lane, Ballymoney in 1910.

JOHNSTON GRAVE no. 16

Mary Ann Johnston
daughter of Samuel Mallett of Balligan
and the beloved wife of
Henry Johnston
of Ballymoney by whom this stone
has been raised to her memory
Her two infant children
sleep on her bosom

1 Henry Johnston
.. +Mary Ann Mallett 1819 - 1846
*2nd Wife of Henry Johnston:
.. +Nancy Love 1824 -
...... 2 Matilda Johnston 1849 -
...... 2 Mary Jane Johnston 1850 -
...... 2 Robert Johnston 1852 -
...... 2 Henry Hamilton Johnston 1858 -
...... 2 Samuel John Johnston 1862 -

Mary Ann Mallett married Henry, son of Hamilton Johnston, in 1843 in 1st Ballymoney Presbyterian Church. His residence was Killinchy at the time of his marriage. In 1846, he was a Baronial Surveyor living in Charles Street.

After the death of Mary Ann, he married Nancy, daughter of Robert and Martha (Culbert) Love of Taghey in 1848 in 1st Ballymoney.

HOPKIN

GRAVE no. 17

Here lyeth t
he body of Ma
ry Hopkin: wh
o ?   ? :Mar
   ?   7

Mary Hopkin was possibly the mother of William (see graves 37, 270).

GALT

GRAVE no. 18

Here
Lyeth the body
of Matthew Galt
who died Novem
ber 1741 aged
55 years

Matthew Galt was a merchant in Ballymoney and was possibly an uncle of Robert Galt (see grave 77).

MORRISON

GRAVE no. 19

In memory of
Benjamin Morrison
late of Secon
who died 18th July 1880
aged 66
also his wife Nancy
who departed this life
aged 82 years

1 William Morrison 1750 -
.... 2 Hugh Morrison
.... +Ann ?
.... 3 Hugh Morrison
.... 3 Susan Morrison
.... +John Twaddle
.... 4 John Twaddle 1852 -
.... 4 Mary Twaddle 1854 -
.... 4 Matthew Twaddle 1856 -
.... 4 Elizabeth Anne Twaddle 1859 -
.... 3 Mary Morrison
.... 3 Martha Morrison
.... +Robert Wilson
.... 3 Margaret Morrison
.... +William Templeton
.... 2 James Morrison
.... +Nancy Love
.... 2 Thomas Morrison
.... 2 Benjamin Morrison 1812 - 1880
.... +Nancy McHenry 1807 - 1889
.... 3 James Morrison 1843 -
.... 3 Mary Jane Morrison 1849 -
.... +Andrew Morrison
.... 4 James Morrison
.... 4 Agnes Morrison
.... 2 William Morrison
.... 2 John Morrison
.... 2 Margaret Morrison
.... 2 Rachael Morrison

This Morrison family settled in Culderry in the early 1700s. William Morrison was born in 1750 and had six sons and two daughters.

Benjamin, a farmer, was the fourth son and married Nancy, daughter of James and Catherine (Scott) McHenry of Ballymoney in 1st Ballymoney Presbyterian Church in 1841. They had a son James and a daughter Mary Jane, who married Andrew Morrison, a boiler maker from Glasgow in 1883 in 1st Ballymoney.

Benjamin and Nancy each died at Secon.

TYLOR

GRAVE no. 20

Here lays th
e body of Ma
ry An Tylor
who departe
d this life N
ovber
15 1733

The modern spelling of this name is Taylor. There were Taylor families at Carnately for many years.

RAINEY GRAVE no. 21

Erected by
Mrs Mary Murtagh
Omaha, U.S. America
To the memory of her father
Archibald Rainey
Late of Ballymoney
Who died 17th December 1873
Aged 85 years
And also of her mother
Agnes
Who died 19th November 1848
Aged 47 years

1 Archibald Rainey - 1817
.... 2 Archibald Rainey 1788 - 1873
.... +Agnes ? 1801 - 1848
.... 3 Nancy Rainey 1828 - 1908
.... +Samuel Beckett 1815 - 1899
.............................see grave 22
.... 3 Matilda Rainey 1838 -
.... +Daniel Morrison
.... 3 Mary Rainey 1848 -
.... +John Murtagh 1852 -
.... 4 Archy Murtagh 1876 -
.... 4 Agnes Mary Murtagh 1877 -
.... 4 John Murtagh 1880 -
.... 4 James Murtagh 1883 -
.... 4 Nelson R. Murtagh 1886 -
.... 4 Eliza Murtagh 1888 -
.... 2 Jean Rainey
.... 2 Elizabeth Rainey 1800 -
.... +Alexander McKinney
.... 3 Alexander McKinney 1823 -
.... 3 Jean McKinney 1826 -
.... 2 James Rainey 1803 -
.... 2 Arthur Rainey 1806 -

Archibald, son of Archibald Rainey, was born at Ballywindland, and had siblings Jean, Elizabeth, James and Arthur. In 1846, he was a spirit dealer in High Street, Ballymoney. He had daughters Nancy, Matilda and Mary.

Nancy married Samuel Beckett of Ballycormick (see grave 22).

Matilda married Daniel Morrison of Glenhead in 1855 in Trinity Presbyterian Church.

Mary emigrated to U.S.A. in 1865 and married John Murtagh who was also born in Ireland. They had seven children and lived in Douglas, Omaha, Nebraska.

BECKETT

GRAVE no. 22

Erected by
Samuel Beckett
Ballycormick
In memory of his daughters
Margaret
Who died 20 Apr 1884
Aged 18 years
Agnes Williams
who died in 27th
June 1884 aged 32 years
Matilda
Who died 13 July 1885
Aged 24 years
Also the above
Samuel Beckett
Who died 12th Jun 1899 aged 83 years
His wife Nancy
Who died
15th March 1908 aged 79 years

1 Samuel Beckett 1815 - 1899
.. +Nancy Rainey 1828 - 1908
.... 2 Agnes Williams Beckett 1852 - 1884
.... 2 Jane Taylor Beckett 1854 -
.... 2 Mary Beckett 1856 -
.... 2 Samuel John Beckett 1859 - 1901
.... 2 Margaret Beckett 1865 - 1884
.... 2 Matilda Beckett 1871 - 1885

Samuel Beckett was a farmer at Ballycormick, third son of John and Jean (possible Taylor) Beckett (see graves 183, 184, 185).

He married Nancy, daughter of Archibald Rainey, a publican in Ballymoney (see grave 21) in Trinity Presbyterian Church in 1851. They had a family of Agnes, Jane Taylor, Mary, Samuel John, Matilda and Margaret. Mary emigrated to Omaha and married a man called Stills.

BOYD GRAVE no. 23

Here lieth the body of
Robert Boyd
late of Macfin
who departed this life
the 24th Janry 1802
aged 58 years

1 Robert Boyd 1743 - 1802
.... 2 John Boyd
.... 2 Mary Boyd
.... 2 Robert Boyd 1779 - 1865
.... +Hannah ?
.... 2 Samuel Boyd 1790 -
.... +Mary Dinsmore 1794 -
.... 3 Mary Boyd 1820 -
.... 3 Margaret Boyd 1822 -
.... 3 Robert Boyd 1819 -
.... +Sarah Jane Burnside 1820 -
.... 4 Robert Wallace Boyd - 1924

Robert Boyd, a farmer at Macfin, had children Robert, John, Mary and Samuel. Robert married Hannah. Samuel married Mary, daughter of Andrew and Margaret (Dinsmore) Dinsmore of Ballywattick, in 1816 and had three known children. Of these, Robert married Sarah Jane, daughter of James and Jane (Moore) Burnside of Macfin whose son Rev. Robert Wallace Boyd was Vicar of Kilrowan, Carrick on Shannon, Co. Leitrim.

MCKINLAI

GRAVE no. 24

Memento mori
Here lyeth the
body of John Mc
Kinlai who de
parted this life
The 2 of March
The year of our
Lord 1778 aged 4? years

There were at least three McKinlai (modern spelling is McKinlay) families in the Ballymoney area who had children baptised in 1st Ballymoney Presbyterian Church in the mid 1700s.

William had a daughter Mary.

Archibald had daughters, Margaret and Martha.

John had a son Archibald born in 1756.

DUNLOP GRAVE no. 25

1 Thomas Dunlop 1853 - 1925
.. +Ellen Doherty 1852 -
...... 2 Margaret Jane Dunlop 1874 -
...... 2 Annie Dunlop 1881 - 1882
...... 2 James Dunlop 1882 -
...... 2 Anne Dunlop 1885 -
...... 2 Thomas Dunlop 1886 -
...... 2 Samuel Dunlop 1887 -
...... 2 Jane Dunlop 1889 -

No details(only name in concrete surround)

Although there are no details on the gravestone, I have checked the Book of Internment for the Old Churchyard 1882-1932 and found the family of Thomas Dunlop who married Ellen Doherty in 1873 at St. Patrick's Parish Church. Thomas seems to have come to Ballymoney around the time he got married as he was not present in the church in 1871. Thomas was a labourer and lived in Townhead Street at the time of his marriage but was living at Roddenfoot when he had his children.

MISKELLY

GRAVE no. 26

To the memory of
John Miskelly
late of Ballindreen
by his daughter
Mrs Judges
of Philadelphia

There are several Miskelly families in the area, mainly from Carnfeogue in the Derrykeighan/Stranocum area. The name was often shortened to Kelly so John Miskelly is likely to be from the same family as the Kelly family of grave 27.

KELLY   GRAVE no. 27

In loving memory of
Hugh Kelly
who died 8th May 1893
also of his wife Jane Small
who died 13th Nov 1910
aged 88 years
and of their children
Rosanna died April 1849
aged 11 months
Robert died June 1855
aged 3 months
Mary Jane died June 1864
aged 11 years
William died 31st Oct 1924
Grace Ann Kelly
died 5th September 1935
Isabella Kelly
died 18th February 1950

1 William Kelly
.. +Jenny Jordan 1792 - 1818
...... 2 Jane Kelly 1811 -
...... 2 Jane Kelly 1816 -
...... 2 Hugh Kelly 1818 - 1893
.... +Jean Small 1822 - 1910
.... 3 Mary Jane Kelly 1845 - 1862
.... 3 Rosanna Kelly 1848 - 1849
.... 3 William Small Kelly 1850 - 1924
.... 3 Robert Kelly 1851 - 1867
.... 3 Rosanna Kelly 1853 - 1864
.... 3 Robert Kelly 1855 - 1855
.... 3 Isabella Kelly 1858 - 1950
.... 3 Grace Ann Kelly 1861 - 1935

William and Jane Kelly had three children who were baptized in St. Patrick's Parish Church. William was not present in the town in 1803. Jane was the daughter of James and Jane (Anderson) Jordan of Main Street, Ballymoney (see graves 229, 230).

Their son Hugh married Jane, daughter of William and Rose Ann (Craith) Small of Ballywattick in 1844 in 1st Ballymoney Presbyterian Church. Hugh was a saddler in Church Street, and later Main Street, Ballymoney.

MURPHY

GRAVE no. 28

Erected
by Clarke Murphy
In memory of his wife
Lizzie
Who died 12th Oct 1891
Aged 38 years
Also his daughter
Martha E.
Who died 31st Dec 1876
Aged 16 months
Mary E.
Who died 6th Sep 1890
Aged 13 years
His son Clarke
Who died 3rd April 1897
Aged 10 years
the above
Clarke Murphy J.P.
Died 3rd July 1916
Aged 61 years

1 James Murphy
...... 2 Clarke Murphy 1853 - 1918
.... +Elizabeth Laverty 1853 - 1891
.... 3 Martha E. Murphy 1875 - 1876
.... 3 Mary Ellen Murphy 1877 - 1890
.... 3 Elizabeth Murphy 1879 -
.... 3 Martha Murphy 1882 -
.... 3 James Murphy 1883 -
.... 3 Clarke Murphy 1886 - 1897
.... 3 Catherine Murphy 1889 -
.... 3 Johnston Murphy 1891 - 1916
...... *2nd Wife of Clarke Murphy:
.... +Martha Anne White 1867 – 1913
.... 3 Margaret Murphy 1903
.... 3 Robert Murphy 1896 - 1918
.... 3 Clarke Murphy 1900 - 1959
...... *3rd Wife of Clarke Murphy:
.... +Matilda Johnston or McMichael

Clarke Murphy was the son of James and Elizabeth Murphy and had at least one sister Elizabeth.
He married three times. His first wife was Elizabeth Laverty (1853-1891) who died of kidney disease and they had eight children. The youngest, Johnston, died in WW1. He then married Martha Ann, daughter of Robert Nevin White, in 1894 at Dervock Reformed Presbyterian Church and had three children. Their eldest son Robert died in WW1. He lastly married Matilda McMichael in 1915 in St. James Presbyterian Church.
He lived in Charlotte Street until about 1880 when he moved to Main Street, Ballymoney and was a Justice of the Peace in the town.

STEWART

GRAVE no. 29

This stone was erected by John Stewart in Memory of his wife who died the 26th Febry 1830 aged 70 years

CASSIDY

GRAVE no. 30

Henry Cassidy
died 16th Nov 1899 aged 83 years
His wife Catherine Ross
died 29th July 1914
aged 87 years
Also their daughters
Mary Jane and Catherine Anne
Elise relict of Thomas Nelson
of Bellicentre, Ohio, U.S.A
who died 26 Nov 1911
Hester Johnston
Died 11th May 1931 aged 73 years

1 Henry Cassidy 1816 - 1899
.. +Catherine Ross 1827 - 1914
.... 2 Catherine Anne Cassidy
.... 2 Mary Jane Cassidy
.... 2 Elise Cassidy 1853 - 1911
.... +Thomas Nelson 1845 -
.... 2 Hester Johnston Cassidy 1856 - 1931
.... 2 Eliza Small Cassidy 1860 - 1904
.... 2 Henrietta Cassidy 1861 -

Henry Cassidy, a farmer of Garryduff, was the eldest son of Alexander and Elizabeth (Small) Cassidy. He married Catherine, daughter of John and Esther (Johnston) Ross of Milltown in 1846 in Ballymoney (see grave 31). He was a teacher and lived in the Garvagh area for a time where some of his children were born.

Elise married Thomas Nelson, a farmer from Hardin, Ohio in 1884 in Garvagh Presbyterian Church and emigrated. They had no family.

Henrietta owned a kindergarten school in Cheshire where her sister Hester lived for a time. They retired to Portstewart. The family were Methodists.

ROSS GRAVE no. 31

Memonto Mori
Here lieth the the remains of
Mary Henry Robert and
Hugh Ross July the 24th 1817
Ester and John Ross
late of Ballymoney
who died respectively 1837 and
1846

1 John Ross
.. +Catherine ?
.... 2 James Ross 1795 -
.... 2 Andrew Ross 1798 -
.... 2 John Ross 1801 - 1845
.... +Ester Johnston - 1837
.... 3 Fanny Ross 1823 -
.... 3 John Ross 1825 -
.... 3 Catherine Ross 1827 - 1914
.... +Henry Cassidy 1816 - 1899
.... 3 Andrew Ross 1829 -
.... 3 Mary Jane Ross 1831 -
.... 3 Matty Ross 1834 -
.... 3 Robert Alexander Ross 1836 -
.... 2 Mary Ross 1802 - 1817
.... 2 Robert Ross 1804 - 1817
.... 2 Henry Ross 1807 - 1817
.... 2 Hugh Ross 1807 - 1817
*2nd Wife of John Ross:
.. +Jenny Picken

John and Catherine Ross of Milltown had a family of seven, four of whom seem to have died in 1817. Their son John, a miller at Milltown, Ballymoney married Esther Johnston and also had seven children (see grave 30).

HENRY

GRAVE no. 32

J   H
In memory of Margaret Henry late of Drumaheskey who departed this life the 18th Nov 1827 aged 59 years
Also her husband James Henry who departed this life on the 18th February 1837 aged 61 years

James and Margaret Henry of Drumahiskey had at least six children, Mary, Sarah, Margaret, John, Ann and James.

```
1 James Henry 1775 - 1837
.. +Margaret ? 1768 - 1827
...... 2 Matthew Henry
.......... +Catherine Lilley
............... 3 Jean Henry 1808 -
................... +Samuel Cooper 1805 -
....................... 4 John Cooper 1839 -
............... 3 Mary Henry 1810 -
............... 3 John Henry 1812 -
................... +Annie Spear
............... 3 Martha Henry 1815 -
................... +William Cooper
....................... 4 James Cooper 1818 -
............... 3 Matthew Henry 1818 -
............... 3 Daniel Henry 1820 - 1899
................... +Elizabeth Love 1834 - 1900
....................... 4 Mary Henry
....................... 4 Matthew Henry 1857 -
....................... 4 Margaret Jane Henry 1859 -
....................... 4 James Lyle Henry 1861 -
....................... 4 John Henry 1864 -
....................... 4 Catherine Henry 1866 -
....................... 4 Anne Henry 1870 -
....................... 4 Matilda Henry 1877 -
...... 2 Mary Henry
...... 2 Sarah Henry 1798 -
.......... +Alexander McMaster
...... 2 Margaret Henry 1800 -
.......... +Archibald Holmes
...... 2 John Henry 1802 -
...... 2 Ann Henry 1802 -
...... 2 James Henry 1805 -
```

HENRY

GRAVE no. 33

Here ly
eth the body
of John Henry
who depart
ed this life
the 10th day
Mar 1779
aged 82 years

Here
lyeth the
body of James
Henry who
departed this
life the 7th
day of Decem
ber 1774 aged
89 years

This Henry family is possibly from Drumahiskey (see graves 32, 34).

HENRY

GRAVE no. 34

? Interred the
body of Matthew Henry
who died the 18th of Jany
1784 aged 42 years
Also five of his children
Likewise of Detlif Orr
who died July 30th 1782
aged 38 years

These are probably the parents of James Henry (see grave 32).

FULTON

GRAVE no. 35

No details on gravestone

1 John Fulton
.. +Elizabeth ? 1810 - 1892
...... 2 Eliza Jane Fulton
.... +Charles Shaw
...... 2 Daniel Fulton 1841 -
.... +Catherine Thompson 1842 -
...... 2 Hugh Fulton 1844 - 1894
.... +Jane Eason 1845 -
.... 3 Alexander Fulton 1869 -
.... +Agnes?
.... 4 Agnes Fulton 1892 -
.... 4 Samuel Fulton 1894 -
.... 4 David Fulton 1895 -
.... 4 Rose Trainor Fulton 1896 -
.... 4 Hugh Fulton 1898 -
.... 3 Hugh Fulton 1871 -
.... +Bessie ?
.... 4 Hugh Fulton 1908 -
.... 4 Elizabeth Fulton 1916 -
.... 3 Jane Fulton 1873 - 1894
.... +Alexander Morrison 1873 - 1937
.... 4 Agnes Morrison 1892 -
.... 4 Jane Morrison 1894 -
...... 2 Letitia Fulton 1848 -
.... +Thomas Neill 1843 -

John Fulton was a tailor in Ballymoney and married Elizabeth. They had at least three children. Hugh, also a tailor, married Jane Eason (daughter of Alexander) in 1867 in St. Patrick's Parish Church and had Alexander, Hugh and Jane who were all born in Townhead Street.

This son Hugh married Bessie, and was a bootmaker in Main Street, but by 1916 he was a merchant. They had two children Hugh and Elizabeth.

UNREADABLE   *GRAVE no. 36*

Memento Mori
?
? depar
ted this life
December t-e
28 ? ? 77

HOPKINS

GRAVE no. 37

Sacred
to the memory of
William Hopkins late
of Ballymoney who
departed this life
15 day of December 1816
aged 54 years

1 William Hopkins 1761 - 1816
.. +Eliza 1773 - 1851
...... 2 Mary Hopkins 1790 - 1831
.... +James Hunter 1782 - 1864
               see grave 107
...... 2 Hannah Hopkins
.... +David Torrens
...... 2 Jane Hopkins 1799 - 1859
.... +Robert Jordan 1784 - 1864
               see grave 230
...... 2 Ann Hopkins 1801 -
...... 2 William Hopkins 1803 - 1863
.... 3 William Hopkins 1825 - 1854
...... 2 James Hopkins 1808 -
...... 2 John Hopkins 1811 -
...... 2 Samuel Hopkins 1813 -

William Hopkins was a grocer and yarn dealer at Main Street, Ballymoney. His wife Eliza (1773-1851) was present in Main Street as a grocer in 1824 and 1846. They had family of eight.
His daughter Mary married James, son of John and Agnes Hunter of Secon.
His daughter Hannah married David Torrens of Drumreagh in 1827 in 1st Ballymoney Presbyterian Church.
His daughter Jane married Robert Jordan, a merchant of Main Street, Ballymoney (see graves 229, 230).

SPENCE

GRAVE no. 38

Here lieth
the remains of
Edward Spence
of Currysisken who
departed this life the
12th day of Novr 1798
Aged 56 years. And
three of his children
Also his wife Agnes
who departed this life
4th May 1832 aged 84 years

1 Edward Spence 1742 - 1798
.. +Agnes 1748 - 1832
...... 2 Samuel Spence
.... +Nancy Wright
...... 2 Edward Spence

Edward and Agnes Spence had two known children, Edward and Samuel. Samuel married Nancy, daughter of Joseph and Mary (Curry) Wright of Culbrim.

MCFARLAND

GRAVE no. 39

Erected
In memory of James McFarland
Landhead
Who died 29th April 1885
Aged 90 years
Also his beloved wife
Margaret
Who died 15th July 1864
Aged 66 years
Daniel, their son
Died 22nd March 1898
aged 73 years
Jane, their daughter
died 5th January 1910
Aged 85 years
Margaret, their daughter
died 11th August 1917 aged 86 years

1. James McFarland 1793-1885
.. +Margaret Lamont 1798 - 1864
...... 2 Jane McFarland 1824 - 1910
...... 2 Daniel McFarland 1836 - 1899
...... 2 James Henry McFarland 1828 - 1903
.... +Mary Mansfield 1828 - 1903
...... 2 Margaret McFarland 1830 - 1917
...... 2 Isabella McFarland 1833 -
...... 2 John McFarland 1836 - 1894
.... +Lucy B. Teasdale

James McFarland married Peggy Lamont on 17th May 1823 at St. Patrick's Parish Church, Ballymoney. She was possibly the daughter of Robert and Jennet Lamont of Ballygan. They attended 1st Ballymoney Presbyterian Church where their children were baptised. They lived at Carnany before moving to farm at Landhead.

Daniel, a bachelor, continued farming at Landhead after his parents died. His brothers James and John emigrated to South Dakota, sister Isabella died young and sisters Jane and Margaret moved to Queen Street, Ballymoney.

MCHUGH

GRAVE no. 40

Erected
by Samuel Kennedy
of Ballymoney
In memory of
Patrick McHugh R.I.C.
Who died 14th Novr 1884
aged 44 years

Patrick McHugh was a policeman in Ballymoney, a bachelor, who died of tuberculosis. The witness to his death was Samuel Kennedy, a publican in Church Street, Ballymoney.

MACDERMOTT

GRAVE no. 41

In memory of
William MacDermott
Cullermoney
who died 5th April 1890
aged 79 years
Also his wife Margaret
who died 28th June 1892
aged 72 years
Their son William MacDermott
Lic.R.Coll.Phys.and Surgs., Edin
Late of Coxhoe, Durham, England
who died 12th May 1893
aged 37 years
Their son Clarke MacDermott
who died 18th July 1911
aged 51 years
Their daughter
Mary Anne MacDermott
who died 13th July 1933
aged 80 years
Their daugther
Sara Jane MacDermott
who died 22nd April 1936
aged 78 years
Also their daughter
Margaret MacDermott
who died 29th December 1942
aged 81 years.

1 John MacDermott
.... 2 William MacDermott 1810 - 1890
.... +Margaret Archibald
.... 3 Mary Ann MacDermott 1853 - 1933
.... 3 William MacDermott 1855 - 1893
.... 3 Sara Jane MacDermott 1857 - 1936
.... 3 Clarke MacDermott 1860 - 1911
.... 3 Margaret MacDermott 1860 - 1942
.... 2 Clarke MacDermott 1790 - 1878
.... 2 Peggy Jane MacDermott
.... +Samuel Mullans

The McDermott family were farmers at Roseyards and attended Roseyards Presbyterian Church. William married Margaret, daughter of Nathaniel Archibald of Bellisle, Dervock, in 1846 in Roseyards Presbyterian Churchyard.

MCDERMOTT

GRAVE no. 42

Erected
to the memory of
Clarke McDermott
of Cullermoney
who died 11th October 1878
aged 88 years

Clarke was the son of John, brother of William (see grave 41), a bachelor and a farmer at Roseyards.

MCDERMOT

GRAVE no. 43

To
the
memory of Will
McDermot who
departed this life
the 26th August
1786 aged 75 years

His wife Agnes
who departed this
life 12 of Nov
1782 aged 76 years

This is the same branch as the other McDermott families of Cullermoney (see graves 41, 42).

MCKEAGUE

GRAVE no. 44

In loving memory of
Thomas MacAfee
eldest son of
Andrew McKeague
Ballywindland
Died June 4th 1885
aged 25 years
Mary his only daughter
Died 5th January 1888
aged 21 years
John
His second son
Died September 11th 1891
aged 27 years

Left side

John McKeague
Died May 14th 1839
aged 57 years
Also his wife Mary
Died September 19th 1861
aged 62 years

MCKEAGUE

GRAVE no. 44

Right side

Jane MacAfee
Beloved wife of
Andrew McKeague
Died 15 th January 1913
aged 83 years
Andrew McKeague
Died 8th February 1916
Aged 82 years

1 Benjamin McKeague
.. +Martha Curry
.... 2 John McKeague 1789 - 1839
.... +Mary White 1799 - 1861
.... 3 Andrew McKeague 1833 - 1916
.... +Jane MacAfee 1829 - 1913
.... 4 Thomas McAfee McKeague 1861 - 1885
.... 4 John McKeague 1863 - 1891
.... 4 Mary McKeague 1866 - 1888
.... 4 William McAfee McKeague 1868 - 1931
.... +Rose Ann Ross Thomson 1870 - 1959
.... 3 Mary McKeague
.... +Samuel Boyd 1828 - 1862
.... 4 John Boyd 1859 -
.... 4 Samuel Boyd 1861 -
.... 3 Benjamin McKeague
.... 2 Andrew McKeague 1776 - 1854
.... +Mary 1783 - 1811
.... 3 Ann McKeague 1808 - 1811
.... 3 Benjamin McKeague 1810 - 1898
.... 2 Mary Ann McKeague 1788 - 1864
.... 2 Benjamin McKeague
.... +Agnes Steen

John McKeague was the son of Benjamin and Martha (Curry) McKeague and he married Mary White. The family were farmers at Lower Ballywindland.

Andrew married Jane, daughter of Thomas and Martha (Knox) MacAfee of Currysisken in 1860 in 1st Ballymoney Presbyterian Church. Their three eldest children died leaving only a son William who married Rose Ann, daughter of Adam and Anne (McElderry) Thomson of Church Street, Ballymoney in 1905 in Trinity Presbyterian Church.

Their daughter married Samuel, son of John Boyd of Ballywindland in 1859 in St. James Church.

HUNTER

GRAVE no. 45

Here lieth
The body of John
Hunter who de
parted this life
15th of November
1754 aged 50 years
also his wife Ma
ry Hunter who
departed this life
Febry the 4th 1781
aged ?? years

This is most likely to be the brother of William Hunter of Dunluce (see grave 49). It is not known why this Hunter family was buried in Ballymoney, rather than closer to their home. It is possible that William's wife, Margaret Orr, was from Ballymoney as there are two Orr graves next to the Hunters.

HUNTER

GRAVE no. 46

Here lie the remains of
Adam Hunter
of Ballymagarry Esq. who departed this life
the 13th January 1819 in the 70th year of his age
During a long and active life
He was eminently conspicuous for piety
charity and hospitality. By his death
society have lost a valuable member
The poor a benevolent and beautiful friend
Conjugal love has erected this testimony
To the memory of a most kind
and affectionate husband
By the side of her beloved husband
lie the remains of
Jane relic of the late
Adam Hunter Esq.
Who died on the 20 Jan 1828 in the 71st
year of her age

Adam Hunter was born on 26th March 1748 and was the agent to the estate of the Earl of Antrim. He was granted the desmesne of Ballymagarry in the parish of Dunluce containing 326 acres. He was a wealthy man, also owning property in Deffrick and houses in Ballymoney. He was the son of William and Margaret (Orr) Hunter of Dunluce (see grave 49).

He had no family and when he died he left £100 in his will to Dunluce Church in a bond.

MCCEUITY GRAVE no. 47

Erected to
to the memory of Ann McCeuity
of Ballymoney who departed
this life the 9th June 1821 aged
51 years. This stone was erected
by her daughter Frances
who also
Lyeth the remains of Thomas
  Hunter   ?   ?
  above   ?   ?
  of Thomas   ?
  ?   d aged   ?

The surname McCeuity is unusual for Ballymoney and does not show up on any records that I can find. It may be significant that it is in the middle of the Hunter graves. It is possible that Frances married Thomas Hunter.

HUNTER GRAVE no. 48

Here
Lieth the remains of
Thomas Hunter late of
Gortnee who departed
this life in the year of our
Lord 10th May 1829 aged 62
years.
Also his wife
Rachael Hunter who departed
this life March 12th 1850 aged 81
years

1 William Hunter 1702 - 1748
.. +Margaret Orr 1716 - 1784
...... 2 Ian Hunter 1740 -
...... 2 Hugh Hunter 1745 - 1765
...... 2 Thomas Hunter 1746/47 - 1829
.... +Rachael Corkidale
.... 3 William Hunter 1791 -
.... 3 Rose Hunter 1793 -
.... 3 Adam Hunter 1795 -
.... 3 John Hunter 1797 -
.... 3 Jane Hunter 1799 - 1869
.... +John Haughey 1795 - 1877
.... 4 Margaret Jane Haughey 1824 - 1893
.... +James Huey Pollock - 1869
.... 4 John Haughey 1826 - 1899
.... 4 Rachael Haughey 1835 - 1839
.... 3 Margaret Hunter 1801 -
.... 3 Hugh Hunter 1803 -
...... 2 Adam Hunter 1748 - 1819
.... +Jane ? 1756 - 1828
...... 2 Margaret Hunter 1752 -
...... 2 Jane Hunter 1752 - 1785
.... +? Kirk
...... 2 William Hunter 1753 -
...... 2 John Hunter 1755 -
...... 2 James Hunter 1756 -
...... 2 May Hunter 1758 -

Thomas Hunter was born in Dunluce on 8th March 1847. He was the elder brother of Adam (grave 46) and son of William and Margaret Hunter (grave 49). He married Rachael Corkidale on the 31st October 1790 and had seven children.

Their daughter Jane married John Haughey of Bushmills and had three children. One of these Margaret Jean married James Huey Pollock of Ballymoney in 1859.

HUNTER   GRAVE no. 49

Memento Mori
Here lyeth the body of
William Hunter who de
parted this life the 9th
of July 1748 aged 46
Also Hugh Hunter
his son who died the 23rd
of November aged 20 years
And Margaret his wife
who departed this life
the 11 day of November
1784 aged 68 years

```
1 William Hunter 1702 - 1748
.. +Margaret Orr 1716 - 1784
...... 2 Ian Hunter 1740 -
...... 2 Hugh Hunter 1745 - 1765
...... 2 Thomas Hunter 1746/47 - 1829
.......... +Rachael Corkidale
............... 3 William Hunter 1791 -
............... 3 Rose Hunter 1793 -
............... 3 Adam Hunter 1795 -
............... 3 John Hunter 1797 -
............... 3 Jane Hunter 1799 - 1869
................... +John Haughey 1795 - 1877
............... 3 Margaret Hunter 1801 -
............... 3 Hugh Hunter 1803 -
...... 2 Adam Hunter 1748 - 1819
.......... +Jane ? 1756 - 1828
...... 2 Margaret Hunter 1752 -
...... 2 Jane Hunter 1752 - 1785
.......... +? Kirk
...... 2 William Hunter 1753 -
...... 2 John Hunter 1755 -
...... 2 James Hunter 1756 -
...... 2 May Hunter 1758 -
```

William Hunter married Margaret Orr on 28th February 1739 and had a family of eleven.

Their son Hugh died in Larne on 23rd November 1765 and their daughter Jane Kirk otherwise Hunter died in Larne on 26th February 1785.

Many of these details were found in an old Bible.

ORR

GRAVE no. 50

Memento Mori
Here lith the body
of William Orr who
departed this life
the 13th day of December 1777 aged 84 years
Also Isabella his wife
who died January the 11th
1787 aged 73 years
Likewise the body of
William Orr their son
who departed this life
the 16th Octr 1801 aged 61
Also
Flora Orr his wife who
died the 7th November 1801
aged 58 years

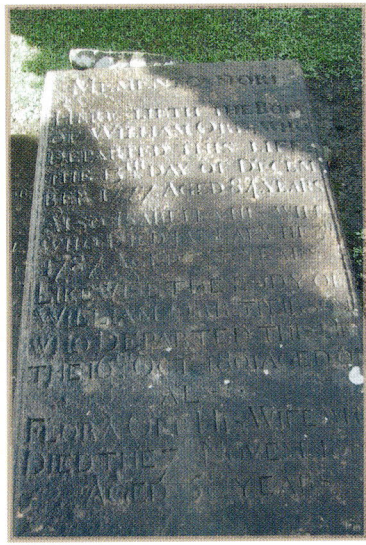

1 William Orr 1693 - 1777
.. +Isabella ? 1713 - 1787
...... 2 William Orr 1740 - 1801
.... +Flora ? 1743 - 1801
.... 3 William Orr 1778 - 1856
.... +Mary Mitchell
......................see grave 51
.... 3 Mary Orr 1782 - 1864
.... +John White
.... 4 William White 1814 - 1866
.... 4 Flora White 1817 -
.... +William Munnis 1818 - 1866
.... 4 John White 1819 -
.... 4 Martha Thomasine Matilda White 1821 -
.... +Thomas Adair
.... 3 Flora Orr
.... +Robert Rowan
.... 4 George Washington Rowan

This Orr family were merchants in Ballymoney.

Mary Orr married John White, a woollen draper in Main Street, Ballymoney. She had three children and died at Greenville, Cookstown at the home of her daughter Martha who had married Thomas Adair in 1845.

Their daughter Flora married Rev. William, son of Rev. William and Alice (Lyle) Munnis of Carncullagh, Dervock (and Minister of Roseyards Presbyterian Church) in 1853 in Portstewart Presbyterian Church. William was Minister of the Free Church, Marykirk, Scotland. Their son William moved to Brooklyn, New York where he died.

Flora Orr married Robert Rowan who was a wine and spirit merchant in Main Street, Ballymoney.

ORR
GRAVE no. 51

Sacred
to the memory of
William Orr
who departed this life 19th April
1856
Aged 77 years
Therefore be ye also ready
for in such an hour ? Ye think not
the son of man cometh   Matt xxiv

On side

Erected
to the memory
of Jane

1 William Orr 1778 - 1856
.. +Mary Mitchell
...... 2 William Mitchell Orr 1812 - 1856
.... +Susannah MacAfee 1815 - 1894
.... 3 Matilda MacAfee Orr 1852 -
.... 3 William Thomas Orr 1855 - 1883
...... 2 James John Orr 1819 -
.... +Elizana Cameron 1820 - 1862
.... 3 Mary Mitchell Orr 1844 -
.... +Jonathan Lovett Bennett
.... 4 Anna Edith Bennett 1870 -
.... 4 George Bennett 1881 -
.... 4 Walter Edmund Bennett 1873 -
.... 3 Elizabeth Orr 1849 - 1932
.... +Samuel Lyle 1841 - 1919
.... 4 William Gordon Lyle 1871 -
.... 4 John McIntosh Lyle 1873 -
.... 4 Henry H.M. Lyle 1875 -
.... +Jessie
.... 4 James Cameron Lyle 1877 -
.... 4 Mary Elizabeth Lyle 1878 -
.... +Alexander Warden
.... 4 Norman Wood Lyle 1885 -
...... 2 Hetty Orr
.... +Neil Kilpatrick
.... 3 Mary Ann Mitchell Kilpatrick 1833 -
.... 3 James Mitchell Kilpatrick 1835 -

William Orr of Ballymoney married Mary Mitchell and had children William Mitchell, James John and Hetty.

William Mitchell Orr was a woollen draper in Ballymoney. He married Susannah MacAfee, daughter of Thomas and Martha (Knox) McAfee in 1848 in 1st Ballymoney Presbyterian Church.

James John married Elizana, daughter of Daniel and Grace (Scott) Cameron of Ballymoney in 1842 in 1st Ballymoney Presbyterian Church. Their daughter Mary Mitchell married Jonathan Lovett Bennett, a merchant in Dublin, in 1865 in 1st Ballymoney Presbyterian Church. Their other daughter Elizabeth married Rev. Samuel, son of Gordon and Elizabeth (Lyle) Lyle of Knockanboy, Dervock. They moved to Wentworth, Ontario.

ANDERSON

GRAVE no. 52

Sacred
To the memory of
Elizabeth Anderson
daughter of the late
John Orr of Ballymoney
She departed this life
the 9th day of March 1878
aged 35 years

Elizabeth Anderson was the wife of John Anderson who was a baker in High Street, Ballymoney. His father John died on 5th June 1860 in High Street and his mother Sarah in 1867. They had a daughter Sarah and a son John who died in 1865 in Woolwich.

MARTIN

GRAVE no. 53

Erected
by
Alexander Martin
to the memory
of his wife Elizabeth
who departed this life
Oct 30th 1870 aged 73 years
The above Alexander
died 15th July 1873 aged 75 years
Their sons
John, Sergeant in the Inniskillings
who died 20th August 1890
aged 72 years
Thomas, 4th May 1913
aged 76 years

1 Alexander Martin 1798 - 1873
.. +Elizabeth Campbell 1797 - 1870
...... 2 John Martin 1818-1890
...... 2 Alexander Martin 1827 -
...... 2 Daniel Martin 1831 -
...... 2 Elizabeth Martin 1836 -
...... 2 Thomas Martin 1836 - 1913

Alexander Martin married Elizabeth Campbell in St. Patrick's Parish Church in 1822 and had family of John, Martha, Alexander, Daniel, Elizabeth and Thomas who were baptised in 1st Ballymoney Presbyterian Church.

John was born at Newbuildings and when he died he was married and a farmer in Cummingston (or Ballymenagh). His brother Thomas was single and died in Ballymoney.

UNREADABLE

GRAVE no. 54

N
T-e
Mat
?77
wh
rte
Life
T-e 2

MCCOLLUM

GRAVE no. 55

Here lyeth
The body of
Hugh McCol
lum who dep
arted this
Life t-e 26th day
of Feb 1779
Also the body
of his wife Helle
n   ?

In 1740 there were three McCollums in Ballymoney, Hugh, William and John. In 1766, Alexander, and two Johns were recorded. Hugh McCollum was a merchant in Ballymoney in the 1700s.

PINKERTON

GRAVE no. 56

In memory
of
Samuel Pinkerton, Knowhead
died 22 July 1838 aged 44
and
Robert Pinkerton, Knowhead
died 28 Jun 1846 aged 59
and Robert his son
died 26 Novr 1880 aged 53
and Nancy Pinkerton
died 23rd Jany 1876 aged 88

1 Robert Pinkerton 1787 - 1846
.. +Agnes Hunter 1788 - 1876
...... 2 James Pinkerton 1814 - 1876
.... +Nancy Hamilton 1810 -
...... 2 John Pinkerton 1817 - 1869
...... 2 Rachael Pinkerton 1821 - 1859
.... +William MacAfee 1813 - 1861
    see grave 100
...... 2 Robert Pinkerton 1827 - 1880
...... 2 William Pinkerton 1829

Samuel was the brother of Robert Pinkerton. They were born at Secon and are possibly sons of James. Robert married Agnes, daughter of John and Agnes Hunter of Secon.

Their son James married Nancy, daughter of Hugh and Jean Hamilton of Moneygobbin in 1843 in 1st Ballymoney Presbyterian Church and had no family. They attended the Unitarian Church and are buried with James's brother John in St. Patrick's Parish Churchyard. They farmed at Knowhead, Moneygobbin and this farm was left to their sister Rachael's children.

Their daughter Rachael married William, son of Thomas and Martha (Knox) MacAfee of Currysisken in 1843 (see grave 100).

PINKERTON

GRAVE no. 57

Erected
to the memory of
Samuel Pinkerton of
Secon who departed this life
Decr 1815 aged 81 years
Also his wife Jane Cristy
who died 26th March 1791
aged 64 years
Also his son John
who died 23rd September 1824
aged 62 years
His wife Abigail Wallace
who died 22nd April 1832
aged 48 years

```
1 Samuel Pinkerton 1728 - 1813
.. +Jane Cristy 1727 - 1791
...... 2 Jane Pinkerton 1752 -
.......... +Robert McKay
...... 2 Mary Pinkerton 1754 -
.......... +Alexander McKay
............... 3 Mary McKay 1803 -
............... 3 Alexander McKay 1805 -
............... 3 Mary McKay 1811 -
...... 2 David Pinkerton 1760 -
.......... +Rachael
............... 3 David Pinkerton
............... 3 Samuel Pinkerton
............... 3 Jean Pinkerton
............... 3 Agnes Pinkerton
............... 3 Daniel Pinkerton 1812 -
...... 2 John Pinkerton 1766 - 1824
.......... +Abigail Wallace 1784 - 1832
............... 3 Agnes Pinkerton 1805 -
................... +James Hart
............... 3 Samuel Pinkerton 1807 - 1887
................... +Ellen Sharpe
............... 3 Mary Pinkerton 1809 -
................... +George McKay
............... 3 James Pinkerton 1811 - 1892
................... +Eliza Burnside 1810 - 1895
............... 3 John Pinkerton 1813 - 1848
................... +Nancy Pinkerton 1804 - 1865
............... 3 Abigail Pinkerton 1815 - 1900
................... +John Hamill 1805 - 1877
```

The Pinkerton family lived in Secon from the the 1600s and spread into many nearby townlands such as Forttown, Ballygobbin, Moneygobbin, Coldagh, Claughey, Ballinamoney, Landhead, Ballaghmore and Dunaverney.

This Samuel was the son of Samuel senior of Secon and he married Jane Cristy, possibly of Ballywatt. Two daughters, Jane and Mary married two McKays from Secon. Each branch called sons Samuel, John and Robert which has led to confusion in some of the relationships.

Samuel and Jane's son John married Abigail, daughter of James and Agnes Wallace of Booton.

Their daughter Agnes married James, son of William and Mary Hart of Secon and another daughter Mary married George McKay of Secon.

PINKERTON

GRAVE no. 57

Their eldest son Samuel married Ellen Sharpe of Ballylig, Ramoan and they farmed at Coldagh.

Their son James married Eliza, daughter of Alexander and Ann (Moore) Burnside of Secon in 1847 in Ballymoney Unitarian Church. Many of the Pinkerton families were Unitarian.

Another son John married Nancy Pinkerton and he died young due to a fall from a horse. This family is buried in the Parish Churchyard. A great, great grandson of theirs, also called John, presently lives in Secon.

Their daughter Abigail married John, son of Robert and Jean (Wallace) Hamill of Dunaverney in 1847 in the Unitarian Church and they are also buried in the Parish Churchyard. Their son Robert went to work in a bank in Clones and returned with tuberculosis which killed all his siblings apart from one brother John.

Robert married Nancy, daughter of Robert and Isabella (Wallace) Dick of Garry in 1851 in the Unitarian Church. They farmed at Ballaghmore and are buried in Knock Road Cemetery, Ballymoney.

```
............... 3 Robert Pinkerton 1818 - 1903
.................. +Nancy Dick 1826 - 1914
...... 2 Samuel Pinkerton 1770 - 1863
.......... +Margaret
............... 3 Samuel Pinkerton 1796 -
.................. +Mary Young
............... 3 John Pinkerton 1799 -
.................. +Sally Moore
............... 3 James Pinkerton 1801 -
............... 3 Sarah Pinkerton 1803 -
............... 3 Sheriff Pinkerton 1804 -
```

PINKERTON

GRAVE no. 58

Erected
in memory of James Pinkerton
late of Coleraine
Died 21st Jany 1827 aged 25 years
Also Samuel Pinkerton
late of Forttown
died 10th March 1872
aged 81 years
Also his wife Jane
died 24th Febry 1873 aged 83 years

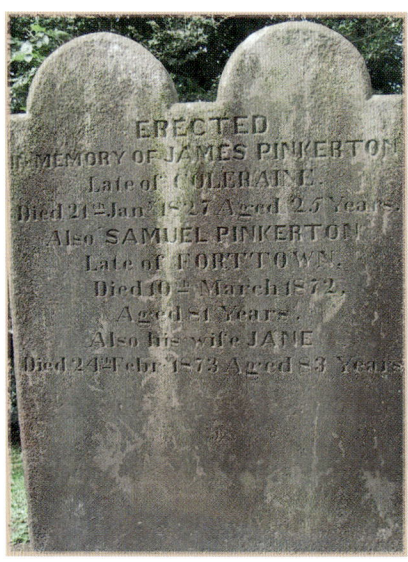

1 Samuel Pinkerton 1790 - 1872
.. +Jean McCrellis 1789 - 1873
...... 2 Matilda Pinkerton 1815 -
.... +Samuel Gilmore
.... 3 George Gilmore 1837 -
...... 2 Peggy Ann Pinkerton 1817 -
...... 2 Jenny Pinkerton 1820 -
.... +James Hart
...... 2 Peggy Pinkerton 1820 -
.... +William Nevin
...... 2 Samuel Pinkerton 1822 -
...... 2 John Pinkerton 1824 - 1906
...... 2 James Pinkerton 1829 -
.... +Rose Ann Thompson 1829 -
.... 3 John Thompson Pinkerton 1857 -
.... 3 Mary Ann Pinkerton 1862 -
.... 3 Mary Jane Pinkerton 1867 -
...... 2 Sheriff Moore Pinkerton 1834 - 1904
.... +Sarah Jane Lyons 1842 - 1882
.... 3 Jane Anna Pinkerton 1878 - 1960
.... +Samuel McLean 1874 - 1961

    Samuel Pinkerton married Jean McCrellis of Kirkmoyle about 1814. He was possibly born in Secon and had eight children.

    Matilda married Samuel Gilmore of Aghadowey in 1836, Jenny married James Hart of Secon in 1845; Peggy married William Nevin of Galvally in 1852; James married Rose Ann Thompson of Ballygabbin in 1856 and Sheriff Moore married Sarah Ann, daughter of Hugh and Nancy (Leslie) Lyons in 1877. They each married in 1st Ballymoney Presbyterian Church other than Peggy who married in St. Patrick's Parish Church.

    Sheriff had only one child, a daughter Jane Anna, who married Samuel, son of William John and Isabella (Cochrane) McLean in 1901 and they continued to farm at Forttown.

ADAMS

GRAVE no. 59

Lizzie Stewart
wife of Robert Adams
Ballymoney
Died 9th Feb 1890
Their son
Alexander Erskine
Died 30th September 1900
aged 12 years
Also Robert Adams
who died 7th April 1931
aged 69 years

1 Robert Adams 1862 - 1931
.. +Elizabeth Stuart 1862 - 1890
...... 2 Alexander Erskine Adams 1888 - 1900
...... 2 Mary Young Adams 1889 - 1960
.... +William Drain McKeown 1884 - 1960
.... 3 Robert Adams McKeown 1916 - 1988
.... +Joan Dickey 1921 - 2007
.... 3 James Johnson McKeown 1921 - 1992
.... +Marion Winifred Pyper
.... 3 William Drain McKeown 1929 - 2005
.... +Iris Knox

Lizzie Stewart (or Stuart), wife of Robert Adams, of Church Street, Ballymoney was born in 1862, daughter of Moore and Martha (Erskine) Stuart of Carnany. She died of consumption followed two years later by her son Alexander.

Robert was the son of David and Mary (Young) Adams of Claughey (see grave 60) and worked as a watchmaker in Church Street. He was known to cycle to Dublin in order to obtain parts and was very involved in the Masonic order. His business was taken over by his daughter Mary Young Adams who married William, son of Daniel and Sarah (Johnston) McKeown in 1916. The shop evolved into an electrical business which only closed in 2006.

ADAMS

GRAVE no. 60

In memory of
David Adams
Claughey
died 20th Feby 1877
Aged 55 years
His sons
Archibald
Died 5th Oct 1861
Aged 2 years
William
Died 13th Novr 1873
Aged 20 years
His daughter
Jane
Died 1st Octr 1893
Aged 35 years
His wife Mary Young
Died 11th Augt 1896
Aged 68 years
and was interred in
Mount Moriah Cemetery
Philadelphia

1 David Adams 1818 - 1877
.. +Mary Young 1828 - 1896
...... 2 David Adams
...... 2 William Adams 1853 - 1873
...... 2 Jane Culbertson Adams 1857 - 1893
.... +George Kirkpatrick
.... 3 George Kirkpatrick 1880 -
.... +Selena Morrison 1880 -
.... 3 Nancy Kirkpatrick 1878 -
.... 3 Jane Kirkpatrick 1880 -
.... 3 Martha Kirkpatrick
.... 3 Mary Young Kirkpatrick 1880 -
.... 3 John Kirkpatrick 1882 -
.... 3 Alexander Kirkpatrick 1892 -
...... 2 Archibald Adams 1859 - 1861
...... 2 Robert Adams 1862 - 1931
.... +Elizabeth Stuart 1862 - 1890
..........see grave 59
...... 2 Alexander Adams 1864 -
...... 2 Mary Ann Adams 1868 -

David was the son of Archibald and Mary (Kennedy) Adams, miller of Claughey Mill. He married Mary, daughter of William and Jane (Culbertson) Young of Trench in 1852 in 1st Ballymoney Presbyterian Church.

Their daughter Jane married George, son of John and Isabella (Torrens) Kirkpatrick of Polintamney in 1876 in Trinity Presbyterian Church.

Their son Robert married Elizabeth Stuart (see grave 59).

GETTY

GRAVE no. 61

In loving memory
of
The Getty family

1 John Getty
.. +Mary Ann
...... 2 Alexander Getty 1795 - 1897
.... +Martha Dobbin - 1850
.... 3 Matilda Getty 1823 -
.... 3 Margaret Getty 1823 - 1897
...... 2 Andrew Getty 1798 - 1863
...... 2 John Getty 1801 -
...... 2 James Getty 1803 - 1875
...... 2 Robert Getty 1805 -
.... +Nancy Hamill 1807 - 1894
.... 3 Matthew Getty 1838 - 1879
.... 3 Robert Getty 1841 -
.... 3 Mary Getty 1843 -
...... 2 Matthew Getty 1808 -
.... +Jennet McKeown
.... 3 Catherine Getty 1830 -
...... 2 Sarah Getty 1810 - 1886
...... 2 David Getty 1814 - 1887
.... +Matilda Edwards 1814 - 1888
.... 3 Sarah Getty 1850 -
.... +George Picken 1833 - 1897
.... 3 David Getty 1853 -
.... 3 Matilda Getty 1857 -
.... +James McKay
.... 3 Catherine Getty 1858 -
.... 3 John Getty 1860 -
.... +Matilda Jane Brown
...... 2 Catherine Getty 1816 - 1881
.... +Daniel McIlreavy 1814 - 1872
.... 3 John McIlreavy 1836 - 1914
.... 3 Annie McIlreavy 1841 - 1867
.... 3 Margaret McIlreavy 1843 - 1860
.... 3 Sarah McIlreavy 1844 - 1861
.... 3 Catherine McIlreavy 1847 - 1930
.... 3 Matilda McIlreavy 1850 - 1874
.... 3 Daniel McIlreavy 1851 - 1872
.... 3 William McIlreavy 1855 - 1901

This is possibly the family Getty of Ballywattick, as several members of these are noted in the Internment book for the Old Churchyard.

Alexander married Martha Dobbin and emigrated to Pennsylvania. Robert married Nancy Hamill of Ballywattick in 1837. Matthew married Jennet of Ballywattick in 1828. David married Matilda, daughter of David Edwards, in 1850 and remained at Ballywattick as a farmer. Catherine married Daniel, son of John and Hannah (Quigg) McIlreavy of Heagles and Booton in 1835 and emigrated to New York. They each married in 1st Ballymoney Presbyterian Church.

GIVEN

GRAVE no. 62

Sacred
To the memory of Robert Given
late of Booton who departed th
is life Sept., the 5th 1841 aged 78 years
Also
His son John who departed this
life Dec the 24th 1841 aged 41 years

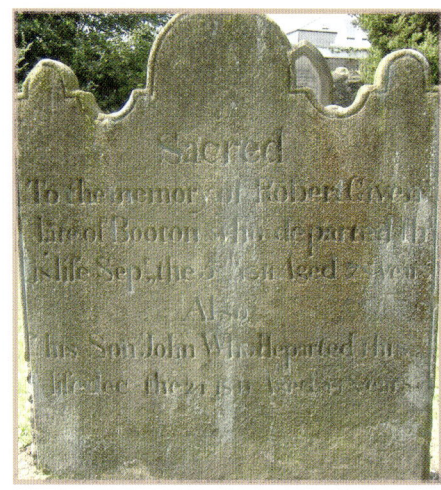

1 Robert Given 1763
.. +Mary ?
...... 2 Ann Given 1795 -
.... +James Cooper
.... 3 Letitia Cooper 1824 -
...... 2 Elizabeth Given 1797 -
...... 2 John Given 1800 - 1841
...... 2 James Given 1801 -
...... 2 Jean Given 1802 -
.... +Alexander McLoud
.... 3 Nancy McLoud 1824 -
...... 2 Robert Given 1804 -
.... +Margaret Adams 1807 -
.... 3 Elizabeth Given 1837 -
.... 3 Mary Ann Given
.... 3 Jane Given 1840 -
.... 3 Robert Wallace Given 1842 -
...... 2 James Given 1806 -
...... 2 William Given 1808 -
...... 2 Mary Given 1810 -
...... 2 Joseph Given 1812 - - 1841

Robert and John Given were living at Booton in 1803. I suspect that they might be related to the Given family of Lisconnan.

Their son married Margaret, daughter of James and Martha Adams of Newbuildings in 1830 in 1st Ballymoney Presbyterian Church.

GERROW

GRAVE no. 63

Memento
Mori
Here lieth the
Body of John Gerrow
who departed this
life the 1st day of Oc
tober 1773. aged 80
years.
Also Mary his
daughter who depar
ted this life the 20th
day of January 1780
aged 36 years

There was a Gerrow family who lived at Newhill, Ballymoney in the 1800s.

William, son of William, married Jane Keers and had at least six children. Alexander married Ann, daughter of John and Jenny (Small) Getty of Kilmoyle in 1848 in Ballymoney Unitarian Church and his brother Robert married her sister Nancy in 1859. They were weavers. Robert and his family lived at Millquarter and later emigrated to America.

Mary Gerrow married Nathaniel, son of Alexander and Katie Culbert of Roddenfoot (see grave 416).

William married Jane Keers and they lived at Newhill.

1 William Gerrow
...... 2 Mary Gerrow
.... +Nathaniel Culbert
.... 3 Catherine Culbert 1812 -
.... 3 Eliza Culbert 1814 -
.... 3 Rose Culbert 1816 -
.... +William Forbis
.... 3 Alexander Culbert 1817 -
.... 3 John Culbert 1818 -
.... 3 William Culbert 1821 -
.... 3 Mary Jean Culbert 1826 -
.... 3 Martha Culbert 1829 -
.... 3 Sally Ann Culbert 1831 -
...... 2 William Gerrow
.... +Jane Keers 1792 - 1864
.... 3 James Gerrow 1820 - 1874
.... 3 William Gerrow 1822 -
.... 3 Nehemiah Gerrow 1824 -
.... 3 Alexander Gerrow 1825 -
.... +Ann Getty 1824 -
.... 3 Archibald Gerrow 1829 -
.... 3 Robert Park Gerrow 1832 -
.... +Nancy (or Anna) Getty 1826 -
...... 2 Martha Gerrow
.... +William Keers
.... 3 Jean Keers 1825 -
.... 3 Mary Ann Keers 1831 -
.... 3 David Keers 1833 -
.... 3 John Keers 1836 -
.... 3 Robert Keers 1839 -

MCAFEE

GRAVE no. 64

Here
Lieth the remains of
Robert McAfee
Late of Newbuildings who
Departed this life the 1st of
November 1832 aged 81 years
Also his wife
Martha McAfee
who departed this life the
19th April 1822 aged 70 years

1 Robert McAfee 1751 - 1832
.. +Martha 1752 - 1822
...... 2 Jean McAfee
.... +John Hayes - 1860
.... 3 Robert Hayes 1861 - 1939
.... +Maria Smith 1876 - 1947
.... 3 Martha Hayes 1822 -
.... +Robert Smyrell
             3 James P. Hayes 1824 - 1880
.... +Jessie Gordon 1820 - 1898
.... 3 John Hayes 1828 - 1874
.... 3 Jane Hayes 1831 -
.... 3 William Hayes
.... +Elizabeth Boyd
...... 2 Elizabeth McAfee

Robert and Martha McAfee were farmers at Newbuildings North, Ballymoney. Their daughter Jean married John Hayes, also of Newbuildings (see graves 66, 67).

Date Stone found inside the tower

MCELDERRY

GRAVE no. 65

Robert McElderry Leitrim
died 1832
Sarah Lyle his wife
died 1850
and their sons

Thomas McElderry	Samuel McElderry
Ballymoney	Leitrim
1788-1872	died 1844
Elizabeth Nevin	Mary Jane his wife
his wife	died 1840
died 1865	John, their son 1900

The earliest McElderry recorded in the area who lived in Leitrim, outside Ballymoney, is Patrick (1690-1756). He had at least five children, Elizabeth, Margaret, Patrick, John and Mary.

This Patrick (1720-1777) married Margaret and had children Mary, Jean, Robert, Thomas and Patrick. Thomas and Patrick emigrated to Baltimore, U.S.A.

Robert married Sally, daughter of John Lyle of Magheradonnell and had a family of eight. The family worshiped at Roseyards Presbyterian Church. John married Mary, daughter of Francis McKinley of Conagher (who was hanged in Coleraine for his part in the 1798 rebellion) and emigrated to Bristol, Pennsylvania. Patrick (1783-1866) married Betty Lyle, had three daughters. He stayed and farmed at Leitrim. Robert (1784-1821) emigrated to Jamaica. Sarah married James, son of James and Jane (McElderry) Lyle of Magheradonnell. Samuel (1786-1844) married Mary Jane Patrick, had a son John and farmed at Leitrim. Jane married James Neill in 1818 at Roseyards Presbyterian Church and had three children John, Samuel and Sally.

Their youngest son Thomas moved to Ballymoney and became a merchant and successful businessman. He married Elizabeth, daughter of Robert and Alice (Lyle) Nevin of Kilmoyle, Dervock. He died in Charles Street, Ballymoney.

There are still McElderry families living in the area. There is also a McElderry business in Ballymoney.

MCELDERRY

GRAVE no. 65

1 Thomas McElderry 1786 - 1871
.. +Elizabeth Nevin 1801 - 1867
...... 2 Sally McElderry 1826 -
.... +James Lyle
.... 3 Thomas Lyle 1848 -
.... +Margaret Annie Knox 1850 - 1911
...... 2 Jane McElderry 1827 - 1916
.... +David Boyd 1816 - 1892
.... 3 Samuel Burnside Boyd 1849 - 1929
.... 3 Sarah Boyd 1851 -
.... 3 Thomas Lyle Boyd 1853 - 1891
.... 3 John Boyd 1856 -
.... 3 Elizabeth Nevin Boyd 1858 - 1941
.... +William Howard Campbell 1858 - 1910
.... 3 Annie McElderry Boyd 1861 -
.... +John Stewart 1861 - 1913
.... 3 David Boyd 1864 - 1917
.... 3 Alice Lyle Boyd 1868 - 1948
...... 2 Robert McElderry 1829 - 1865
...... 2 William McElderry 1831 - 1866
...... 2 Anne McElderry 1833 - 1928
.... +Adam Thomson 1822 - 1900
.... 3 Rose Anna Thomson 1861 - 1865
.... 3 Thomas McElderry Thomson 1863 - 1863
.... 3 Thomas McElderry Thomson 1865 -
.... +Minnie Redpath
.... 3 James Ross Thomson 1866 - 1963
.... +Annie Thomson Todd 1871 - 1930
.... 3 Robert Benjamin Thomson 1868 - 1957
.... +Mary Stewart 1890 - 1965
.... 3 Rose Ann Ross Thomson 1870 - 1959
.... +William McAfee McKeague 1868 - 1931
.... 3 David Thomson
.... +Emily Galloway
...... 2 Thomas McElderry 1835 - 1911
.... +Alice Jane Knox 1848 - 1927
.... 3 Elizabeth Nevin McElderry 1869 - 1885
.... 3 Margaret McElderry 1870 - 1962
.... 3 Thomas Lyle McElderry 1872 -
.... +Harriette E. Smyth
.... 3 Alice Howard McElderry 1873 - 1952
.... 3 Annie McElderry 1874 - 1968
.... +Robert Dick Megaw 1868 - 1947
.... 3 Matilda Knox McElderry 1875 -
.... +J. N. Turnbull
.... 3 Sara Lyle McElderry 1877 - 1961
.... 3 Jane Isabel McElderry 1878 - 1897
.... 3 Robert Andrew McElderry 1880 - 1970
.... +Jennie Constance Moffett 1893 - 1973
.... 3 John Henry McElderry 1881 -
.... +Ina Symes
.... 3 Samuel Burnside Boyd McElderry 1885 - 1984
.... +Mildred Mary Orme 1884 - 1974
...... 2 Elizabeth McElderry 1837 - 1916
...... 2 John McElderry 1840 - 1935
.... +Matilda Knox 1845 - 1925
.... 3 Elizabeth Nevin McElderry 1868 -
.... 3 Robert Knox McElderry 1869 - 1949
.... 3 Thomas McElderry 1870 -
.... 3 Margaret Edith McElderry 1872 - 1957
.... 3 William McElderry 1873 - 1967
.... 3 Jane Burnside Boyd McElderry 1874 - 1961

HAYES

GRAVE no. 66

IHS
In loving memory
of Caroline Hayes
died 23rd July 1911

1. Robert Hayes 1861 - 1939
.. +Maria Smith 1876 - 1947
...... 2 Martha Mason Hayes 1897 -
.... +Samuel McMillan
...... 2 Robert Hayes 1898 -
...... 2 Emily Elizabeth Hayes 1903 -
.... +Thomas Law McCaughan
.... 3 Robert McCaughan - 1982
.... +Maud McDermott 1932 - 1995
.... 3 Thomas McCaughan
.... 3 John McCaughan
.... 3 Hayes McCaughan
.... +Zillah Calvin
.... 3 Margaret McCaughan
.... +Don Procter
.... 3 May McCaughan
.... +Lyle Nevin
...... 2 Jane McMillan Hayes 1906 -
.... +William McGrath
...... 2 Caroline Hayes 1909 - 1911
...... 2 Thomas Hayes 1913 -
...... 2 William Yorke Hayes 1913 -

Caroline Hayes was the daughter of Robert and Maria (Smith) Hayes of Newbuildings. Caroline was born on the 23th September 1909 (see grave 67).

HAYES

GRAVE no. 67

Erected
?
? Newbuildings
died ?
?
died ? who
Also their sons
John Hayes Newbuildings
11th Feb 1874 aged 46 years
James Hayes
died 22 August 1880
aged 54 years
Robert Hayes
24th April 1887
aged 67
His wife Matilda Hayes
died 25th July 1899
John Hayes
died 20th Jany 1939

1 John Hayes - 1860
.. +Jean McAfee
...... 2 Robert Hayes 1820 - 1887
...... 2 Martha Hayes 1822 -
.... +Robert Smyrell
.... 3 Jane Smyrell 1848 -
.... +William Adams 1836 -
.... 3 Matilda Smyrell 1850 -
.... 3 [2] George Smyrell 1852 -
.... +Elizabeth Killough
.... *2nd Wife of [2] George Smyrell:
.... +[1] Margaret Gordon Hayes 1851 -
.... *3rd Wife of [2] George Smyrell:
.... +Jane Smyrell 1860 -
...... 2 James P. Hayes 1824 - 1880
.... +Jessie Gordon 1820 - 1898
.... 3 Janey Hayes 1855 -
.... +David Boyd Keers 1847 -
.... 3 [1] Margaret Gordon Hayes 1851 -
.... +[2] George Smyrell 1852 -
.... 3 John P. Hayes 1853 -
.... 3 Mary E. Hayes 1859 -
...... 2 John Hayes 1828 - 1874
...... 2 Jane Hayes 1831 - 1889
...... 2 Robert Hayes 1861 - 1939
.... +Maria Smith 1876 - 1947
.... 3 Martha Mason Hayes 1897 -
.... +Samuel McMillan
.... 3 Robert Hayes 1898 -
.... 3 Emily Elizabeth Hayes 1903 -
.... +Thomas Law McCaughan
.... 3 Jane McMillan Hayes 1906 -
.... +William McGrath
.... 3 Caroline Hayes 1909 - 1911
.... 3 Thomas Hayes 1913 -
.... 3 William Yorke Hayes 1913 -

John Hayes was living at Newbuildings North in 1817 he was married to Jean, daughter of Robert and Martha McAfee, also of Newbuildings.

Their eldest daughter Martha married Robert Smyrell of Ballymaconnelly in 1846 in 1st Ballymoney Presbyterian Church.

Their second son James married Jessie, daughter of Nathaniel Gordon of Carnany, in 1851 in St. James Presbyterian Church.

Their youngest son Robert married Maria Smith in 1897 in Tamlaght O'Crilly Parish Church.

SMALL　　　　　　　　　　　　　　　　　　　　　GRAVE no. 68

John Small
late of Kirkhills
died 7th February 1882
aged 71 years
Also his son
Robert Small
died 24th April 1878
aged 20 years
Also his daughter Lizzie
died 10th January 1884
aged 31 years
And his wife Mary Ann died 2 Jan 1901
Also
Their son James Small died 31st March 1933
Also his wife Mary Jane died 7 Mar 1929
Also their children
William died 20th October 1892
Jane
died 15th April 1912
Mary died 12th November 1935

1 John Small 1810 - 1882
.. +Mary Ann Young 1814 - 1902
...... 2 James Small 1848 - 1933
.... +Mary Jane Smyth 1860 - 1929
.... 3 Elizabeth Small 1884 - 1966
.... +Robert Erskine 1879 - 1969
.... 3 John Small 1886 - 1951
.... +Anna Mary Richmond 1898 - 1995
.... 3 Robert Small 1888 - 1949
.... 3 William Small 1889 - 1892
.... 3 Mary Small 1891 - 1935
.... 3 Jane Small 1895 - 1912
.... 3 Anna Small 1897 - 1986
.... +William John Coulter 1876 - 1944
.... 3 Isabella Small 1898 - 1979
.... 3 William Small 1902 - 1972
.... +Mary Edith Bell 1907 - 1995
...... 2 Isabella Small 1850 - 1935
.... +John Jameson 1837 - 1887
.... 3 Samuel Jameson 1877 - 1900
.... 3 John Jameson 1879 - 1880
.... 3 William Jameson 1881 - 1949
.... +Emily Macauley 1888 - 1979
.... 3 James Small Jameson 1883 - 1971

SMALL

GRAVE no. 68

John Small was the son of James Small of Kirkhills. He married Mary Ann, daughter of Robert and Mary (Bateson) Young of Ballymoney in 1846 in 1st Ballymoney Presbyterian Church (see grave 392).

Their daughter Lizzie married John McIlroy of Cloughmills in 1st Ballymoney in 1881 but died in 1884 of tuberculosis. Her brother Robert who was was studying medicine in Belfast also died of tuberculosis.

Isabella married John Jameson, farmer of Drumart, in 1st Ballymoney in 1876. This Jameson family is not related to the other two graves in the Old Churchyard. They are buried in Kilraughts Old Churchyard. After her husband died, Isabella and her family emigrated to Canada. She died in Vulcan, Alberta.

William emigrated to South Africa and died in Capetown.

James married Mary Jane, youngest daughter of Samuel Chestnutt and Jane Moore (Woodside) Smyth of Stroan, Dervock. He stayed and farmed the home farm at Kirkhills. Their children, William, Mary and Jane died young at Kirkhills. Elizabeth married Robert Erskine of Dunaverney (see grave 236). John went to Canada for a time with his Jameson cousins but returned to marry and farmed at Drumart. Robert continued to farm at Kirkhill until retirement when he sold the farm and moved to Newhill Road, Ballymoney with his sisters Anna and Isabella.

.... +Ada Sophia Wright 1889 - 1976
.... *2nd Wife of James Small Jameson:
.... +Grace Elizabeth 1891 - 1956
.... *3rd Wife of James Small Jameson:
.... +Margaret Lillian Johnston 1883 - 1941
.... 3 Robert Jameson 1885 -
.... +Sarah Gilmour Macauley 1890 - 1978
.... 3 Annie Jameson 1886 - 1971
.... +Robert Edgar Lyman 1883 - 1979
...... 2 Elizabeth Small 1852 - 1884
.... +John McIlroy
.... 3 Janie McIlroy 1883 -
...... 2 William Small 1855 - 1939
.... +Chris Stewart - 1970
...... 2 Robert Small 1857 - 1878

SMALL

GRAVE no. 69

Here was interred
The body of the late
John Small
of Churchill who
departed this life
the 18th May 1816
aged 76 years

1 John Small 1740 - 1816
...... 2 James Small 1780 - 1866
.... 3 John Small 1810 - 1882
.... +Mary Ann Young 1814 - 1902
.......................see grave 68
.... 3 James Small 1808 -
.... +Margaret Murphy
.... 4 Rosetta Small 1831 - 1916
.... +James Boyle 1828 - 1896
.... 4 Robert Small 1833 -
.... 4 Mary Small 1835 -
.... +Alexander Stewart 1833 - 1918
.... 4 Margaret Small 1837 -
.... +William McQuilken
.... 4 Hugh Small 1838 - 1865
.... 4 Benjamin Small 1843 - 1915
.... 4 Elizabeth Small 1840 -
.... +John Ferguson 1818 - 1902
.... 3 Elizabeth Small
.... 3 William Small
.... +Jane Sharpe
.... 3 Benjamin Small
...... 2 William Small 1771 - 1867
...... 2 Jane Small 1787 - 1817

John Small was the son of John and Anna Small of Kirkmoyle (see grave 213). The Small family came from England as soldiers to protect the river Bann. They prospered in the area and this John moved to Kirkhills in the late 1700s.

John had family of William, James and Jane.

James had a son John who married Mary Ann Young of Ballymoney (see grave 68). He also had a son James who married Margaret Murphy of Turnarobert in 1827 in Armoy Presbyterian Church and their children. Nothing is known of Robert, Rosetta, Mary and Margaret emigrated to U.S.A., Hugh died young and Benjamin farmed at Ballyratahan in Dervock. Elizabeth married John, son of James and Ann Ferguson of Conagher in 1876 in St. James Presbyterian Church, who became very wealthy and moved to Coleraine.

SMALL

GRAVE no. 70

Memento Mori
This stone is erected to
Jane Small
of Churchills who
departed this life Janry
14th 1817 aged 29 years
In life beloved and
death lamented

Jane was the daughter of John Small (see grave 69) and sister of William and James (see grave 68). Kirkhills is the modern name for Churchills.

WEIR

GRAVE no. 71

Erected
to the memory of
Isabella (Wallace) Weir
who died at Newbuildings
the 6th of October 1858 aged
72 years
Her husband
Joseph Weir
? ? July 1876 aged
90 years
and their grand-daughter
Isabella Wallace Loudon
died 17th Dec. 1944 aged 84 years

1 Joseph Weir 1786 - 1876
.. +Isabella Wallace 1786 - 1858
...... 2 Mary Weir 1815 -
.... +Hugh Fisher
...... 2 Samuel Weir 1816 -
...... 2 Thomas Weir 1821 -
...... 2 Joseph Weir 1824 -
...... 2 Isabella Weir 1824 - 1917
.... +Francis Loudon 1828 - 1916
.... 3 Mary Loudon 1858 -
.... 3 Isabella Wallace Loudon 1860 - 1944
.... 3 Eliza Jane Loudon 1862 -
.... 3 William J. Loudon 1868 - 1925
.... 3 Martha Loudon 1870 - 1892
.... 3 Maggie Loudon 1873 - 1903
...... 2 Jane Weir
...... 2 Mary Weir 1826 -

    Ebby or Isabella Wallace, daughter of Samuel and Mary Wallace of Newbuildings North, Ballymoney, married Joseph Weir in 1813. Their daughter Isabella married Francis, son of William Loudon in 1857 in 1st Ballymoney Presbyterian Church. At the time of marriage Francis was a merchant in Ballybogey. They had five daughters and one son William J. who died a bachelor in Coleraine.

WALLACE GRAVE no. 72

Here lieth the body of
Robert Wallace
late of Newbuildings
who departed this life
the 17th July 1798
Aged 81 years. Also
his son Samuel Wallace
who departed this life
the 7 March 1827 aged
82 years

1 Robert Wallace 1717 - 1798
.... 2 Samuel Wallace 1745 - 1827
.... +Mary
.... 3 Thomas Wallace
.... +Mary Ramsay
.... 4 Samuel Wallace 1810 -
.... 4 Margaret Wallace 1812 -
.... 4 Hugh Wallace 1814 -
.... 4 Robert Wallace 1816 -
.... 4 Thomas Wallace 1819 -
.... 4 William Wallace 1819 -
.... 4 Mary Wallace 1821 -
.... 4 Eliza Wallace 1824 -
.... 3 Robert Wallace
.... 3 Isabella Wallace 1786 - 1858
.... +Joseph Weir 1786 - 1876
                           .see grave 71
.... 4 Jane Weir
.... 4 Mary Weir 1826 -

It is possible that the Wallace families of Newbuildings are related to the Wallaces of Booton (see graves 273, 274).

SINCLAIR   GRAVE no. 73

Memento
Mori
Here lieth the
body of James
Sinclair who de
parted this life
the 21st day of
June 1779 aged 71
years

1 James Sinclair 1708 - 1779
...... 2 James Sinclair 1751 - 1852
.... +Jane
.... 3 Jenny Sinclair 1803 -
.... 3 Peggy Ann Sinclair 1806 -
.... 3 James Sinclair 1809 - 1894
.... +Sarah Kirkpatrick 1816 - 1882
.... 4 Jane Sinclair - 1933
.... +John McAyeal 1830 - 1902
.... 4 John Sinclair 1848 -
.... 4 Sarah Sinclair 1852 - 1923
.... +Henry Robinson 1845 - 1905
.... 5 Mary Kirkpatrick Robinson 1890 - 1965
.... 5 Jane Robinson 1886 - 1944
.... 4 James Sinclair 1853 - 1920
.... 4 Mary Sinclair 1855 - 1861
.... 4 Anne Sinclair 1858 - 1920

The Sinclair family were farmers at Druckendult for many years. There were at least four generations named James.

James married Sarah, daughter of John and Jane (Wallace) Kirkpatrick of Ballynagashel, Kilraughts in 1847 in Kilraughts Presbyterian Church.

Their daughter Jane married John, son of Alexander and Sarah (Fullerton) McAyeal of Tullaghgore.

Their daughter Jane married Henry, son of Henry and Jane (Warnock) Robinson of Newbuildings in 1884 in 1st Ballymoney Presbyterian Church (see grave 364).

SINCLAIR — GRAVE no. 74

In
loving memory
of
James Sinclair
of Druckendult
who died 27th March 1894
his wife Sara
died 17th January 1882
their children
Annie
died 2nd February 1920
Jane Sinclair McAyeal
died 27th December 1933
Jane Robinson
died 14th May 1944
aged 58 years

See grave 73

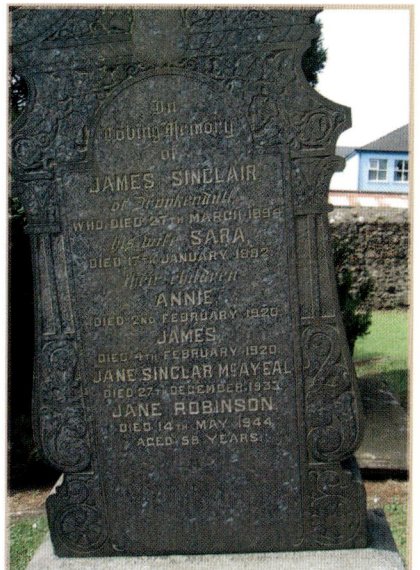

1 James Sinclair 1809 - 1894
.. +Sara Kirkpatrick 1816 - 1882
...... 2 Jane Sinclair - 1933
.... +John McAyeal 1830 - 1902
...... 2 John Sinclair 1848 -
...... 2 Sarah Sinclair 1852 - 1923
.... +Henry Robinson 1845 - 1905
.... 3 Jane Robinson 1886 - 1944
.... 3 Mary Kirkpatrick Robinson 1890 - 1965
...... 2 James Sinclair 1853 - 1920
...... 2 Mary Sinclair 1855 - 1861
...... 2 Anne Sinclair 1858 - 1920

NEVIN

GRAVE no. 75

Erected
to
the memory of
Samuel Nevin
of Claughey
who died 29th Decr 1893
aged 65 years
Also James Nevin
who died 15th May 1905
aged 41 years
and Annie Nevin
beloved wife of the above
James Nevin
who died 10th January 1947
aged 85 years

1 James Nevin 1792 -
.. +Nancy Ferrier
...... 2 James Nevin 1826 -
...... 2 Samuel Nevin 1827 - 1893
.... +Matilda Nevin 1839 - 1907
.... 3 James Nevin 1863 - 1905
.... +Annie Nevin 1861 - 1947
.... 4 Samuel Ferrier Nevin 1885 -
.... +Elizabeth Robinson
.... 4 Rachael Eliza Nevin 1889 -
.... +Joe McCaw
.... 4 William Nevin 1892 -
.... 4 John Nevin 1894 -
.... +Margaret Tweed Armour 1904 -
.... 4 Jeannie Matilda Neil Nevin 1896 -
.... +William Tweed Kennedy 1895 -
.... 4 Anne Nevin 1898 -
.... +David Thompson
.... 4 Thomas McElderry Nevin
.... +Minnie White
.... 4 Margaret Dunlop Nevin 1887 - 1977
.... +Robert Patterson 1875 - 1952
.... 3 Agnes Nevin 1865 - 1937
.... +William John Cooper
.... 4 John Nevin Cooper 1888 -
.... 4 Daniel Stirling Cooper 1890 -
.... 4 Annie Hamilton Cooper 1891 -
.... 4 Matilda Nevin Cooper 1900 -
.... 4 Samuel Burnside Boyd Cooper 1903 -
.... 4 Jane Neil Cooper 1903 -
.... 3 John Nevin 1867 -
...... 2 Matilda Nevin 1829 -

Samuel Nevin was the son of James and Nancy (Ferrier) Nevin of Claughey. He married Matilda, daughter of John and Jane (Neill) Nevin of Kilmoyle in 1862 in Trinity Presbyterian Church.

Their eldest son James married Annie, daughter of William and Margaret Dunlop (Nevin) Nevin of Kilmoyle in 1884 in 1st Ballymoney Presbyterian Church.

Their daughter Agnes married William John, son of Daniel and Anna (Stirling) Cooper of Bendooragh in 1888 in 1st Ballymoney Presbyterian Church.

NEVIN

GRAVE no. 76

Erected
to
the memory of
Samuel Nevin
of Claughey
who died 27th Decr 1876
aged 80 years
Also his daughter
Esther
who died 11th January 1899
aged 86 years
his son James
who died 24th May 1907
aged 60 years
and Hugh who died in infancy

1 John Nevin 1756 - 1808
...... 2 Jean Nevin 1790 -
.... +Alexander Gamble
.... 3 Sarah Gamble 1818 -
.... 3 John Gamble 1823 -
.... 3 Peter Gamble 1825 -
.... 3 Peter Gamble 1827 -
.... 3 Jenny Gamble 1830 -
.... 3 Matilda Gamble 1832 -
...... 2 James Nevin 1792 -
.... +Nancy Ferrier
..............see grave 75
...... 2 Mary Nevin 1794 -
.... +Thomas Thompson
...... 2 Samuel Nevin 1796 - 1876
.... +Martha Swan 1802 - 1899
.... 3 Esther Nevin 1844 - 1860
.... 3 James Nevin 1847 - 1907
.... 3 Hugh Nevin 1851 - 1852

Samuel Nevin was the son of John and brother of James (see grave 75). He married Martha Swan and had a family of at least three none of whom seemed to marry.

One sister Jean married Alexander, son of Peter and Mary Gamble of Polintamney. His other sister married Thomas Thompson in 1821 in 1st Ballymoney Presbyterian Church.

GALT

GRAVE no. 77

To the memory
of Robert Galt of
Ballymoney who died
26th August 1845
aged 76 Years

There was a grocer named Robert Galt present in Main Street, Ballymoney in 1824 and 1846.

There is also a will in the Public Record Office of Northern Ireland (PRONI) of a Robert Galt who died 14th May 1846 with probate on 3rd March 1847. It mentions his wife Margaret and seven children, all minors. The house in Main Street was sold to John Anderson and Margaret and her children emigrated to America.

Robert's father was a merchant in Ballymoney.

BOYD

GRAVE no. 78

To the memory of
John Boyd
late of Forttown
who departed this life
5th Feby 1851 aged 76 years
Also his son
Matthew
who died April 26th 1851
aged 10 years
Margaret, wife of John Boyd
died 20th December 1868
aged 69 years

1 John Boyd 1778 - 1854
.. +Margaret Cherry 1799 - 1868
...... 2 James Boyd 1835 - 1909
.... +Martha Hunter Forsythe 1837 - 1907
...............see grave 78
...... 2 John Boyd 1838 - 1907
.... +Margaret Gordon Lyle 1845 - 1875
.... 3 Mary Gordon Lyle Boyd 1865 - 1955
.... 3 Joseph Douglas Boyd 1867 -
.... +Margaret Smith Bell
.... 3 Margaret Cherry Boyd 1868 - 1909
.... 3 James Boyd 1870 - 1956
.... +Annie Wilson 1869 - 1954
...... 2 Joseph Douglas Boyd 1840 -
.... +Martha J. Rodgers
...... 2 Matthew Boyd 1841 - 1851

    John Boyd, a farmer at Forttown, married Margaret, daughter of John Cherry of Myroe House, Limavady at her home in 1834. They had children James, John, Joseph Douglas and Matthew.
    John married Margaret Gordon, daughter of Thomas and Mary Ann (Gordon) Lyle, a merchant in Church Street, Ballymoney in 1864 in 1st Ballymoney Presbyterian Church. John had a drapery business at 20, Church Street, Ballymoney. They are buried in St. Patrick's Parish Churchyard, Ballymoney.
    James Douglas Boyd married Martha Rodgers in 1864 in 1st Limavady Presbyterian Church.
He lived in Limavady and became a Justice of the Peace.

BOYD

GRAVE no. 79

Erected
by
James Boyd
Forttown
In memory of his wife
Martha Hunter Forsythe
who died 11th March 1907
aged 69 years
Here also lies
the above named James Boyd
who died 7th April 1909
aged 73 years

1 James Boyd 1835 - 1909
.. +Martha Hunter Forsythe 1837 - 1907
...... 2 Margaret Cherry Boyd 1861 -
...... 2 John Boyd 1862 - 1955
.... +Rachael Anderson 1878 - 1966
.... 3 Annie Matthews Boyd 1912 - 1978
.... +John Fulton Jamison 1915 - 1975
.... 3 Martha Forsythe Boyd 1918 -
.... +Robert Samuel Baird 1911 -
.... 3 James Boyd 1910 -
.... 3 John Boyd 1913 -
.... +Margaret Mary Moore Forsythe 1921 -
.... 3 William Brown Forsythe Boyd 1917 -
.... +Nancy Jean Lamont 1927 -
.... 3 Margaret Boyd 1922 - 1922
.... 3 Charles Anderson Boyd 1915 -
.... +Elizabeth Wallace Forsythe 1918 -
...... 2 Robert Boyd 1865 - 1925
.... +Elizabeth Lamont Jellie 1870 - 1924
.... 3 Clarence Boyd
.... 3 Robert Forsythe Boyd
...... 2 Mary Gordon Lyle Boyd 1866 - 1955
...... 2 Margaret Cherry Boyd 1868 - 1948
.... +Alexander Hill 1863 - 1933
.... 3 Myra Boyd Hill 1896 - 1964
.... 3 Eveline Martha Forsythe Hill 1898 -
.... 3 James Boyd Hill 1903 -
.... +Doreen Warnock
...... 2 Annie Wilson Boyd 1869 - 1954
...... 2 James Boyd 1870 - 1956
...... 2 Mary Brown Boyd 1873 - 1953

James, son of John and Margaret (Cherry) Boyd married Martha Hunter Forsythe, daughter of Robert and Mary (Brown) Forsythe of Forttown in 1860 in 1st Ballymoney Presbyterian Church. They had a family of twelve children.

Their eldest son John married Rachael, daughter of Charles and Annie (Matthews) Anderson of Culcrum in 1908 in Ballyweaney Presbyterian Church. He worked the home farm at Forttown. Two of their sons (Charles and John) married their second cousins, the Forsythe sisters who lived next door to them.

Their second son Dr. Robert Boyd was a ship's surgeon as a young man and sailed to America, along the West Coast of Africa and up the Congo River. He then practised in Portadown and Belfast. He then married Elizabeth Jellie of

BOYD

GRAVE no. 79

Moneyrea in 1897. They had sons Dr. Clarence Boyd, who was in Singapore when it fell during WW2, and Robert Forsythe Boyd.

Their youngest son James emigrated to U.S.A.

Their daughter Margaret married Alexander, son of Joseph and Mary (Boyd) Hill of Kirkhills in 1893 in Carncullagh Presbyterian Church.

Mary (Minnie) married Adam Wales, son of James and Mary (Wales) McClure of Strone, Dervock in 1867 in Bushmills Presbyterian Church.

Jane married John, son of James and Matilda (Cochrane) Knox of Ballymoney in 1861 in 1st Ballymoney Presbyterian Church.

Their other daughters were unmarried.

```
.......... +Adam Wales McClure 1873 - 1924
............... 3 James McClure 1910 -
............... 3 Frederick Boyd McClure 1912 -
............... 3 John Knox McClure 1915 - 1982
...... 2 Isabella Boyd 1875 - 1941
...... 2 Martha Boyd 1878 -
...... 2 Elizabeth Curry Boyd 1883 - 1953
...... 2 Jane Boyd 1871 -
.......... +John Knox 1866 -
............... 3 James Boyd Knox 1898 -
.................... +Ieria H. 1901 - 1985
............... 3 Minnie Brown Knox 1900 -
.................... +John Stuart
............... 3 Jeannie Knox 1902 - 1968
```

GETTY

GRAVE no. 80

In memory of the ?
James Getty
of Kirkmoyle who died the
8th February 1784 aged 74 years
Also Hannah his wife
who died the 4th of November
1766 aged 58 years
Andrew Getty
their son who died the 6th Dec 1814
James Getty   ?   ?   ?
and
and Jennet Getty his wife who
died December 1820
Aged 73
James Getty late of Heagles
died 7th Sept 1861
Jane Getty died 14th May 1880
John Getty Heagles
died 6th September 1910 aged 60
years
His wife Mary Jane
died 29th Nov 1926 aged 88 years

1 James Getty 1709 - 1784
.. +Hannah 1708 - 1766
...... 2 James Getty 1745 – 1825
          see grave 81
...... 2 John Getty 1747 - 1825
.... +Mary Moore 1748 – 1801
          see grave 82
...... 2 David Getty 1749 - 1813
.... +Mary Taggart 1747 - 1825
...... 2 Andrew Getty 1755 - 1814
.... +Jane
.... 3 James Getty 1784 - 1861
.... +Jane Steele - 1880
.... 4 John Getty - 1910
.... +Mary Jane Cooper 1836 - 1925
.... 4 James Getty 1824 -
.... +Mary Small
.... 4 Mary Getty 1825 -
.... 3 John Getty 1786 - 1859
.... 3 Mary Getty
.... 3 Ann Getty - 1843
.... 3 dau Getty 1788 -
.... +Hamill
.... 4 Ann Hamill
.... 3 dau Getty 1790 -
.... +William Orr 1786 -

Getty families can be traced in the Ballymoney area as far back as the early 1600s. This branch lived at Kirkmoyle and Heagles. The names James and John appear in every family in every generation, so some of these relationships may not be accurate.

Andrew, youngest son of James and Hannah moved to Heagles, probably to the Moore farm.

His son James married Jane Steele in 1822 in St. Patrick's Parish Church and his son John married Mary Jane, daughter of John and Jenny (Adams) Cooper of Kilmoyle.

GETTY

GRAVE no. 81

To the memory
of James Getty of
Kirkmoyle who died ?
J ? ? 1825 aged 80 years
Also his wife
Nancy Getty died
11th Jul 1841 aged 85
years
Also Mary ? ? of James Getty
? ? ?

1 James Getty 1745 - 1825
.. +Agnes ? 1756 - 1841
...... 2 James Getty
.... +Margaret McKeown
.... 3 Mary Getty 1806 -
.... 3 Ann Getty 1808 -
.... 3 Jean Getty 1810 -
.... 3 Andrew Getty 1812 -
.... 3 Hannah Getty 1815 -
.... 3 James Getty 1817 -
.... 3 Margaret Getty 1820 -
...... 2 Andrew Getty
.... +Mary Norris
.... 3 Ann Getty 1832 -
.... 3 John Getty 1834 -
.... 3 Isabella Getty 1836 -
.... 3 Elizabeth Getty 1838 -
.... 3 James Getty 1840 -
...... 2 Agnes Getty

James Getty was the son of James and Hannah Getty of Kirkmoyle (see grave 80). In 1817, he had two children, Andrew and Agnes living with him.
They possibly had a son James who married Margaret McKeown.
Andrew married Mary Norris of Ballynag in 1831 in 1st Ballymoney Presbyterian Church.

GETTY

GRAVE no. 82

In Memory of
John Getty
of Kirkmoyle who died 20 Sep
1825 aged 78. Also his wife
Mary
who died March the 21st 1801
aged 52
Moore Getty
Their youngest son ? a
Sentiment of that dear C?
this stone to their memory
Who also is interred here
died 29th May 1869
aged 81 years
Also Nancy his wife
died 6th May 1845
Aged 53 years
Likewise his daughter
Nancy Ann Getty
who died 19th December 1885
aged 56 years
James Getty
Died 19th Jan 1895
aged 77 years
Jane Douglas Getty
Died 5th June 1926
aged 75 years

1 John Getty 1747 - 1825
.. +Mary Moore 1748 - 1801
...... 2 Hannah Getty
...... 2 Mary Getty
...... 2 Moore Getty 1787 - 1869
.... +Nancy Cooper 1791 - 1845
.... 3 James Getty 1815 - 1895
.... +Jane Douglas 1850 - 1926
.... 4 Moore Getty 1871 - 1871
.... 4 James Moore Gladstone Getty 1879 - 1951
.... +Annie Kerr McIlmoyle - 1974
.... 4 John Getty 1881 - 1972
.... 4 Anna Jeanette Boyce Getty 1884 - 1967
.... 3 John Getty 1819 -
.... 3 John Getty 1821 - 1891
.... +Margaret Patterson - 1902
.... 4 Mary Getty 1863 -
.... 4 Matilda Getty 1865 -
.... 4 Moore Nelson Getty 1869 -
.... 4 Jane Douglas Getty 1872 - 1902
.... 4 Margaret Getty 1874 -
.... 4 James Getty 1876 - 1895
.... 4 John Getty 1879 -
.... 4 Caroline Getty 1881 -
.... 3 Mary Getty 1823 -
.... 3 Moore Getty 1827 - 1894
.... +Mary Nelson
.... 4 Frances Sophia Getty 1862 - 1956
.... 4 Anne Getty 1864 - 1927
.... 4 Wilhemina Muir Getty 1866 - 1960
.... 4 Mary Robina Getty 1869 - 1944

GETTY   GRAVE no. 82

John, son of James and Hannah Getty of Kirkmoyle married Mary, daughter of James Moore of Heagles about 1786. Their son John married Jenny Small and Moore married Ann (or Nancy) Cooper of Kilmoyle.

Moore's eldest son James married Jane, daughter of Samuel and Margaret Jane (Boyce) Douglas in 1869 in Ballycarry Non Subscribing Presbyterian Church near Larne, where his brother Moore was minister. The Douglas family were originally from Maine, near Limavady but had moved to Glenstall.

John Getty married Margaret Patterson of Culderry in 1861 and they farmed at Heagles.

Rev. Moore married Mary Nelson in 1861 in Ballycarry.

Their daughter married John, son of John and Mary (Taggart) McCaughan of Kilmahamoge, Ballintoy in 1848 in St. Patrick's Parish Church, Ballymoney. Most of this family emigrated to U.S.A.

Their youngest daughter Jane married Alexander Jackson of Drumbane, NewtonLimavady in 1860 in the Remonstrant Meeting House, Ballymoney.

```
                    +Alfred Turner
           3 Hannah Getty 1828 -
              +John McCaughan 1825 -
                 4 John Moore McCaughan 1850 - 1920
                 4 James McCaughan 1852 -
                    +Miss Cooper
                 4 William Charles McCaughan
                 4 Margaret McCaughan
                    +James Currie
                 4 Mary Jane McCaughan 1853 -
                    +Isaac Sweeton 1854 -
                 4 Sarah McCaughan
                 4 Frances McCaughan 1862 -
                    +James Irwin 1852 -
                 4 Agnes McCaughan
           3 Nancy Ann Getty 1829 - 1885
           3 Jane Getty 1831 -
              +Alexander Jackson
     2 John Getty
        +Jean
           3 James Getty 1808 - 1817
           3 Moore Getty 1806 -
           3 Mary Getty 1810 -
           3 Hannah Getty 1812 -
           3 Jean Getty 1815 -
```

MCCRELLIS

GRAVE no. 83

To the memory of John McCrellis late of Kirkmoyle who departed this life the 15th February 1838
Aged 82 years
Also his beloved wife Martha who departed this life the 5 Apr 1851
Aged 96 years
? ? ? ? cted by
There ? ? ? ?
Elizabeth
Samuel McCreelis
Died 18th November 1881?
Thomas McCreelis
Died 21st February 1902
aged 82 years

1 John McCrellis 1755 - 1838
.. +Martha ? 1755 - 1851
...... 2 John McCrellis 1793 -
...... 2 Samuel McCrellis 1795 -
.... +Jean Hamill
.... 3 Matilda McCrellis 1824 -
.... 3 Thomas McCrellis 1826 - 1902
.... 3 Samuel McCrellis 1829 - 1891
.... +Margaret Anderson
.... 3 James McCrellis 1834 -
.... 3 John McCrellis 1842 - 1900
...... 2 Mary McCrellis 1797 -
.... +Robert Thompson 1797 -
.... 3 Mary Ann Thompson 1829 -
.... +James Taggart
.... 3 Alexander Thompson 1828 -
.... +Margaret Anne Stephenson
.... 3 Roseann Thompson
...... 2 Matthew McCrellis 1799 -
.... +Esther Trimble
...... 2 Elizabeth McCrellis 1801 - 1877
.... +Daniel McMullan 1812 - 1893
...... 2 Jean McCrellis 1801 -
.... +William Thompson 1799 - 1868
.... 3 John Thompson 1824 -
.... 3 Elizabeth Thompson 1829 -
.... +James Biggart 1827 -
.... 3 Janey Thompson 1832 -
.... +William Thompson
.... 3 Francis Thompson 1833 -
.... 3 James Boyle Thompson 1837 -
.... 3 Robert Thompson 1840 -
.... 3 Mary Ann Thompson 1842 -
.... +James Dickey
.... 3 Hugh Thompson
.... +Ellen Walker

John and Martha McCrellis farmed at Kirkmoyle. Their son Samuel, a farmer at Secon, married Jean Hamill, and their son Samuel married Margaret Anderson in 1882 in Benvarden Presbyterian Church.

Their daughter Mary married Robert, son of Hugh and Rose Thompson of Ballygobbin in 1826. Matthew married Esther Trimble of Tullycapple in 1828. Elizabeth married Daniel McMullan, son of Charles in 1849 and they continued to farm at Kirkmoyle. Jean married Hugh Thompson of Ballygobbin, brother of Robert, in 1825. They each married in 1st Ballymoney Presbyterian Church.

MCMULLAN

GRAVE no. 84

Erected
by
Daniel McMullan
of Kirkmoyle
to the memory of his wife
Elizabeth McMullan
who died 21st June 1877 aged 76 years
John McCrellis Kilmoyle
Died 7th October 1900 aged 58 years

Daniel McMullan, son of Charles, married Elizabeth McCrellis in 1849 but did not appear to have any children. He was a farmer at Kirkmoyle where the McCrellis family also farmed. John who was buried in the same grave was their nephew. Daniel died on 11th March 1893 at Kirkmoyle (see grave 83).

BOYD

GRAVE no. 85

Underneath lie the
Body of Daniel Boyd
late of Culbrim who
departed this life the
25 day of Decemr 1778
aged 78 years. Also Mary
Ann his wife who de
parted this life the 29
of May 1773 aged 71 years
? ? ?   Margaret Boyd

    The townland of Culbrim can also be spelled as Coolebreen or Kulbrin and is at the side of the River Bann next to Macfin. In 1803 there was a John Boyd and in 1817 an Abraham.   There were other Boyd families at Macfin. In 1825, at the time of the Tithe applotment, there was only a Samuel.
    Abraham and Mary Jane had two daughters baptised in St. Patrick's Parish Church, Ballymoney. Mary was born in 1817 and Jane in 1819.

MCALONAN GRAVE no. 86

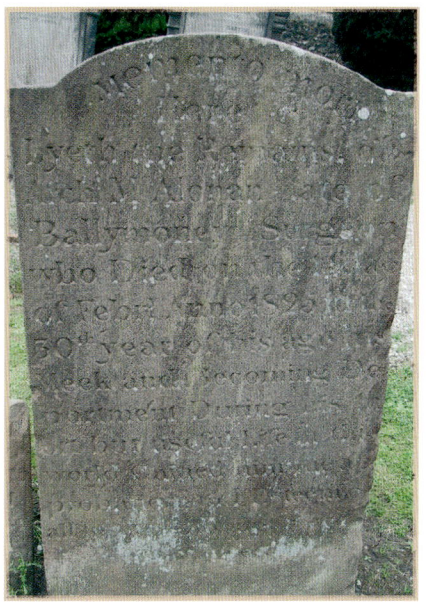

Memento Mori
Here
Lyeth the remains of
Archd McAlonan late of
Ballymoney surgeon
who died on the 4th
Febry anno 1825 in his
30th year of his age
Meek and becoming De
portment During his sh
ort but useful life in this
world gained him the ap
proval ? ? esteem
all ? ? ? ? ?

Archibald was the son of Archibald McAlonan, a publican of Church Street, Ballymoney, and Agnes. He had brothers Samuel (b.1805), Robert (b.1807) and sisters Rachael and Jean.

Archibald was a doctor.

The McAlonan name also appears in the Kilraughts area. Some of the family may have moved there to farm.

THOMPSON

GRAVE no. 87

Memento Mori
Here lieth the bo
dy of Mary Thompson
wife of William
Thompson of Gre
enshields who de
parted this life the
30th day of Septem
ber 1773 aged 23
years and three
of their children

1 William Thompson
.. +Mary 1750 - 1773
*2nd Wife of William Thompson:
.. +Letitia
...... 2 George Washington Thompson 1787 - 1840
.... +Jane Galbraith 1789 - 1863
.... 3 William Marshall Thompson 1820 - 1906
.... +Matilda Robinson
.... 3 John Galbraith Thompson 1821 - 1911
.... 3 Letitia Thompson 1824 -
.... 3 Sarah C. Thompson 1826 -
.... 3 Elizabeth Thompson 1829 - 1918
.... 3 Jane Thompson 1831 - 1900
.... 3 George Washington Thompson 1832 - 1885
...... 2 Alexander Marshall Thomson 1781 - 1873
.... +Jean Stewart
.... 3 Mary Ann Thomson 1817 -
.... 3 Jean Thomson 1820 -
.... 3 Charles Stuart Thompson 1826 - 1874
.... 3 Letitia Marshall Thomson 1830 -
...... 2 Jean Thomson

This is possibly the first wife of William Thompson of Greenshields. He was married again to Letitia. They had at least three children.

Their son George Washington Thompson married Jane, daughter of John and Letitia (Marshall) Galbraith of Druckendult and emigrated to Illinois ca. 1840.

Another son Alexander Marshall Thompson married Jean Stewart and they also emigrated to Illinois.

UNREADABLE

GRAVE no. 88

THOMPSON

GRAVE no. 89

?
?
?
?
And his son
William R?
Late of Ballymoney
Died   ?   1861
Aged 83 years

THOMPSON

GRAVE no. 90

Momento
Mori Here lyes
The body of Eliz
Thompson wife of
John Thompson
who departed th
is life the 21st of
?ber 1751 aged 36

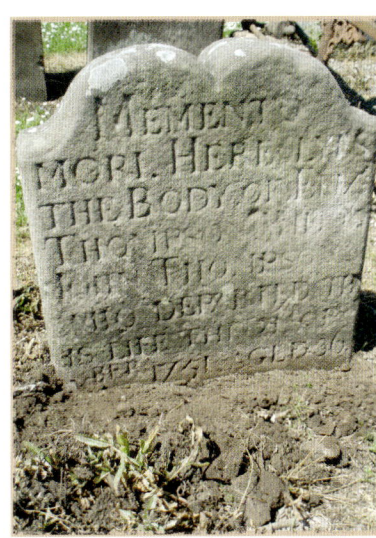

THOMPSON

GRAVE no. 91

Unreadable

THOMPSON

GRAVE no. 92

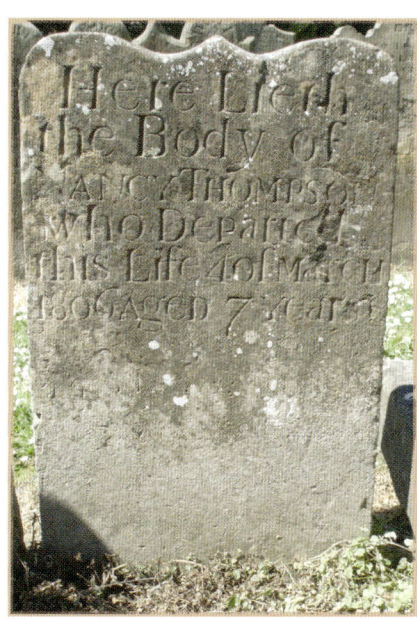

Here lieth
the body of
Nancy Thompson
who departed
This life 4 of March
1806 aged 7 years

MCAFFEE

GRAVE no. 93

Here lieth
The body of
James McAffee
late of Curryshiskin
who departed this life
the 2nd of June 1800 aged
74 years also his wife
Jennit MacAfee
who departed this
life the 8th March 1802

1 James MacAfee 1726 - 1800
.. +Jinnet - 1802
...... 2 Robert MacAfee 1760 - 1833
.... +Mary Ann ?
.... 3 James MacAfee 1808 - 1882
.... +Jane Boyd 1802 - 1889
.... 4 John MacAfee 1832 - 1862
.... 4 Elizabeth MacAfee 1835 -
.... 4 Elizabeth MacAfee 1837 - 1860
.... 4 Robert Boyd MacAfee 1840 - 1896
.... +Sarah Luke
.... 4 Margaret MacAfee 1842 - 1863
.... 4 James Alexander MacAfee 1852 -
.... 3 Mary MacAfee 1810 -
.... +Andrew Knox 1800 -
.... 4 William Knox 1821 - 1874
.... +Isabella McKay
.... 4 Robert Knox 1822 - 1863
.... 4 Margaret Knox 1825 - 1898
.... +Joseph Boyd 1817 - 1898
.... 4 Mary Ann Knox 1827 - 1907
.... +Andrew Wright 1817 - 1872
.... 4 Andrew Wright Knox 1829 -
.... 4 Andrew Knox 1832 -
.... 4 John Leslie Knox 1834 -
.... +Jane Moody 1840 -
.... 4 James Knox 1836 -
.... +Eliza Jane Boyd
.... 3 Daniel MacAfee 1812 -
.... 3 William MacAfee 1813 - 1898
.... +Susan Wilson 1825 - 1906
....   see grave 128

It is reputed that four MacAfee (McDuffee, McAffee, McAfee) brothers came to Ulster from Scotland in the 17th century. The two eldest settled at Park, near Dunluce, the third at Currysisken, near Ballymoney, and the youngest settled at Englishtown near Coleraine.

Thomas, either a son or grandson of the settler at Currysisken had four sons, James, Samuel and Robert/John? This Robert/John was executed at Coleraine in 1798 for his part in the uprising.

Robert's eldest son James married Jane, daughter of John and Elizabeth Boyd of Ballywindland in 1828. Their sons emigrated; John to Nevada where he drowned and Robert to Colac, Victoria where he was a teacher. Their daughters died young.

Their daughter Mary married Andrew, son of William and Margaret Knox of Currysisken in 1821 in 1st Ballymoney Presbyterian Church.

Postcard ca. 1920s

MACAFEE

GRAVE no. 94

Erected
to the memory of
Martha MacAfee Currysisken
who fell asleep trusting in the
saviour she had long known
and loved on the 23rd August 1858
Aged 72 years
Her children rise up and call her
blessed. Her husband also and he
praiseth her.   ProverbsXXXI 28
Also Thomas MacAfee
late of Currysisken
who departed this life December
16th 1866
Aged 82 years

1 Thomas MacAfee 1784 - 1866
.. +Martha Knox 1786 - 1858
...... 2 Samuel MacAfee 1812 - 1812
...... 2 William MacAfee 1813 - 1861
.... +Rachael Pinkerton 1820 – 1899
              see grave 100
...... 2 Susannah MacAfee 1815 - 1894
.... +William Mitchell Orr 1812 - 1856
.... 3 Matilda MacAfee Orr 1852 -
.... +R. Glover
.... 3 William Thomas Orr 1855 - 1883
...... 2 Margaret MacAfee 1818 - 1900
.... +Robert Knox 1809 - 1851
.... 3 Andrew Knox 1843 - 1844
.... 3 Matilda Knox 1845 - 1925
.... +John McElderry 1840 - 1935
.... 3 Alice Jane Knox 1847 - 1847
.... 3 Alice Jane Knox 1848 - 1927
.... +Thomas McElderry 1835 - 1911
.... 3 Margaret Annie Knox 1850 - 1911
.... +Thomas Lyle 1848 - 1915
.... 3 Bessie Knox 1851 - 1880
.... +George Knox Galloway 1844 -
...... 2 Thomas MacAfee 1820 - 1914
.... +Erina Maingay
.... 3 Erina MacAfee
.... 3 Frances MacAfee
.... 3 Thomas MacAfee
...... *2nd Wife of Thomas MacAfee:
.... +Harriett Lowry
...... 2 Matilda MacAfee 1823 - 1862

Thomas was the eldest son of Samuel and Shusanna (Dinsmore) MacAfee, brother of James (see grave 93). His brother John stayed at Currysisken but died unmarried. Joseph emigrated in 1811 and died in Ohio in 1816. Samuel emigrated in 1817 and moved to South Carolina in 1824. James emigrated in 1815 and also moved to South Carolina in 1824.

Thomas married Martha Knox and had a family of eight. He died at Springfield at the home of his daughter Margaret (Mrs Robert Knox). He was an elder in 1st Ballymoney Presbyterian Church where most of children married.

MACAFEE

GRAVE no. 94

Their daughter eldest Susanhah married William Mitchell, son of William and Mary (Mitchell) Orr in 1848. He was a woollen draper in High Street, Ballymoney.

Their second daughter Margaret married Robert, son of Andrew and Alice (Howard) Knox of Culramoney in 1840. They were farmers at Springfield, near Culramoney.

Their son Thomas had a long and distinquished career as a Presbyterian minister in Ardglass, Co. Down from 1846 to 1905.

Another daughter, Matilda, married Thomas Carson of Ballylig in 1848.

A daughter Nancy married James, son of James and Elizabeth (Workman) Hamill in 1852, who was a mechanic and then a jeweller in Main Street, Ballymoney. Their two sons, the Rev. Professor Thomas Macafee Hamill and the Rev. James Macafee Hamill became prominent ministers in the Presbyterian Church.

Their youngest daughter Jane married Andrew McKeague of Ballywindland in 1860.

```
.......... +Thomas Carson
............... 3 Joseph Carson
............... 3 Martha Carson
............... 3 Margaret Carson
............... 3 Thomas Carson
.................. +Selina Watson
............... 3 John Carson
.................. +Miss Morrow
............... 3 Anne Carson
...... 2 Nancy MacAfee 1826 - 1914
.......... +James Hamill 1824 - 1911
............... 3 Thomas McAfee Hamill 1853 - 1919
.................. +Mary Isobel McFarland
............... 3 Marianne Hamill
.................. +Robert Allen Beatty 1859 - 1933
............... 3 Martha Knox Hamill 1860 - 1954
.................. +William Charles Pollock 1865 - 1941
............... 3 Agnes MacAfee Hamill 1862 - 1907
............... 3 Harriet Hamill 1864 - 1946
............... 3 James MacAfee Hamill 1866 - 1912
.................. +Margaret Dickson
............... 3 Margaret Knox Hamill 1869 - 1869
...... 2 Jane MacAfee 1829 - 1913
.......... +Andrew McKeague 1833 - 1916
                 see grave 44
```

WHITE

GRAVE no. 95

Here
Lieth the B
ody of Margaret
White who
Died December
10th 1750

CURRY

GRAVE no. 96

**Momento Mori
Here lyeth the
body of Andrew
Curry who dep
arted this life
April the 1st 1766**

1 Andrew Curry 1686 - 1766
.. +Mary Ann Lamont
...... 2 Mary Curry
.... +Joseph Wright - 1817
.... 3 Thomas Wright 1780 - 1860
.... +Sarah Boyd 1790 - 1891
.... 3 Andrew Wright 1781 - 1857
.... 3 Mary Ann Wright 1767 - 1860
.... +Gideon Keers 1753 - 1832
.... 3 Joseph Wright
.... +Sarah Stirling 1781 - 1822
.... 3 Sallie Wright
.... +James Lyons 1768 - 1830
.... 3 Jane (or Mary) Wright
.... +Robert Culbertson
.... 3 Nancy Wright
.... +Samuel Spence
...... 2 Martha Curry
.... +Benjamin McKeague
              see grave 44
...... 2 John Curry

Andrew Curry of Ballygan married Mary Ann Lamont also of Ballygan. Their daughter Martha married Benjamin McKeague of Ballywindland (see grave 44). Another daughter Mary married Joseph Wright of Culbrim (see graves 158, 160, 161).

John Curry was present in 1740 and 1766. There are also two baptisms recorded for children of John, James in 1753 and Marmaduke in 1756.

DINSMOOR

GRAVE no. 97

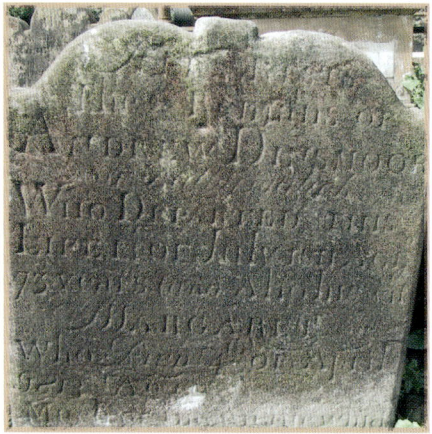

The remains of
Andrew Dinsmoor
Ballywattick
who departed this
life 18 of July 1811 aged
73 years
Margaret
who died 4th April
1813 aged 62 years
M ? ? ? which

1 Andrew Dinsmore 1737 - 1811
.. +Margaret Dinsmore 1750 - 1813
...... 2 Susan Dinsmore 1788 -
.... +James Neill 1785 -
.... 3 Catherine Neill
.... 3 James Neill
.... 3 Jane Neill 1812 - 1896
.... 3 Margaret Neill 1813 -
.... 3 Ann Neill 1816 -
.... 3 Rachael Neill 1819 -
.... 3 Mary Neill 1821 -
.... 3 William Neill 1823 -
...... 2 Rachael Dinsmore 1790 - 1837
.... +John Hunter 1784 - 1823
.... 3 William Hunter 1811 - 1877
.... 3 Andrew Hunter 1813 -
.... 3 John Hunter 1817 - 1887
.... 3 Margaret Hunter 1820 -
...... 2 Jean Dinsmore 1792 -
.... +Joseph Small 1788 -
.... 3 Jean Small 1804 -
.... 3 Hannah Small 1805 - 1889
.... +Francis McKinley 1798 -
.... 3 Margaret Small 1807 - 1882
.... 3 Jennet Small 1809 -
.... 3 Joseph Small 1815 -
.... 3 Andrew Small 1817 -
.... 3 James Small 1820 - 1900
.... 3 Robert Small 1823 - 1870
.... 3 Mary Jean Small 1824 -
.... 3 Joseph Small 1838 -
...... 2 Mary Dinsmore 1794 -
...... 2 Andrew Dinsmore
...... 2 John Dinsmore
...... 2 Robert Dinsmore 1770 - 1830
...... 2 James Samuel Dinsmore 1771 - 1846
...... 2 William Dinsmore
...... 2 Andrew Dinsmore

    Andrew Dinsmoor (or Dinsmore) was the son of Samuel of Ballywattick. He married Margaret, daughter of Robert Dinsmoor of Ballywattick, about 1786. He had previously been married and had at least five children, Robert, James Samuel, William, Andrew and John. Only Robert stayed on the farm at Ballywattick and the rest emigrated.

    Their daughter Susan married James Neill of Druckendult, had eight children and emigrated to Philadelphia with some of their family.

    Their daughter Rachael married John, daughter of John and Agnes Hunter of Secon and emigrated to York, Pennsylvannia about 1815.

    Their daughter Jean married Joseph, son of Joseph and Jane Small of Ballywattick and emigrated to Monroe, Indiana about 1830.

    Their daughter Mary married Samuel, son of Robert Boyd of Macfin in 1818 in 1st Ballymoney Presbyterian Church (see grave 23).

BLAIRE

GRAVE no. 98

Here lys the bo
dy of John Blaire
who departed this
Life ?
?   ?   Tho
mas Blaire who
Departed ?   ?
Also Jean Blaire
Who departed ?

1 Adam Blair - 1770
.. +Rose - 1781
...... 2 John Blair - 1734
...... 2 Adam Blair 1718 - 1790
...... 2 Margaret Blair 1738 - 1813
.... +Hugh Orr - 1818
.... 3 Alexander Orr 1765 -
...... 2 Mary Blair 1739 -
.... +William Erskine
...... 2 Ann Blair 1740 - 1824
...... 2 Rose Blair 1744 -
...... 2 Elizabeth Blair 1746 -
         +Alexander Erskine
         see grave 238
         2 James Blair 1746 - 1808
...... 2 Catherine Blair 1748 - 1824
...... 2 Martha Blair 1748 - 1817
.... +William Glass - 1817
         see grave 133
...... 2 Sarah Blair 1750 -
.... +John Mitchell
.... 3 Rose Mitchell
...... 2 Elinor Blair 1752 -
...... 2 Redonaxella Blair 1754 -
...... 2 Jane Blair 1758 - 1833
.... +William Dinsmore 1755 – 1818
...... 2 Rachael Blair 1759 - 1836
.... +John Adams 1761 - 1818
         see grave 307

Adam Blair was a merchant in Ballymoney and had a large family. Several of his daughters married Ballymoney merchants.

Elizabeth married Alexnder Erskine and Mary married William Erskine, brothers from Dunaverney. Alexander was a farmer and William lived in the town.

Margaret married Hugh Orr, a builder in Ballymoney. Martha married William Glass who was a grocer in Main Street. Jane married William Dinsmore, son of Robert of Ballywattick (see grave 102). Rachael married John Adams, a butcher in Main Street.

Their son Adam was educated at Glasgow University and became a Presbyterian Minister. He died near Lisburn in 1790.

There is an old deed dated 1785 where Rose leaves property in Main Street to her twelve daughters. There is no mention of sons.

It is said that Adam had also sons James, Robert and Thomas who emigrated to Pennsylvania.

JOHNSON

GRAVE no. 99

Interred here
Jane wife to Hugh Johnson
of Ballymoney
who departed this life
25th July 1839 aged 69
Also
five of their children
Also the above Hugh Johnson
who depd this life 9th Oct 1851
Aged 82

Hugh Johnston was a tailor and lived at the head of town in Ballymoney at the east side, according to Miller's list of inhabitants.
He married Jane and had known children of Ruth, John, Elizabeth, Agnes and Jean.

MCAFEE

GRAVE no. 100

William McAfee
Currysisken
?   1861

?

?

Also his wife
Rachael Pinkerton McAfee
died November 10th 1899
Aged 79 years

1 William MacAfee 1813 - 1861
.. +Rachael Pinkerton 1820 - 1899
...... 2 Thomas MacAfee 1844 - 1925
.... +Mary Anne Dunne 1847 - 1878
.... 3 Mary Jane Steen MacAfee 1873 -
.... +John Boyd 1851 - 1910
.... 3 William MacAfee 1875 - 1941
.... +Rachael Jocelyn Crawley 1880 -
.... 3 John B. MacAfee 1876 - 1880
.... 3 Thomas Boyd MacAfee 1877 - 1963
.... +Muriel Kathleen Allen 1887 - 1961
...... *2nd Wife of Thomas MacAfee:
.... +Ellen Thomson 1843 - 1912
...... 2 Robert MacAfee 1846 -
...... 2 Nancy MacAfee 1849 - 1921
.... +William John Knox 1841 - 1888
.... 3 Mary Peacock Knox 1873 -
.... +James Dunlop Black
.... 3 William MacAfee Knox 1876 - 1948
.... +Anna Pinkerton Knox 1883 - 1963
.... 3 Rachael Evaleen Knox 1878 -
.... +William Jones
.... 3 Jane Sinclair Knox 1881 -
.... 3 Robert Sinclair Knox 1882 -
.... 3 Annie Knox 1883 -
...... 2 William John MacAfee 1851 -
...... 2 Rachael MacAfee 1853 -
.... +W. W. Prince
...... 2 Margaret MacAfee 1855 - 1930
.... +Samuel Burnside Knox 1845 - 1920
...... 2 Matilda MacAfee 1857 -
.... +John Boyd 1851 - 1910
...... 2 James MacAfee 1856 - 1900
.... +Mary Harrington

William was the son of Thomas and Martha (Knox) McAfee (or MacAfee) of Currysisken. He married Rachael, only daughter of Robert and Nancy (Hunter) Pinkerton of Secon and Knowehead, Ballymoney in 1843. William resided for a time after his marriage at Culbrim but returned home to Currysisken after the death of his father.

Their eldest son Thomas married Mary Ann, daughter of John and Mary Jane (Steen) Dunne of Dartries, Articlave in 1872 in Dunboe Presbyterian Church and had four children. After her death in 1878, Thomas remarried Ellen, daughter of James Thompson of Cullycapple, Aghadowey in 1880 in 1st Ballymoney Presbyterian Church. He remained on the home farm.

MCAFEE

GRAVE no. 100

    Their other three sons, Robert, William John and James all emigrated to Pittsburgh.

    Their daughter Nancy married William John, son of Robert and Mary (Peacock) Knox of Currysisken in 1872 in 1st Ballymoney Presbyterian Church.

    Their daughter Rachael married W.J. Prince and lived in Allegheny, Pennsylvania.

    Their daughter Margaret married Samuel Burnside, son of Alexander and Jane (Burnside) Knox of Secon. Margaret was his second wife and had previously lived in Phildelphia. When she was widowed she lived with her sister Matilda in Belfast.

    Their daughter Matilda married Rev. John, son of Joseph Boyd of Ballywindland in 1872 in 1st Ballymoney Presbyterian Church. He was minister of Portaferry Presbyterian Church.

DINSMORE

GRAVE no. 101

Here lieth the body
of the late Samuel
Dinsmore of Bally
wattick who departed
this life the 12 Nov 1829
Aged 68 years —
Also his son Robert
who departed this
life 18th April
1818 aged 18 years

1 Samuel Dinsmore 1761 - 1829
.. +Mary Brewster 1762 - 1847
...... 2 William Dinsmore 1785 -
.... +Elizabeth
.... 3 Mary Dinsmore 1812 -
.... 3 Samuel Dinsmore 1814 -
.... 3 Andrew Dinsmore 1816 -
...... 2 Andrew Dinsmore 1787 -
.... +Margaret
.... 3 Susan Hannah Dinsmore 1816 -
...... 2 Margaret Dinsmore 1789 -
.... +Archibald McIlreavy 1785 -
.... 3 Mary Jean McIlreavy 1823 -
.... +Samuel Johnston
.... 3 Margaret McIlreavy 1825 -
.... 3 Daniel McIlreavy 1827 -
.... 3 Rachael McIlreavy 1828 -
...... 2 Bette Dinsmore 1791 -
...... 2 Samuel Dinsmore 1792 - 1816
...... 2 James Dinsmore 1795 -
...... 2 Mary Dinsmore 1799 -
.... +Samuel Johnston
...... 2 Robert Dinsmore 1800 - 1818
...... 2 Jennie Dinsmore 1803 -
.... +Robert Small 1800 -
...... *2nd Husband of Jennie Dinsmore:
.... +Samuel McAllister
...... 2 Rachael Dinsmore 1806 - 1842
.... +James McAffee 1809 - 1862
.... 3 William James McAffee 1841 -
.... 3 Samuel James McAffee 1839 -
...... 2 Matilda Dinsmore 1808 -
.... +Campbell McCurdy 1804 -
...... 2 John Dinsmore 1810 - 1892
.... +Margaret Small 1807 - 1882
.... 3 Samuel Dinsmore 1834 -

Samuel, son of Robert Dinsmore of Ballywattick, married Mary, daughter of Andrew Brewster of Glenhall, Co Londonderry, in 1783 and had twelve children. Their son Robert died young and all but their two daughters emigrated.

Margaret married Archibald, son of Andrew McIlreavy of Ballywattick in 1821 in 1st Ballymoney Presbyterian Church and moved to Portstewart.

Mary married Samuel Johnston of Dunluce in 1826 in 1st Ballymoney Presbyterian Church.

Their youngest son John stayed at home at Ballywattick, but in 1838 he emigrated to Monroe, Indiana with his family and his mother. The Ballywattick farm was sold to Archibald Usher. John married Margaret, daughter of Joseph and Jean (Dinsmore) Small of Ballywattick in 1832 in 1st Ballymoney Presbyterian Church. Margaret's parents also emigrated to Monroe, Indiana.

DINSMORE

GRAVE no. 102

Consigned to the tomb
in 63rd year of age
Here liest remains of Wm
Dinsmore late of Ballywattick
A man distinquished by plenty
of morals and integrity of
health impressed with a
due sense of religion, his
practice was regulated by its
dictates firmly believing the
truths of the gospel his whole life
E ?   ?   ?
of Christian   ?

1 Robert Dinsmore 1720 -
...... 2 Margaret Dinsmore 1750 - 1813
.... +Andrew Dinsmore 1737 - 1811
                see grave 97
...... 2 William Dinsmore 1755 - 1818
.... +Jane Blair 1758 - 1833
...... 2 Molly Dinsmore 1757
.... +Thomas McIlhose
.... 3 Robert McIlhose
.... 3 Matthew McIlhose
.... 3 Margaret McIlhose
.... 3 James McIlhose
.... 3 Andrew McIlhose 1796 - 1860
...... 2 Samuel Dinsmore 1761 - 1829
.... +Mary Brewster 1762 - 1847
                see grave 101
...... 2 Martha Dinsmore 1763 -
.... +Alexander Culbertson
.... 3 James Culbertson - 1888
.... 3 William Culbertson
.... 3 Margaret Culbertson
.... 3 Martha Culbertson
.... 3 Alexander Culbertson 1801 -
.... +Isabella Brown 1815 -
...... 2 James Dinsmore 1767 - 1842
.... +Jane Curry 1805 -

The first Dinsmore (or Dinsmoor) to settle in Ballywattick was John, second son of the Laird of Achenmead in Scotland. He was born in 1650, left for Ireland in his 17th year, married in 1670, was widowed at 70 years and died in his 99th year. His eldest son John emigrated to America where he was one of the founders of the Londonderry settlement in New Hampshire.

His second son Robert was a prominent man in the Presbyterian Church and his son Robert is the father of the William buried here. William lived in Philadelphia for a time before returning to live in Ballymoney. He owned houses and outbuildings in Main Street, Ballymoney and had considerable wealth.

He married Jane, daughter of Adam and Rose Blair of Ballymoney, but had no children.

Of his sisters, Margaret married her cousin Andrew Dinsmore of Ballywattick (see grave 97), Molly married Thomas McIlhose of Carncullagh and Martha married Alexander Culbertson of Ballywattick.

Of his brothers, Samuel married Mary Brewster (see grave 101) and James married Jane Curry.

BOYD

GRAVE no. 103

In loving memory of
Robert Boyd of Ballywindland
who died on the 25th May 1895
Aged 73 years
Also his wife Jane Moore
who died at Portstewart
on the 15th August 1913
Aged 77 years

1 Samuel Boyd 1782 - 1862
.. +Jean Crilly
...... 2 Thomas Boyd 1814 -
...... 2 Rebecca Jane Boyd 1816 -
...... 2 John Boyd 1818 -
...... 2 Robert Boyd 1822 - 1895
.... +Jane Moore 1836 - 1895
.... 3 Jane Anna Boyd 1873 -
.... 3 Margaret Boyd 1875 -
...... 2 Thomas Boyd 1827 - 1847
...... 2 Samuel Boyd 1828 - 1862
.... +Mary McKeague
.... 3 John Boyd 1859 -
.... 3 Samuel Boyd 1861

Robert, son of Samuel and Jean (Crilly) Boyd, married Jane, daughter of Hugh Moore of Pullans, in 1861 at Terrace Row Pres. Church. They had daughters Jane Anna and Margaret. Robert was a doctor and died in Belfast.

Robert had two brothers called Thomas who both died young. There was a tradition that when a child died, the next baby was called the same name (see grave 104).

His youngest brother Samuel married Mary, daughter of John and Mary (White) McKeague of Ballywindland (see grave 44).

BOYD

GRAVE no. 104

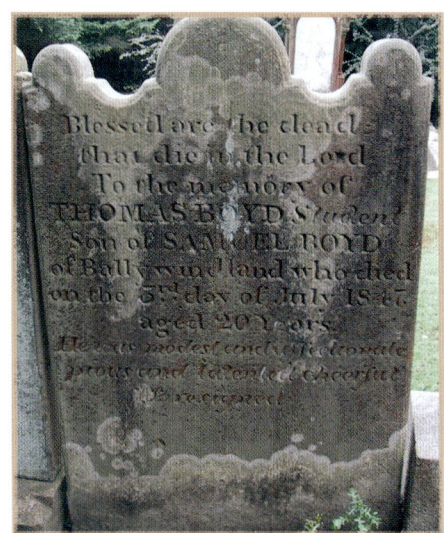

Blessed are the dead
that die in the Lord
To the memory of
Thomas Boyd student
son of Samuel Boyd
of Ballywindland who died
on the 3rd day of July 1847
Aged 20 years
He was modest and affectionate
pious and talented cheerful
? resigned

Thomas was the son of Samuel and Jean (Crilly) Boyd (see grave 103).

BOYD

GRAVE no. 105

Erected
to the memory of
Elizabeth
wife to John Boyd
of Ballywindlan
who died 21st October 1845
Aged 70 years
Also his daughter Margaret
who died 1st January 1828
Aged 17 years
Also the above John Boyd who
died on the 1st Decr 1848 aged 72 years

1 John Boyd 1776 - 1848
.. +Elizabeth 1775 - 1845
...... 2 Jane Boyd 1802 - 1889
.... +James MacAfee 1808 - 1882
.... 3 John MacAfee 1832 - 1862
.... 3 Elizabeth MacAfee 1835 -
.... 3 Elizabeth MacAfee 1837 - 1860
.... 3 Robert Boyd MacAfee 1840 - 1896
.... +Sarah Luke
.... 3 Margaret MacAfee 1842 - 1863
.... 3 James Alexander MacAfee 1852 -
...... 2 Sally Boyd 1803 -
...... 2 John Boyd 1806 - 1855
...... 2 Alexander Boyd 1808 - 1892
...... 2 Margaret Boyd 1810 - 1828
...... 2 Joseph Boyd 1813 -
...... 2 Joseph Boyd 1817 - 1898
.... +Margaret Knox 1825 - 1898
.... 3 John Boyd 1851 - 1910
.... +Mary Jane Steen MacAfee 1873 -
.... 3 Andrew Knox Boyd 1853 - 1898
.... 3 Mary Boyd 1858 -
.... 3 Alexander Boyd 1862 - 1943
.... +Mary Henrietta Small 1877 - 1925
.... 3 Margaret Jane Boyd 1865 -
.... +William Warnock
.... 3 Lizzie Boyd
.... +John McDonnell

John Boyd was a farmer at Ballywindland and brother of Joseph and Samuel (see grave 103).

Their daughter Jane married James, son of Robert and Mary Ann MacAfee of Currysisken in 1828 in 1st Ballymoney Presbyterian Church (see grave 93).

Their son Joseph married Margaret, daughter of Andrew and Mary Ann (MacAfee) Knox of Culderry in 1845 in 1st Ballymoney Presbyterian Church.

MCCURDY

GRAVE no. 106

Moore McCurdy
died 23rd November 1906
aged 79 years

1 Joseph McCurdy
.. +Mary Knox
.... 2 Jenny McCurdy 1821 - 1884
.... 2 Moore Taylor McCurdy 1825 - 1906
.... +Ellen Leslie 1847 - 1921
.... 3 Margaret McCurdy 1876 - 1911
.... 3 Ellen McCurdy 1878 -
.... 3 Esther McCurdy 1880 -
.... 2 Eliza McCurdy 1827 - 1900
.... 2 Margaret McCurdy 1829 - 1919
.... 2 Samuel McCurdy 1830 -

Moore Taylor McCurdy was the son of Joseph McCurdy, a labourer, and Margaret Knox and had sisters Jenny, Eliza and Margaret and a brother Samuel. They were all born at Drumaheglis except Jenny who was born in Ballymoney.

Moore married Ellen, daughter of John Leslie of Balnamore in 1866 in St. James Presbyterian Church, Ballymoney. They had at least three daughters, Margaret, Ellen and Esther. At the time of his marriage he was a smith in Balnamore. He was living in Balnamore at the time of his death.

HUNTER

GRAVE no. 107

Them also which sleep in Jesus
will God bring with him

Mary wife to James Hunter of Secon
Died 10th Feb 1831 aged 40 years
Also John their son died May 1825
aged 4 years
and Nancy their daughter
17th Sepr 1828 aged 15 years
James Hunter
Died 2nd March 1864 aged 81 years

1 John Hunter
.. +Agnes 1753 - 1823
...... 2 James Hunter 1782 - 1864
.... +Mary Hopkins 1790 - 1831
.... 3 Nancy Hunter 1813 - 1828
.... 3 William Hunter 1816 - 1895
.... +Anna Stewart 1843 - 1923
              see grave 108
.... 3 John Hunter 1821 - 1825
.... 3 Eliza Hunter 1823 -
.... 3 James Hunter 1826 -
.... 3 Nancy Hunter 1828 - 1916
.... 3 Mary Hunter 1831 -
.... +Edward Fullerton 1806 - 1894
.... 4 William Wilson Fullerton 1872 -
.... +Jane Getty 1876 -
.... 4 Mary Eliza Fullerton 1874 - 1952
.... +Andrew Curry 1867 - 1951
...... 2 John Hunter 1784 - 1823
.... +Rachael Dinsmore 1790 - 1837
...... 2 Agnes Hunter 1788 - 1876
.... +Robert Pinkerton 1787 - 1846
...... 2 Alexander Hunter 1795 - 1820
...... 2 Margaret Hunter 1797 -

    James, eldest son of John and Agnes Hunter of Secon, married Mary, daughter of William and Eliza Hopkins of Ballymoney. He lived in Ballymoney until Mary's death in 1831. He moved to Ballywattick where he died.

    Their son William married Anna Stewart, daughter of James Lynch of Portrush in 1869. Their daughter Mary married Edward, son of William and Elizabeth (Wilson) Fullerton in 1869 in the Unitarian Church in Ballymoney. They had two children, William Wilson who married Jane, daughter of John and Mary Jane (Cooper) Getty of Heagles in 1898 and Mary Eliza who married Andrew, son of Marmaduke and Ann (Shaw) Curry of Newbuildings North in 1897.

    His brother John married Rachael, daughter of Andrew and Margaret Dinsmore, emigrated and died in York, Pennsylvania.

    His sister Agnes married Robert, son of James Pinkerton of Secon. They moved to farm at Knowehead.

HUNTER

GRAVE no. 108

William Hunter
Ballywattick
Died 22nd July 1895
aged 79 years
Also his daughter
Mary
Born 11th September 1870
Died 27th August 1904

1 William Hunter 1816 - 1895
.. +Anna Stewart Lynch 1843 - 1923
...... 2 James Hunter
...... 2 Mary Hunter 1870 - 1904
...... 2 Martha Hunter

William was the eldest son of James and Mary (Hopkins) Hunter. He was born in Ballymoney and moved to Ballywattick to farm. He married Anna Stewart, daughter of James Lynch, in 1869 in 1st Ballymoney Presbyterian Church and had three known children. Their son James was still farming at Ballywattick at the time of his mothers death.

MOORE

GRAVE no. 109

Here lieth the body of
Jean Moore
who departed this
life the 28th November
1803 aged 72 years
Wife to
Robert Moore of Cloney
who departed this
life the 6 Nov
1806 aged 82 years

1 Robert Moore 1729 - 1806
.. +Jean McAuley 1733 - 1803
...... 2 Mary Moore
.... +Brice Wales
.... 3 Adam Wales 1795 - 1881
.... 3 Jenny Wales 1799 - 1870
...... 2 William Moore 1758 - 1825
.... +Ellen Glenn 1773 - 1807
.... 3 Robert Moore 1801 - 1847
.... 3 John Moore 1803 - 1851
.... 3 Mary Moore 1794 - 1890
.... 3 Martha Moore 1796 - 1838
.... 3 Eleanor Moore 1799 -
.... 3 Jane Moore 1805 - 1885
...... 2 Anne Moore 1764 - 1845
.... +John Given 1762 - 1825
.... 3 Robert Given 1795 - 1822
.... 3 Jane Given 1797 -
.... 3 Ann Given 1799 -
.... 3 Benjamin Given 1800 -
.... 3 John William Given 1805 - 1880
.... +Matilda Sharpe 1807 - 1889
...... 2 Esther Moore 1777 - 1847
.... +James Boyle 1773 - 1835
.... 3 Robert Boyle 1801 - 1862
.... 3 Ann Jane Boyle 1804 - 1874
.... +James Boyle 1782 - 1854
.... 3 James Boyle 1806 - 1882
.... 3 Eliza Boyle 1811 - 1889
.... 3 Helen Marion Boyle 1813 - 1884
.... 3 Matilda Boyle
.... 3 Hessie Boyle
.... 3 Wellington Boyle 1815 -
.... 3 Henry Boyle

Robert was the brother of James Moore and uncle of James Moore senior (see graves 2, 111). He was born at either Heagles, Ballymoney or Kilraughts, son of Archibald and Mary (Neal) Moore of Ballymacwilliam, Kilraughts, and died at Cloney, Dunluce.

He married Jean McAuley and had at least four children; Mary who married Brice Wales of Cavanmore, William of Priestland who married Ellen, daughter of William and Martha (Miller) Glen of Glenvale, Anne who married John Givin of Lisconnan, Dervock and Esther who married Rev. James Boyle, minister of Dunluce Presbyterian Church, Bushmills from 1801 to 1835.

MOORE

GRAVE no. 110

Erected in memory of
James Moore jun
Late of Dunluce
who departed this life on the 8th
Day of June 1843 aged 48 years
And
Mary Jane his daughter
who died 26 May 1847 aged
19 years

1 James Moore 1745 – 1833
...... 2 Agnes Moore 1777 -
...... 2 Anne Moore 1778 -
.... +Alexander Burnside 1778 - 1865
.... 3 Jean Burnside 1808 -
.... 3 Eliza Burnside 1810 - 1895
.... +James Pinkerton 1811 - 1892
.... 3 Mary Burnside 1812 -
.... 3 Samuel Burnside 1814 -
.... 3 James Moore Burnside 1816 - 1891
.... 3 Jane Burnside 1807 - 1864
.... +Alexander Knox 1804 - 1884
.... 4 James Alexander Knox 1841 - 1924
.... 4 William Hugh Knox 1843 - 1923
.... +Fannie M. Kirkpatrick 1864 -
.... 4 Samuel Burnside Knox 1845 - 1920
.... +Margaret MacAfee 1855 - 1930
.... *2nd Wife of Samuel Burnside Knox:
.... +Nancy Pinkerton 1842 - 1912
.... 3 John Burnside 1820 - 1903
.... +Mary Jane Templeton 1829 - 1910
.... 4 John Templeton Burnside 1858 - 1939
.... +Margaret Houston Wilson 1864 - 1946
.... 4 James Moore Burnside 1860 -
.... +Ellen McGorm
.... 4 Jane Templeton Burnside 1863 - 1932
.... 4 Alexander Burnside 1865 -
.... +Mary Gertrude Black
.... 4 Anna Moore Burnside 1868 - 1934

James Moore senior, was born at Heagles, outside Ballymoney in 1745 and died in Dunluce in 1833. He had at least seven children, Agnes; Anne who married Alexander Burnside of Secon, Mary who married Edward McCurdy of Eagry, Bushmills, Jane who married James Burnside of Secon and Macfin and brother to Alexander, Robert, Rachael who married Alexander Boyd of Knockans, Finvoy and James who married Mary Jane.
    Nothing more is known of James and Mary Jane.

MOORE

GRAVE no. 110

```
.......................... +Francis Carter
....................... 4 Eliza Burnside 1870 - 1951
.......................... +Robert Holmes 1867 - 1945
...... 2 Mary Moore 1780 - 1859
.......... +Edward McCurdy 1776 - 1810
...... 2 Jane Moore
.......... +James Burnside 1784 -
............... 3 Samuel Burnside 1813 - 1890
............... 3 Eleanor Burnside 1816 -
............... 3 Sarah Jane Burnside 1820 -
.................. +Robert Boyd
....................... 4 Robert Wallace Boyd - 1924
...... 2 Robert Moore
...... 2 Rachael Moore
.......... +Alexander Boyd 1791 - 1870
............... 3 David Boyd 1822 - 1898
............... 3 William Moore Boyd 1824 - 1857
............... 3 Robert Boyd 1828 - 1910
............... 3 John Boyd
............... 3 Mary Boyd - 1909
.................. +William Smyrell
....................... 4 William Smyrell 1854 -
....................... 4 Alexander Boyd Smyrell 1856 - 1932
....................... 4 Ellen Smyrell 1858 -
.......................... +Henry Young Henderson
....................... 4 Jane Smyrell 1860 -
.......................... +George Smyrell 1852 -
....................... 4 Mary Smyrell 1863 -
....................... 4 Rachael Ann Smyrell 1866 - 1967
....................... 4 Robert Smyrell 1868 - 1901
....................... 4 Matilda Smyrell 1872 -
.......................... +Thomas Bamford
............... 3 Ellen Boyd - 1855
............... 3 Rachael Boyd
.................. +Samuel Smyth 1831 - 1922
...... 2 James Moore 1794 - 1843
.......... +Mary Jane
............... 3 Mary Jane Moore 1828 - 1847
```

MOORE

GRAVE no. 111

Underneath lies the mortal remains
of James Moore Senr
late of Dunluce
Who departed this life the
11th of March 1833 aged 87 years

1 Archibald Moore 1678 - 1771
.. +Mary Neal 1692 - 1759
...... 2 James Moore 1722 -
.... see grave 109
.... 3 James Moore 1745 - 1833
.... 3 Anne Moore 1746 - 1794
.... +Robert Nevin 1741 - 1824
.... 3 Mary Moore 1748 - 1801
.... +John Getty 1747 - 1825
...... 2 Robert Moore 1729 - 1806
.... +Jean McAuley 1733 - 1803
.... 3 Mary Moore
.... see grave 110
...... 2 Margaret Moore 1737 - 1810
.... + Archibald Moore 1736 - 1786
.... 3 James Moore 1769 - 1834
.... + Anne Cramsie 1778 - 1850
.... 3 Jane Moore 1779 - 1842
.... + William Getty 1780 - 1865
.... 3 David Moore
.... 3 Archibald Moore
.... 3 Hugh Moore
...... 2 Mary Moore
.... +David Watt
.... 3 Fergus Watt 1743 -
.... 3 Samuel Watt 1746 -
...... 2 David Moore
.... +? Wallace
.... 3 Robert Moore 1753 - 1832
.... +Margaret 1748 - 1823
...... 2 John Moore

James Moore senior was born at Kilraughts, son of Archibald and Mary (Neal) Moore and grandson of Archibald Moore. He had brothers Robert, Archibald of Ballymacwilliam, who is buried at Old Kilraughts Churchyard, David of Crosstagherty and John of Mullan and sisters Margaret, who married her cousin Archibald Moore, son of David of Kilraughts and Mary who married David Watt.

He had three known children. James junior, Anne and Mary. Anne married Robert, son of Hugh and Jane (Jamison) Nevin of Kilmoyle, Dervock. She died in 1794 and Robert Nevin was married again to Esther Patrick of Carncullagh. The Nevin family are buried in Derrykeighan Old Churchyard. Mary Moore married John Getty of Kirkmoyle and they are buried in grave 82.

WHITE

GRAVE no. 112

Erected
by
Robert White, Coleraine
in memory of
His father Robert White
Colebreene
who died 18th April 1882
Aged 67 years
Also his mother Martha
who died 10th June 1880
Aged 63 years
Also his brother John
who died 20th Decr 1879
Aged 26 years
and his sister Sarah
who died Sept 1856
aged 2 years
Also
His daughter Martha
who died 28th Jany 1870
aged 10 days
Also Maggie Ann
who died 16th August 1879
aged 6 years
Also Robert John
who died 17th Jany 1881
aged 6 years
and Agnes White
who died 28th Jany 1881
aged 2 years
The above Robert N. White
5th February 1901 aged 58 years
He is not lost but gone before
and Margaret M White died 5th Dec 1933
of Hamilton, Ontario
beloved parents of JM and WH White

1 Robert White 1814 - 1882
.. +Martha 1817 - 1880
...... 2 Robert White 1842 - 1901
.... +Margaret
.... 3 Martha White 1870 - 1870
.... 3 Maggie Ann White 1873 - 1879
.... 3 Robert John White 1875 - 1881
.... 3 Agnes White 1878 - 1881
...... 2 John White 1853 - 1879
...... 2 Sarah White 1854 - 1856

I have failed connect this family with the rest of the Whites in the area. The White families all seem to originated from Artigoran and Macfin spreading to Ballymoney, Culbrim, Currysisken, Drumaheglis, Forttown and Taghey.

WHITE

GRAVE no. 113

Erected
By John White
? ?
?
?
Mary
th Nov ?   ? aged 6?
Also her husband John White
who died 27th August 1885
Aged 88 years

1 John White
.. +Mary ?
...... 2 Robert White 1789 -
.... +Nancy Thomson
.... 3 Rose White 1822 -
.... 3 Mary White 1830 -
.... 3 John White 1832 -
.... 3 Jane White 1833 -
.... 3 William Thomson White 1836 -
...... 2 Martha White 1791 -
.... +William Smith
...... 2 William White 1793 -
.... +Ellen Biggart 1814 -
.... 3 John White 1834 -
.... 3 William White 1836 -
.... 3 Robert White 1837 -
.... 3 Hannah White 1839 -
.... 3 Solomon White 1841 -
.... 3 Jane White 1842 -
.... 3 Marshall White 1847 -
...... 2 Jean White 1795 -
...... 2 John White 1797 - 1885
.... +Mary Hemphill 1801 - 1885
.... 3 Martha White 1834 -
.... 3 Mary White 1836 -
.... 3 Elizabeth Jane White 1842 - 1907
...... 2 Mary White 1802 -
...... 2 Elizabeth White 1804 -
.... +Robert Biggart 1803 -
...... 2 Margaret White 1808 -
.... +William Campbell 1802 -
...... 2 James White 1811 -
.... +Mary Getty 1817 -

John White was the son of John and Mary White of Artigoran. He had siblings Robert, who married Nancy Thomson; Martha who married William Smith of Broughshane; William who married Ellen Biggart; Mary who was unmarried, Elizabeth who married Robert Biggart; Margaret who married William Campbell of Macfin and James who married Mary Getty of Taghey.

He married Mary Hemphill of Culbrim, daughter of James, in 1st Ballymoney Presbyterian Church in 1833 and had three daughters, Martha, Mary and Elizabeth Jane, none of whom married. Mary and her daughter Mary died at Drumaheglis.

WHITE
GRAVE no. 114

Martha White
who departed   ?
October 1809 Aged 52 years
William White of
who departed this life the 6 December
1832   aged 73 years
also their eldest son
who departed this life 8th April
1856 aged 70 years
John youngest son of the above
John White
died 1st March 1853 aged 38 years
Mary White
wife of John White Sr
died 5th Apr 1864 aged 82 years

1 William White 1759 - 1832
.. +Martha 1757 - 1809
...... 2 John White 1785 - 1856
.... +Mary Orr 1782 - 1864
.... 3 William White 1814 - 1866
.... 3 Flora White 1817 -
.... +William Munnis 1818 - 1866
.... 3 John White 1819 - 1858
.... 3 Martha Thomasine Matilda White 1821 -
.... +Thomas Adair

   John, son of William and Martha White married Mary, daughter of William and Flora Orr of Ballymoney (see grave 50).
   John was a woollen draper in Main Street, Ballymoney and died in Portstewart. His wife Mary died in Cookstown at the home of her daughter Martha.
   Their eldest son William emigrated and died in Brooklyn, New York.
   Their daughter Flora married Rev. William, son of Rev. William and Alice (Lyle) Munnis of Carncullagh, Dervock (and Minister of Roseyards Presbyterian Church) in 1853 in Portstewart Presbyterian Church. William was Minister of the Free Church, Marykirk, Scotland.
   Their daughter Martha married Thomas Adair, a merchant od Greenvale, Co. Tyrone in 1845 in 1st Ballymoney Presbyterian Church.

WHITE

GRAVE no. 115

To the memory of
Nancy
wife of William White Currysisken
who died 7th June 1856
in her 61st year

1 William White 1784 - 1868
.. +Ann McNaul 1795 - 1856
...... 2 James White 1818 - 1854
...... 2 Robert White 1820 -
...... 2 Samuel White 1823 -
.... +Margaret C. Shaw
.... 3 William Shaw White 1851 - 1856
.... 3 Samuel Robert White 1856 - 1858
...... 2 William White 1824 - 1860
...... 2 John White 1828 -
...... 2 Matthew White 1829 - 1903
.... +Sarah Picken - 1893
.... 3 Annie Jane White 1856 - 1903
.... +James Johnston
.... 3 William White 1858 - 1903
.... 3 Eliza Martha White 1859 - 1868
.... 3 John White 1861 - 1903
.... 3 Mary White 1863 -
.... 3 Joseph White 1865 - 1903
.... 3 Fanny White 1866 - 1867
.... 3 Fanny Young White 1868 - 1903
.... 3 Robert Johnston White 1870 -
.... +Grace Ann Knox 1869 -
.... 3 Samuel White 1874 -
.... +Emily Mabin
...... 2 Joseph White 1833 -
...... 2 Mary Ann White 1836 -
.... +Robert Johnston

William, son of William and Mary White of Macfin, married Nancy (or Ann) McNaul about 1816. They farmed at Macfin, where their children were born, but they died at Currysisken.

Their sons James and William emigrated to Pittsburg, U.S.A. Samuel was a draper in Coleraine and married Margaret Shaw in 1850 in 1st Ballymoney Presbyterian Church. Matthew married Sarah, daughter of John and Agnes (McCay) Picken of Taghey, in 1856 in 1st Ballymoney Presbyterian Church. Mary Ann married Robert Johnston of Stallbridge, England in 2nd Coleraine Presbyterian Church.

THOMSON   GRAVE no. 116

Here lieth the remains
of
Elizabeth
wife of James Thomson
of Duneyverney
Who departed this life
2nd October 1841
aged 60 years
William Thomson
Dunaverney
died 20th August 1890 aged
68 years
Also his wife Mary Boyd
who died on 10th May 1905
aged 77 years

1 James Thomson 1780 – 1859.
+Elizabeth Bateson 1781 - 1841
.... 2 William Thomson 1821 - 1890
.... +Marianne Boyd 1828 - 1905
.... 3 James Thomson 1852 - 1932
.... +Martha Stewart 1864 - 1943
.... 4 Mary Boyd Thomson 1888 -
.... 4 William Thomson 1889 - 1917
.... 4 Annie Stewart Thomson 1891 -
.... 4 Maud Stewart Thomson 1894 -
.... 4 Margaret Houston Thomson 1896 -
.... 4 James Stewart Thomson 1899 -
.... 3 John Boyd Thomson 1854 - 1915
.... 3 Elizabeth Bateson Thomson 1856 - 1921
.... +James White 1853 -
.... 4 John Knox White 1885 -
.... 4 William Bateson Thomson White 1886 -
.... 4 Hugh Boyd White 1888 -
.... +Mary Haughey
.... 3 William Bateson Thomson 1858 -
.... 3 David Thomson 1860 - 1909
.... 3 Samuel Boyd Thomson 1862 - 1941
.... +Bessie Hill Adams - 1895
.... 3 Robert Thomson 1864 - 1941
.... +Margaret Conn Hamilton 1872 - 1906
.... 4 Alice Hamilton Thomson 1894 - 1982
.... 3 Sarah Boyd Thomson 1870 - 1929
.... +William James Ramsay 1850 - 1905
.... 4 William James Ramsay 1900 - 1981
.... +Mary Wallace 1902 - 1994
.... 4 Hugh Ramsay 1904 - 1977
.... +Evelyn Elizabeth Hazlett 1907 - 1985
.... 3 William Boyd Thomson 1871 - 1930

    James Thomson was a farmer at Dunaverney (as it is now spelt) but was not born there. I strongly suspect that he was a son of William and Violet Thomson of Booton. He married Elizabeth, daughter of William and Jenny Bateson of Ballymoney (grave 392) in 1820 in 1st Ballymoney Presbyterian Church and only had one child.
    William Thomson married Marianne (or Mary Anne), daughter of John and Sarah (Burnside) Boyd of Knockans, Finvoy in 1851 in Finvoy Presbyterian Church. They had a large family of nine.

WALKER

GRAVE no. 117

Erected
in memory of
Alexander Walker, Ballymoney
who died the 5th May 1848 aged 46 years
and his son Alexander Walker
who died 18th July 1878 aged 42 years
Also his wife Sarah Jane
who died 16th June 1893 aged 80 years
and their grandson John Walker
who died 25th Nov 1903 aged 19 years
Their grandson Alexander
died 17th August 1910 aged 34 years
Their son William
died 18th August 1915 aged 75 years
His wife Matilda
died 9th February 1915 aged 69 years
Matilda Walker
died 13th Nov 1918 aged 31 years
William Walker
died 17th May 1939 aged 61 years
Margaret Walker
died 2nd Feby 1957 aged 80 years
James Walker
died 6th Oct 1959 aged 79 years

1 Alexander Walker 1802 - 1848
.. +Sarah Jane Martin 1813 - 1893
...... 2 William Walker 1840 - 1915
.... +Matilda Rice 1845 - 1915
.... 3 Alexander Walker 1874 - 1910
.... +Charlotte Thompson
.... 3 Margaret Walker 1877 - 1957
.... 3 James Walker 1879 - 1959
.... 3 John Walker 1884 - 1903
.... 3 Matilda Walker 1886 - 1918
.... 3 William Walker 1872 -
...... 2 Alexander Walker 1836 - 1878
...... 2 Catherine Walker 1841 -
.... +Samuel Shales

Alexander, son of James Walker of Drumscie, married Sarah Jane Martin of Inchinagh in 1836 in 1st Ballymoney Presbyterian Church. Their son Alexander died young and their son William, a blacksmith, married Matilda, daughter of Dennis and Anne (Lusk) Rice of Pharos, Loughguile in 1871 in 1st Ballymoney Presbyterian Church.

Their grandson Alexander, a blacksmith, married Charlotte Thompson of Ballymoney in 1898 in Carncullagh Presbyterian Church.

THOMPSON

GRAVE no. 118

Sacred to the memory of
David Thompson
late of Greenshields
who died 26th July 1823
aged 45 years
Also Elizabeth Thompson
who died 28 August 1841
aged 61 years
Likewise their brother
Robert Thompson
late of Islandmore
who died 25th December 1868
aged 90 years

1 Adam Thomson 1757 - 1817
.. +Agnes 1752 - 1821
see grave 228
...... 2 David Thomson 1777 - 1823
.... +Elizabeth 1780 - 1841
...... 2 Robert Thomson 1778 - 1868
...... 2 Benjamin Thomson 1780 - 1838
.... +Rose 1786 – 1861
  see grave 119
...... 2 Adam Thomson 1784 - 1864
.... +Elizabeth Rogers 1808 - 1834
...... *2nd Wife of Adam Thomson:
.... +Sarah Gault 1813 -
...... 2 Jane Thomson 1785 - 1850
.... +James Cramsie 1786 - 1855
...... 2 Samuel Thomson 1789 - 1796
...... 2 Ann Thomson 1795 - 1796
...... 2 James Thomson 1798 - 1866
.... +Alicia Greene 1800 - 1868

David and Robert Thompson were the sons of Adam and Agnes Thompson and were born at Greenshields. Adam was a merchant in Ballymoney and died there in 1817. He had a large family some of whom were farmers and some merchants, all of whom prospered. The name was also spelt in many records as Thomson.

THOMPSON

GRAVE no. 119

Sacred to the memory of
Benjamin Thompson
late of Ballymoney
who departed this life 8th May 1838
aged 57 years
Also his daughter Rose Anna
aged 5 years
David McCurdy Thompson
died 7th Feb 1856 aged 25 years
Rose Thompson
Relict of Benjamin Thompson
died 22nd Feb 1861 aged 74 years
Rose Anna Thompson
Born 18th Feb 1861 died 11th January 1885
Thomas McElderry Thompson
Born 8th Apr 1863 died 5th Nov 1863
children of Adam & Anne Thompson

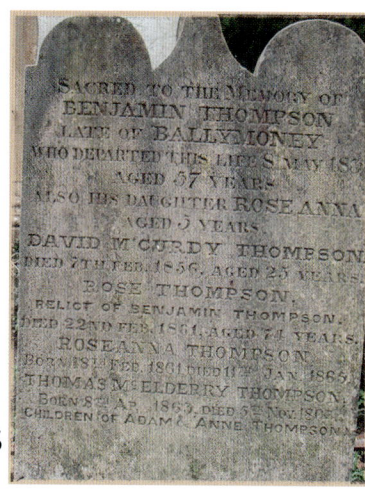

1 Benjamin Thomson 1780 - 1838
.. +Rose 1786 - 1861
.... 2 James Ross Thomson 1816 - 1901
.... 2 Rose Anna Thomson 1820 - 1825
.... 2 Adam Thomson 1822 - 1900
.... +Anne McElderry 1833 - 1928
.... 3 Rose Anna Thomson 1861 - 1865
.... 3 Thomas McElderry Thomson 1863 - 1863
.... 3 Thomas McElderry Thomson 1865 -
.... +Minnie Redpath
.... 4 James Ross Thomson
.... 4 Margaret Thomson
.... 4 Marion Thomson
.... 3 James Ross Thomson 1866 - 1963
.... +Annie Thomson Todd 1871 - 1930
.... 4 Andrew Todd Thomson 1903 -
.... +Isabella Orr
.... 4 Annie McElderry Thomson 1903 - 1928
.... 4 James Ross Thomson 1905 - 1984
.... 4 John Patrick Thomson 1906 - 1986
.... 4 Jane Kyle Thomson 1907 - 1986
.... 3 Robert Benjamin Thomson 1868 - 1957
.... +Mary Stewart 1890 - 1965
.... 4 Anne Ross Thomson 1904 -
.... 4 Jane Stewart Thomson 1905 - 1966
.... +Robert Andrew Wilson
.... 4 William Stewart Thomson 1907 - 1914
.... 4 Adam Thomson 1906 - 1980
.... +Helen L.
.... 4 David Thomson 1912 -

THOMPSON

GRAVE no. 119

Benjamin Thompson (or Thomson) was born at Greenshields and married Rose abt 1815. Their first son James Ross was born at Greenshields and they must have moved into Ballymoney c.1819 as the rest of their children were born there. He was a boot and shoemaker in Church Street, Ballymoney.

His eldest son, John Ross went to Glasgow University, became a well known surgeon and is buried in Knock Road Cemetery in Ballymoney. He never married.

Their eldest daughter Rose Anna died young but their second daughter, also Roseanna, married Archibald McCurdy of Lismorluss near Bushmills in 1848 in St. James Presbyterian Church, Ballymoney. She had three children but died just after the birth of her son Benjamin McCurdy in 1854.

Their second son Adam married Anne, daughter of Thomas and Elizabeth (Nevin) McElderry of Ballymoney in 1858 in Trinity Presbyterian Church, Ballymoney. They had a large family and lived in Church Street, where Adam was a merchant.

Their youngest son David McCurdy died in 1856 in Main Street of a malignant sore throat aged 25 years.

3 Rose Ann Ross Thomson 1870 - 1959
 +William McAfee McKeague 1868 - 1931
  4 Jean McAfee McKeague 1911 - 1999
   +James Gamble Donaghy 1905 - 1976
    5 Patricia Donaghy
  4 Mary McKeague 1912 -
   +Thomas MacAfee Boyd 1898 -
    5 John Denis Boyd
3 David Thomson
 +Emily Galloway
  4 Robert B. Thomson
  4 Annie Caroline Thomson
  4 Rita Thomson
2 Roseanna Thomson 1826 - 1854
 +Archibald McCurdy 1807 - 1885
  3 Mary McCurdy 1849 - 1916
   +William John Rankin 1849 - 1925
    4 Rose Thompson Rankin 1886 - 1952
    4 Elizabeth Erskine Rankin 1889 - 1919
  3 Samuel McCurdy 1851 - 1932
   +Annie Scott 1854 - 1886
    4 Annie Scott McCurdy 1886 - 1965
     +William J. Borland 1883 - 1937
  3 Benjamin Thompson McCurdy 1854 -
2 David McCurdy Thomson 1830 - 1856

TEMPLETON

GRAVE no. 120

To the memory of
Robert Templeton, Moneycannon
who died on the 26th March 1852 aged 62 years
Also John Templeton
who died on the 8th July 1859 aged 76 years
Also Jane Templeton, Mullans
who died on the 6th Decr 1862 aged 70 years
Also her husband Arthur Templeton
who died on the 5th Jany 1869 aged 88 years
Also Jane Templeton
who died on the 20th Novr 1875 aged 86 years

1 Arthur Templeton 1778 - 1869
.. +Jane Burnside 1792 - 1862
...... 2 Mary Jane Templeton 1829 - 1910
.... +John Burnside 1820 - 1903
.... 3 John Templeton Burnside 1858 - 1939
.... +Margaret Houston Wilson 1864 - 1946
.... 3 James Moore Burnside 1860 -
.... +Ellen McGorm
.... 3 Jane Templeton Burnside 1863 - 1932
.... 3 Alexander Burnside 1865 -
.... +Mary Gertrude Black
.... 3 Anna Moore Burnside 1868 - 1934
.... +Francis Carter
.... 3 Eliza Burnside 1870 - 1951
.... +Robert Holmes 1867 - 1945
...... 2 Sarah Templeton
.... +James McKay
.... 3 Maggie McKay
.... +Dr. McIlfatrick
...... 2 Robert Templeton
.... +Catherine Isabella Ogilvy
.... 3 Robert Ogilvy Templeton

Arthur Templeton married Jane Burnside, daughter of Samuel and Sarah (Bingham) of Secon. They had at least three known children. Rev. Robert Templeton was a Presbyterian minister in Hillsborough, married Catherine Isabella Ogilvy and had a son Robert Ogilvy.

Their daughter Sarah married James, son of Marshall McKay of Kilrea, in 1862 in Kilrea Presbyterian Church and had at least one daughter Maggie who married Dr. McIlfatrick.

Another daughter Mary Jane married John of Secon, son of Alexander and Anne (Moore) Burnside of Secon. They are buried in Knock Road Cemetery, Ballymoney (see grave 120).

TEMPLETON

GRAVE no. 121

Sacred
? Templeton
? departed
? 3 182?
? years

TAMPLETON

GRAVE no. 122

Here lieth the
Body of Jam
es Tampleto
n who depa
rted this li
fe the 6 1777

This name is also known as Templeton (see graves 120, 121). In 1740, there were James, James, John and Robert Templeton present in Ballymoney Parish. In 1766 there was a J. Templeton.

BELL

GRAVE no. 123

Here lieth the body
of
Isabella Bell of Prospect
who departed this life on the the 8th
day of Jany 1802 aged 78 years
And her husband
David Bell
who departed this life on the 17th
day of Dec 1815 aged 89 years
Sarah daughter of John Bell
died 6th May 1865 aged 84 years
Also Jane her sister
who died 8th July 1865 aged 82 years
Likewise Alice Bell her sister
who died 14 Dec 1878 aged 87 years

1 David Bell 1726 - 1815
.. +Isabella 1723 - 1802
.... 2 John Bell 1751 - 1844
.... +Alicia 1749 - 1824
.... 3 Jane Bell 1783 - 1865
.... 3 Sarah Bell 1781 - 1865
.... 3 William Bell 1787 - 1859
.... +Mary Matthews
.... 4 Sarah Bell 1812 -
.... 3 James Bell 1785 - 1855
.... 3 Alice Bell 1791 - 1878
.... 3 Elizabeth Bell 1795 - 1856

The Bell family were farmers at Prospect and were present from the 1660s. They were members of St. Patrick's Parish Church (see grave 124). Prospect is about about a mile from Ballymoney, and was originally called Cloughcorr.

BELL

GRAVE no. 124

Here lieth the body
of
Alicia Bell late of Prospect
who departed this life
29th March 1824 aged 74 years
And
John her husband who died
2nd September 1844 aged 93
Also
James Bell his son who died
27 December 1855 aged 70
Likewise his daughter
Elizabeth Bell who died
24th March 1856 aged 60
Also his son William Bell
who died 25th August 1859
aged 72 years

1 David Bell 1726 - 1815
.. +Isabella 1723 - 1802
.... 2 John Bell 1751 - 1844
.... +Alicia 1749 - 1824
.... 3 Jane Bell 1783 - 1865
.... 3 Sarah Bell 1781 - 1865
.... 3 William Bell 1787 - 1859
.... +Mary Matthews
.... 4 Sarah Bell 1812 -
.... 3 James Bell 1785 - 1855
.... 3 Alicia Bell 1791 - 1878
.... 3 Elizabeth Bell 1795 - 1856

Alicia Bell was the wife of John, son of David and Isabella Bell of Prospect. They had six known children. Jane, Sarah and William all died at Portbradden, near Ballintoy. William married Mary Matthews and had one known child.

Alice died in Linenhall Street, Ballymoney.

James Bell was land agent, in succession to his father, to James E. Leslie Esq. of Leslie Hill. He had made a very considerable collection of antiquities, which were sold after his death at Prospect. Some of them were purchased by the postmaster of the time, Mr Wilson, who then presented them to the trustees of the Town Hall in Ballymoney. He was also a contributor to the first series of the Ulster Journal of Archaeology.

TODD

GRAVE no. 125

Sacred
to the memory of the
late Hugh Todd of
Ballygan
who departed this life
4 Jany 1812 aged
72 years
Also Agnes his wife who
died 7 May 1820 aged
82 years

In 1803, there was a Hugh Todd present in Ballymoney town and a Gabriel Todd present at Ballygan. A Gabriel Todd had daughters Elizabeth born about 1754, Agnes in 1756 and John in 1757. Another Gabriel Todd had daughters Grace Bell (b.1805) and Jean (b.1807) but had died before 1817.

HARPOUR

GRAVE no. 126

James Harpour
Drumnafivey 1807
aged 75 years

The name Harpour is also spelt Harper. There were two burials recorded in the early 1800s, James buried on 8th November 1820 aged 85 years and John buried 20th October 1808 aged 42 years.

The family is possibly related to the Fergusons of Clintyfinnan (see grave 127) as Harper was used as a middle name. In 1803, James Harper senior and junior were present at Drumafivey.

FERGUSON

GRAVE no. 127

Erected
By order of the late
Hugh Ferguson
of Cluntyfinnan in memory of his
mother Ruth Ferguson who died
29th May 1858 aged 76 years
Also his brother
Robert Ferguson
who died 15th May 1878 aged 69 years
Also the above
Hugh Ferguson
who died 21st January 1877 aged 77 years

1 James Ferguson 1773 - 1864
.. +Ruth 1782 - 1858
...... 2 Robert Ferguson 1808 - 1878
...... 2 Hugh Ferguson 1809 - 1887
...... 2 James Harper Ferguson 1814 - 1901
.... +Elizabeth Anne Woodside 1828 - 1914
.... 3 Elizabeth Nevin Ferguson 1863 - 1941
.... +James Campbell 1844 - 1900
...... 2 Sally Anne Ferguson
.... +John Stewart
.... 3 Hugh Ferguson Stewart 1848 - 1933
.... +Eliza Jane Kerr 1861 - 1953

    Ruth Ferguson was the wife of James Ferguson who was buried in Armoy Parish graveyard. There was a Margaret Ferguson in Clintyfinnan (as it is commonly known) in 1803. It is next to the townland of Drumafivey, near Stranocum.
    Another son James Harper Ferguson married Elizabeth Anne, daughter of Robert and Elizabeth (Nevin) Woodside of Strone, Dervock in 1862 in Dervock Reformed Presbyterian Church and farmed at Moyaver near Clintyfinnan.
    Their daughter Sally Ann married John Stewart of Ballykenver in 1847.

MCAFEE

GRAVE no. 128

Erected by
William McAfee of Ballymoney
In memory of his daughter Eliza
who died 10th June 1864 aged 17 years
Her two infant brothers
William aged 10 months
and Alexander aged 14 months
Also interred here His daughter Lucy died 5th March
1892 aged 33 years
His son Alexander B.A.
Lic. Coll. Surgeons, Edinburgh, distinguished surgeon
? Cape Colony died 13th July 1875 aged 21?
also ? ? ?
William McAfee
died 14th April 1898
aged 85 years
His wife Susan McAfee
died 19th June 1906 aged 80 years
Their daughter Susanna
died 19th March 1908 aged 60 years
Their son John Wilson
died at Valparaiso, Chile
on 15th September 1920

1 William MacAfee 1813 - 1898
.. +Susan Wilson 1825 - 1906
...... 2 Mary Jane MacAfee 1845 - 1879
.... +Charles Lyle 1841 - 1888
.... 3 Mary Lyle 1871 -
.... 3 Thomas Lyle 1873 -
.... 3 William MacAfee Lyle 1875 - 1877
.... 3 Charles Gordon Lyle 1878 - 1935
.... +Florence Jane Seabrook - 1963
.... 3 William MacAfee Lyle 1878 -
...... 2 Lizzie MacAfee 1847 - 1864
...... 2 Susanna MacAfee 1847 - 1908
...... 2 Matilda Leslie MacAfee 1852 - 1935
.... +Thomas Knox

MCAFEE

GRAVE no. 128

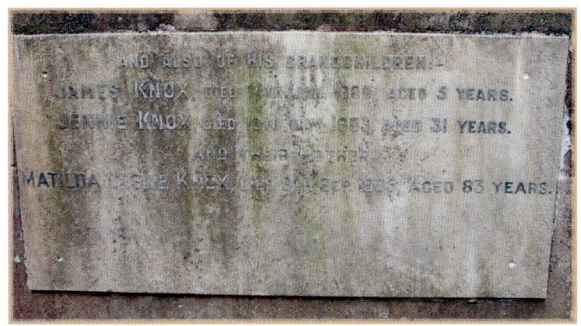

And also of his grandchildren
James Knox died 14th Jan 1880 aged 5 years
Jennie Knox died 10th May 1903 aged 31 years
And their mother
Matilda Leslie Knox, died 9th September 1935
aged 83 years

.... 3 Jeannie Knox 1871 - 1903
.... 3 William Knox
.... 3 James Knox 1875 - 1880
...... 2 William MacAfee 1854 - 1855
...... 2 Louisa MacAfee 1858 - 1892
...... 2 Alexander MacAfee 1864 - 1865
...... 2 Eliza MacAfee 1866 -
.... +Adam Moss
.... 3 Frank Dudley Moss 1900 -
.... 3 William Arthur Moss 1902 -
...... 2 John Wilson MacAfee - 1920
...... 2 Alexander MacAfee

William, son of Robert and Mary Ann McAfee of Currysisken married Lucy, daughter of Andrew and Lucy Wilson. He was a spirit dealer in Main Street, Ballymoney.

Their eldest daughter Mary Jane married Charles, son of Thomas and Mary Ann (Gordon) Lyle in 1868 in 1st Ballymoney Presbyterian Church. Thomas was a merchant and Charles was a hotel keeper in Church Street. Charles and Mary Jane died when their family were young and are buried in St. Patricks Parish Churchyard.

Matilda married Thomas, a spirit dealer in Portglenone, and son of Rev. John and Jenny (Knox) Knox of Culramoney and Portglenone, who was in 1870 in 1st Ballymoney Presbyterian Church.

Eliza married Dr. Adam, son of David and Agnes (Watson) Moss in 1897 in 1st Ballymoney Presbyterian Church and moved to Lancashire.

MARTIN GRAVE no. 129

In loving memory of
John Martin, Ballinamoney
who died 30th Dec 1887
Aged 76 years
Also his wife Martha
who died 7th Nov. 1882
and their son John
who died 7th Sept. 1888
Aged 38 years
And his wife Margaret
who died 22nd Feb. 1936
Aged 85 years
Also their grandson
James N. Martin
who died 1st Nov. 1894
Aged 11 years

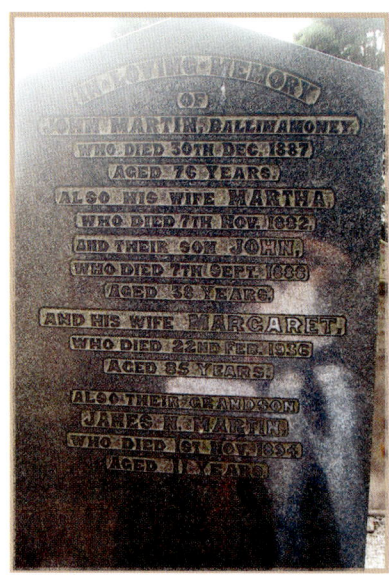

1 John Martin 1811 - 1887
.. +Martha Moore 1813 - 1882
...... 2 Letty Martin 1833 -
...... 2 David Martin 1836 - 1879
.... +Matilda Speare - 1905
.... 3 David Cochrane Martin 1857 -
.... 3 William James Martin 1859 -
.... +Margaret Lyons
.... 3 Matilda Martin 1862 - 1924
.... 3 Jane (Maggie J.?) Martin 1864 -
.... 3 Alexander Martin 1866 - 1924
.... 3 Samuel George Martin 1877 -
...... 2 Jane Martin 1837 - 1872
.... +Daniel Taylor 1826 -
.... 3 John Taylor 1859 -
.... 3 Matilda Taylor 1861 - 1862
.... 3 William Taylor 1862 -
.... 3 Joseph Taylor 1866 -
.... 3 Jacob Taylor 1867 -
.... 3 James Cramsie Taylor 1871 -
.... +Sarah Taylor 1872 -
.... 3 Daniel Taylor
.... +Margaret Blair
...... 2 Matilda Martin 1839 - 1929
.... +John Matthews - 1920
...... 2 William Martin 1847 -
...... 2 John Martin 1850 - 1888
.... +Margaret Lees 1851 - 1936
.... 3 Martha Moore Martin 1873 - 1955
.... +John Thompson McCracken 1860 - 1946
.... 3 Margaret Jane Martin 1875 - 1951

    John, son of William and Jane (Cochrane) Martin of Moneycannon married Martha daughter of John and Letitia (Watt) Moore of Drumaheglis. They were farmers at Ballinamoney.

    Their son David married Matilda, daughter of Samuel Speare of Polintamny and they farmed at Moneycannon.

    Their daughter Jane married Daniel, only son of John and Martha (Boyd) Taylor of Ballinamoney in 1857 in 1st Ballymoney Presbyterian Church.

MARTIN

GRAVE no. 129

Their daughter Matilda married John, son of Samuel Matthews of Polintamny in 1866 in 1st Ballymoney Presbyterian Church and emigrated to Australia.

Their second son John married Margaret, daughter of John Lees of Grangemore, Articlave, and his sister Mary Moore married Isaac, son of John Lees, both in 1872 in 1st Ballymoney Presbyterian Church.

John's youngest son James Nevin died aged 11 years from scarletina.

```
................... +John Stuart Cochrane 1870 -
............... 3 John Martin 1877 - 1951
............... 3 William Martin 1879 - 1949
............... 3 Samuel Martin 1881 -
............... 3 James Nevin Martin 1883 - 1894
............... 3 Mary Ann Martin 1886 -
................... +John Cochrane Martin 1874 - 1946
............... 3 Elizabeth J. Martin 1888 - 1968
................... +John Graham 1870 - 1954
...... 2 Mary Moore Martin 1852 - 1916
.......... +Isaac Leese
```

ADAMS

GRAVE no. 130

Here lieth the body of
Martin Adams
Ballymoney who
Departed this life the 8th
of January in the year
of 1806 aged 44 Years
Also
his daughter Matilda Adams
who died the 27th March 1822
aged 21
And his wife Jane who died
6th January 1842 aged 72 years
And their daughter Sarah
who died the 18th April 1855
aged 56 years

Martin and Jane Adams lived in Church Street, Ballymoney. Martin was a maltster. They had three children Sarah (1799-1855), Matilda (1801-1822) and Hugh (b.1803).

TWEED

GRAVE no. 131

In
loving memory
of
William Tweed
who died 26th October 1892
Aged 60 years
Also his wife Mary
of Pleasurestep
who died 1st January 1911
Aged 79 years

1 William Tweed 1833 - 1892
.. +Mary Stewart 1831 - 1911
...... 2 John Tweed
...... 2 Mary Tweed
.... +James Kennedy
.... 3 Margaret Stewart Kennedy 1894 -
.... 3 William Tweed Kennedy 1895 -
.... +Jeannie Matilda Neil Nevin 1896 -
.... 3 Samuel Guiler Kennedy
.... 3 Charlotte Kennedy
.... 3 John Stewart Kennedy
.... +May Glenn
.... 3 Hugh Kennedy
.... 3 Mary Kennedy
.... 3 James Kennedy

William, son of John and Mary (McIlhernon) Tweed of Ballymacwilliam, married Mary, daughter of John and Catherine Stewart of Loughabin, Kilraughts in 1863 in Kilraughts Presbyterian Church.. They moved to Enagh to farm, where William died of a broken neck due to a fall from a horse.

Their daugher Mary married James, son of William and Charlotte (Long) Kennedy of Drumreagh in 1893 in 1st Kilraughts Presbyterian Church. Her mother Mary died in Crannagh at her daughter's home.

GLASS

GRAVE no. 132

Interred here
Helen Glass
died October 1807
aged 7?

Helen was possibly the sister of William Glass of Ballymoney. William was a builder and grocer and lived at Main Street. He married Martha, daughter of Adam and Rose Blair (see grave 98). They had a son Robert (see grave 133).

GLASS

GRAVE no. 133

Interred here
Margaret
the beloved wife of
Robert Glass aged ?
1855.   Also
Two of their daughters
Robert Glass
Died 6th Octr 1862
Aged 82 years

1 Robert Glass 1780 - 1862
.. +Margaret Johnston - 1855
.... 2 William Glass
.... +Christina MacDougall
.... 3 Catherine Glass 1861 -
.... 3 John Glass 1863 -
.... 3 Jane Glass 1865 -
.... 2 James Glass
.... 2 Robert Glass
.... 2 Helen Glass 1819 -
.... +Richard Craig
.... 2 Margaret Glass 1821 -

    Robert Glass was the son of William and Martha (Blair) Glass and lived at Charlotte Street, Ballymoney. He was a tailor and a member of the Unitarian Church.

    He married Margaret Johnston and they had at least five known children. Their son William worked with the Inland Revenue. Robert John moved to Belfast in 1842. Helen married Richard Craig of Belfast in 1844.

    He left a will which mentions his son and two surviving daughters. He also mentions grandchildren Robert James Glass, Robert, John and Margaret Brown, and Robert and Mary Bell.

STEWART

GRAVE no. 134

Here rest the remains of
John Stewart of Louhgab
bin who departed this life
20th November 1824 Aged
80 years. Also Elisabeth
his wife who departed
this life 12 October 1831
Aged 81 years
And his son William who
died on the 9th September 1856
Aged 71 years

1. John Stewart 1744 -1824
.. +Elizabeth 1750 - 1831
...... 2 John Stewart 1779 - 1869
.... +Catherine 1794 - 1870
.... 3 John Stewart 1825 -
.... +Elizabeth Tweed 1830 -
.... 4 Annie Stewart 1871 -
.... 4 William James Stewart 1873 -
.... +Jane Anna Morton 1879 -
.... 4 Jane Stewart 1876 -
.... 4 Ann Stewart 1879 -
.... 3 Mary Stewart 1831 - 1911
.... +William Tweed 1833 - 1892
                see grave 131
.... 3 William Stewart 1825 - 1908
.... +Jane Tweed 1836 - 1922
.... 4 John Stewart 1861 - 1913
.... +Annie McElderry Boyd 1861 -
.... 4 William Stewart 1863 - 1942
.... +Eleanor Moore Kirkpatrick 1862 - 1930
.... 4 Robert Stewart 1866 -
.... 4 Catherine Stewart 1871 -
.... +Hugh Wallace McCammon
.... 4 Jennie Stewart 1874 -
.... +Robert Smyth Robinson
.... 4 Charles Stewart 1877 -
.... +Margaret Campbell Huey
.... 4 Samuel Finlay Stewart 1884 - 1972
.... +Maud Isobel Armour 1890 - 1976
.... 4 Mary Stewart 1890 - 1965
.... +Robert Benjamin Thomson 1868 - 1957
.... 4 Elizabeth Stewart
.... +William Henry Lyle 1872 -
...... 2 William Stewart 1785 - 1856

This Stewart family were farmers in Loughabin (spelling error on the gravestone) in the Kilraughts area for many generations. They were prominent members of Kilraughts Presbyterian Church.

Their eldest son John and his family are buried in Kilraughts Old Churchyard. He married Catherine and they had three known children who all married Tweeds.

John married Elizabeth, daughter of John and Jennie (Arthur) Tweed of Killogue in 1868.

His sister Mary married William, son of John and Mary (McIlhernon) Tweed of Ballymacwilliam, Kilraughts (see grave 131).

His brother William married William Tweed's sister Jane in 1860 in 1st Kilraughts Presbyterian Church and they moved to Larchfield, Kilraughts to another farm.

ROWAN

GRAVE no. 135

Robert Rowan Esq.
of Garry and Bellisle, died at Douglas, and was interred at Kirk Malew in the Isle of Man
A.D.1832 aged 78 years
There also was interred his wife Eliza Rowan, daughter of
Hill Wilson Esqr.
of Purdysburn, Co. of Down
who died at Castletown, Isle of Man
A.D.1817 aged 64 years
And his daughter Eliza who died
A.D.1802 aged 14 years
His daughter Elinor, First wife of the Honourable
Deemster Heywood
died at Douglas A.D.1820 aged 28 years
and was interred at
Kirk Couchan, Isle of Man
Robert Willson Rowan
Mount Davys
? ? ?

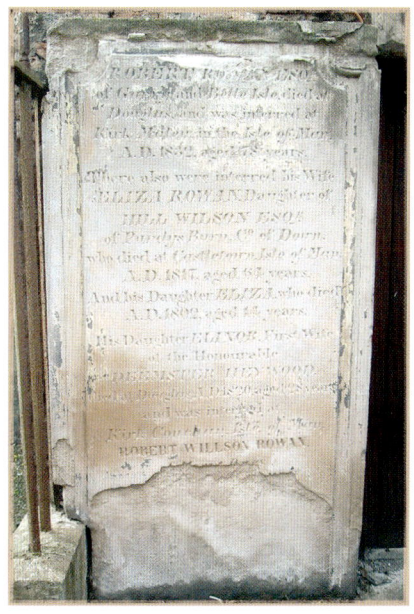

1 Robert Rowan 1754 - 1832
.. +Eliza Willson 1753 - 1817
...... 2 John Rowan 1778 - 1865
.... +Dorothea Shaw Ogilvy
...... *2nd Wife of John Rowan:
.... +Eliza Honoria MacManus - 1810
.... 3 Robert Rowan 1810 -
.... +Anna Minnit
...... 2 Hill Willson Rowan 1779 - 1863
...... 2 Robert Rowan 1781 -
...... 2 Charles Rowan 1783 - 1852
...... 2 Frederick Rowan 1785 -
...... 2 Edward Rowan 1787 -
.... +Elizabeth Legge
...... 2 Eliza Rowan 1788 - 1832
...... 2 William Rowan 1789 - 1879
.... +Martha Spong 1788 - 1874
...... 2 Elinor Rowan 1791 - 1820
.... +John Joseph Heywood 1790 - 1856
.... 3 Elinor Heywood 1820 -

Robert was the son of John and Rose (Stewart) Rowan of Mullans and Garry and High Sheriff of Antrim.

Robert was an officer in the Antrim militia at the Battle of Wexford in the 1798 Irish Rebellion. In 1777 he married Eliza, daughter of Hill Willson of Purdysburn.

Their youngest daughter Elinor married the Honorable John Joseph Heywood of the Isle of Man, Deemster for the Isle of Man for 33 years. They had one daughter Elinor.

JAMISON

GRAVE no. 136

Erected
To the memory of
William Jamison
late of Drunkendult who died
on the 15th Jany 1815 aged 72
Also his wife Margret who
died on the 16th October 1829
Aged 82 years
And their daughter Jane Graham
late of Bendooragh who died
on the 12th January 1849 aged
72 years

There were no Jamisons at Druckendult (as it should be spelt) in 1803. This William may be related to the Jameson family of Drumart, which is the next townland.

ROWAN

GRAVE no. 137

Middle

Dorothea Shaw
John Rowan D.S. ?
All   ?   ?
second   ?   ?
of Bally?   ?
Capt.   ?   ?
She died ? this   ?
Erected by his   ?
John Rowan ? Garry ?
Latterly of Mount Davys
in the county of Antrim
Born 30th March 1778

Exemplary in every relation of life
loved and respected by all ? es
just courteous dispassionate
and consistent man?
Sorely tried while still young.
By the loss of a wife whom devotedly loved
and to whose only child.
His affectionate was henceforth transferred
He died humbly relying on the merits
of his saviour 19th December 1855

1 John Rowan 1778 - 1855.
+Dorothea Shaw Ogilvy 1778 – 1849
*2nd Wife of John Rowan:
.. +Eliza Honoria MacManus ?- 1810
...... 2 Robert Rowan 1810 -
.... +Anna Minnit
.... 3 John Joshua Rowan 1838 -
.... 3 Alexander MacManus Rowan 1841 -
.... 3 Eliza Hester Rowan 1843 -
.... 3 Mary Dorothea Rowan
.... 3 Anna Rowan
.... 3 Robert Rowan

Right

Eliza Honoria
First wife of John Rowan Esq. Of Garry
in the county of Antrim
and eldest daughter
of Alexander McManus
of Mount Davys in the County of Antrim
Lieutenant Colonel of the Antrim
and Major of Volunteer
in the year 1780
She departed this life 18th May 1810
This tablet was
Erected by her affectionate husband
Marks the resting place
of her mortal remains

ROWAN

GRAVE no. 138

Below

To the memory of Letitia
Relict of Rev. Robert Rowan
of Mullans and Drumhead heiress
of John Stewart Garry and Drumart
A descendant of the Stewarts of Bute
Died full of years A.D. 1794

1 John Stewart 1678 -
. +Letitia Rowan
...... 2 Letitia Stewart 1711 - 1794
.... +Robert Rowan
.... 3 John Rowan 1733 - 1768
.... +Rose Stewart
.... 4 Letitia Rowan
.... 4 Rose Rowan
.... 4 Charlotte Rowan
.... 4 Margaret Rowan
.... 4 Charles Rowan
.... 4 John Rowan - 1796
.... 4 Hellena Rowan
.... +S. Boyd
.... 4 Robert Rowan 1754 - 1832
.... +Eliza Willson 1753 - 1817
.... 3 Archibald Rowan
.... 3 Stewart Rowan
.... 4 Rose Rowan
.... 4 Robert Rowan
.... 3 William Rowan
.... 3 Margaret Rowan
...... 2 Mary Stewart 1712 -

Rev. Robert, son of Rev. John and Margaret (Stewart) Rowan of Ballynagappog, Co. Down, married Letitia, daughter of John and Letitia Stewart of Garry in 1732.

John, son of Robert and Eliza (Willson) Rowan of Garry and Ahoghill, married Eliza Honoria MacManus, eldest daughter of Lt. Col. And Hester Henrietta (O'Neill) MacManus of Mount Davys, Co. Antim. They had one child, Rev Robert Rowan of Mount Davys, who succeeded, on the death of his uncle Alexander MacManus, to part of the MacManus estate.

He married Dorothea Shaw Ogilvy, relict of T. Blair of Whitehaven, Belfast. She died at Merville, Carnmoney, Belfast.

GREER

GRAVE no. 139

Sacred
to the memory of
James Greer Esq Late of Turners Grove
in the county of Armagh who departed
this life at O'Hara Brook in this Parish
the 7th August 1812 Aged 67 years
Also his wife
Katherine Greer
who died 11th December 1866

It is not known why James Greer is buried here. His wife Katherine died at Moneymore in 1866 aged 86 years.

LECKY

GRAVE no. 140

Semper Parartas

Sacred to the memory
of
Thomas Lecky Esqr
who departed this life
the 1st day of May 1785
Aged 75 years
And
Elizabeth his wife
daughter of the Revd.
Thomas Warburton
She departed this life
the 6th day of June 1784
Aged 60 years

Thomas and Elizabeth Lecky had a daughter Elizabeth who married George Hutchinson of Ballymoney (see grave 142). The Lecky family resided in Cloyfin at Beardiville House and the families remained very close for the next 150 years. George's eldest daughter Matilda married Hugh Lecky III.

The Leckys owned a house in Main Street, Ballymoney which George Hutchinson inherited on his marriage to Elizabeth.

HUTCHINSON

GRAVE no. 141

Sacred
to the memory of
Elizabeth
wife of George Hutchinson of
Ballymoney
who departed this life on the 5th
May 1825 A.D.
Also
to the memory of
Elizabeth their daughter
who departed this life on the 5th
March A.D. 1818
aged ? years
Almighty God
? to their memory

1 George Hutchinson 1761 - 1845
.. +Elizabeth Lecky - 1825
...... 2 Thomas Lecky Hutchinson 1793 - 1845
.... +Catherine Sinclaire 1799 - 1884
.... 3 Thomas Hutchinson 1823 - 1825
.... 3 George Augustus Hutchinson 1825 - 1857
.... 3 Elizabeth Hutchinson 1827 -
.... +Shakspere Wood
.... 3 Matilda Jane Hutchinson 1829 - 1914
.... 3 Catherine Hutchinson 1831 - 1914
.... 3 Thomas Lecky Hutchinson 1833 - 1886
.... 3 Amelia Adelaide Hutchinson 1834 -
.... +Thomas H. Gelston
.... 3 John Sinclaire Hutchinson 1835 – 1919
.... +Elizabeth - 1924
.... 3 Harriet Hutchinson 1836 - 1908
...... 2 Elizabeth Hutchinson 1788 - 1818
...... 2 Mary Hutchinson
...... 2 Matilda Hutchinson
.... +Hugh Lecky
.... 3 George Lecky
.... +Harriett Dobbs

George, son of Archibald and Elizabeth (Forsythe) Hutchinson, married Elizabeth, daughter of Rev. Thomas and Elizabeth (Warburton) Lecky (see grave 140).

They had a son and three daughters. Thomas Lecky Hutchinson married Catherine Sinclaire in 1822 in Belfast. Matilda married Hugh Lecky of Beardiville in 1837 in Taney Church.

Thomas and Catherine had nine children. Their eldest son Thomas died as an infant. Their second son George died at Glenlynden, Rice Lake, Upper Canada in 1857. Their eldest daughter Elizabeth married Shakspere Wood in 1859 in London. Their fourth daughter Amelia married Thomas Gelston of Whiteabbey in 1860 in Portrush. Their youngest son, John Sinclaire married Elizabeth, lived near Ballycastle and is buried in Ramoan Parish Churchyard with his sister Harriet. Their daughters Matida Jane and Catherine are buried with their father in Ballymoney Parish Churchyard.

HUTCHINSON

GRAVE no. 142

Sacred to the memory
of
George Hutchinson
of
Ballymoney

Obit. 1st July 1845

George Hutchinson was born in 1761, second son of Archibald and Elizabeth (Forsythe) Hutchinson of Stranocum. His elder brother, Richard, inherited Stranocum House and the surrounding estate in 1795.

Richard and George were young men, who were asked by the local magnates to lead units of the Dunluce Cavalry, or local mobile forces. These forces were raised from local land owners, farmers and townspeople. Richard was a Captain and George was also commissioned in that unit as a Lieutenant.

In 1803 Richard died of tuberculosis leaving wife, Sarah Forde and four young children. Richard had two sons, Archibald, who died in 1828 and James, who inherited the estate. He married Charlotte Forde and died in 1848, without issue. This led to the Ford family inheriting the Stranocum estates, despite the usual practice of the trustees directing the inheritance to the eldest surviving male relative. This matter took many years to resolve and was a source of friction between the Ford Hutchinsons and George Hutchinson's family.

George married Elizabeth Lecky in 1785 and their eldest son Thomas Lecky was born in 1793. After a private education George studied law and became a Justice of the Peace in Ballymoney.

With some considerable assistance from Elizabeth's inheritance, George's family fortunes improved George practised careful husbandry, accumulating nearly 3000 acres, a similar size to the Stranocum estate. His eldest son

HUTCHINSON

GRAVE no. 142

Thomas Lecky, who was a qualified lawyer on the Rolls in Dublin, was able to enjoy the fruits of George's hard work.

The family lived in the Manor House in Main Street. This house was damaged during the 1798 rebellion and was restored at Government expense of about 800 pounds sterling.

Some Ballymoney families were unable to forget George's actions in the rebellion, however George was friendly with a number of Catholics in the neighbourhood. This is evidenced by his donation of some land for a new church and a petition from a number of Catholics recognizing his support of their community.

George lived to a very old age. He drafted a Memorial document, which was to be sent to the Chief Secretary for Ireland asking for a pension as recompense for his work assisting the Government in the rebellion. The request was never sent as his family told him he did not need the money.

In 1845, he died and was buried in the Old Churchyard in Ballymoney. He outlived his wife Elizabeth, his daughters Mary and Elizabeth, and son Thomas Lecky, who died on the 5th March 1845 and is buried in Ballymoney Parish Churchyard.

(Contributed by Peter Hutchinson, grgrgrandson of George Hutchinson).

```
1 Archibald Hutchinson
.. +Elizabeth Forsythe
...... 2 Richard Hutchinson 1758 - 1808
.......... +Sarah Forde
............... 3 Archibald Hutchinson - 1828
.................... +Charlotte Waring
............... 3 James Hutchinson
.................... +Charlotte Forde
............... 3 Elizabeth Hutchinson
............... 3 Sarah Hutchinson
...... 2 George Hutchinson 1761 - 1845
.......... +Elizabeth Lecky - 1825
           see grave 142
...... 2 James Reynolds Hutchinson 1764 -
...... 2 Elizabeth Hutchinson 1766 - 1845
```

STEWART

GRAVE no. 143

Sacred
to the memory of
Samuel Stewart
late of Cabra who dep
arted this life on the 14th
June Anno 1830 aged
47 years

Samuel and Nancy Stewart had a daughter Elizabeth born in 1813 in Cabra. She married Samuel Arthur in 1838 in 1st Ballymoney Presbyterian Church. Samuel possible had a sister Mary who married John Hopkins of Cabra, and another sister Phoebe who was living with the Hopkins family in 1817. Samuel wasn't living in Cabra in 1803. However, there were two Samuel Stewarts present nearby in Enagh.

MCMASTER

GRAVE no. 144

Erected by James McMaster Ballymoney
in
memory
of
His beloved son
James
who died 27th April 1879
Aged 18 years
Also six of his children
who died young
Also his daughter
Mary Stuart
died 12th Feb 1898
Aged 30 years
Also his daughter Tillie
died 11th April 1901
Aged 21 years
The above James McMaster
who died 7th June 1913
Aged 78 years
And his wife Catherine
who died 9th January 1923
Aged 83 years

1 James McMaster 1835 - 1913
.. +Catherine Rainey 1839 – 1923
...... 2 James Lyle McMaster 1861 - 1879
...... 2 John McMaster 1865 -
...... 2 Mary McMaster 1867 - 1898
.... +William Young Stuart 1863 - 1936
.... 3 Female Stuart 1891 - 1891
.... 3 James Stuart 1892 - 1893
.... 3 Archibald Stuart 1893 - 1969
.... +Theresa Gascoyne 1922 - 2005
.... 3 Catherine Stuart 1895 - 1985
.... +James McKinney
.... 3 Mary McMaster Stuart 1898 - 1980
.... +Samuel Rosborough - 1982
...... 2 Matilda McMaster 1870 - 1901
...... 2 Sarah Jane McMaster 1872 -
...... 2 John McMaster 1876 -
.... 3 James McMaster 1918 -
.... +Mary Dorothy McLean 1918 -
.... 3 Doris Patricia McMaster 1924 -
.... +David Acheson Lindsay
...... 2 Matilda McMaster 1879 - 1901

James, son of James and Martha (McDowell) McMaster, married Catherine, daughter of John and Mary (Walker) Rainey of Bendooragh in 1859 in 1st Ballymoney Presbyterian Church.

His daughter Mary married John Young, son of Thomas and Margaret (Robinson) Stuart of Newbuildings in 1856 in 1st Ballymoney Presbyterian Church. She died after the birth of her fifth child.

Only one child, John, survived to old age.

MARSHALL

GRAVE no. 145

In grateful remembrance
of the Revd Doctor
Alexander Marshall
Presbyterian Minister
of Ballymoney
for 27 years
His mourning parishioners
and some others
have erected this stone
to his memory
He was truly pious
liberal in his principles
Lived, beloved
and died lamented
By good men
of every persuasion
He departed this life
the 10th of April 1799
aged 50 years
Mary his wife and their
infant child are also
interred here

Rev. Alexander Marshall was the son of George Marshall, a farmer at Ray. He went to Glasgow University in 1766 and was licensed to preach by Limavady Presbytery in 1770. He was ordained in Ballymoney in 1772, filling a four year vacancy after the death of the previous minister, Rev. Robert Smylie.

The present church became too small and he was responsible for the construction of a new Presbyterian meeting house in 1777 where it still stands today. He was honoured with a doctor of Divinity Degree and was chosen as Moderator of the General Synod of Ulster in 1795.

The 1798 rebellion in Ireland tore the families of Ballymoney apart and although Dr. Marshall tried his best to support his people, it affected him badly and he died in 1799.

SMYLIE

GRAVE no. 145a

Sacred
to the memory of the
Rev. Robert Smylie. 8
years Minister of the Dissenting
Congregation of Ballymoney
He practiced those devine truths
which he recommended to his
Hearers. He died on the 31 of
August 1767 in the 35 year of his age
This stone is erected by order of
his affectionate spouse. March 1812
N.B. This is erected here as
Mr McBride, Mr Smylie and Mr. Marshall
occupy the same grave

Robert Smylie was the eldest son of Robert and Mrs Smylie of Ardstraw. He was educated at Glasgow University and was ordained in Ballymoney in 1759. He was described as having a delicate constitution and died after only being minister for eight years.

Rev. Robert McBride was the son of Rev. John McBride, minister of 1st Presbyterian Church in Rosemary Street, Belfast from 1694 to 1718. He was educated in Scotland and Holland and was ordained in Ballymoney in 1716. He died in Main Street, Ballymoney in 1759, in his 73th year of age, and although buried in the Old Graveyard, a marble tablet was erected in the Parish church nearby, which was an unusual tribute for a Presbyterian minister.

PARK

GRAVE no. 146

Eliza Park
wife of the Reverend Robert Park
died 16th January 1828
aged 31 years
John Park
their infant child died 26th Nov 1827
aged 16 months
Martha Park
died 20th August 1851 aged 8 years
Mary Park
died April 30 aged 11 years

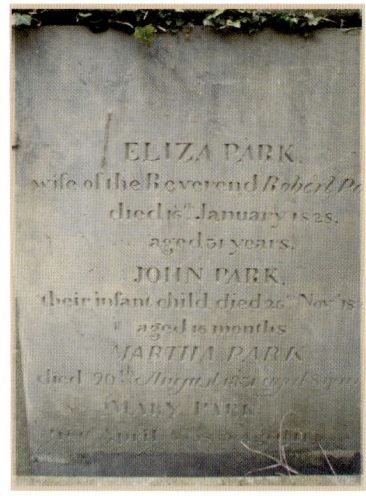

1 Robert Park 1794 - 1876
.. +Eliza Brown 1796 - 1828
.... 2 Mary Park 1819 - 1830
.... 2 Martha Park 1823 - 1831
.... 2 Margaret Park 1825 -
.... 2 John Park 1826 - 1827
*2nd Wife of Robert Park:
.. +Margaret Burriss 1803 - 1888
    see grave 146a

Rev. Robert Park was born in Stewartstown, Co. Tyrone in 1794 the son, and sixth child of Mr and Mrs John Park. He was educated at Glasgow University and came to Ballymoney in 1817 after the resignation and death of Rev. Benjamin Mitchell in 1815.

He married Eliza Brown from Connor and all four children of this marriage died in childhood.

He was a very popular minister and many children in his congregation were called after him. He kept meticulous records including a census of his congregation in 1817 and thorough baptismal and marriage details, which have been a major research tool used in this book.

He resigned from his ministry in 1866, due to age and ill health. Later in the same year the congregation obtained an assistant and successor in Rev. Alexander Patton. Rev. Park died at his home in Charlotte Street in 1876 and in the same year a memorial tablet was erected inside the church in his memory.

PARK

GRAVE no. 146a

In loving remembrance
Re. Robert Park A.M.
For nearly sixty years minister of
Presbyterian Church Ballymoney
born 15 April 1794
died 10 May 1876
Also of his beloved wife
Margaret
who died 18th Sept 1888
aged 83 years

1 Robert Park 1794 - 1876
.. +Eliza Brown 1796 - 1828
   see grave 146
*2nd Wife of Robert Park:
.. +Margaret Burriss 1805 - 1888
.... 2 John Park 1838 - 1910
.... +Margaret Lyons
.... 3 dau Park 1868 -
.... 2 Richard Burriss Park 1840

After the death of the Eliza, Rev. Robert Park's first wife, he married Margaret Burriss, by whom he had two sons. She died in Ballinahinch in 1888. Their elder son John became Professor of Logic and Metaphysics in Queens College, later Queens University, Belfast.

MILLAR

GRAVE no. 147

To the memory of
John Millar late of
Ballymoney who depar
ted this life the 3rd day
of May 1799 aged 70 years
Also Thomas Millar his
son who departed this
life the 20th day of Dece
mber 1803 aged 44 years

In 1803, John, Samuel and William Miller (or Millar) were living in Ballymoney. John Miller was a yeoman and baker. In 1817, there was a widow Miller with children Agnes and George. This George is probably the man who compiled Miller's list of Ballymoney naming all the residents of the town. He married Sibella McMichael of Bendooragh in 1835 and moved to Belfast.

Miller mentions in his list Samuel Miller, a soap boiler who lived at the Head of town, and whose daughter Mary married John Given of Ballymoney in 1815 in St. Patrick's Parish Church (see grave 110) and Billy Miller, a shoemaker who lived in Meetinghouse Lane.

PATTON

GRAVE no. 148

Erected
in memory of
Robert Patton of Cuppidale
who died 29th December 1864
aged 77 years
Also his daughter
Mary Anne Bamford
who died 29th Jan 1866
aged 35 years
Also his wife Jane
who died 29th April 1879
aged 90 years
Daniel Patton
died 24th Nov 1936 aged 55 years
Margaret Patton
died 24th April 1950
Mary Patton
died 24th Oct 1965 aged 60 Years
Drumaheagles

1 Robert Patton 1787 - 1864
.. +Jane White 1788 - 1879
...... 2 Hamilton Brown Patton 1816 - 1901
...... 2 James Patton 1820 - 1902
...... 2 Robert Patton 1822 - 1909
...... 2 Thomas Patton 1823 -
.... +Fanny Stuart
.... 3 Charles Robert Stewart Patton 1864 -
.... +Elizabeth Simpson
.... 4 Hamilton Patton 1907 -
.... 4 William Robert Simpson Patton 1909 -
...... 2 Ellen Patton 1824 - 1909
...... 2 Alexander Patton 1827 -
.... +Jane Sloss
...... 2 Mary Anne Patton 1830 - 1866
.... +James Bamford
.... 3 Jeannette Clarke Bamford 1866 -

Robert, son of Robert Patton, was born at Drumaheglis, married Jane White and was a farmer. He moved to Balnamore for a few years and then to Cuppindale (Cuppidale or Cubbindale), near Stanocum about 1830.

Their youngest daughter Mary Anne married James Bamford of Claragh in 1864 in 1st Ballymoney Presbyterian Church, had a daughter in 1866, but died 19 days later.

Their son Thomas married Fanny, daughter of Robert Stuart of Roseyards, in 1862 in 1st Ballymoney Presbyterian Church and their son Robert married Elizabeth, daughter of Samuel Simpson of Derrykeighan, in 1906 in Benvarden Presbyterian Church.

Their son Alexander married Jane, daughter of James Sloss of Magherafelt in 1866 in Garryduff Presbyterian Church. He was a draper at the time of his marriage.

BURNSIDE

GRAVE no. 149

The body of
Samuel Burnside
of Macfinn lies here
He died the 14th day
of April 1805 closing
An industrious and useful
Life of 76 years

1 Samuel Burnside 1729 - 1805
.. +Sarah Bingham
...... 2 David Burnside
...... 2 William Burnside 1775 - 1814
...... 2 Alexander Burnside 1778 - 1865
.... +Anne Moore 1778 - 1864
　　　　see grave 109
...... 2 James Burnside 1784 -
.... +Jane Moore
　　　　see grave 109
...... 2 Mary Burnside 1787 - 1877
.... +David Boyd 1795 - 1878
.... 3 Mary Boyd 1818 - 1891
.... 3 Samuel Burnside Boyd 1820 - 1897
.... 3 Jane Boyd 1823 - 1904
.... +Joseph Keers 1804 - 1885
.... 3 Sarah Boyd 1825 - 1911
.... 3 Elizabeth Boyd 1828 - 1907
.... +Hugh Fulton 1834 - 1910
...... 2 Robert Burnside 1790 -
.... +Margaret McAllister
.... 3 Margaret Hill Burnside
...... 2 Jane Burnside 1792 - 1862
.... +Arthur Templeton 1778 - 1869
　　　　see grave 120
...... 2 Sarah Burnside 1794 - 1876
.... +John Boyd 1787 - 1864
.... 3 David Boyd 1816 - 1892
.... +Jane McElderry 1827 - 1916

　　There is a tradition in this family that the original name of Burnside was Wallace i.e. Wallace of the Burnside.
　　The earliest Burnside known at Macfin was James who died in 1739 and married Jane McAfee. They had at least five known children, Samuel, Thomas, David, Elizabeth and Jane.
　　Samuel married Sarah Bingham, daughter of Mary McGregor and granddaughter of Alexander McGregor of Maynock, Co. Derry. Alexander was a brother of Rev. James McGregor, minister of Aghadowey from 1701 to 1718, who emigrated to New Hampshire with about 600 of his congregation and founded a new colony called New Londonderry.
　　Their eldest son William joined General Simon Bolivar's force which fought for independence of Venezuela, was taken prisoner, cast into a jail in Caracas and shot by the Spaniards some time between 1814 and 1819.

BURNSIDE

GRAVE no. 149

    Their sons Alexander and James married Ann and Jane, daughters of James Moore of Dunluce (see grave 109).

    Another son Robert married Margaret McAlister of Aghadowey and emigrated.

    Their eldest daughter Mary married David and her sister Sarah married John, sons of David and Mary (Gardiner) Boyd of Knockans Finvoy and are buried in Finvoy Presbyterian Churchyard. John and Sarah Boyd's daughter Marianne married James Thomson of Dunaverney (see grave 116).

    Their daughter Jane married Arthur Templeton of Moneycannon in 1826 (see grave 120).

    Their son Samuel died unmarried in Lynchburg, Virginia in 1850 and sons David and Thomas died in Philadelphia.

    There are still Burnsides living in the Ballymoney area.

.... 3 Sarah Boyd 1819 - 1841
.... 3 Samuel Burnside Boyd 1822 - 1847
.... 3 William Gardiner Boyd 1825 - 1889
.... 3 Marianne Boyd 1828 - 1905
.... +William Thomson 1821 - 1890
.... 3 Elizabeth Boyd
.... +William Hayes
.... 3 John Boyd 1834 - 1912
.... +Margaret Ann Smyth 1846 - 1925
.... 3 Elizabeth Boyd 1830 -
.... +William Wallace
...... 2 Samuel Burnside 1796 - 1850
...... 2 Thomas Burnside 1790 -

SPEERS

GRAVE no. 150

Erected by
James Speers
In memory of his father
John Speers
who died 5th August 1838
aged 48 years
Also of his sons
John Arthur
who died 14th Sept 1873
aged 20 years
And
Hugh Moore
who died 16th May 1874
aged 14 years
James Speers
who died 20th Sept 1894
aged 72 years
Jane Speers
died 25th March 1895
aged 78 years

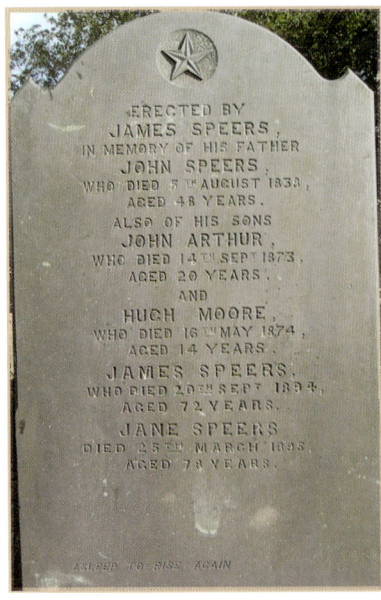

1 John Speers 1790 - 1838
.. +Margaret Tonner
.... 2 James Speers 1822 - 1894
.... +Jane Neill 1816 - 1895
.... 3 William Speers 1847 -
.... 3 Margaret Speers 1850 -
.... 3 John Arthur Speers 1852 - 1873
.... 3 Jane Speers 1854 -
.... 3 James Speers 1857 -
.... 3 Hugh Moore Speers 1860 - 1874
.... 3 Joseph Speers 1862 -
.... 2 Nancy Speers 1822 -
.... 2 John Speers 1825 -
.... +Jane Stevenson
.... 3 William Speers 1849 -
.... 3 Sarah Speers 1855 -
.... 2 William Speers 1828 -

John Speers was a shoemaker in Ballymoney, as was his son James who lived in Charlotte Street. John married Margaret Tonner and had children John, Nancy and William as well as James.

James married Jane, daughter of Joseph Neill, a labourer, in St. James Presbyterian Church in 1845. They had eight children, William, Mary Anne, Margaret, John Arthur, Jane, James, Hugh Moore and Joseph. James died in Ballymoney in 1894 and Jane died in Dublin in 1895.

John junior, a nailer, married Jane, daughter of James Stevenson, land steward, a dressmaker and had family of William and Sarah.

BOYD

GRAVE no. 151

Inspe dormie
Near this lyes
interred the re
mains of Thomas Bo
yd Junr of Cullor
money who in the
morning of life obe
yed the summons of
mortality 13 of Oct
1781 aged 21 years

MACAFEE

GRAVE no. 152

MACAFEE

This is the grave of the family of Robert and Jean (Knox) Macafee or McAfee of Bootown.

James McAfee, a teacher, married Margaret, daughter of James and Betty (Jamison) Lyle of Orble, Dervock in 1852 in Billy Parish Church. Their son William Hugh was the owner of a well known hardware shop in Church Street.

Robert McAfee married Roseann Hamill of Secon in 1842 in St. James Presbyterian Church. He was born at Bootown but died at Ballywattick and was a carpenter.

Samuel McAfee, a farmer, married Elizabeth, daughter of Andrew and Mary (Black) McLaughlin of Newbuildings in 1854 in St. James Presbyterian Church.

1 Robert McAfee 1777 - 1861
.. +Jean Knox 1784 - 1860
...... 2 James McAfee 1809 - 1885
.... +Margaret Lyle 1826 - 1910
.... 3 Eliza Jane McAfee 1855 - 1904
.... 3 Robert John McAfee 1857 - 1890
.... 3 James Lyle McAfee 1860 - 1954
.... 3 Hessie Ann McAfee 1863 - 1941
.... 3 William Hugh McAfee 1867 - 1928
.... 3 William Charles McAfee 1865 -
.... 3 Maggie Knox McAfee 1870 -
...... 2 William McAfee 1809 -
.... +Elizabeth Cooper
.... 3 James McAfee 1832 -
.... 3 Robert McAfee 1834 -
.... 3 William McAfee 1837 -
...... 2 Robert McAfee 1811 - 1890
.... +Roseann Hamill 1816 - 1879
.... 3 Eliza McAfee 1842 - 1904
.... 3 William McAfee 1844 - 1922
.... +Elizabeth Thompson 1865 - 1919
.... 3 Jane McAfee 1846 - 1913
.... 3 Hugh McAfee 1849 -
.... 3 Thomas McAfee 1851 - 1926
.... 3 Robert McAfee 1853 -
.... 3 Mary McAfee 1855 -
.... 3 Nancy McAfee 1857 - 1916
.... 3 Anna McAfee - 1911
...... 2 Hugh McAfee 1814 -
...... 2 John McAfee 1816 -
...... 2 Jean McAfee 1818 -
...... 2 Archy McAfee 1820 -
...... 2 Samuel McAfee 1825 - 1903
.... +Elizabeth McLaughlin 1831 - 1895
.... 3 Andrew McAfee 1855 -
.... +Annie McGoogan
.... 3 dau McAfee 1861 -
.... 3 Samuel McAfee 1866 -
.... 3 John Boyd McAfee 1869 -
.... 3 Robert McAfee
.... 3 James McAfee 1872 - 1892
.... 3 William McAfee 1865 -
.... 3 Anne McAfee
...... 2 Knox McAfee 1825 -

MCAFEE

GRAVE no. 153

William McAfee
Bootown
Died December 15th 1853
His wfe
Jane Boyd McAfee
Died December 22nd 1853
Their children
James McAfee
Died 12th February 1890
Mary McAfee
Died 1st March 1895
Margaret Jane McAfee
Died 8th March 1897

1 William McAfee - 1853
.. +Jane Boyd - 1853
...... 2 Elizabeth McAfee 1816 -
...... 2 Margaret Jane McAfee 1820 - 1897
...... 2 Mary McAfee 1822 - 1895
...... 2 James McAfee 1826 - 1880

This McAfee family (also spelt McFee, MacAfee, McDuffee) were living in Booton in 1817 near Robert and Jean (Knox) McAfee, but I can not find a direct relationship (see graves 152, 154) but there is a possibility that they were brothers due to the proximity of the graves. He had a sister Isabella and an aunt Elizabeth living with them in 1817. There was a probate of a will in 1804 of a William McAfee of Bootown, Dunluce, so he may have been their father.

MCDUFFEE

GRAVE no. 154

Here lyeth the
Body of Archd Mc
Duffee who depar
ted this life the
21st Febry 1800 aged
23 years

Although I have no actual evidence, I suspect this may be the brother of Robert, William and Isabella McAfee of Bootown (see graves 152, 153). This McAfee name was spelt McDuffee in the 1803 agricultural census.

WILLSON   GRAVE no. 155

Sacred
To the memory of David Willson late of Toloughgore who departed this life April 21 1808 aged 82 years. Also his wife Grizzey Willson who departed this life April 5th 1806 aged 71 years

1 David Willson 1726 - 1808
.. +Grizzey ?
.... 2 David Wilson 1775 - 1854
.... +Elizabeth White 1779 - 1851
.... 3 James Wilson 1806 - 1879
.... 3 Martin Wilson 1810 - 1838
.... 3 Jane Wilson 1812 - 1836
.... 3 David Wilson 1815 - 1904
.... +Elizabeth Douglas 1830 -
.... 3 Nancy Wilson 1819 -
.... 2 Mary Wilson
.... +William Kidd 1771 - 1833
.   see grave 156
.... 2 Elizabeth Wilson - 1836
.... +William Fullerton 1765 - 1847
.... 3 Sarah Fullerton 1799 - 1886
.... +Alexander McAyeal 1800 - 1886
.... 3 Christian Fullerton 1801 -
.... 3 Daniel Fullerton 1803 - 1884
.... +Rose Ann Cooper 1805 - 1867
.... 3 Jennet Fullerton 1803 - 1868
.... 3 Edward Fullerton 1806 -

The Willson (or Wilson) family of Tullaghgore (as it is now spelt) were no longer present in 1817.
There was a David Wilson in Artigoran married to Elizabeth White and I suspect that he is a son of the above David. Grizzey was another version of the name Christian which appeared frequently through the related families. Two daughters of David senior married other farmers in Tullaghgore.
Elizabeth married William Fullerton and a family of Sarah, Christian, Daniel, Jennett and Edward.
Mary married William Kidd and had a family of ten (see grave 156).

KIDD

GRAVE no. 156

Sacred
To the memory of William
Kidd of Toloughgore
who departed this life
October 5th
1832 aged 62 years. Also his
daughter Grizzy who depar
ted this life Dec the 22
1819 aged 24 years

1 William Kidd 1771 - 1833
.. +Mary Wilson
...... 2 Christian Kidd 1795 - 1819
...... 2 James Kidd 1798 -
...... 2 Elizabeth Kidd 1800 -
.... +John Patterson
.... 3 Mary Patterson 1841 -
...... 2 David Kidd 1802 - 1880
...... 2 Letitia Kidd 1804 -
...... 2 Martha Kidd 1806 -
...... 2 Mary Kidd 1808 -
...... 2 William Kidd 1810 -
...... 2 Edward Kidd 1813 -
...... 2 Martha Kidd 1817 -

William Kidd was not present in 1803 in Toloughgore (or Tullaghgore) and the family seem to have disappeared from the area after he died. He married Mary Wilson, daughter of David and Grizzy Wilson (see grave 155).

His daughter Grizzy was also known as Christian. His son David emigrated about 1840 to Pennsylvania and died there in 1880. Only one daughter seems to have married in the Ballymoney area. Elizabeth married John Patterson of Moneycannon in 1836 in 1st Ballymoney Presbyterian Church and had a daughter Mary.

MCCURDY

GRAVE no. 157

In memory of
James McCurdy
who died 17th Jany 1867
Aged 77 years
His wife Mary and their daughter
Sarah. Their daughter Jane
died 20th Sept 1884
Aged 63 years
John Stewart
died 11 Feb 1892 Aged 73 years
His wife Mary Stewart
died 26 January 1914
Aged 94 years

1 James McCurdy 1789 - 1867
.. +Mary Love
...... 2 John McCurdy 1814 -
...... 2 Jean McCurdy 1815 -
...... 2 James McCurdy 1817 -
...... 2 Sarah McCurdy
...... 2 Mary McCurdy 1820 - 1914
.... +John Stewart 1818 - 1892
...... 2 Hugh McCurdy 1826 -
...... 2 Andrew L. McCurdy 1823 -
.... +Annie McClure 1839 - 1914

James McCurdy married Mary Love and lived at Newhill, Ballymoney. He was a ploughman.
John, son of David Stewart, a farmer, was Master of Ballymoney workhouse. He married Mary, daughter of James McCurdy, in St. Patrick's Parish Church in 1866. She was a nurse and died in Queen Street, Ballymoney

WRIGHT

GRAVE no. 158

In
memory of
John Wright
Culbrim
who died 28th Oct 1894
aged 81 years

1 Joseph Wright
.. +Sarah Stirling 1781 - 1822
...... 2 Joseph Wright 1811 -
...... 2 John Wright 1813 - 1894
...... 2 Stirling Wright 1815 -
...... 2 Andrew Wright 1817 - 1872
.... +Mary Ann Knox 1827 - 1907
...... 2 James Wright 1819 -
...... 2 Sarah Wright 1822 -
.... +Samuel McAfee

John Wright, a farmer and bachelor, was the second son of Joseph and Sarah (Stirling) Wright of Culbrim and grandson of Joseph and Mary (Curry) Wright. His mother died just after the birth of her youngest child Sarah, who married Samuel McAfee of Ballymoney.

CALDERWOOD

GRAVE no. 159

Here lieth the body of
Alexander Calderwood who
died 10th December 1749
aged 7? years
Also rests his wife aged 90
and two of their chil
dren who died in infancy
?
?
Margaret   ?   ?
died 31st May 1776 aged 23
and
Andrew Calderwood son ?
?
died the 17th Feb 1783 aged 75 years
Like Mary wife to the
above named Andrew who
died the 10th August 1799
aged 84 years
Also Andrew her son
who died the 10 of March 1799
aged 35 years

This Calderwood family seem to be quite wealthy as births recorded in 1st Ballymoney Presbyterian Church recorded Andrew as a Mr. Baptisms were recorded for children of Andrew, Alexander, John, William and Matthew.

In the 1734 map of Ballymoney town there were one James and three Alexander Catherwoods. This was an alternate spelling of Calderwood.

In 1740 there were Alexander, David and John in the parish of Ballymoney. In 1803, there were families in Cuppindale, Balnacree and Ballymoney.

In Miller's list, there was a Jack Catherwood, a gentleman, and Alex and Andy Catherwood, bricklayers, living at Piper Row (now Charlotte Street).

In 1817, there were Calderwood families at Cuppindale, Calhame, Coldagh Whitesstown and Leitrim.

WRIGHT

GRAVE no. 160

Erected
in memory of
Andrew Wright
late of Culbrim who departed
this life on the 11th March 1857
aged 75 years

1 Joseph Wright - 1817
.. +Mary Curry
...... 2 Thomas Wright 1780 - 1860
.... +Sarah Boyd 1790 - 1891
...... 2 Andrew Wright 1781 - 1857
...... 2 Mary Ann Wright 1767 - 1860
.... +Gideon Keers 1753 - 1832
...... 2 Joseph Wright
.... +Sarah Stirling 1781 - 1822
...... 2 Sallie Wright
.... +James Lyons 1768 - 1830
...... 2 Jane (or Mary) Wright
.... +Robert Culbertson
...... 2 Nancy Wright
.... +Samuel Spence

    Andrew Wright was the son of Joseph and Mary (Curry) Wright. He was born and died at Culbrim. His mother Mary was the daughter of Andrew and Mary Ann (Lamont) Curry of Ballygan.

    Their son Thomas married Sarah, daughter of Samuel and Elizabeth Boyd of Ballymoney in 1818 and they emigrated to U.S.A. with most of their children.

    Their daughter Mary Ann married Gideon, son of William and Mary (Neely) Keers of Slaveny, Finvoy.

    Their son Joseph married Sarah Stirling (see grave 158).

    Their daughter Sallie married James Lyons of Drumaheglis (see grave 199).

    Jane married Robert Culbertson of Artigoran.

    Their youngest daughter Nancy married Samuel, son Edward and Agnes Spence of Currysisken and had no family (see grave 38).

WRIGHT

GRAVE no. 161

In memory
of
Andrew Wright
who died 25th February 1872
Aged 55 years
Also his sons
Joseph Wright
who died 21 May 1863
Aged 2 years
Andrew Wright
who died 18th May 1896
aged 33 years
His wife Mary Ann
who died 9th October 1907
aged 80 years

1. Andrew Wright 1817 - 1872
.. +Mary Ann Knox 1827 - 1907
.... 2 Sarah Wright 1850 -
.... +John Anderson
.... 3 James Anderson
.... 3 Andrew Wright Anderson
.... 2 Mary Wright 1851 -
.... +Robert Love 1853 -
.... 3 Ella Boyd Love 1882 -
.... 3 Andrew Wright Love 1884 - 1963
.... +Edith Kennedy
.... 3 Mamie Love 1886 -
.... 3 Janie Wright Love 1889 -
.... 3 Robert Love
.... 2 Andrew Wright 1853 - 1886
.... 2 Margaret Wright 1856 -
.... +Thomas Caldwell
.... 3 John Caldwell
.... 3 Andrew Wright Caldwell
.... 3 Thomas Knox Caldwell
.... 3 William Launcelot Caldwell
.... 3 Marian Caldwell
.... 3 Maggie Wright Caldwell
.... 3 Misae Caldwell
.... 3 Rebecca Caldwell
.... 3 Eleanor Caldwell
.... 2 Mary Ann Wright 1858 -
.... 2 Joseph Wright 1861 - 1863
.... 2 Jane Wright 1863 -
.... 2 Annie Leslie Wright 1865 -
.... +Christopher Ludlow Grabham 1860 -
.... 3 Andrew Knox Grabham 1902 -
.... 3 Mary Scott Grabham 1903 -
.... 3 Joseph Francis Wright Grabham 1904 -

Andrew Wright, son of Joseph and Sarah (Stirling) Wright married Mary Ann, daughter of Andrew and Mary (MacAfee) Knox of Currysisken in 1849 in 1st Ballymoney Presbyterian Church. They had eight children.

UNREADABLE

GRAVE no. 162

Large stone with no writing
Overturned and next to Wright grave

WYLIE   GRAVE no. 163

To the memory of Robert Wylie Late of Artigoran who departed this life the 12th day of December 1829 aged 81 years

1 Robert Wylie 1748 - 1829
.. +Elizabeth
...... 2 Hugh Wylie 1792 - 1866
...... 2 Jean Wylie 1796 -
...... 2 Elizabeth Wylie 1798 - 1886
...... 2 James Wylie 1800 -
.... +Hannah Black
.... 3 Jane Wylie 1836 -
.... 3 Robert Wylie 1838 -
...... 2 Margaret Wylie 1802 -
...... 2 John Wylie 1803 - 1873
...... 2 Matilda Wylie

Robert and Elizabeth Wylie had family of Hugh, Jean, Elizabeth, James, Margaret, John and Matilda.
Robert was a farmer at Artigoran
He had a brother John and his father was possibly Hugh.
   Their son Hugh was a weaver, their son James a farmer, was the only child to marry. He married Hannah Black, of Coleraine, in 1834 in 1st Ballymoney Presbyterian Church. Their daughter Elizabeth was a schoolmistress.

UNREADABLE

GRAVE no. 164

Small metal plaque with no name

MCMASTER

GRAVE no. 165

Erected
to the memory of
Robert McMaster
Born the 16 of May 1817
Died the 9 November 1862

Robert Park McMaster was the eldest child of James and Eleanor (Scott) McMaster. He was born at Calhame and died at Muckamore. He married Anne, daughter of James Sterling and Jane (Nevin) Moore of Ballyboyland in 1848 in St. James' Presbyterian Church. They had nine children.

1 James McMaster 1794 - 1868
.. +Eleanor Scott
.... 2 Robert Park McMaster 1817 - 1862
.... +Anne Moore - 1903
.... 3 Robert Moore McMaster 1849 -
.... +Malinda McCaughern - 1910
.... 3 Ellen McMaster 1850 -
.... +George Betty
.... 3 Jane Nevin McMaster 1852 -
.... +John George Thompson
.... 3 James McMaster 1853 -
.... 3 Margaret McMaster 1855 -
.... 3 Hugh McMaster 1856 - 1899
.... 3 Annie Stirling McMaster 1858 -
.... +James Hanna
.... 3 Agnes McMaster 1861 -
.... 3 David Moore McMaster 1862 -
.... 2 Mary Ann McMaster 1820 -
.... +William Barr
.... 2 Nancy McMaster 1822 -
.... +John Craig
.... 2 Ellen McMaster 1824 -
.... +Robert Culbert 1819 -
.... 3 Nancy Culbert 1851 -
.... 3 Ellen Culbert 1852 -
.... 3 Roseann Culbert 1853 -
.... 3 Mary Culbert 1859 - 1866
.... 3 Alexander Culbert 1860 - 1861
.... 3 Elizabeth Culbert 1865 -
.... 3 Robert Culbert 1867 - 1868
.... 2 James McMaster 1826 -
.... 2 Hugh McMaster 1828 -
.... 2 John Galt Smith McMaster 1831 -
.... 2 Letitia Smith McMaster 1836 -
.... +James Moore 1836 -
.... 3 Quintin Moore 1861 -
...2 Jane McMaster

MCMASTER

GRAVE no. 166

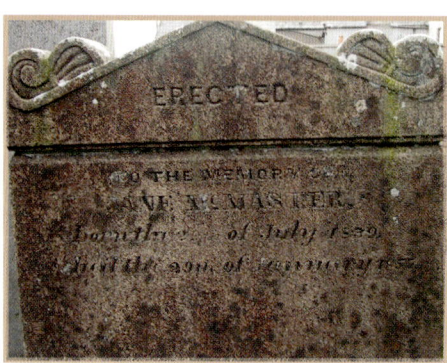

Erected
to the memory of
Jane McMaster
Born the 29th of July 1839
Died the 29th of January 1857

1 James McMaster 1794 - 1868
.. +Eleanor Scott
...... 2 Robert Park McMaster 1817 - 1862
.... +Anne Moore - 1903
.... see 165
...... 2 Mary Ann McMaster 1820 -
.... +William Barr
...... 2 Nancy McMaster 1822 -
.... +John Craig
...... 2 Ellen McMaster 1824 -
.... +Robert Culbert 1819 -
...... 2 James McMaster 1826 -
...... 2 Hugh McMaster 1828 -
...... 2 John Galt Smith McMaster 1831 -
...... 2 Letitia Smith McMaster 1837 -
.... +James Moore 1836 -
...... 2 Jane McMaster 1839 - 1857

Jane was the youngest daughter of James and Eleanor (Scott) McMaster and she died at Balnamore after a few days illness. Her death was recorded in the Coleraine Chronicle. Her father was a mill owner and a prominent member of St. James Presbyterian Church.

BROWN

GRAVE no. 167

Erected
in
Loving memory of
John Brown
late of Portrush
who died 9th Sept 1878
Aged 77 years
Also his wife
Jane Taylor
who died 29th Aug 1854
Aged 55 years
And his wife
Sarah Anne Lyle
who died 12 Novr 1898
Aged 82 years

1 John Brown
.. +Ann
...... 2 Ann Brown 1795 -
.... +Thomas Fleming
...... 2 Mary Brown 1797 -
.... +David McAula
.... 3 Jean McAula 1826 -
.... 3 Elizabeth McAula 1828 -
.... 3 Isabella McAula 1835 -
...... 2 Adam Brown 1799 -
...... 2 John Brown 1801 - 1878
.... +Jane Taylor 1799 - 1854
...... *2nd Wife of John Brown:
.... +Sarah Ann Lyle 1816 - 1898
...... 2 James Brown 1806 -
...... 2 Elizabeth Brown 1809 -
...... 2 Matthew Brown 1810 -
...... 2 Jane Brown 1813 -
...... 2 Elizabeth Brown 1816 -

John, son of John and Ann Brown, married Jane Taylor, and then after her death married Sarah Anne, daughter of John and Elizabeth (Lyle) Lyle of Cuppindale in Carncullagh Presbyterian Church in 1855. Sarah died in Antrim. John was a farmer at Scroggie which is part of the townland of Cabra.

John's sister Ann married Thomas Fleming in 1829 and his sister Mary married David McAula of Cloynt.

HART   GRAVE no. 168

Erected
by
John Hart Coolderry
In memory of his sister
Matilda
wife of Samuel Christy
Died 23rd August 1895
Also the sons of John Hart
Damhead
Thomas Hart
Died 10th September 1923
Aged 1 year and 10 months
William James Hart
Died 8th August 1924
Aged 4 years
John Hart
Died 28th June 1935
Aged 12 years
John Hart, Damhead
Died 23rd November 1959 Aged 80 years
Elizabeth Hart
Died 14th April 1962 Aged 70 years

1 John Hart 1787 - 1875
.. +Agnes Quigg 1789 - 1877
.... 2 William H. Hart 1819 - 1887
.... 2 Mary Hart 1821 - 1869
.... 2 John Hart 1823 - 1915
.... 2 Matilda Hart 1825 - 1895
.... +Samuel Christy
.... 2 Jean Hunter Hart 1827 -
.... 2 Thomas Hart 1829 - 1900
.... 2 Robert Park Hart 1833 - 1911
.... +Mary Jane Donaghy 1853 -
.... 3 Nancy Hart 1877 -
.... 3 John Hart 1878 - 1959
.... +Elizabeth Stirling 1892 - 1962
.... 4 Robert Hart 1917 -
.... 4 Dorothy Elizabeth Hart 1918 -
.... +John Harbison
.... 4 William James Hart 1920 - 1924
.... 4 Thomas Hart 1921 - 1923
.... 4 John Hart 1923 - 1935
.... 3 James Donaghy Hart 1880 - 1975
.... +Sarah Getty 1885 - 1978
.... 4 John Alexander Hart 1917 -
.... 4 Mary Jane Hart 1914 -
.... +Harold Burnside Holmes 1901 - 1979
.... 4 Archibald Getty Hart 1922 -
.... +Ellen Bolton Torrens 1933 - 1972
.... 3 Mary Hart 1884 -
.... 3 Matilda Hart 1886 -
.... 3 Thomas Hart 1887 -
.... 3 Eliza Jane Knox Hart 1893 -
.... 3 Rose Ann Hart 1896 -
.... 3 Thomas Hart 1891 -
.... +Anna Margretta Clark Gilmore 1889 -
.... 4 Elizabeth Rosemary Hart 1924 -
.... +John Alfred Small 1921 - 1990
.... 4 Noel Hart

HART

GRAVE no. 168

John Hart was born at Secon and married Agnes, daughter of Henry Quigg of Heagles, about 1817 and had a family of seven. They were farmers at Culderry (Coolderry).

Matilda married Samuel Christy of Bushmills in 1853 in Bushmills Presbyterian Church and died at her family home of Culderry.

Their youngest son Robert Park married Mary Jane, daughter of James and Jane (Park) Donaghy of Moneygobbin, in 1876 in St. James Presbyterian Church. They had nine children. Their oldest son John married Elizabeth Stirling in 1916 in Ballyrashane Presbyterian Church and they had five children, three of whom died young.

GETTY

GRAVE no. 169

Here lieth the body
of James Getty late of Tau
ghy who departed this life
the 22 of June A.D. 1804
Aged 62 years

1 James Getty 1742 - 1804
.. +Mary
...... 2 Henry Getty 1790 -
.... +Mary Brown
.... 3 James Getty 1807 -
.... +Elizabeth Kilpatrick 1805 - 1873
.... 3 Matthew Getty 1810 -
.... +Sally Culbertson 1812 - 1877
.... 3 John Getty 1812 -
.... 3 Robert Getty 1820 - 1890
.... +Ann Matilda Culbertson 1820 - 1890
.... 3 Ann Getty 1823 -
.... 3 William Getty 1829 -
.... 3 Rose Getty 1815 -
.... +Alexander Gibson 1810 - 1842
.... *2nd Husband of Rose Getty:
.... +Thomas Smith 1813 - 1879
.... 3 Mary Getty 1817 -
.... +James White 1811 -
...... 2 Mary Getty
...... 2 Fanny Getty
...... 2 Margaret Getty
...... 2 John Getty
.... +Mary Picken
.... 3 John Getty 1818 -
.... 3 James Getty 1820 -
.... 3 Mary Getty 1823 -
.... 3 Jennett Getty 1813 - 1891
.... +Richard Martin 1813 - 1893
...... 2 Robert Getty
...... 2 Matthew Getty 1790 - 1855
.... +Rachael Poole
...... 2 Anne Getty
...... 2 Rose Getty

James and Mary Getty of Taughey had a family of nine children and were farmers. James left a will naming all his children.

His son Henry married Mary Brown in 1807 in 1st Ballymoney Presbyterian Church and had a large family most of whom emigrated, apart from Robert who married Matilda Ann, daughter Robert and Mary (Wright) Culbertson of Artigoran in 1850 in St. Patrick's Parish Church. They lived at Orble outside Dervock.

John married Mary Picken of Taghey in 1809 and had four known children. Their youngest daughter Jennet married Richard, son of Thomas and Ann (Getty) Martin of Artigoran in 1843 in 1st Ballymoney Presbyterian Church. Their son James emigrated to Melbourne, Australia and the letters he wrote home are in PRONI.

Matthew married Rachael Poole in 1813 in St. Patrick's Parish Church and was a weaver. They had children Roseanna, William John, James, Nancy and Samuel.

WRIGHT

GRAVE no. 170

Beneath this stone rests
John Wright
late Presbyterian Minister of
the parish of Donegore for 50 years
The entertained, comprehensive
and elevated opinion of the ex
cellence of the Christian religion
free from bigotry on the one
hand and supersticion on the
other. Liberal in his sermons
exemplary in his life and con
verstion, a cheerful companion
and ? ? ? friend
He died on the 1 day of May
1807 aged 85 years

John Wright was born at Culbrim and was the brother of Joseph Wright (see graves 158, 159, 161).

HOLMES

GRAVE no. 171

In memory of
Alexander Holmes
of Ballymoney
The faithful servant of the late
Dr. and Mrs Reynolds
He died 23 Feb 1862
Aged 70 years

This may be the son of Alexander and Mary Ann Holmes who were living at Leslie Hill in 1817. The Dr. Reynolds is John who was a surgeon in High Street, Ballymoney.

MATTHEWS

GRAVE no. 172

Here lieth the remains
of Neal Matthews of
Craigatimpin who died
26th Apr 1827 aged 78
Also his wife Mary Anne
who died 22 May 1822
And their son Daniel
who died 22 July 1818
Aged 21 years

The Matthews family were present in Craigatempin in 1803, but seem to have disappeared by 1825 at the time of the Tithe applotments. There were also Matthews families at Calhame which is a neighbouring townland, so there is a high possibility that they were related.

COOPER

GRAVE no. 173

Here lieth the remains of Mary Cooper late of Kilmoyle who died 20th May 1825 aged 40 years. Also her grand daughter Mary McCoock who died in infancy Also her husband William Cooper late of Kilmoyle who died 5th June 1854 aged 91 years

1 Cooper
.... 2 William Cooper 1763 - 1854
.... +Mary 1785 - 1825
.... 3 Samuel Cooper 1798 -
.... 3 William Cooper 1800 -
.... 3 Benjamin Cooper 1802 -
.... 3 John Cooper 1804 - 1887
.... +Elizabeth Wylie 1830 – 1917
 see grave 174
.... 3 James Cooper 1808 -
.... 3 Mary Eliza Cooper 1811 - 1874
.... 3 Sarah Cooper 1813 -
.... 2 James Cooper
.... +Mary Taggart
.... 3 John Cooper 1800 -
.... +Jenny Adams
.... 3 Thomas Cooper 1802 -
.... 3 Rose Ann Cooper 1805 - 1867
.... +Daniel Fullerton 1803 - 1884
.... 3 Elizabeth Cooper 1807 -
.... 3 Sarah Cooper 1810 -
.... +Matthew Brown
.... 2 John Cooper
.... +Mary ?
.... 3 Mary Cooper 1800 -
.... 3 Samuel Cooper 1803 -
.... 3 James Cooper 1805 -
.... 3 Peggy Jean Cooper 1809 -

James, John and William Cooper appear together living at Kilmoyle in both 1803 and 1817. Not much is known about John apart from having a wife Mary and four children, Mary, Samuel, James and Peggy Jean.

James married Mary Taggart and had family of John, Thomas, Rose Ann, Elizabeth and Sarah. John married Jenny, daughter of James and Martha Adams of Newbuildings North in 1834. Rose Ann married Daniel, son of William and Elizabeth (Wilson) Fullerton of Tullaghgore in 1827 and emigrated to Illinois. Sarah married Matthew Brown of Clough in 1834. They all married in 1st Ballymoney Presbyterian Church.

William and Mary Cooper had a family of seven but only one child's marriage was found. John Cooper married Elizabeth Wylie (or Wiley) (see graves 7, 174).

GETTY

GRAVE no. 174

In loving memory
of
Mary Getty of Kilmoyle
Her mother
Elizabeth Cooper
who died 2nd October 1917
And her sister Sarah
who died 5th July 1940
Also her husband
David Getty
who died 17th August 1948
And his wife
Margaret Jane
who died 12th January 1951

1 John Cooper 1804 – 1887
. +Elizabeth Wylie 1830 - 1917
.... 2 Sarah Eliza Cooper 1863 - 1948
.... 2 Maria Cooper 1865 - 1942
.... +William Orr Robinson 1860 - 1950
.... 3 James Howard Robinson 1889 - 1966
.... +Margaret Rea Marks 1888 - 1972
.... 3 Robert John Robinson 1891 - 1961
.... +Annie Gault
.... 3 Robinson
.... +John Speers
.... 2 Mary Cooper 1866 - 1914
.... +David Getty 1864 - 1948
.... 3 David John Cooper Getty 1908 - 1991
.... +Margretta Cunningham 1921 - 1996
.... 3 Elizabeth Mary Getty 1906 - 2001
.... +Albert John Hanna 1902 - 1968

John Cooper married Elizabeth daughter of Robert and Elizabeth (Stewart) Wylie (or Wiley) of Dunaverney (graves no.7, 173). They had 3 daughters, Sarah, Maria and Mary.

Maria married William Orr Robinson, farmer of Tamlaght, Rasharkin in 1888 in Rasharkin Presbyterian Church. William Orr was named after his grandmother's brother William Orr who was hanged in Carrickfergus after the 1798 rebellion. William emigrated to Canada to join the police, but returned home in 1887 to look after the family farm.

Mary (known as Minnie) married David Getty, who had been working on the family farm at Kilmoyle, in 1905 in St. James Presbyterian Church. After Minnie died he was remarried again Margaret, daughter of Samuel Getty, in 1917 in Trinity Presbyterian Church.

REYNOLDS

GRAVE no. 175

Here lieth the body
of John Reynolds who
departed this life in
Jany 1766 aged 49 years
Also
Abigail his wife his
son Thomas and daugh
ter Frances are near
this place interred
and
On the 2 day of June
1784 was deposeted be
neath this stone with
all due military honours
The remains of his son
William Reynolds sur
geon to the Ballymoney
Volunteer Company
aged 35 years
And also James Reynolds
surgeon who departed
this life April the 1
1815 aged 51 years
He lived esteemed
and died regretted
Also Elizabeth his wife who
died 4 Sept 1840 aged 85 years

1 John Reynolds 1716 - 1766
.. +Abigail
...... 2 Frances Reynolds
...... 2 Thomas Reynolds
...... 2 William Reynolds 1759 - 1784
...... 2 James Reynolds 1764 - 1815
.... +Elizabeth
.... 3 John Reynolds

William, James and John junior were all surgeons in Ballymoney. It is possible that they were related to the Reynolds family of Drumafivey, who are buried in Kilraughts Old Churchyard as many of them were also surgeons.

MCKEESOCK

GRAVE no. 176

Here lieth
the body of
John McKeesock
who departed this
life Jany 25th 1810 aged
79 years.   Also his
wife Nancy who
departed 3th Feb 1810
aged 71 years

1 John McKeesock 1727 - 1810
.. +Nancy 1728 - 1810
.... 2 Edward McKeesock 1778 - 1829
.... +Mary
.... 3 William McKeesock 1806 - 1874
.... +Anne
.... 3 Mary McKeesock 1808 -
.... 3 John McKeesock 1811 -
.... +Mary Jane Drain
.... 4 Edward McKeesock 1836 -
.... 4 James McKeesock 1837 -
.... 4 Hugh McKeesock 1839 -
.... 4 Robert McKeesock 1842 -
.... 4 David McKeesock 1844 -
.... 3 Catherine McKeesock 1815 -
.... 3 Flora McKeesock 1820 -
.... 2 John McKeesock 1770 - 1845

John and Nancy McKeesock had a son John who died in 1845 (aged 75) in Charlotte Street and another son Edward, who married Mary, and was a publican in Main Street Ballymoney.

Edward had sons William and John and daughters Mary Catherine and Flora. William, a nailer, married Anne and is buried in St. Patrick's Parish Churchyard. John, a sawyer, married Mary Jane Drain in 1834 in St. Patrick's Parish Church and had five children.

DORRANS

GRAVE no. 177

Sacred to the
memory of
Mary Sandford
daughter to Alex Dorrans
of Ballymoney who departed
this life on the 1st of November
1827 in the 21 year of her age
Her husband James Sandford
has placed this small token here
in commemoration of her
many virtues and of his sincere
sorrow in her death
James Dorrans died 30th June 1890
aged 80 years
His wife Mary
Died Jan 1884 aged 68 years
George Miller died 5th June 1897
aged 68 years. His wife Margaret
died 5th May 1872 aged 28 years
Also their infant son James
He that giveth to ? ?
? ? ? to the Lord

1 Alexander Dorrans
.. +Hannah
...... 2 Mary Dorrans 1806 - 1827
.... +James Sandford
.... 3 Alexander Sandford 1827 -
...... 2 James Dorrans 1810 - 1890
.... +Mary Hunter
.... 3 John Dorrans 1832 -
.... 3 Mary Dorrans 1834 -
.... 3 Hannah Dorrans 1836 -1867
.... 3 Margaret Jane Dorrans 1843 - 1872
.... +George Millar 1829 - 1897
.... 4 Mary Millar 1866 -
.... 4 James Dorrans Millar 1869 -
.... 3 Mary Pinkerton Dorrans 1851 -
.... 3 William James Dorrans 1856 -

Alex Dorrans was a publican in Main Street, Ballymoney and was married to Hannah. They had two children.

Mary married James Sandford of Drumachose in 1825 in 1st Ballymoney Presbyterian Church and had a son Alexander in 1827.

James was a house agent in Ballymoney and married Mary Hunter. Their daughter Margaret (or Peggy) was a seamstress and married George, son of Alick Millar in 1866 in St. Patrick's Parish Church. He was head railway porter in Ballymoney and they lived in no. 21 Meetinghouse Lane. They had two children, Mary who was born in 1866 and James Dorrans who was born in 1869.

TAYLOR

GRAVE no. 178

Erected
To the memory of
Martha A. Taylor
who died 12th May 1877 aged 26 years
Also her brother
William
who died 7th May 1879
aged 32 years
Also Alexander
Father of the above
who died 5th February 1883
aged 68 years

1 Alexander Taylor
.. +Ann Stewart
.... 2 Jean Taylor
.... 2 Alexander Taylor 1813 - 1883
.... +Betty Kyle 1819 - 1892
.... 3 William Taylor 1846 - 1879
.... 3 Hugh Taylor 1849 - 1923
.... +Margaret Warnock
.... 3 Martha Ann Taylor 1851 - 1877
.... 3 Elizabeth Taylor 1854 -
.... +David Kyle
.... 2 John Taylor

Alexander Taylor was the son of Alexander and Ann (Stewart) Taylor of Carneatly. He married Elizabeth Kyle and they had four children, William, Hugh, Martha Ann and Elizabeth.

Hugh married Margaret, daughter of James Warnock of Culduff in 1885 in 1st Ballymoney Presbyterian Church. Elizabeth married David Kyle of Frocess in 1885, also in 1st Ballymoney.

FORSYTHE

GRAVE no. 179

Erected
to the memory of
Robert Forsythe
Forttown
who died 9th October 1860,
aged 63 years
also his wife
Mary Brown
who departed this life
29th December 1890
aged 81 years
William B. Forsythe
died 30th April 1913
Aged 66 years
also Elizabeth Wallace
wife of W. B. Forsythe
died 20th December 1922 aged 77 years

1 Robert Forsythe 1807 – 1869
. +Mary Brown 1809 - 1890
...... 2 Isabella Forsythe 1835 - 1921
.... +James Campbell 1828 - 1881
.... 3 Elizabeth Campbell 1866 -
.... +Robert Love
...... 2 Martha Hunter Forsythe 1837 - 1907
.... +James Boyd 1835 - 1909
.... 3 Margaret Cherry Boyd 1861 -
.... 3 John Boyd 1862 - 1955
.... +Rachael Anderson 1878 - 1966
.... 3 Robert Boyd 1865 - 1925
.... +Elizabeth Lamont Jellie 1870 - 1924
.... 3 Mary Gordon Lyle Boyd 1866 - 1955
.... 3 Margaret Cherry Boyd 1868 - 1948
.... +Alexander Hill 1863 - 1933
.... 3 Annie Wilson Boyd 1869 - 1954
.... 3 James Boyd 1870 - 1956
.... 3 Mary Brown Boyd 1873 - 1953
.... +Adam Wales McClure 1873 - 1924
.... 3 Isabella Boyd 1875 - 1941
.... 3 Martha Boyd 1878 -
.... 3 Elizabeth Curry Boyd 1883 - 1953
.... 3 Jane Boyd 1871 -
.... +John Knox 1866 -
...... 2 Jane Forsythe 1839 - 1925
.... +John Curry 1835 - 1929
.... 3 Elizabeth Rankin Curry 1875 - 1960
...... 2 Samuel Hunter Forsythe 1842 -

Robert Forsythe was a farmer at Forttown and married Mary, daughter of William and Isabella (Borland) Brown of Ballinaloob in 1834 in 1st Ballymoney Presbyterian Church. He was born at Ballyleighery, Co. Derry and had gone as a child to live with aunt and uncle Samuel and Martha (Forsythe) Hunter at Forttown and was left the farm as they had no children.

FORSYTHE   GRAVE no. 179

    Their eldest daughter Isabella married James, son of John and Elizabeth Campbell of Carncullagh in 1861 in First Ballymoney and had a daughter Elizabeth, who married Dr. Robert Love of Ahoghill.

    Their second daughter married James, son of John and Margaret (Cherry) Boyd of Forttown in 1860 in First Ballymoney and had a large family.

    Jane married John, son of Martin and Elizabeth (Rankin) Curry of Ballyversal in 1874 in Trinity Presbyterian Church. Samuel emigrated to America and was never heard from again.

    Their youngest son William, married Elizabeth, daughter of James and Ellen (Moore) Wallace of Knockahollet in 1874 in Ballyweaney Presbyterian Church.

```
...... 2 Mary Brown Forsythe 1844 - 1849
...... 2 William Brown Forsythe 1848 - 1913
.......... +Elizabeth Wallace 1845 - 1922
............... 3 Robert Forsythe 1875 - 1952
................... +Margretta Elizabeth Orr 1889 - 1957
............... 3 James Wallace Forsythe 1876 - 1935
................... +Mary Tweed McMillan
............... 3 Ellen Moore Forsythe 1878 - 1949
................... +Charles Anderson 1868 - 1946
............... 3 Mary Brown Forsythe 1879 - 1888
............... 3 Samuel Hunter Forsythe 1881 - 1957
................... +Julia Ellen Henderson 1888 - 1942
............... 3 John Curry Forsythe 1883 - 1884
............... 3 William Brown Forsythe 1883 - 1933
............... 3 John Curry Forsythe 1884 -
............... 3 Elizabeth Wallace Forsythe 1889 - 1934
............... 3 Margaret Moore Forsythe 1887 -
................... +Thomas Millen
............... *2nd Husband of Margaret Moore Forsythe:
................... +Thomas Millen 1877 -
```

NEIL   GRAVE no. 180

This
stone was
erected by Catherine Neil
? the remains of
John Neil of Druckendult
who departed this life
on the 27th day of March
in the year of our lord 1837
aged 87 years
Also her husband John Neil
who departed this life on
the 28th day of August in
the year of our lord 1845 (?1815)
aged 51 years

This John Neil is probably the brother of William (see grave 181). There other Neil families living nearby in Dunaverney and Carnany, who may have been related.

In the remains of an old register in 1st Ballymoney Church the baptisms of James (1753), Thomas (1757) and William (1757), children of a James Neil are recorded.

NEIL

GRAVE no. 181

Sacred
to the memory of William
Neil of Druckendult who
departed this life Janry 18
1836 aged 78 years

1 James Neill 1785 -
.. +Susan Dinsmore 1788 -
...... 2 Margaret Neill 1813 -
.... +Alexander Murphy
...... 2 Ann Neill 1816 -
...... 2 Rachael Neill 1819 -
...... 2 Mary Neill 1821 -
...... 2 William Neill 1823 -

William and John Neil were living at Druckendult in 1803. In 1817, William was living with Widow Neil and there was another family of James and Susan (Dinsmore) Neil (or Neill).

MCKEAG

GRAVE no. 182

Memento Mori
On the 13 of June
1788 was interred
here the remains
of the Rev. Patr
ick McKeag aged
38 years

BECKETT

GRAVE no. 183

BECKETT

1 John Beckett 1773 - 1844
.. +Jean poss Taylor
...... 2 Philip Beckett 1798 - 1875
.... +Ann 1793 - 1871
            see grave 184
...... 2 John Beckett 1800 - 1881
.... +Nancy Workman
.... 3 Samuel Workman Beckett 1830 - 1901
.... 3 Bess Beckett 1832 -
.... 3 Rose Ann Beckett 1834 -
.... 3 Matilda Beckett 1843 -
.... 3 John Beckett 1846 -
.... 3 Washington Workman Beckett 1850 -
.... 3 Anna Beckett 1853 -
...... 2 William Beckett 1805 - 1872
.... 3 Oliver Beckett 1827 - 1893
.... +Roseann Culbertson 1834 - 1864
.... *2nd Wife of Oliver Beckett:
.... +Mary Kelly 1836 - 1881
.... *3rd Wife of Oliver Beckett:
.... +Matilda Donaghy 1834 -
...... *2nd Wife of William Beckett:
.... +Eliza Thomson 1804 - 1880
...... 2 Mary Beckett 1807 -
...... 2 Jennett Beckett 1808 -
...... 2 Robert Beckett 1810 -
...... 2 Oliver Beckett 1814 - 1901
.... +Martha Adams 1825 - 1914
.... 3 Jane Beckett 1852 -
.... 3 Alexander Beckett 1853 - 1941
.... 3 John Beckett 1855 -
.... 3 James Beckett 1856 - 1890
.... 3 Maria Beckett 1858 -
.... 3 Martha Beckett 1860 -
.... 3 Sarah Moore Beckett 1862 -
.... 3 Oliver Beckett 1864 -
...... 2 Samuel Beckett 1815 - 1899
.... +Nancy Rainey 1828 - 1908
...... 2 Hannah Beckett 1816 -

There are several Beckett families in the area probably all originating from Ballycormick.

John's eldest son Philip moved to Lislagan (see grave 184). His third son William had a son Oliver, from his first marriage and then remarried Eliza, daughter of William Thomson of Booton in 1827 in 1st Ballymoney Presbyterian Church. They are buried in St. Patrick's Parish Churchyard. His fifth son Oliver married Martha, daughter of James Adams of Milltown in 1851 in St. Patrick's Parish Church. His sixth son Samuel married Nancy Rainey (see grave 22).

BECKETT

GRAVE no. 184

Erected
by
Philip Beckett
in memory of his son
Alexander
late of Lislagan
who departed this life
17th June 1852 aged 28 years
Also here lie the remains
of Ann mother of the above
Alexander and the beloved wife
of Philip Beckett of Lislagan
who departed this life 6th May
1871 aged 78 years
Also the above Philip Beckett
who departed this life 14th Feb 1875
aged 76 years

1 Philip Beckett 1798 - 1875
.. +Ann 1793 - 1871
...... 2 Alexander Beckett 1822 - 1852
...... 2 John Beckett 1825 -
.... +Grace Ann Nicholl
...... *2nd Wife of John Beckett:
.... +Eliza Archibald 1851 -
...... 2 James Beckett 1827 -
...... 2 Adam Blair Beckett 1828 -
.... +Elizabeth Coulter
.... 3 Sarah Anne Beckett 1859 -
.... 3 Thomas Beckett 1870 -
.... 3 Sarah Beckett 1871 -
...... 2 Sarah Hill Beckett 1829 -
.... +James McCreath
...... 2 Oliver Beckett 1839 -
.... +Margaret Nicholl 1838 -
.... 3 Margaret Anne Beckett 1867 -

Philip was the eldest child of John and Jane Beckett. He was born at Ballycormick, was a farmer at Lislagan, but died in Dervock. He was a publican in Dervock.

His eldest son Alexander lived at Ballybrakes, but died in Lislagan.

BECKETT

GRAVE no. 185

? to the memory
? who departed
? the 12 January
? the 52 year of his age
Also
?n Beckett
who died on the ?
? ?07 aged 1 year
? erected to the
by his mother
Beckett als Cristy
and wife to the above named
? as a ? ? of his
? ? in life and
? ? at their decease

1 Philip Beckett 1775 - 1828
.. +Jean Cristy - 1863
...... 2 Elizabeth Beckett 1803 -
.... +David Kennedy
...... 2 Sarah Beckett 1806 -
.... +John Boyd 1803 -
...... 2 Oliver Beckett 1809 -
...... 2 Mary Beckett 1811 -
.... +James Junk
...... 2 John C. Beckett 1813 - 1841
...... 2 Philip Beckett 1815 -
...... 2 Jean Beckett 1819 -
...... 2 Matilda Beckett 1821 -
...... 2 Nancy Beckett 1821 -
...... 2 Alexander Beckett 1824 -

This is the grave of Philip Beckett of Drumart who married Jean Cristy. He was possibly the brother of John Beckett of Ballycormick.

Their eldest daughter Elizabeth married David Kennedy of Drumboe in 1820. Their second daughter Sarah married John Boyd of Ballybrakes in 1826. Mary married James Junk of Moneymore in 1830. They all married in 1st Ballymoney Presbyterian Church.

Their son John was a doctor and died in Falmouth, Jamaica in 1841.

LONG   GRAVE no. 186

To the memory of
John Long
who died   ? ?
aged 27 years
Also his ? ?
Hanna
who died 24 ? 1877
at Brisbine ? aged 2?
Also their mother
Sarah Long
who died 4th November 1889
aged 67 years
and her husband
Daniel Long
who died 29th December 1891
aged 85 years
Ellen Long
died 22 July 1893 aged 33
Catherine Long
died 28th July 1895

1 John Long
. +Hanna ? - 1877
...... 2 Daniel Long 1806 - 1891
.... +Sally Douthart 1822 - 1889
.... 3 John Long 1849 - 1876
.... 3 Mary Long 1852 - 1924
.... 3 Catherine Long 1856 - 1895
.... 3 Sarah Long 1858 -
.... 3 Ellen Long 1860 - 1893
.... 3 William Long 1862 - 1898
.... 3 Bella Long

Daniel, son of John and Hanna Long, was a farmer and corn dealer at Bravellan. He married Sarah, daughter of William and Mary (Connelly) Douthart of Bravellan in 1st Ballymoney Presbyterian Church in 1848.

Their daughter Mary died in Belfast and Catherine, Ellen (a teacher) and William all died in Ballymoney as did their parents.

HAY

GRAVE no. 187

Erected
by John Hay Ballymoney
In memory of his son John
who died 15th June 1865
Aged 2 years
and 9 months
Also his daughter Eliza
who died 16th March 1868
aged 1 year and 9 months
and his daughter Margaret
who died 15th May 1876
aged 15 years and 11 months
John Hay
died 8th February 1877
aged 47 years

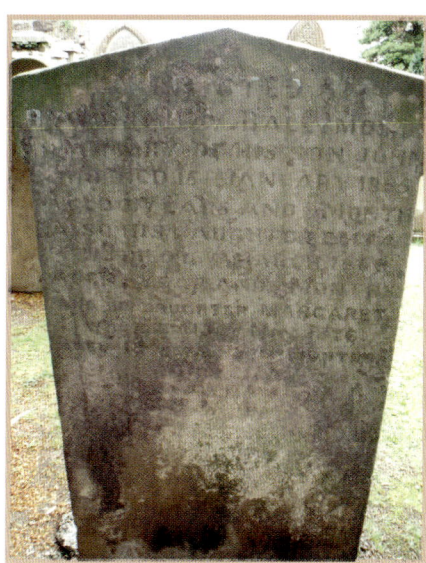

1 Edward Hay 1806 -
.. +Sarah Rainey 1803 -
...... 2 Andrew Hay 1829 -
...... 2 James Hay 1830 -1895
.... +Mary Rainey
.... 3 Sarah Hay 1854 -
.... 3 Mary Hay 1855 -
.... 3 Margaret Jane Hay 1859 -1931
.... 3 Nancy Hay 1863 -
...... 2 John Hay 1830 - 1877
.... +Mary McFarland 1829 -
.... 3 Mary Jane Hay 1854 -
.... 3 Sarah Hay 1856 -
.... 3 Martha Hay 1858 -
.... 3 Margaret Hay 1860 - 1876
.... 3 John Hay 1862 - 1865
.... 3 Ellen Hay 1864 -
.... 3 Eliza Hay 1866 - 1868
...... 2 Mary Jane Hay 1833 -
...... 2 Margaret Hay 1834 -
...... 2 Sarah Hay 1835 -
...... 2 Edward Hay 1837 -
.... +Margaret McNeill
.... 3 Andrew Hay 1865 -
.... 3 John Hay 1866 -
...... 2 Sarah Hay 1839 -

John, a mechanic in Ballymoney, was the son of Edward and Sarah (Rainey) Hay. He was born at Drumskea. He married Mary, daughter of James and Jane McFarland of Ballymoney, in 1853 in 1st Ballymoney Presbyterian Church.

MCQUILLAN

GRAVE no. 188

Erected
by Jane McQuillan
In memory of her beloved son
George
who departed this life the
28th August
1864 aged 18 years
Also her mother Jane Haltridge
who died 2nd June 1864
aged 80 years

Jane was the daughter of Robert and Jane Haltridge of Ballymoney. She married John McQuillan of Antrim in 1842 in 1st Ballymoney Presbyterian Church (see grave 189).

Her mother Jane had a grocery, milliner and dressmaking business in Main Street, Ballymoney in 1846. In 1856, the business was described as grocer, ironmonger and hardware merchant and in 1864 it was a toy shop.

HALTRIDGE

GRAVE no. 189

Sacred to the memory of
Robert Haltridge
who departed this life the year
of our lord March 17 1842 aged 64
And also his daughter Jane died
Nov 15 1818 aged 6 years

1 Robert Haltridge 1778 – 1842
. +Jane 1784 - 1864
.... 2 Esther Haltridge 1806 -
.... +Randal Neillie
.... 3 John Neillie 1827 -
.... 3 Jane Neillie 1830 -
.... 2 Elizabeth Haltridge 1810 -
.... +Arthur Connor
.... 2 Robert Haltridge 1808 -
.... 2 Jane Haltridge 1812 - 1818
.... 2 John Haltridge 1814 -
.... 2 Jane Haltridge 1818 -
.... +John McQuillan
.... 3 George McQuillan 1846 - 1864

    Robert, a shoemaker in Piper Row, Ballymoney, son of John and Ester Haltridge, married Jane and had at least five children. Their eldest daughter Esther married Randal Neillie, a publican of Main Street, Ballymoney. Their second daughter married Arthur Connor in 1826 and their youngest Jane married John McQuillan of Antrim in 1842.
    Their son John may have been a coach builder in Coleraine as there is a notice in the Coleraine Chronicle of his wife's death in 1860.

CAMAC

GRAVE no. 190

In memory of
Mary
Daughter of Robert Camac of Garry
who died 26th Novr 1861
aged 14 years
Also his son William
who died 28th March 1873
aged 21 years

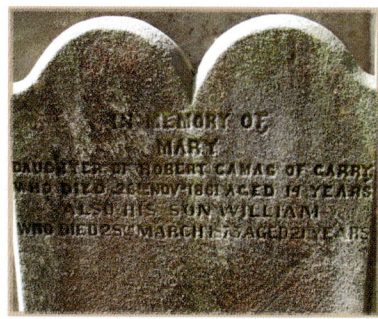

1 Robert Camac 1812 - 1887
.. +Mary Jane Adams 1817 - 1901
...... 2 James Moore Camac 1843 - 1920
...... 2 Rose Camac 1845 - 1910
...... 2 Mary Camac 1847 - 1861
...... 2 William Camac 1851 - 1873
...... 2 Matilda Adams Camac 1851 - 1932
.... +William John Hale 1851 - 1928
.... 3 Samuel James Clark Hale 1880 - 1956
...... 2 Matthew Adams Camac 1853 - 1903
...... 2 Robert Camac 1856 - 1924
.... +Anna Matilda Hale 1868 - 1918
.... 3 Robert Camac 1889 - 1955
.... 3 William John Camac 1895 - 1955
.... 3 Frances Jane Camac 1896 - 1972
.... 3 James Clarke Camac 1898 - 1978
.... 3 Moore White Camac 1902 -
.... +Margaret 1903 -
.... 3 Clarke Camac 1904 - 1971
.... 3 David Adams Camac 1908 - 1972
.... +Margaret Law Lamont 1907 - 1977

Robert, son of William and Jane (Caldwell) Camac, married Mary Jane, daughter of John & Mary Adams of Ballyboyland. Only two of their children married. She had a brother Matthew and when he died her sons James and Matthew farmed at Ballyboyland and died there.

Matilda married William John, son of Robert Hale of Ballyrock and Drumart in 1879 in Roseyards Presbyterian Church.

Robert married Anna Matilda, daughter of James Clark and Fanny (Craig) Hale of Drumart and niece of William John Hale. Their youngest son David Adam Camac married Margaret, daughter of John and Nanay (McConagie) Lamont of Glennylough in 1944 in Roseyards. Their eldest son still farms in Garry.

BAIRD

GRAVE no. 191

Erected by
James Baird Ballymoney
In memory of his beloved wife
Sarah Anne
who died 3rd Oct 1868 aged 29 years
Also his daughter
Sarah Anne
who died 15th February 1867
aged 1 year
And 6 months
Also in memory
of James Baird
Born 25th April 1831
Died 16th September 1875

1 James Baird
...... 2 James Baird 1831 - 1875
.... +Sarah Ann Robinson 1841 - 1868
.... 3 James Baird 1861 -
.... 3 John Baird 1862 -
.... +Jane Ann Robinson
.... 4 Mary Jane Baird 1884 -
.... 4 Jane Baird 1885 -
.... 4 Sarah Jane Baird 1886 -
.... 4 Annie Baird 1888 -
.... 4 Margaret Eleanor Hunter Baird 1889 -
.... 4 Maud Baird 1891 -
.... 3 Mary Jane Baird 1863 -
.... +James McCurdy
.... 3 Sarah Ann Baird 1865 - 1867
...... *2nd Wife of James Baird:
.... +Jane Murray
...... 2 Robert Baird

James, son of James Baird, was a spirit merchant in Ballymoney. He married Sarah Anne, daughter of John and Jane (McLester) Robinson of Newbuildings in 1861 in 1st Ballymoney Presbyterian Church. Sarah Anne died in Linenhall Street, Ballymoney in 1868 and James was remarried in 1870 in 1st Ballymoney Church to Jane, daughter of James Murray.

Their son John married Jane Anne, daughter of John and Mary (Smyth) Robinson or Newbuildings in 1884 in First Ballymoney.

Their daughter Mary Jane married James, son of James McCurdy, in 1882 in St. Partick's Parish Church. James was a grocer in Ballycastle.

HAMILL

GRAVE no. 192

?
Daniel Hamill ? Heagles
who departed ? ? 1862
? ?
his daughter Eliza Jane
died 25th Jany 1869
aged 18 years

1 Daniel Hamill 1803 - 1861
.. +Jane McKeown 1812 - 1888
...... 2 Mary Jane Hamill
...... 2 Samuel Wallace Hamill 1849 - 1931
.... +Amanda Sager 1858 - 1935
.... 3 Agnes J. Hamill 1879 - 1974
.... 3 Wallace Lee Hamill 1880 -
.... 3 Safronia Ellen Hamill 1882 - 1945
.... 3 Grover Cleveland Hamill 1884 -
.... 3 Adelbert S. Hamill 1886 - 1906
.... 3 Bessie E. Hamill 1888 -
.... 3 Robert E. Hamill 1890 -
.... 3 Lawrence P. Hamill 1892 -
.... 3 Hazel Margaret Hamill 1895 - 1970
...... 2 James Bell Hamill 1850 - 1906
.... +Jennie Henderson 1856 - 1916
.... 3 Daniel Hamill 1878 - 1966
.... 3 Alfred Hamill 1880 -
.... 3 Samuel W. Hamill 1882 - 1967
.... 3 Sadie Hamill 1885 - 1966
.... 3 Ida Hamill 1887 - 1977
.... 3 John A. Hamill 1893 - 1944
.... 3 Eliza Hamill 1898 - 1898
.... 3 Charles R. Hamill 1899 - 1957
...... 2 Eliza Jane Hamill 1851 - 1869
...... 2 Robert Hamill 1853 - 1915
.... +Harriet 1857 -
.... 3 Grace S. Hamill 1900 - 1986
.... 3 Lydia Hamill 1888 -
.... +John Rothlisberg 1883 - 1916

    Daniel, farmer of Heagles, and son of Robert and Jean (Wallace) Hamill of Dunverney married Jane, daughter of Robert and Bess (McAula) McKeown of Forttown om 1847 in the Unitarian Church in Ballymoney. Although the grave states that Daniel died in 1862, the Coleraine Chronicle has the date as 1861. After Daniel's death his widow emigrated to U.S.A. and died in Wattsberg, Washington.

BOYLE

GRAVE no. 193

To the memory of
William Boyle
Cuppidale
who departed this life 10th Jany 1869
Aged 24 Years
Also
mother Mary who died 5th
May 1878 aged 70 years

Erected
by his brother John

The death of William Boyd Boyle was reported in the Coleraine Chronicle. He died from diabetes and may also have had a brother Charles who was witness at his death.

CAMPBELL

GRAVE no. 194

Erected
to the memory
of John Campbell
late of Top
who died 1st October
1851 aged 76 years
Also
His wife Ann
who died 8th April
1861 aged 81 years

John Campbell was a farmer at Topp in 1803, and John and Thomas were present in 1825.

BOYLE

GRAVE no. 195

To the memory of the late
Thomas Boyle of Toop, who
lived in the fear of God @
by all appearance died in
his favour on the 9th of Febry
1827 aged 71 years

In 1803 and 1825, Thomas and John Boyle were living at Topp Upper. By 1833, the farm had been taken over by James Knox.

SMITH

GRAVE no. 196a

Front Erected
to the memory of
Samuel Smith
late of Bendooragh
died on the 25th November
1857 aged 60 years

1 Samuel Smith 1716 - 1794
.. +Jean 1733 - 1796
...... 2 James Smith - 1818
.... +Nancy 1777 - 1845
.... 3 Samuel Smith 1797 - 1857
.... 3 William Smith 1802 -
.... +Jennett Sherrard
.... 3 James Smith 1805 -
.... +Agnes Dickie
.... 3 Elizabeth Smith 1807 -
...... 2 Samuel Smith
.... 3 Nathaniel Smith 1801 -
.... +Mary Dunlop
.... 3 Samuel Smith 1803 -

Samuel and Jean Smith had at least two children, James and Samuel.

James and Nancy Smith of Bendooragh had at least four children, baptised in 1st Ballymoney Church. William (1802) married Jennett Sherrard of Bravellan in 1826 and had a son James in 1831. James married Nancy Dickey of Drumreagh in 1828 and had children Betty (1829) and Samuel (1830). Elizabeth was born in 1807.

Samuel had sons Nathaniel and Samuel. Nathaniel married Mary Dunlop of Drumscie in 1823 and had two children Elizabeth and Samuel.

SMITH   GRAVE no. 196b

Back

Memento Mori
Here lieth the
body of Sml Smith
who departed this
Life 16 July 1794
Aged 78 years
Also his wife Jean
who departed this
Life 10 March 17
96 aged 66 years
Also James Smith aged ?
Who died 13th March
1818 and Nancy his
wife who died on the
? Feb 1845 aged 67

SMYTH

GRAVE no. 197

Here lieth the body
of Marey Smyth
who departed
May the 22 1807
aged 72 years

This is possibly a sister of Samuel Smyth (or Smith) who lived at Bendooragh (see grave 196).

LYONS

GRAVE no. 198

Erected
to the memory of
Hugh Lyons, Heagles
His wife Annie Leslie
and
Their daughters
Hannah and Matilda

1 Hugh Lyons
.. +Nancy Leslie 1812 - 1909
...... 2 Hannah Lyons 1837 - 1903
...... 2 John Lyons 1840 -
...... 2 Matilda Lyons 1842 - 1899
...... 2 Margaret Wright Lyons 1850 -
.... +Andrew Moore
.... 3 Andrew Knox Moore
...... 2 Sarah Jane Lyons 1842 - 1882
.... +Sheriff Moore Pinkerton 1834 - 1904
.... 3 Jane Anna Pinkerton 1878 - 1960
.... +Samuel McLean 1874 - 1961

Hugh, son of James and Sallie (Wright) Lyons of Drumaheagles married Nancy Leslie of Ballymoney in 1834 in 1st Ballymoney Presbyterian Church. He was a carpenter in Ballymoney.

Their daughters Hannah, Matilda and Mary Ann died in Ballymoney and were unmarried. Their son John emigrated to U.S.A. Another daughter Margaret Wright married Andrew Moore of Newtonards.

Their daughter Sarah Jane married Sheriff Moore, son on Samuel and Jean (McCrellis) Pinkerton of Forttown in 1877 in 1st Ballymoney Presbyterian Church.

LYONS

GRAVE no. 199

Sacred
to the memory of
James Lyons
Late of Drumaheagles
who departed this life
the 18th July 1830
Aged 62 years

1 James Lyons 1768 - 1830
.. +Sallie Wright
...... 2 Hugh Lyons
.... +Nancy Leslie 1812 - 1909
          see grave 198
...... 2 Ann Lyons
...... 2 John Lyons
...... 2 James Lyons
.... +Maria Wright 1823 -
...... *2nd Wife of James Lyons:
.... +Matilda Perry
.... 3 Sarah Lyons 1835 -
.... 3 Hanna Lyons 1837 -
.... 3 Samuel Lyons 1840 -
.... 3 Eliza Anne Lyons 1842 -
.... 3 Thomas Lyons 1844 -

James Lyons of Drumaheglis married Sallie, daughter of Joseph and Mary (Curry) Wright of Culbrim and had four known children.
Hugh married Nancy Leslie of Ballymoney (see grave 198).
Ann and John emigrated to U.S.A.
James junior married Matilda daughter of Samuel Perry of Ballymoney in 1833 in 1st Ballymoney Presbyterian Church and was a farmer at Drumaheglis. They attended the Unitarian Church. Matilda's father was a spirit dealer at Main Street. He married secondly Maria, daughter of Thomas and Sally (Boyd) Wright of Culbrim.

SMOLL

GRAVE no. 200

Erected
In memory of John Smoll
of Ballymoney
Age 70 years
Also his wife Elise
Also his daughter
Elizabeth Cassidy of Garryduff
who died 4th January 1883
aged 92 years

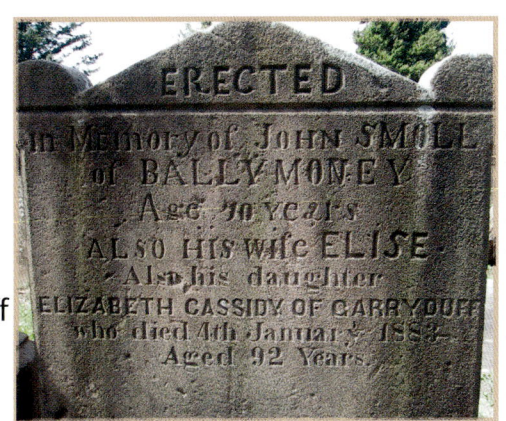

1 John Small
.. +Elise ?
...... 2 John Small 1788 - 1858
...... 2 Elizabeth Small 1791 - 1883
.... +Alexander Cassidy
.... 3 Catherine Cassidy
.... +Robert Gilmour
.... 3 Hugh Cassidy 1817 -
.... 3 Alexander Cassidy 1818 - 1894
.... +Martha Lamont 1825 -
.... 3 Jean Cassidy 1821 -
.... 3 James Gamble Cassidy 1823 - 1872
.... 3 Ann Cassidy 1826 -
.... 3 Elizabeth Cassidy 1829 -
.... +Daniel Loughridge
.... 3 John Cassidy 1833 - 1898
.... +Mary Lowry 1833 -
.... 3 Henry Cassidy 1816 - 1899
.... +Catherine Ross 1827 - 1914

Although the name is Smoll, the original name was Small. All the Smalls families in the area originated from Kirkmoyle.

Elizabeth married Alexander Cassidy, a farmer of Garryduff and their children were baptised in 1st Ballymoney Presbyterian Church. Their daughter Catherine married Robert Gilmour of Culduff in 1839 and their son Alexander married Martha, daughter of Richard and Mary (Greer) Lamont of Greenshields in 1848 both in 1st Ballymoney Presbyterian Church. Elizabeth married Daniel, son of John Loughridge of Inchinagh in 1861 and John married Mary, daughter of William Lowry of Inchinagh in 1854 in St. James Presbyterian Church. Henry married Catherine Ross (see grave 30).

CASSIDY

GRAVE no. 201

Erected
in memory of
James Gamble Cassidy
Late of Garryduff
who died 29th March 1872
aged 48 years
Also his brother John
who died 17th Aug 1898
Aged 64 years
Also his daughter
Martha aged 13 years
Also his daughter
Eliza S. Cassidy
who died 10th Apr 1904

.1 Alexander Cassidy
.. +Elizabeth Small 1791 - 1883
...... 2 Catherine Cassidy
.... +Robert Gilmour
...... 2 Hugh Cassidy 1817 -
...... 2 Alexander Cassidy 1818 - 1894
.... +Martha Lamont 1825 -
.... 3 James Cassidy
.... +Annie Eliza Cochrane
.... 3 Mary Cassidy
.... +Alexander Campbell
.... 3 Annie Elizabeth Cassidy
.... 3 John Cassidy
.... +Annie Jane Gault
.... 3 Martha Cassidy - 1897
.... +James Gault - 1941
...... 2 Jean Cassidy 1821 -
...... 2 James Gamble Cassidy 1823 - 1872
.... 3 Martha Cassidy
.... 3 Eliza S. Cassidy 1864 - 1904
...... 2 Ann Cassidy 1826 -
...... 2 Elizabeth Cassidy 1829 -
.... +Daniel Loughridge
...... 2 John Cassidy 1833 - 1898
.... +Mary Lowry 1833 -
.... 3 Jennie Henry Cassidy 1856 -
.... +John Arthur Tweed 1843 -
.... 3 Annie H. Cassidy
.... +Robert Tweed
...... 2 Henry Cassidy 1816 - 1899
.... +Catherine Ross 1827 - 1914
.   see grave 30

James Gamble was the son of Alexander and Elisa (Small) Cassidy and had two known children.

MACGILL

GRAVE no. 202

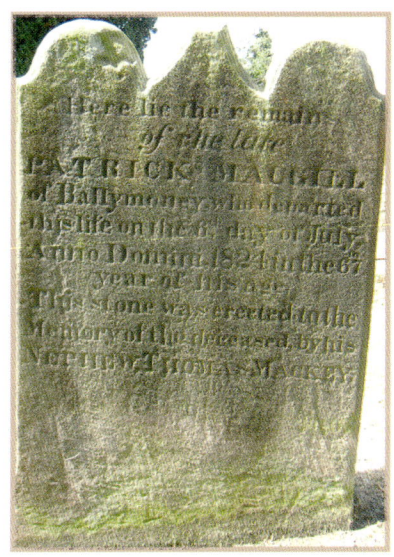

Here lie the remains
of the late
Patrick Macgill
of Ballymoney who departed
this life on the 6th day of July
Anno Domini 1824 in the 67th
year of his age
This stone was erected to the
Memory of the deceased, by his
Nephew, Thomas Mackey

There was a Patrick Macgill present in 1803 at Turnagrove, Loughguile.

Thomas Mackey was the master of the Erasmus Smith Free School in Church Street Ballymoney and Episcopalian. He died at the School House in 1870 aged 83 years.

A Free school in Ballymoney was established in 1808 for the education of the poorer classes. The Church of Ireland controlled the school, although it was open to all religions. By 1824, it had sixty six boys and fifty four girls enrolled.

MOORE

GRAVE no. 203

Sacred to the memory
of
James Moore
Late of Drumaheagles
Who departed this life 20
May 1832 aged 23 years

1 John Moore
.. +Letitia Watt
...... 2 Samuel Moore 1799 -
...... 2 Charles Moore 1801 -
...... 2 Elizabeth Moore 1803 -
...... 2 John Moore 1805 -
...... 2 James Moore 1807 - 1832
...... 2 Mary Moore 1810 - 1832
...... 2 Martha Moore 1813 - 1882
...... 2 Jean Moore 1819 - 1891

James Moore was the son of of John and Letitia (Watt) Moore of Drumaheaglas and brother of Mary Moore (see grave 204).

DOUGLAS

GRAVE no. 204

Sacred to the memory
of
Mary Douglas alias Moore
late of Drumaheagles
who departed this life 2 June
1832 aged 22 years
Also her husband John Douglas
who died 29 December 1851
Aged 57 years

1 John Douglas 1794 – 1851
.. +Mary Moore 1810 - 1832
...... 2 Elizabeth Douglas 1830 -
.... +David Wilson 1815 - 1904
.... 3 Annie Wilson
.... +John McIlmoyle
.... 3 John Wilson 1850 - 1934
.... +Hannah M. Williamson 1851 - 1931
.... 3 James Wilson
.... 3 Nancy Wilson
.... 3 Robert Wilson
.... 3 Josiah Wilson
.... 3 David Wilson 1853 - 1899

John Douglas married Mary, daughter of John and Letitia (Watt) Moore of Drumaheglis in 1828 in 1st Ballymoney Presbyterian Church.

Their daughter Elizabeth married David, son of David and Elizabeth (White) Wilson of Artigoran in 1849 in 1st Ballymoney Presbyterian Church.

MOORE

GRAVE no. 205

Erected
by
Henry Moore, Uxbridge Mass
In memory of his father
Robert Moore of Burnquarter who
Departed this life 18 April 1843
Aged 56 years.   ~   Also
Sarah Moore his daughter who
died 29th April 1829 aged 20 years
Also Henry Moore son of
James Moore, Burnquarter who
died April 1835 aged
3 months

KENNEDY

GRAVE no. 206

J. Kennedy

Small metal plaque- no more information

There is no other J. Kennedy recorded in the Interment Book 1888- 1932 apart from the family from Leaney (grave 5).

DARCUS

GRAVE no. 207

Erected in memory
of
Charlott. J. Darcus,
Ballybrake,
Who died 1st May 1880,
Aged 54 years.
Also
Ellen. J. Darcus,
Who died 4th July 1875,
Aged 16 years.
Charles Darcus, Jun,
Died 10th May 1910
Aged 53 years

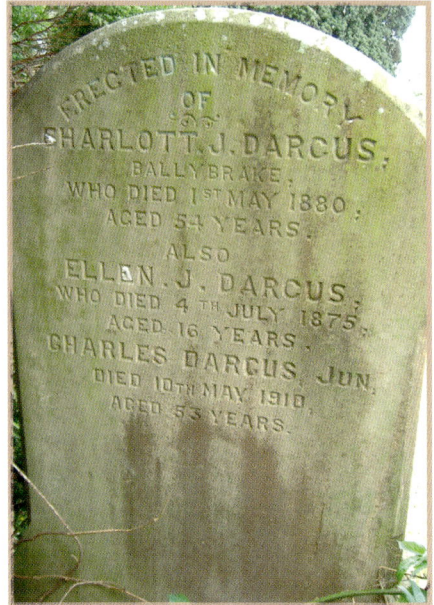

1 William Darcus
.. +Ellen McKeague
...... 2 David Darcus 1821 -
...... 2 Charles Darcus 1825 - 1905
.... +Charlotte Jane McNaughton 1826 - 1880
.... 3 William Darcus 1851 -
.... 3 James Alexander Darcus 1853 - 1925
.... 3 Charles Darcus 1856 - 1910
.... +Marjory 1851 - 1926
.... 3 Mary Darcus 1858 -
.... 3 Ellen J. Darcus 1859 - 1875
.... 3 William John Darcus 1860 -
.... 3 John Darcus 1862 -
.... 3 Elizabeth Darcus 1864 -
.... +Mr Wilson
...... 2 Catherine Darcus 1824 -
...... 2 Peggy Ann Darcus 1820 -
...... 2 William Darcus 1827

    Charles, son of William and Ellen (McKeague) Darcus, married Charlotte Jane, daughter of Charles McNaughton in 1849 in Ballymoney Register Office. He was a servant in Coldagh at the time of his marriage. Their first two children were born in Castle Street, Ballymoney and the rest at Coldagh. By 1871, Charles was described as a farmer and road contractor and living at Milltown. He died at Castle Street.
    His son Charles and wife Marjory died at Ballybrakes. Most of his other children emigrated.

SMALL
GRAVE no. 208

Here lieth the
Body of Joseph Small
of Ballywattick
Who departed this life the
26 Day of June 1797
aged 76 years
Also his wife Jane
Small who died the
17 of July 1815 aged 76
years

1 Joseph Small 1720 - 1797
.. +Jane 1739 - 1815
...... 2 Samuel Small - 1817
.... +Jean Todd
.... 3 Joseph Small
.... +Jean Craith
.... 3 William Small - 1846
.... +Rose Ann Craith
.... 3 John Small 1778 - 1815
...... 2 John Small
.... 3 John Small
.... +Jennet
.... 3 Agnes Small
.... +Robert Dinsmore 1770 - 1830
.... 3 Joseph Small 1782 -
.... +Jean Dinsmore 1785 -

Joseph and Jane Small of Ballywattick had two known children.
    Their son Samuel married Jean Todd. Their sons Joseph and William married daughters of Nathaniel and Rose (McLeesh) Craith of Ballymoney.
    Their son John had three known children. His son John married Jennet, farmed at Ballywattick and had four children. His daughter Agnes married Robert, son of Andrew Dinsmore of Ballywattick and their family all emigrated to U.S.A. His son Joseph married Jean, daughter of Andrew and Margaret (Dinsmore) Dinsmore, and half sister to Robert. They farmed for a time at Moneygobbin before emigrating to Monroe, Indiana.

SMALL

GRAVE no. 209

Here lieth
the body of
John Small late
of Ballywatick
who departed this
Life the 20 of March
1815 in the 36 year
of his age

John was the son of Samuel and Jean (Todd) Small of Ballywattick (see grave 208) and brother of Joseph and William.

SMALL

GRAVE no. 210

In memory of
William Small, Ballymoney
formerly of Ballywattick
Died 8th June 1904 aged 70 years

```
1 Samuel Small
.. +Jean Todd
...... 2 Joseph Small
.......... +Jean Craith
............... 3 Samuel Small 1808 - 1891
................... +Elizabeth Jane Jamison 1816 - 1900
............... 3 Nathaniel Small 1811 -
............... 3 Rose Ann Small 1819 - 1871
................... +George Alexander Knox 1796 - 1874
...... 2 William Small - 1846
.......... +Rose Ann Craith
............... 3 Samuel Small 1815 - 1870
................... +Sarah Jane Love 1815 - 1881
............... 3 Jean Small 1822 - 1910
................... +Hugh Kelly 1818 - 1893
............... 3 Mary Small 1829 - 1898
................... +William Jamison 1814 - 1876
............... 3 Peggy Ann Small 1831 -
............... 3 William Small 1834 - 1904
............... 3 Isabella Small 1838 - 1896
................... +William James Knox 1842 - 1916
...... 2 John Small 1778 - 1815
```

William, was the son of William and Rose Ann (Craith) Small of Ballywattick. He was a carrier in Ballymoney, a bachelor, and died in Main Street.

His brother Samuel married Sarah Jane, daughter of Robert and Martha (Culbert) Love of Taghey in 1843 in 1st Ballymoney Presbyterian Church.

His sister Jean married Hugh, son of William and Jenny (Jordan) Kelly of Ballymoney in 1844 in 1st Ballymoney.

His sister Mary married William, son of Daniel Jamison of Carrowcrin, Armoy in 1853, also in 1st Ballymoney.

His sister Isabella married William James Knox, a farmer at Ballywattick, in 1877 in Trinity Presbyterian Church. They are buried in Knock Road Cemetery.

SMALL

GRAVE no. 211

In
Memory of
William Small
Killmoyle
Died 1st Jany 1883
Aged 66 years
His wife Jane
Died 21st April 1878
Aged 42 years
Their children
Benjamin an infant
Robert died 8th Sepr 1875
Aged 17 years
Thomas Glenn
died 19th Sepr 1876 aged 6 years
Joseph Campbell
died 8th Jun 1888 aged 28 years
James Campbell
who ?
9th June 1888 aged 24 years
Jane Campbell
died 11th Decr 1888

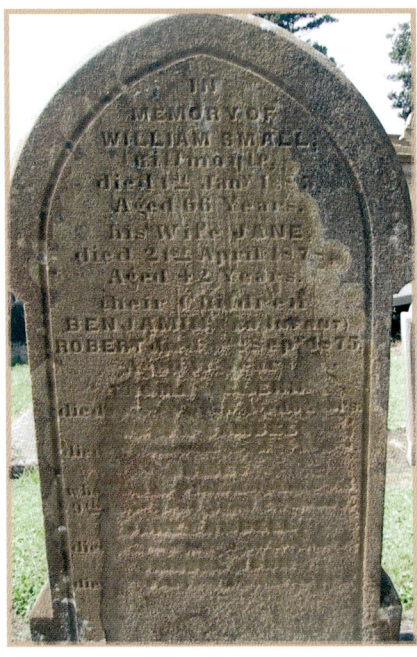

1 Robert Small 1769 - 1851
.. +Agnes Templeton
...... 2 Peggy Anne Small 1808 -
...... 2 Jennet Small 1810 -
.... +Hugh Thompson 1804 -
...... 2 Mary Small 1812 -
.... +Robert Beverland
...... 2 Ann Small 1814 -
...... 2 Matilda Small 1816 -
.... +Thomas Glen
...... 2 William Small 1818 - 1887
.... +Jane Campbell 1836 - 1878
.... 3 Robert Small 1858 - 1875
.... 3 Joseph Campbell Small 1860 - 1888
.... 3 Samuel John Small 1861 - 1889
.... 3 William Small 1863 -
.... 3 James Small 1864 - 1888
.... 3 Jane Campbell Small 1868 - 1888
.... 3 Thomas Glen Small 1870 - 1876
.... 3 Annie Templeton Small 1872 -
.... +Arthur Martin
.... 3 Benjamin Small 1873 - 1873
...... 2 Robert Small 1821 - 1866

William, son of Robert and Agnes (Templeton) Small of Kilmoyle married Jane, daughter of Samuel and Jean (McAlister) Campbell of Ballymoney in 1857 in 1st Ballymoney Presbyterian Church.
Only one of their children married, their daughter Annie Templeton to Arthur Martin in 1894 at Ballywillan Presbyterian Church.

ROSBOROUGH

GRAVE no. 212

Here
Lieth the mortal Remains
of
Martha Rosborough
wife to
Alexr Rosborough
of Ballymoney who
Departed this life ye
6th of Janry 1807 aged
25 years. Also her son
Willm Small Rosborough
Aged 6 months

1 Alexander Rosborough
.. +Martha Small 1781 - 1807
...... 2 Jean Rosborough 1802 - 1880
.... +Richard Hamilton 1785 - 1847
...............see grave 249
...... 2 William Small Rosborough 1804 - 1805
...... 2 Matilda Rosborough 1805 - 1870
.... +James Moore 1800 - 1877
.... 3 Jane Moore
.... +John Small 1809 - 1898
.... 3 Anna Moore 1835 - 1857
.... 3 Matilda Moore 1843 - 1870
.... 3 William Moore - 1913
.... 3 Mary Moore - 1916
.... 3 Margaret Moore - 1926
.... 3 James Moore
.... +Mary Eccles

    Alexander Rosborough, a grocer of Main Street, married Martha, daughter of William and Mary Small of Kilmoyle. Martha died when her youngest child was less than two years old. Their daughters went to Kilmoyle to live with their grandparents after their mother's death.
    Their daughter Jean married Richard, son of Robert and Sarah (Murdock) Hamilton in 1822 in 1st Ballymoney Presbyterian Church. He was post master in Ballymoney.
    Their youngest daughter married James, son of Hugh and Anna Moore of Pullans in 1832 in 1st Ballymoney Presbyterian Church.

SMALL

GRAVE no. 213

This stone
is erected to the
memory of John Small
late of Killmoyle who
Departed this life 16 Novr
1789 aged 84 years
Also his wife Anna S Small
who died 18th February 1773 aged
65 years. Likewise their son
William Small who died
15 Jany 1818 aged 76 years
He was distinguished thro
life for his industry and
integrity which gained him
the esteem of the worthy
and endeared him to
his family and friends
Also in memory of his
wife Martha Small
who departed this life 15
August 1845 aged 95 years

1 John Small 1705 - 1789
.. +Anna 1707 - 1773
...... 2 Martha Small 1735 - 1823
...... 2 James Small 1738 -
.... +Jennett Boyd 1732 - 1822
.... 3 Robert Small
...... 2 John Small 1740 - 1816
.... 3 James Small 1780 - 1866
.... 3 William Small 1771 - 1867
.... 3 Jane Small 1787 - 1817
...... 2 Benjamin Small 1741 - 1823
...... 2 William Small 1742 - 1818
.... +Martha 1750 - 1845
.... 3 Robert Small 1769 - 1851
.... +Agnes Templeton
.... 3 James Small 1780 - 1869
.... +Hannah Getty 1788 -
.... 3 Matilda Small
.... 3 Martha Small 1781 - 1807
.... +Alexander Rosborough

All the Small families in the area are reputed as having come from the same original family who arrived as soldiers to guard the River Bann and then settled here. The earliest source found are John and James Small in the 1740 census. The original family were farmers at Kirkmoyle (Kilmoyle), Ballywattick and Kirkhills (author's family). They had at least five known childen.

James married Jennet Boyd in 1770 in 1st Ballymoney Presbyterian Church and a son Robert who may have been the Robert Small who was a farmer at Taghey.

Benjamin was a farmer at Kilmoyle and on retirement moved to Ballymoney with his sister Jean.

CAMPBELL

GRAVE no. 214

CAMPBELL

in faint writing which had been plastered over

Samuel Campbell of Ballymoney
Died 19th July 1841
and Benjamin Small in Apr 1841
his daughter Elizabeth Small
24th May 1849
and his son Randal in New Orleans
24th August 1853
and his son Joseph 18 June 1855
and Jane his wife 25th Novr 1870
Her brother
Abraham McAlister died 1870

1 Randal McAlister
...... 2 Jean McAlister 1804 - 1870
.... +Samuel Campbell 1800 - 1841
.... 3 Joseph Campbell 1824 - 1855
.... 3 Benjamin Small Campbell 1826 - 1841
.... 3 Randle Campbell 1831 - 1853
.... 3 William Campbell 1833 - 1915
.... +Sarah Jane Freeman 1850 - 1917
                    see grave 242
.... 3 Jane Campbell 1836 - 1878
.... +William Small 1818 - 1887
                    see grave 211
.... 3 Elizabeth Small Campbell 1838 - 1849
...... 2 Abraham McAlister - 1870

Randal McAlister was a publican in Church Street, Ballymoney. His son Abraham was a bachelor and was also a publican.

His daughter Jean married Samuel, son of Joseph and Mary (Pattison) Campbell in 1823 in 1st Ballymoney Presbyterian Church. Samuel was a whitesmith.

Only two of their children married and the rest died in their youth. Jane married William, son of Robert and Agnes (Templeton) Small of Kirkmoyle in 1857 in 1st Ballymoney Presbyterian Church. William married Sarah Jane Freeman (see grave 242).

MOORE

GRAVE no. 215

In
memory of
William Moore
of Fernalizery
who died 27th February 1806
Aged 90 years
and his wife Martha White
James Moore and his wife
Margaret Killough
and sister Margaret Moore
William Moore
Died 17th May 1894 aged 77 years
his wife Rose Adams
Died 22nd August 1855
James Moore
Died 20th November 1840
Aged 12 years
Two infant sisters Matilda
Mary Moore
Died 21st December 1870
William Moore
Died 1st October 1892
Aged 55 years
John Adams Moore
Died 22nd November 1920
Aged 87 years

1 William Moore 1715 - 1806
.. +Martha White
...... 2 James Moore
.... +Margaret Killough
.... 3 William Moore 1786 - 1864
.... +Rose Adams - 1855
.... 3 Martha Moore 1790 -
.... +Robert White
.... 3 Mary Moore 1793 -
.... +William Brown
.... 3 Agnes Moore 1795 -
.... +Samuel Huey
.... 3 Marshall Moore 1799 - 1849
.... +Jane Maria ? - 1861
...... 2 Margaret Moore

William, son of Quentin Moore, was a a farmer at Fernalizery and married Martha White. His son James married Margaret Killough and they had five known children.

Their eldest son William married Rose Adams of Ballyboyland.

Their daughter Martha married Robert White of Macfin (see grave 114).

Their daughter Mary married John Brown of Cullermoney in 1822 in 1st Ballymoney Presbyterian Church.

Their daughter Agnes married Samuel Huey of Ballynaris in 1820.

Their son Marshall was a Presbyterian minister at Faughanvale and died at Coolafiney.

WHITE

GRAVE no. 216

Erected
to the memory of
James White
of Ballymoney
who died 30th December 1884
Aged 64 years
His wife
Margaret Moore White
Died 25th May 1907
aged 76 years
Their only son
William Moore White
Died 11th March 1930
aged 64 years

1 Robert White
.. +Martha Moore 1790 -
...... 2 James White 1820 - 1884
.... +Margaret Moore 1830 - 1907
.... 3 Martha Moore White 1863 -
.... 3 William Moore White 1865 - 1930
...... 2 Robert White 1826 -
...... 2 John White 1829 -

Robert was the son of William and Mary White of Macfin and brother of William (see grave 115) and James. He married Martha, daughter of James and Margaret (Killough) Moore of Fernalizary (see grave 215), moved to Ballymoney and became a grocer in Church Street.

They had two children who never married. William continued with his fathers business.

MOORE

GRAVE no. 217

In loving memory
of David Moore
Ballyboyland
Died 28th April 1900
and his wife Sarah
Died 15th October 1924
Also their daughter Jane
Died 25th September 1952
and their son David R.
Died 13th January 1962
Laurence Moore
Died 10th May 1972

1 Lawrence Moore 1787 - 1868
.. +Jenny 1790 - 1860
...... 2 James Moore 1815 - 1869
.... +Mary Ross - 1911
...... 2 Thomas Moore 1821 - 1891
.... +Margaret McKeown - 1880
.... 3 Maggie Toland Moore 1862 - 1905
.... +James Hopkins McAllister 1865 - 1925
.... 3 [2] James Moore
.... +[1] Rachael Moore 1879 -
...... 2 Lawrence Moore 1840 -
.... +Martha Warnock
...... 2 David Ross Moore 1825 - 1900
.... +Sarah McCurdy 1846 - 1924
.... 3 Jane Ross Moore 1878 -
.... 3 [1] Rachael Moore 1879 -
.... +[2] James Moore
.... 3 Alice McElderry Moore 1880 - 1969
.... +James Hanna 1883 - 1971
.... 3 Sarah Annie Moore 1883 -
.... +Thomas McCullough
.... 3 David Ross Moore 1885 - 1962
.... 3 Lawrence Moore 1890 - 1972
...... 2 Margaret Moore
.... +James Kennedy
...... 2 Jane Moore
.... +James Nevin
.... 3 William John Nevin 1863 - 1934
.... 3 Rachael Nevin
.... +Robert Clarke
.... 3 David Nevin
.... 3 James Nevin
.... 3 Jeannie Nevin
.... 3 Margaret Nevin
.... 3 James Nevin

David, son of Lawrence and Jenny Moore of Ballyboyland married Sarah McCurdy in 1876 in Carncullagh Presbyterian Church.

Their daughter Rachael married her cousin James, son of Thomas and Margaret (McKeown) Moore of Greenshields in 1908 in Dervock Reformed Presbyterian Church.

Alice married James, son of John Hanna of High Street, Ballymoney in 1912 in Roseyards Presbyterian Church and they are buried in Knock Road Cemetery.

Sarah Anne married Thomas, son of Abraham McCullough of Armagh, in 1911 in Carncullagh Presbyterian Church.

Their three other children did not marry. Laurence, their youngest son, was possible the last burial in the old churchyard.

CALDERWOOD

GRAVE no. 218

Here
Lyeth interred
The remains of
Alexr Calderwood
who departed this
Life the 6th Octor
1782 aged 18 years

There were Calderwood families in Ballymoney, Cuppindale and Balnacree in 1803 (see grave 159).

SHIELDS

GRAVE no. 219

Erected by
Mary Morrison
in memory
of her aunt
Margaret Shields
who died
16 August 1892

1 Hugh Shanks
.. +Mary 1812 - 1887
...... 2 Margaret Shanks 1836 -
...... 2 Matty Shanks 1840 -
.... +Thomas McDowell 1840 - 1895
.... 3 James McDowell 1869 - 1907
.... 3 Hugh Shanks McDowell 1871 -
.... +Mary Jane Cairns
.... 3 John Shanks McDowell 1873 -
.... 3 Thomas McDowell 1875 - 1888
.... 3 Mary Elizabeth McDowell 1878 -
.... +John O'Neill
...... 2 Eliza Shanks 1843 -
.... +William Pattison
...... 2 Martha Shanks 1846 - 1900
...... 2 Mary Shanks 1848 -
.... +Patrick Haughey
...... 2 Alicia Shanks 1850 -
.... +John Morrison
.... 3 Jane Morrison 1874 -
.... 3 Samuel Morrison 1875 -
.... 3 Mary Morrison 1877 -
.... 3 Margaret Morrison 1878 -

Margaret Shields, a widow, died in Union Street, Ballymoney aged 72 of old age. She was interred by Thomas McDowell, who was a postman. She left a will mentioning her niece Martha, wife of Thomas McDowell and a grandniece Jane Morrison.

I couldn't find a marriage for Margaret Shields, but I suspect that her maiden name was Shanks. Her niece Martha was the daughter of Hugh and Mary Shanks of Castle Street, Ballymoney. Hugh was a stone mason. They were members of St. Patrick's Parish Church.

Her grandniece Jane Morrison was the daughter of John and Alicia (Shanks) Morrison of Castle Street who married in 1872 in St. James Presbyterian Church.. John was a tailor.

MCCUTCHION

GRAVE no. 220

Sacred
?
James McCutchion
?
?
Also   ?

I have only found one family of this name (see grave 221).

MCCUTCHION

GRAVE no. 221

Adam McCutchion
who died 12th March 1780
aged 74 years
Also of Margaret and Jane
His first and second wife
and four of his children
?
?

There was a family of McCutchion (or McKutchin) in Claughey in 1817.

1 David McCutchion
.. +Sally Clarke
…… 2 John McCutchion
………. +Mary Cairns
…………… 3 Mary McCutchion 1834 -
…………… 3 David McCutchion 1836 -
…… 2 Margaret McCutchion
………. +James McAlister
…………… 3 David McAlister 1836 -
…………… 3 John McAlister 1836 -
…………… 3 James McAlister 1837 -
…… 2 Sally McCutchion 1818 -
………. +James Crawford
…………… 3 Sarah Jane Crawford 1840 -
…………… 3 John Crawford 1841 -
…………… 3 Matilda Crawford 1842 -
…………… 3 Elizabeth Crawford 1843 -
…… 2 Elizabeth McCutchion 1821 -
…… 2 Rose Ann McCutchion 1823 -
…… 2 Mary McCutchion 1826 -
…… 2 Jean McCutchion 1829 -
…… 2 Mary McCutchion 1832 -
………. +John Steele
…………… 3 William Steele
…………… 3 Daniel Campbell Steele
…………… 3 Matthew Steele
…………… 3 Margaret Steele
…………… 3 John Steele
…… 2 Matty McCutchion 1837 -

Council workers clearing the undergrowth

HAMILTON

GRAVE no. 222

Sacred to the memory of
Jane wife to H McCurdy Hamilton
and daughter to the Rev. Jas Brown
who departed this life on the 5 day
of April 1843 aged 41 years. Also
Her infant daughter aged seven days
Also James Brown Hamilton
who died 15 June 1863 aged 27 years
Mary McCurdy Hamilton
and wife of the late Hugh McCurdy Hamilton
and wife of the Rev R.S. Coffey Mullingar
who passed away on 20 May 1911

In memory of
Hugh McCurdy Hamilton
who died at Ballymoney 17th Feby 1867
aged 65 years
Also
Alexander MacLeod Stavely Hamilton
Born December 10th 1850
Died at sea February 8th 1880
and Mary Hamilton
widow of Hugh McCurdy Hamilton
and Eldest daughter of the late
Rev. W.J. Stavely D.D.
died 1st July 1895 aged 83 years

1 Hugh McCurdy Hamilton 1801 - 1867
.. +Jane Brown 1802 - 1843
...... 2 John McCurdy Hamilton 1834 - 1915
.... +Eliza Thorburn 1848 - 1882
.... 3 Hugh Alexander Hamilton 1873 -
.... 3 John Thorburn Hamilton 1874 -
.... 3 Elizabeth Dorothea Hamilton 1876 -
.... 3 James Brown Hamilton 1878 -
.... 3 Jane Brown Hamilton 1880 -
.... 3 Arthur Wallace Hamilton 1881 -
...... *2nd Wife of John McCurdy Hamilton:
.... +Margaret Hamilton 1852 -
...... 2 James Brown Hamilton 1835 - 1863
...... 2 Hugh McCurdy Hamilton 1837 - 1907
.... +Frances Stuart Lougheed 1843 - 1868
.... 3 Jane Brown Hamilton 1865 - 1932
.... +Alexander Peden
...... 2 William Hamilton 1839 - 1902

HAMILTON

GRAVE no. 222

Hugh McCurdy, a merchant in Ballymoney, son of Archibald and Jane (McCurdy) Hamiton married Jane, daughter of Rev. James and Jane (Adams) Brown in 1832. Rev. James Brown was born in Ballinaloob, son of John and Jane (Moore) Brown. He was minister of Garvagh Presbyterian Church. Hugh and Jane had five children and Jane died just after the birth of her fifth child. Hugh remarried Mary, daughter of William John and Jane (Adams) Stavely in 1845 in 1st Ballymoney Presbyterian Church. They had one child Alexander McLeod Stavely Hamilton, who married his cousin Jane Adams, daughter of Rev. Alexander McLeod and Margaret (Cameron) Stavely, minister of Kilraughts Reformed Presbyterian Church.

From Hugh's first marriage, his eldest son John married Eliza, daughter of John Thorburn of Carlow. He was educated at Edinburgh University and was ordained minister at Donore, Dublin where he remained until retirement in 1902.

Their third son Hugh also became a Presbyterian minister, graduating from Edinburgh University and was ordained as minister of Templepatrick. He married Frances Stuart, daughter of Rev. Robert and Elizabeth (Stuart) Loughead, minister of Trinity Presbyterian Church, in 1864 in Belfast.

Their son William, a woollen draper in Ballymoney, married Alice, daughter of Robert and Margaret (Conn) Nevin in 1867 in Terrace Row Presbyterian Church, Coleraine.

Their only daughter Mary married Rev. Robert Steele, son of William and Elizabeth (Steele) Coffey, in 1867. Rev. Coffey was minister in Eire, Bradford, England and U.S.A.

Their youngest son, Thomas Bones, a merchant in Ballymoney, married Jane Eccles Gilmour in 1878 in Terrace Row Presbyterian Church, Coleraine.

.... +Alice Nevin 1842 - 1931
.... 3 James Brown Hamilton 1868 - 1958
.... +Elizabeth Scott Leitch 1875 - 1959
.... 3 Robert Nevin Hamilton 1871 - 1940
.... 3 Margaret Conn Hamilton 1872 - 1906
.... +Robert Thomson 1864 - 1941
.... 3 Hugh McCurdy Hamilton 1875 - 1963
.... +Ida Marion Wylie - 1949
.... 3 William Hamilton 1878 - 1958
.... 3 Jane Brown Hamilton 1880 - 1969
...... 2 Mary McCurdy Hamilton 1840 - 1911
.... +Robert Steele Coffey 1843 - 1913
.... 3 Hugh McCurdy Hamilton Coffey 1868 - 1943
.... +Norah Grandage 1874 - 1911
...... 2 Thomas Bones Hamilton 1843 - 1932
.... +Jane Eccles Gilmour 1850 - 1910
.... 3 Alice Hamilton 1878 -
.... +James Alexander Hazlett
.... 3 James Gilmour Brown Hamilton 1879 -
.... 3 Thomas Bones Hamilton 1884 -
.... +Marian Emily Gault 1890 -
.... 3 Hugh McCurdy Hamilton 1886 - 1897
.... 3 Janet Eccles Gilmour Hamilton 1888 - 1973
*2nd Wife of Hugh McCurdy Hamilton:
.. +Mary Stavely 1812 - 1895
...... 2 Alexander McLeod Stavely Hamilton 1850 - 1880
.... +Jane Adams Stavely 1854 - 1930
.... 3 Alexander Hamilton 1876 -
.... 3 Frederick William Hamilton 1880 -

MCCURDY

GRAVE no. 223

Sacred
to the memory of
Letitia McCurdy Jun
who departed this life
on the 2nd Jany 1785
in the 18th year of her age
Also Letitia McCurdy sen
who died the 8th Sept 1805
Aged 76 years
Also
John McCurdy her
husband who departed
this life the 10th Aug 1822
Aged 96 years
Likewise the remains
of their daughter
Mary McCurdy who
departed this life the 15
August 1840 aged 79 years

1 John McCurdy 1729 - 1822
.. +Letitia Hamilton 1729 - 1805
...... 2 Jane McCurdy - 1844
.... +Archibald Hamilton 1769 - 1837
.... 3 John Hamilton 1799 - 1873
.... +Charlotte Parks
.... 3 Hugh McCurdy Hamilton 1801 - 1867
.... +Jane Brown 1802 - 1843
.... *2nd Wife of Hugh McCurdy Hamilton:
.... +Mary Stavely
               see grave 222
.... 3 William Hamilton 1807 - 1886
.... +Anna Patterson 1816 - 1888
...... 2 William McCurdy
...... 2 Hugh McCurdy
...... 2 Mary McCurdy 1761 - 1840
...... 2 Letitia McCurdy 1767 - 1785

    Jane, daughter of John and Letitia (Hamilton) McCurdy married Archibald, eldest son of Robert and Sarah (Murdock) Hamilton. They had four sons. The eldest son was killed in infancy by falling from the back of a boy who was carrying him. The child's head struck a nail and he died instantly. John, the second son, was born in Coleraine. Archibald and Jane separated for a time. Archibald moved to Ballymoney and Jane to Garvagh, where she opened a millinery store which prospered. After a separation of six years they had a temporary reunion and they had their son William.

HAMILTON

GRAVE no. 224

At an early period was here interred the remains of James Hamilton of Cloughcorr now Prospect Also of his son John Hamilton and grandson Hugh Hamilton of Moneygobbin who departed this life ? 26 1748 aged 79 ? ? wives Ann and Mary ? ? ? their offspring Mary Stewart Hamilton wife of William Hamilton of Moneygabin who departed this life the 5 of Jun 1814 aged 80 years

1 John Hamilton
...... 2 Hugh Hamilton 1669 - 1748
.... +Mary
...... *2nd Wife of Hugh Hamilton:
.... +Ann
.... 3 Letitia Hamilton 1729 - 1805
.... +John McCurdy 1726 - 1822
.... 4 Jane McCurdy - 1844
.... +Archibald Hamilton 1769 - 1837
.... 4 William McCurdy
.... 4 Hugh McCurdy
.... 4 Mary McCurdy 1761 - 1840
.... 4 Letitia McCurdy 1767 - 1785
.... 4 James McCurdy 1789 - 1867
.... +Mary Love
.... 3 William Hamilton 1730 - 1817
.... +Mary Stewart 1734 - 1814
                    see graves 225 and 226
.... 3 John Hamilton 1731 - 1810
.... 4 Elizabeth Hamilton 1757 -
.... 4 Mary Hamilton 1759 -

James Hamilton was present in Cloughcorr in 1666. In 1740, a Hu was present in the area.
  Hugh's daughter Letitia married John McCurdy and their daughter Jane married Archibald, son of Robert and Sarah (Murdock) Hamilton. Robert Hamilton is probably related to the Moneygobbin Hamilton family but I haven't found a definite link. Robert was Episcopalian whereas Hugh was Presbyterian.

HAMILTON

GRAVE no. 225

Here lieth interred
Alexander Hamilton, surgeon
late of Ballymoney
who died the 9th day of January 1813
Aged 50 years
Also Hugh Hamilton of Moneygobbin
who died the 22nd of February 1822
Aged 56 years
And his beloved wife Jane Hamilton
who died 15th day of March 1865
Aged 91 years

1 William Hamilton 1730 - 1817
.. +Mary Stewart 1734 - 1814
...... 2 Jane Hamilton 1758 - 1822
.... +William Cramsie
...... 2 Alexander Hamilton 1762 - 1813
...... 2 Hugh Hamilton 1765 - 1822
.... +Jean 1773 - 1865
.... 3 John Thompson Hamilton 1804 - 1875
.... 3 Mary Hamilton 1806 -
.... 3 Nancy Hamilton 1810 -
.... +James Pinkerton 1814 - 1876
.... 3 Jean Hamilton 1812 - 1892
.... 3 William Hamilton 1813 - 1825
.... 3 Elizabeth Hamilton 1815 - 1892
...... 2 Elizabeth Hamilton 1771 -

William, son of Hugh and Ann Hamilton of Moneygobbin, married Mary Stewart and had four known children. Their daughter Jane married William, son of Patrick Cramsie, of Coldagh (see grave 226).

Their son Hugh was a a farmer at Moneygobbin and married Jean (possibly Thompson). Only one child is known to have married. Their daughter Nancy who married James, son of Robert and Agnes (Hunter) Pinkerton of Secon and Knowehead, in 1843 in 1st Ballymoney Presbyterian Church. They farmed at Moneygobbin and had no family.

HAMILTON

GRAVE no. 226

Sacred
to the memory of
Mary Stewart alias Hamilton
who died the 5th day of June 1814
Aged 80 years
and her husband William Hamilton
of Moneygobbin
Died 10th day of March 1817
Aged 86 years
And their grandson William Hamilton
who died 16th day of March 1825
Aged 11 years
John T. Hamilton
Died 5th August 1875
Aged 70 years
Jane Hamilton
Died 23rd June 1892 aged 75 years
Elizabeth Hamilton
Died 7th July 1892 aged 70 years

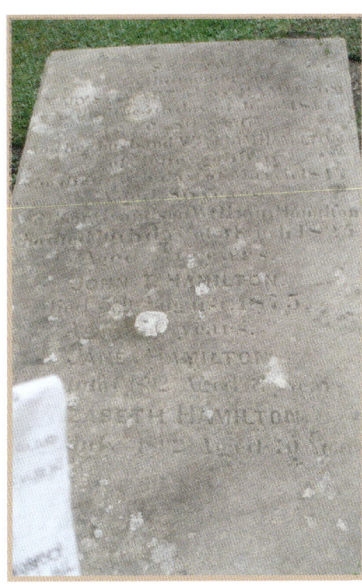

1 William Hamilton 1730 - 1817
.. +Mary Stewart 1734 - 1814
...... 2 Jane Hamilton 1758 - 1822
.... +William Cramsie
.... 3 Alexander Cramsie
.... 3 Anne Cramsie 1801 - 1856
.... 3 Mary Cramsie 1784 - 1865
.... +Charles Oulton 1768 - 1845
.... 4 William Plat Oulton 1809 -
.... 4 Jane Oulton 1810 -
.... 4 Richard Oulton 1812 -
.... 4 John Oulton 1804 -
.... 4 Rachael Oulton 1823 -
.... 4 Plato Oulton 1825 -
...... 2 Alexander Hamilton 1762 - 1813
...... 2 Hugh Hamilton 1765 - 1822
.... +Jean 1773 - 1865
.... 3 John Thompson Hamilton 1804 - 1875
.... 3 Mary Hamilton 1806 -
.... 3 Nancy Hamilton 1810 -
.... +James Pinkerton 1814 - 1876
.... 3 Jean Hamilton 1812 - 1892
.... 3 William Hamilton 1813 - 1825
.... 3 Elizabeth Hamilton 1815 - 1892
...... 2 Elizabeth Hamilton 1771 -

William and Mary (Stewart) Hamilton had four known children and were farmers at Moneygobbin..
Their daughter Jane married William, son of Patrick Cramsie and Miss Moore. Their daughter Mary married Charles Oulton, curate of St. Patrick's Church, Ballymoney, in 1807 in St. Patrick's.

CAMPBELL

GRAVE no. 227

Here lyeth
the body of Samuel Campbell
who died July
the 9th 1793 aged ?
Also his wife
Eliz Campbell
Aged 50 years

1 Samuel Campbell - 1793
.. +Elizabeth ?
...... 2 Joseph Campbell
.... +Mary Pattison
.... 3 Samuel Campbell 1800 - 1841
.... +Jean McAlister 1804 - 1870
                  see grave 214
.... 3 Thomas Campbell 1802 -
.... 3 Joseph Campbell 1804 -
.... +Elizabeth McHenry
.... 3 William Campbell 1808 -
.... +Elizabeth Boyle
.... 3 Elizabeth Campbell 1811 -
.... 3 John Campbell 1813 -
.... 3 Mary Campbell 1818 -
.... 3 Adam Hunter Campbell 1820 - 1893
.... +Martha Caldwell 1811 - 1891
.... 4 Ellen Mary Campbell 1852 -
.... +David McGlade
.... 4 Joseph Campbell 1855 -
...... 2 Samuel Campbell
.... +Agnes Matthews
.... 3 John Campbell 1806 -
.... 3 Samuel Campbell 1809 -
.... 3 Joseph Campbell 1812 -
.... 3 Mary Ann Campbell 1815 -
.... +Robert Steele
.... 3 William Campbell 1817 -
.... 3 Elizabeth Campbell 1820 -
.... 3 Adam Campbell 1822 -
...... 2 William Campbell

Samuel and Elizabeth Campbell of Ballymoney had three known sons.

Joseph, a whitesmith married Mary Pattison and their eldest son Samuel married Jean, daughter of Randle McAlister (see grave 214). Their youngest son Adam Hunter married Martha, eldest daughter of Robert and Sarah (Cameron) Caldwell in 1850 in St. Patrick's Parish Church.

Their second son Samuel married Agnes Matthews and had a family of seven. Their youngest son William was a reed maker in Main Street.

HAMILL
GRAVE no. 228

Here lieth
the remains of Jane Hamill
who departed this life
the 8th Sept 1811 aged 38 years
Also her son Neal Hamill
who died the 9th November
1814 aged 20 years
Likewise her son
Thomas Hamill who
departed this life September
27th 1817 aged 24 years

1 Neal Hamill
.. +Jane ? 1773 - 1811
...... 2 Thomas Hamill 1793 - 1817
...... 2 Neal Hamill 1794 - 1814
...... 2 Mary Hamill 1802 -
...... 2 Nancy Hamill 1807 - 1894
.... +Robert Getty 1805 -
.... 3 Matthew Getty 1838 - 1879
.... 3 Robert Getty 1841 -
.... +Elizabeth Kelly 1861 - 1906
.... 3 Mary Getty 1843 -

Neal Hamill was a farmer at Ballywattick and had at least four children. There was a Neal , son of John Hamill, baptised in 1755.

His daughter Nancy married Robert , son of John and Mary Ann Getty of Ballywattick in 1837 in 1st Ballymoney Presbyterian Church. Their son Robert emigrated to New York about 1857 and was a carpenter. In 1879, he formed a carpentry and building business with his cousin John McElvery in Flatbush, Brooklyn.

JORDAN

GRAVE no. 229

Sacred to the memory
of
James Jordan late of
Ballymoney who died
the 6th of Sept 1818 aged
68 years.   Also Jane his
wife who died the 1st of
March 1813 aged 66 years
Also Catherine Johnston
who died the 9th of November
1811 aged 30 years
also Jane Kelly who died
the 19th of May 1818 aged
26 years

1 James Jordan 1750 – 1818
. +Jane Anderson 1759 - 1813
...... 2 Mary Jordan 1776 - 1818
.... +James Culbertson 1754 - 1810
.... 3 Jane Culbertson 1792 - 1853
.... +William Young 1796 - 1867
...... 2 Jane Jordan 1778 -
...... 2 Catherine Jordan 1781 - 1811
.... +Mr Johnston
...... 2 Robert Jordan 1784 - 1864
.... +Jane Hopkins 1799 - 1859
..............see grave 230
...... 2 John Jordan 1788 -
...... 2 Jenny Jordan 1792 - 1818
.... +William Kelly
.... 3 Jane Kelly 1811 -
.... 3 Jane Kelly 1816 -
.... 3 Hugh Kelly 1818 - 1893
.... +Jean Small 1822 - 1910

    James Jordan married Jane, daughter of Robert and Jane (McKeown) Anderson of Ballymoney in 1774. He was a boot and shoemaker in Main Street, Ballymoney.
    Their daughter Mary married James Culbertson, possibly of Ballywattick. Her husband died in 1810 and their daughter Jane went to live with her grandfather James Jordan in Main Street. Jane married William, son of William and Ann Young of Trench, in 1828 in 1st Ballymoney Presbyterian Church.
    Their daughter Catherine married a Mr. Johnston and died in 1811. Her children James and Mary also went to live with their grandfather in Main Street.
    Their daughter Jenny (or Jane) married William Kelly and had three children. Jane died as an infant, another Jane was living with her mother at her grandfather's house in 1817 and Hugh was born around the time of his mother's death.

JORDAN

GRAVE no. 230

Robert Jordan Ballymoney
Died
12. April 1864 AE 79
His wife
Jane Hopkins, died 8. Feb 1855
AE 63
Their children
Catherine, died 11. May 1851
AE 25
William John died 5. June 1886
AE 49
Jane died 23. Sep. 1897
AE 75
Mary died 1. Feb 1898
AE 73
Marianne died 30. Dec 1899
AE 67
Robert died 16. Dec 1902
AE 74
Bessie, widow of the late Samuel Boyd
Died 11. Sep. 1907 aged 74 years.
James, died 8. Dec. 1909
aged 90 years
His wife, Catherine Stewart
died 28. May 1920, aged 84 years

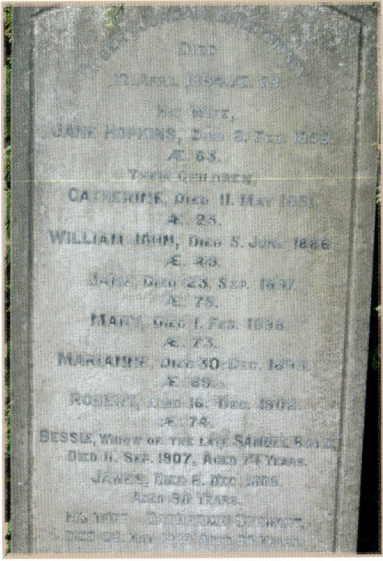

1 Robert Jordan 1784 – 1864
. +Jane Hopkins 1799 - 1859
...... 2 James Jordan 1820 - 1909
.... +Catherine Stewart 1836 - 1920
.... 3 Hugh Stewart Jordan 1862 -
.... 3 William Jordan 1868 -
...... 2 Jane Jordan 1822 - 1897
...... 2 Mary Jordan 1824 - 1898
...... 2 Catherine Jordan 1826 - 1851
...... 2 Robert Jordan 1828 - 1902
.... +Mary Bratt 1834 - 1882
.... 3 Alice Jordan 1863 -
...... 2 Elizabeth Jordan 1832 - 1907
.... +Samuel Boyd
...... 2 Martha Jordan 1835 - 1884
.... +David Perry 1830 -
.... 3 Jane Hopkin Perry 1868 -
...... 2 William John Jordan 1837 - 1886
.... +Rebecca Mary Porter 1848 -
.... 3 William Jordan 1873 -
...... 2 Marianne Jordan 1839 - 1899
.... +Samuel Craig McElroy - 1914
..............see grave 388

Robert, a merchant and son of James and Jane (Anderson) Jordan of Ballymoney married Jane, daughter of William and Eliza Hopkins in 1819 in 1st Ballymoney Presbyterian Church.

Their children James, Catherine and Robert emigrated to U.S.A. In 1851. Catherine died shortly after her arrival and is buried in Long Island. James returned to Ballymoney two years later and set up in business as a building contractor. He married Catherine, daughter of Hugh and Elizabeth (Taggart) Stewart of Kilrea in 1861 in Finvoy Presbyterian Church.

Their daughter Bessie married Samuel, son of William Boyd in 1853 in 1st Kilraughts Presbyterian Church and had four daughters.

Their daughter Martha married David, son of Samuel Perry, in 1866 in 1st Ballymoney and moved to Birkenhead.

BEERS

GRAVE no. 231

Erected
in loving memory
of Margaret Beers
Castle St., Ballymoney
Died 18th Dec. 1929
and her daughter Mary Ann
died 27th Jan. 1946

Margaret was the daughter of Robert and Eliza Beers of Culduff and was baptized in St. Patrick's Parish Church in 1838. Mary Ann Beers was born at Fairhill, Ballymoney in 1869 and was the daughter of Margaret Beers and John Taylor, a farmer from Glennylough.

MITCHELL

GRAVE no. 232

Erected to the memory
of Thos Mitchell A.M.
Of Ballymoney who
departed this life on
the 11th of January 1815
aged 20 years
About the same time
he concluded his
college education
His short life and it is
hoped his preparation
a blessed immortality
Blessed are the dead
who die in the Lord

There were six Mitchells recorded in Ballymoney in 1803, Rev Benjamin, James, John, Robert, Thomas and William.

Thomas was not a son of Benjamin as he married Mary Moore in 1801.

James (or Jack) was married to Esther, was a cooper at the head of town and had children Martha and Archibald present in 1817. These are the most likely parents.

John and Sarah (Blair) Mitchell had one known daughter Rose and would have been too old to have a son born in 1794. There was no Robert present in 1817.

There was a Thomas present in Miller's list who was a blue dyer and Covenanter living in Piper Row but not in 1817.

William and Ann Mitchell had known children of James, Mary (1803), Robert (1805) and Jenny (1807).

UNREADABLE   *GRAVE no. 233*

Small stone – no writing

FERGUSON

GRAVE no. 234

In
memory
of
William Ferguson
late of Drumskey
Died 20th Octr 1895
Mary wife of John Stafford
Died 10th Feb 1907
the said John Stafford
Died 9th March 1919
Aged 86 years
Rose Stafford
Died 10th Nov 1927 aged 48 years

1 James Stafford 1808 - 1870
.. +Ruth 1797 - 1880
.... 2 Rose Stafford 1835 -
.... 2 Mary Stafford 1835 -
.... 2 Jane Stafford 1837 -
.... 2 John Stafford 1833 - 1919
.... +Mary Lamont 1836 - 1907
.... 3 Mary Stafford 1869 - 1951
.... 3 James Stafford 1870 - 1945
.... 3 Frances Anne Stafford 1873 - 1884
.... 3 Rosetta Stafford 1879 - 1927

William, son of John Ferguson, was a farmer at Drumskea. He married Eliza Cromie of Drumskea in 1865 in Drumreagh Presbyterian Church. They had a daughter Jane who married James, son of Joseph Taylor of Carnately in 1894 in Trinity Presbyterian Church. He died in Ballymoney workhouse aged 68.

I can find no relationship between William Ferguson and the Stafford family.

John, son of James and Ruth Stafford, a tailor in Ballymoney married Mary, daughter of John Lamont in 1868 in St. Patrick's Parish Church. They had four children who were all single.

HUNTER

GRAVE no. 235

Erected in memory of
Stephen Hunter,
Ballymoney late of Bushmills
who departed this life 21st June 1838
aged 77 years
and Jane his wife who died 2 March 1834
aged 61 years
In the way of righteousness is life and
In the pathway there of there is no death
Prov. XII 28

Stephen Hunter founded a classical academy at Piper Row (now Charlotte Street) in the early 1800s. According to an old newspaper cutting, preserved in the Historical file at Dalriada School, he was a man of high attainments and the school was attended by the children of a good many of the prominent families of the town and district.

He was a covenanter.

ERSKINE

GRAVE no. 236

In memory of
Adam Erskine, Dunaverney
who died 16th September 1888
Aged 60 years
Also his wife
Maria Wylie
who died 26th July 1932 Aged 91 years
William G. Erskine
Died 6th April 1958, aged 73 years
Alexander C. Erskine
Died 9th Nov. 1964, aged 87 years

1 Adam Erskine 1826 - 1886
.. +Maria Wylie 1841 - 1932
...... 2 Alexander Cameron Erskine 1878 - 1964
...... 2 Robert Erskine 1879 - 1969
.... +Elizabeth Small 1884 - 1966
.... 3 James Wylie Erskine 1917 -
.... +Mary Wallace McMaster 1916 - 2002
.... 3 William Erskine 1919 - 1995
.... +Irene Annetta Getty 1922 - 2003
.... 3 Maria Erskine 1921 -
.... +Robert Simpson 1920 -
.... 3 Adam Alexander Erskine 1923 - 1992
.... 3 Elizabeth Erskine 1926 - 1990
...... 2 William Given Erskine 1885 - 1958

Adam, son of Alexander and Martha (Cameron) Erskine, a farmer at Dunaverney married Maria, daughter of Robert and Elizabeth (Stewart) Wylie (or Wiley), also of Dunaverney in 1876 in 1st Ballymoney Presbyterian Church. Adam died of a perforated stomach ulcer leaving his widow to raise three young children and run a farm. Maria bought the farm next door from another Erskine family and put it into Alexander's name until he was old enough to farm it himself.

Their son Robert inherited another farm at Dunaverney from his uncle James Wylie, but had to pay a share to his aunts. He married Elizabeth (or Lizzie), daughter of James and Mary Jane (Smyth) Small of Kirkhills (see graves 68, 69).

Their eldest son, James Wylie married Mary Wallace, daughter of William Charles and Jane Long (Carson) McMaster of Movenis in 1942 in Drumreagh Presbyterian Church. James worked for a time with the ministry of Agriculture before returning to farm outside Dervock. He emigrated to Australia with his family in the early 1970s, where he still lives.

Their son William married Irene Annetta, daughter of James and Mary (Adams) Getty of Ballyloughbeg, Bushmills in 1948 in Bushmills Presbyterian Church. He farmed at Drumart, moved to Scotland in the 1986, where he died. (These are the author's parents).

Their daughter Myra (or Maria) became a nurse and married Robert, son of Thomas amd Maude (Foster) Simpson of Ballymena.

ERSKINE

GRAVE no. 237

Alexander Erskine
of Dunaverney
Died 6th Novr 1865 aged 83 years
His sister
Margaret
Died 26th March 1859 aged 82 years
His wife
Martha Cameron
Died 31st July 1871 aged 80 years
His son
Alexander Erskine
of Ballymoney
Died 5th Septr 1875 aged 46 years
His daughter
Rose Erskine
Died 22nd June 1880 aged 45 years
His daughter
Elizabeth Erskine
Born 9th April 1833
Died 22nd May 1921
His grand niece Margaret Stuart
Died 18th January 1932

1 Alexander Erskine 1782 - 1865
.. +Martha Cameron 1791 - 1871
...... 2 Adam Erskine 1826 - 1886
.... +Maria Wylie 1841 – 1932
...... 2 Martha Erskine 1827 - 1908
.... +Moore Stuart 1826 - 1903
.... 3 Mary Stuart 1859 - 1946
.... 3 Matilda Stuart 1861 - 1926
.... +Robert Turner - 1922
.... 3 Elizabeth Stuart 1862 - 1890
.... +Robert Adams 1862 – 1931
.... 3 Roseann Stuart 1864 - 1944
.... 3 Thomas John Stuart 1866 - 1952
.... +Sarah Fleming Stuart 1901 - 1976
.... 3 Margaret Stuart 1868 - 1932
.... 3 Sara Jane Stuart 1869 - 1954
.... 3 Adam Moore Stuart 1871 - 1942
.... +Annie Esther Alice Lutz 1877 - 1955
...... 2 Alexander Erskine 1829 - 1875
...... 2 Elizabeth Erskine 1832 - 1921
...... 2 Rose Erskine 1834 - 1880

ERSKINE

GRAVE no. 237

Alexander married Martha, daughter of Archibald and Martha Cameron of Ballymoney in 1825 in 1st Ballymoney Presbyterian Church.

Their eldest son Adam married Maria Wylie (see grave 236).

Their eldest daughter Martha married Moore, son of Thomas and Mary (Moore) Stuart, of Carnany in 1858 in 1st Ballymoney Presbyterian Church. He had previously married Mary, daughter of Henry and Jane (Warnock) Robinson of Newbuildings in 1852. Their daughter Matilda married Robert Turner, a widower and farmer from Tamlaght, Rasharkin in Bushmills Presbyterian Church in 1907. Elizabeth married Robert Adams, watchmaker of Ballymoney (see grave 59). Thomas John stayed on the home farm and married his second cousin Sarah Fleming Stuart in 1937. Margaret lived in Victoria Street with her aunts Elizabeth and Rose and was buried with the Erskines. The rest of the Stuart family are buried in Derrykeighan old graveyard. Sara was a school teacher. Adam Moore (known as Moore) emigrated to U.S.A. in his early twenties as he did not agree with his father's strict religious beliefs.

Alexander, the youngest son of Alexander and Martha, was a merchant in Ballymoney with his Cameron cousins. He was engaged to a Miss Knox, but died of stomach disease. He built a house in Victoria Street and a three storey building next door which was used as an hotel. His sister Elizabeth (or Betty) owned a grocery shop in Victoria Street which she ran with her sister Rose and then her niece Margaret Stuart.

ERSKINE

GRAVE no. 238

ERSKINE

1 Alexander Erskine 1802 – 1887
. +Jean Hamill 1800 -
...... 2 Adam Hamill Erskine 1826 - 1880
.... +Elizabeth Eleanor Martin 1834 - 1872
.... 3 William John Erskine 1857 -
.... 3 Anne Erskine 1860 -
.... 3 Wesley Martin Erskine 1862 - 1914
.... 3 James B. M. Erskine 1862 - 1934
.... 3 Robert Emmett Erskine 1865 -
.... 3 John Alexander Erskine 1870 -
.... 3 Albert Hamill Erskine 1872 - 1930
.... 3 Ellen Jane Erskine 1874 -
...... 2 Alexander Erskine 1827 -
.... Emigrated to U.S.
...... 2 William John Erskine 1828 - 1837
...... 2 Robert Erskine 1829 - 1880
..........Emigrated to U.S.A.
...... 2 Ann Erskine 1834 - 1911
...... 2 William John Erskine 1838 - 1845
...... 2 James Beers Erskine 1842 - 1917
.... +Margaret Crawford 1853 - 1938
.... 3 William John Erskine 1877 - 1904
.... +Lizzie Gilmour 1880 -
.... 3 Jane Hamill Erskine 1880 - 1963
.... +James McBride 1862 - 1919
.... 4 Anna Margaret McBride 1913 - 1988
.... 3 Alexander Erskine 1885 - 1945
.... +Mary Elizabeth Edith Webb 1897 - 1987
.... 3 Male Erskine 1888 - 1888
.... 3 Margaret Sutton Erskine 1889 - 1967
.... +Marshall Moore Thompson 1884 - 1942
.... 3 James Beers Erskine 1892 - 1900

Alexander was the eldest son of William and Ann (Getty) Erskine, farmer in Dunaverney. When he married Jean, daughter of Robert and Jean (Wallace) Hamill in 1825, his father set him up in a weaving business. This branch of the family were known as the weaver Erskines.

Three of their sons emigrated to U.S.A. Their youngest son James took over the business. He married Margaret, daughter of James and Margaret (Sutton) Crawford in 1875 in the Unitarian Church, Ballymoney.

Their son William John married Lizzie Gilmour of Milltown in 1898 and moved to Glasgow.

Alexander, a commercial traveller, married Edith Webb in 1931 in Belfast where he died. Jane married James McBride in 1912 in the Unitarian Church and moved to California where their daughter Anna was born. Jane returned to Ireland after the death of her husband and moved back to Dunaverney. Her sister Margaret also lived there.

GIVIN

GRAVE no. 239

Memorial
of the family of the late John Givin
of Ballymoney
John Givin died at Ballymoney
in 1842 aged 51 years
Mary his wife in 1862 aged 70 years
William their son in 1827 aged 9 years
Samuel in 1844 aged 18 years
And Alexander in 1845 aged 25 years
Jane Givin their daughter died at
New York in 1851 aged 33 years
Also was buried there
Eliza Collins a humble faithful
friend who died in 1857 aged 20 years
Lies here with the family
James Givin their son
Born 11th April 1823
Died at Philadelphia, U.S.A.
9th November 1870

Samuel Given 1758 - 1835
.. +Elizabeth 1759 - 1847
...... 2 John Given 1791 - 1842
.... +Mary Miller 1792 - 1862
.... 3 Jane Given 1817 - 1851
.... 3 William Given 1818 - 1827
.... 3 Elizabeth Given 1819 - 1882
.... +Samuel Gamble 1827 – 1916
.... see grave 240
.... 3 Alexander Marshall Given 1821 - 1845
.... 3 James Given 1823 - 1870
.... 3 Samuel Given 1826 - 1844
...... 2 Alexander M. Given 1798 - 1820
...... 2 James Given 1800 - 1860
.... +Matilda Huey 1807 - 1866
.... see grave 358

John, son of Samuel and Elizabeth Givin of Ballymoney, married Mary, daughter of Samuel Miller, in 1815 in St. Patrick's Parish Church.
  Their only child to marry was Elizabeth (see grave 240). Their son Alexander was a baker.

GAMBLE

GRAVE no. 240

Erected by Samuel Gamble Ballymoney
In memory of
his beloved wife
Elizabeth Givin
Born 11th November 1819
Died 6th June 1882
The said
Samuel Gamble
Born 8th February 1827
Died 19th February 1916

Samuel, son of Alexander and Martha (McIleavey) Gamble married Elizabeth, daughter of John and Mary (Miller) Givin in 1866 in 1st Ballymoney Presbyterian Church. He was a Reformed Presbyterian and they had no children. He was a tradesman.

AGNEW

GRAVE no. 241

Here lyeth the bo
dy of Nivin Agnew
who departed July
the 24 Feb 1690
and the body of Will

Nivin Agnew is possibly related to the Agnew family of Kilwaughter near Larne who were landowners and gentry.

CAMPBELL

GRAVE no. 242

CAMPBELL

1 William Campbell 1833 - 1915
.. +Sarah Jane Freeman 1850 - 1917
...... 2 John Huey Campbell 1872 -
...... 2 Mary McAlister Campbell 1876 -
...... 2 Sarah Jane Campbell 1881 - 1906
...... 2 Elizabeth Campbell 1884 - 1920
...... 2 Joseph Small Campbell 1886 - 1908
...... 2 Samuel Campbell 1888 - 1915
...... 2 Randal Campbell 1892 -
.... +Lizzie Townsend 1893 -
.... 3 Sarah Freeman Campbell 1917 -
.... 3 Elizabeth Townsend Campbell 1918 -
.... 3 Jane Campbell 1920 -
.... 3 Joseph Campbell 1921 -
.... 3 Mary Campbell 1924 - 1925
.... 3 Samuel Campbell 1931 -
.... 3 Margaretta Campbell 1933 -
.... +William Henry Boreland 1930 -
.... 3 William Thomas Campbell 1935 -
.... 3 Ellen Young Campbell 1926 -
.... +Walter Harold Hill 1925 -

This is possibly the burial plot of William Campbell and his family who lived in High Street, Ballymoney.

William was the youngest son of Samuel and Jean (McAlister) Campbell of Ballymoney (see grave 214). He married Sarah Jane, daughter of John and Catherine (Kilpatrick) Freeman in 1871 in Trinity Presbyterian Church.

Their son Randal married Lizzie, daughter of Thomas and Annie (Atkinson) Townsend of Garryduff in 1916 in Garryduff Presbyterian Church. Randal was a tailor and lived in Henry Street.

ANDREWS GRAVE no. 243

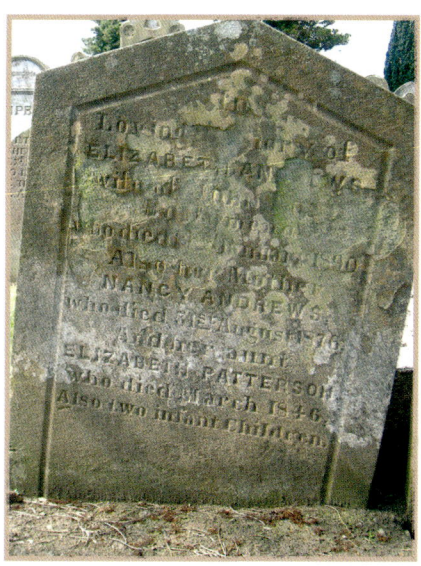

In
loving memory of
Elizabeth Andrews
wife of John Boyd
Ballymena
who died 14th Jan 1890
Also her mother
Nancy Andrews
who died 31 August 1876
And her aunt
Elizabeth Patterson
who died March 1846
Also two infant children

John Boyd, a teacher at Ballygan school, married Elizabeth Andrews, a teacher at Knockintern school in 1843 in 1st Ballymoney Presbyterian Church.

Nancy Andrews died in Ballymena aged 84, at the home of John Boyd.

COCHRAN

GRAVE no. 244

Here lieth
the body of
William Cochran
of Ballygan
who departed this
life the 27th Jan 1811
aged 66 years

There was a William Cochran in the town of Ballymoney in 1803 but no Cochran families at Ballygan. Billy Cochran was sexton of the Meeting House (1st Ballymoney Presbyterian Church).

MCDOWELL

GRAVE no. 245

**John McDowell
Painter**

John Spears McDowell, a painter, married Elizabeth, daughter of David and Margaret Ann (McFarland) McClelland in 1878 in Trinity Presbyterian Church. He had ten children by this marriage. His wfe died in 1904 and he remarried Annie Elizabeth, youngest daughter of James and Eliza Jane (Purdy) McCoubrey in 1905 in St. Patrick's Parish Church and had another eight children.

1 James McDowell 1828 -
.. +Martha Kirkwood
...... 2 John Spears McDowell 1859 - 1922
.... +Elizabeth McClelland 1860 - 1904
.... 3 Mary Elizabeth McDowell 1878 - 1946
.... +Frank McElgin
.... 3 David McDowell 1880 - 1926
.... 3 John Spears Henry Edgar McDowell 1881 -
.... +Ellen McCloy
.... 3 Margaret Jane McDowell 1885 -
.... +James Lorimer Mooney
.... 3 Rosetta McDowell 1889 -
.... 3 Thomas McDowell 1891 -
.... 3 Annie Josephine McDowell 1895 - 1961
.... +Andrew Getty 1894 -
.... 3 James McDowell 1898 -
.... 3 Constance Mary McDowell 1901 - 1918
.... 3 Ellen McDowell 1893 -
...... *2nd Wife of John Spears McDowell:
.... +Annie Elizabeth McCoubrey 1875 -
.... 3 William Francis McDowell 1906 -
.... +Martha
.... 3 Hugh McDowell 1908 -
.... 3 Alexander McDowell 1909 -
.... 3 Quentin McDowell 1911 -
.... 3 Matilda McDowell 1912 -
.... +William George Slocombe
.... 3 Andrew McDowell 1914 - 1916
.... 3 Elizabeth McDowell 1915 -
.... +James Hector Taylor
.... 3 Sarah McDowell 1918 - 1920

MCAYEALE

GRAVE no. 246

1 John McAyeal
...... 2 Daniel McAyeal
.... 3 Robert McAyeal 1748 -
.... +Christian
.... 4 Mary McAyeal
.... +James McCaw
.... 4 Alexander McAyeal 1800 - 1886
.... +Sarah Fullerton 1795 - 1871
.... 4 Elizabeth McAyeal
.... +John McCaw
.... 3 Hugh McAyeal 1750 -
.... 3 Andrew McAyeal 1753 -
.... 4 Thomas McAyeal
.... +Elizabeth Simpson
.... 4 Nancy McAyeal
.... +Thomas Dogherty
.... +Elizabeth Lyons
.... 3 Mary McAyeal 1754 -
.... 3 Alexander McAyeal 1756 -
.... +Margaret
.... 4 Margaret McAyeal 1798 -
.... 4 Martha McAyeal 1800 -
.... 4 John McAyeal 1804 -
.... 4 William McAyeal 1806 -

Here lieth
The remains of Mary McAyeale
who departed this life on
August 15 1708 aged 70 years

This name has many variations of spellings – McAyeale, McYeal, McAyeal. The family were farmers in Tullaghgore for centuries. Daniel was present in 1766 and baptisms of five of his children were found in 1st Ballymoney Presbyterian Church.

Mary, daughter of Robert married James McCaw of Ballywattick in 1820 in 1st Ballymoney and her sister Elizabeth married John McCaw. Her brother Alexander married Sarah, daughter of William and Elizabeth (Wilson) Fullerton of Tullaghgore in 1822 in St. Patrick's Parish Church.

Thomas, son of Andrew McAyeale married Elizabeth daughter of Samuel and Mary Ann Simpson of Forthtown in 1826 in 1st Ballymoney. His sister Nancy married Thomas Dogherty.

BOYD

GRAVE no. 247

?
?
?
Aged
John   ?
?   Jan 17
Also Mary Bell
Daughter of the said
Andrew   ?   Died
?

Nothing more is known of this family.

BOYD GRAVE no. 248

Here lieth the mortal remains of John Boyd
of Ballymoney Mercht who departed this life
11th Feb 1815 aged 86 years

A ? ?
of ? ?
and ? ?
the ? ?
and a s ? ?
He ? ?
more valuable an ? ?
Liberal in his opinions ? ?
Reader be instan? ?
Will make you es? able in ?
happiness in the

HAMILTON   GRAVE no. 249

Beneath this Tablet
is interred all that was mortal of
Richard Hamilton
of Ballymoney, Merchant who
entered into rest on the 19th Feb.
A.D. 1847 aged 63 years
Also of his youngest daughter
Emily Hamilton
who died on the 17th April 1847
aged 4 years
As we have borne this image of this earth
We shall also bear the image of the heaven
Likewise his second daughter
Mary Jane Hamilton
who died on the 26th June 1856
aged 24 years
Blessed are the dead who die in the Lord
Also his third daughter
Sarah Louisa Gilmore
who died 8th March 1864
aged 27 years
Also his son in law John Gawley Gilmore
who died at Ballymoney
13th March 1870 aged 43 years

1 Richard Hamilton 1785 - 1847
.. +Jean Rosborough 1802 - 1880
...... 2 William Orr Hamilton 1823 - 1841
...... 2 Matilda Small Hamilton 1825 - 1905
.... +James Kinnear
              see grave 250
...... 2 Henry West Hamilton 1828 - 1858
.... 3 Mary Hamilton 1856 - 1860
...... 2 Mary Jane Hamilton 1832 - 1856
...... 2 Richard Hamilton 1834 - 1862
...... 2 Sarah Louisa Hamilton 1836 - 1864
.... +John Gawley Gilmore 1826 - 1870
.... 3 Richard Hamilton Gilmore 1862 -
...... 2 William Orr Hamilton 1841 - 1841
...... 2 Anna Hamilton 1842 -
.... +James McIlroy
...... 2 Emily Hamilton 1842 – 1847
...... 2 George Hart Hamilton 1827 -

Richard, son of Robert and Sarah (Murdock) Hamilton of Moneygobbin, married Jean, daughter of Alexander and Martha (Small) Rosborough in 1822 in 1st Ballymoney Presbyterian Church. Richard was an ironmonger and dealer of cutlery as well as postmaster in Ballymoney and lived in Church Street.

Their daughter Matilda married James Kinnear and their son Henry emigrated to Australia where he died (see grave 250).

Their daughter Sarah Louisa married John Gawley Gilmore Esq., a merchant of Balnamore, in 1861 in St. Patrick's Parish Church. They both died young.

Their daughter Anna, twin of Emily who died young, married Dr. James McIlroy of Lavin Cottage in 1872 in 1st Ballymoney Presbyterian Church.

HAMILTON

GRAVE no. 250

Erected
to the memory of Robert Hamilton
Late of Ballymoney who departed
this life 13th Jany 1802 aged 53
Also Sarah Hamilton his wife
Obit. 24th Sepr 1801 aged 56. Also
their sons James Hamilton obit
8th Feby 1806 aged 30. George
Hamilton obit 15th Sept 1815 aged 37
and Thomas Hamilton obit
18th May 1821 aged 37 years
Archibald Hamilton obit 10th Jany
1837 aged 67 years.
John Hamilton obit 18th Feby 1837
aged 65 years
Robert Hamilton Obit 18th Feb. 1827
aged 49 years.
William Orr Hamilton B.L. AM TCD Obit
near Dublin 24th June 1817
aged 38 years
William Orr Hamilton son to
Richard Hamilton Obit 17 May 1841
aged 19 years
William Orr Hamilton infant
Obit June 1841 aged 3 months

HAMILTON

GRAVE no. 250

Robert and Sarah (Murdock) Hamilton had a family of seven sons and a daughter. Their eldest son Archibald married Jane McCurdy. Another son William Orr studied Ancient Classics and became a distinguished scholar in Dublin University. Their only other son to marry was Richard who married Jean Rosborough and named two sons, who died young, after his brother William.

Their only daughter Mary married William McIntyre, an architect and builder, who took contracts all over Co. Antrim for the erection of expensive houses for the nobility and gentry. This family are buried in the Parish Churchyard.

1 Robert Hamilton 1748 - 1802
.. +Sarah Murdock 1745 - 1801
...... 2 Archibald Hamilton 1769 - 1837
.... +Jane McCurdy - 1844
　　　see grave ?
...... 2 John Hamilton 1772 - 1837
...... 2 James Hamilton 1776 - 1806
......2 Robert Hamilkton 1777 - 1827
...... 2 George Hamilton 1778 - 1815
...... 2 William Orr Hamilton 1779 - 1817
...... 2 Richard Hamilton 1785 - 1847
.... +Jean Rosborough 1802 - 1880
............see grave 250
...... 2 Thomas Hamilton 1784 - 1821
...... 2 Mary Hamilton 1776 - 1841
.... +William McIntyre 1772 - 1856
.... 3 Sarah McIntyre 1798 -
.... 3 Jean McIntyre 1803 - 1826
.... 3 Robert McIntyre 1804 - 1844
.... 3 Elizabeth B. McIntyre 1804 - 1897
.... 3 Mary McIntyre 1806 - 1856
.... +James Getty
.... 3 Flora McIntyre 1808 - 1893
.... 3 Sophia O. M. McIntyre 1810 - 1877
.... 3 William Hamilton McIntyre 1812 - 1850
.... +Jane Thomas
.... 3 Thomas McIntyre 1815 - 1863
.... 3 Catherine McIntyre 1820 -
.... +Henry Rowan 1823 -
.... 3 Fanny McIntyre
.... +Thomas Murray

HAMILTON

GRAVE no. 251

Sacred to the memory
of Henry West Hamilton
who died at Bendigo, Victoria
on 13th July 1858
aged 30 years
Also his brother
Richard Hamilton
who died at Ballymoney
15th March 1862 aged 27 years
They that seek me early shall find me
I am the resurrection and the life
Jane Hamilton
wife of Richard Hamilton Senr
and mother of the above
Born 12 August 1802, died 11th May 1880
Also her grand children
Richard Hamilton Kinnear
Born 5th April 1847
Died 22nd Jany 1865
and Jane Kinnear
Born 21st March 1851
Died 24th June 1867

1 Richard Hamilton 1785 - 1847
.. +Jean Rosborough 1802 - 1880
...... 2 William Orr Hamilton 1823 - 1841
...... 2 Matilda Small Hamilton 1825 - 1905
.... +James Kinnear
.... 3 Henry Hamilton Kinnear
.... 3 Mary Hamilton Kinnear
.... +John McCammon
.... 3 James West Kinnear
.... 3 Richard Hamilton Kinnear 1847 - 1865
.... 3 Jane Kinnear 1851 - 1867
...... 2 George Hart Hamilton 1827 -
...... 2 Henry West Hamilton 1828 - 1858
.... 3 Mary Hamilton 1856 - 1860
...... 2 Mary Jane Hamilton 1832 - 1856
...... 2 Richard Hamilton 1834 - 1862
...... 2 Sarah Louisa Hamilton 1836 - 1864
.... +John Gawley Gilmore 1826 - 1870
.... 3 Richard Hamilton Gilmore 1862 -
...... 2 William Orr Hamilton 1841 - 1841
...... 2 Anna Hamilton 1842 -
.... +James McIlroy
...... 2 Emily Hamilton 1842 - 1847

Richard, son of Robert and Sarah (Murdock) Hamilton, was postmaster in Ballymoney. He married Jean, daughter of Alexander and Martha (Small) Rosborough in 1822 in 1st Ballymoney Presbyterian Church.

Their eldest daughter Martha Small married James Kinnear, a merchant of Ballymena, in 1844 in St. Patrick's Church. They had at least five children. She died in Belfast.

Henry West emigrated to Bendigo, Victoria, Australia and died young, as a result of rheumatic fever. His daughter Mary died of diptheria aged three years.

TAGGART GRAVE no. 252

Here lyeth the body
of Jenny Taggart
who departed this
Life the 8 of February
1809 aged 58 years

1 John Taggart
.. +Martha
...... 2 Richard Taggart
.... +Agnes Wallace 1801 -
.... 3 John Taggart 1817 -
.... 3 Robert Taggart 1822 -
.... 3 James Taggart 1825 -
.... +Mary Ann Thompson 1829 -
.... 3 Thomas Taggart 1827 -
.... 3 Nancy Taggart 1830 -
.... +James Thompson
...... 2 John Taggart
.... +Elizabeth Hamilton
.... 3 Samuel Taggart 1820 -
.... 3 Thomas Taggart 1822 -
...... 2 Alexander Taggart

In 1803, John, Richard and William Taggart and their families were living in Tullaghgore. In 1817, families of John, John junior and Richard were living in Forthtown.

NEILL

GRAVE no. 253

Here lyeth the b
ody of John
Neill who dep
arted this
Life May 6 1778
aged 40 years

Neill families have been in the Ballymoney area since the 17th century. John Neile was recorded at Druckendult in 1669. In 1740, present in the area were James, John, James and Thomas and in 1766, Thomas, James, James, John, Hugh, Adam and Adam. In 1766, a James Neil was living at Pharos, Loughguile.

In 1803, Neill families lived at Ballymoney, Cabra, Craigatempin, Cummingston, Druckendult, Dunaverney, Leitrim and Taghey.

This John Neill left a will (see graves 180, 181).

NEILL

GRAVE no. 254

Here lyeth the Body of Thomas Neill who died 24 of May in the year 1779 aged 50 years

This Thomas Neill was recorded in the area in 1760. He may have lived at Dunaverney as there was a Neill family living there in 1817.

Thomas and Margaret (Neill) Neill had children Catherine, Janet, Mary (1806), Margaret, Thomas (1814) and John (1817).

DOHERTY

GRAVE no. 255

In memory of
John R. Doherty
Artigoran who died
15th Feby 1890
aged 65 years
Also
His daughter Jane
died September 1864
aged 6 years

1 John Brown 1804 -
. +Jean Haggerty 1800 -
...... 2 Jean Brown 1822 -
.... +James Culbertson
...... 2 John Brown 1824 -
...... 2 Ebby Brown 1827 -
...... 2 Mary Brown 1829 -
.... +John Doherty 1824 - 1890
.... 3 Jane Doherty 1858 - 1864
.... 3 Joseph Lawence Rentoul Doherty 1870 -
.... 3 Frederick George Alfred Doherty 1873 -
...... 2 Jenny Brown 1832 -
...... 2 James Brown 1835 -

John Doherty, a weaver, married Mary, daughter of John Brown and Jean (Haggarty) Brown of Ballywattick in 1855 in St. James Presbyterian Church.
He died in Artigoran of consumption.

MITCHELL

GRAVE no. 256

Underneath lie the remains of
James Mitchell
Builder, Ballymoney
who died 10th Sept 1831
Aged 29 years

This tomb was erected by
Agnes Mitchell
in memory of her dear husband
Joseph P. Mitchell
Solicitor, who died 28th June
1858, aged 31 years
Agnes Mitchell
died 8th March 1879
Aged 54 years

1 William Mitchell 1775 - 1813
.. +Ann
...... 2 James Mitchell 1802 - 1831
.... +Mary Park - 1851
.... 3 Joseph Park Mitchell 1826 - 1858
.... +Agnes T. Cameron 1825 - 1879
.... 3 Mary Jane Mitchell 1828 -
.... +David Cunningham
...... 2 Esther Mitchell 1803
.... +John Cameron 1792 -
...... 2 Robert Mitchell 1805 -
...... 2 Jenny Mitchell 1807 -
...... 2 Mary Mitchell 1808 -

James, son of William and Ann Mitchell, was a builder in Ballymoney and married Mary Park.
   Their son Joseph Park Mitchell, a solicitor, lived in Charles Street, Ballymoney and died of tuberculosis. He married Agnes Thompson, daughter of Daniel and Grace (Scott) Cameron of Church Street in 1852 in 1st Ballymoney Presbyterian Church in 1852. After her husband died, she was a China, Glass and Earthenware dealer. She died in Rathfarnham, Dublin.
   Their daughter Esther married John, son of Archibald and Martha Cameron of Church Street.

TOLAND

GRAVE no. 257

Erected
In memory of
Archibald Toland, Secon
who died 21st Nov 1888
aged 82 years
His wife Mary Elder
Died 6th Jan 1863
Aged 51 years
Their son Samuel
Died 15th August 1914
aged 78 years
Their son James
Died 6th March 1918
Aged 73 years

1 Archibald Hart Trolland 1806 - 1888
.. +Mary Elder 1811 - 1863
...... 2 Samuel Trolland 1835 - 1914
...... 2 Isabella Trolland 1837 - 1916
.... +Robert Steen Lyons 1838 - 1909
.... 3 Mary Ann Lyons 1874 - 1959
.... 3 James Lyons 1880 - 1918
.... 3 Samuel L. Lyons 1881 - 1957
.... +Mary Gaston 1886 - 1944
.... 4 Margaret Lyons
.... 4 Isobel Lyons
.... 4 Marian Lyons 1930 -
.... +John Fleming 1911 -
...... 2 John Trolland 1842 -
...... 2 James Trolland 1844 - 1918
.... +Anne Hanna 1860 -
.... 3 Samuel Elder Trolland 1881 -
.... +Mary Jane Twaddle
.... 4 Sarah Elizabeth Trolland 1917 -
.... 4 Annie Maud Trolland 1914 - 1984
.... +William James Overend
.... 4 Elizabeth Trolland 1921 - 1924
.... 4 Jack Trolland 1923 - 1927
.... 4 William James Trolland 1918 -
.... +Mary Jane Twaddell
.... 3 Eliza Jane Trolland 1883 -
.... 3 David Trolland 1885 -
.... 3 Mary Trolland 1886 -
.... 3 James Trolland 1888 -
.... 3 Isabella Trolland 1890 -
.... 3 William Trolland 1892 -
...... 2 Matilda Trolland 1850 -

Toland is also known as Trolland. Archibald Hart, son of James and Jean Trolland, married Mary, daughter of John and Isabella Elder of Forttown in 1835 in 1st Ballymoney Presbyterian Church.

Their daughter Isabella married Robert Steen, son of James and Nancy (Lamont) Lyons of Ballygan in 1872 in 1st Ballymoney.

Their son James married Anne, daughter of David and Jane (Sayers) Hanna of Secon in 1892 in St. James Presbyterian Church.

JAMISON

GRAVE no. 258

Erected
in
memory of
Rachael
Beloved daughter of
Robert Jamison
who died 1st Jan 1881
aged 14 years
Also his son
James Reid
who died 23rd April 1887
aged 7 years

1 Robert Jamison 1840 - 1912
.. +Rachael Wallace 1843 - 1912
...... 2 Rachael Jamison 1866 - 1881
...... 2 Mary Jamison 1871 - 1888
...... 2 Thomas Wallace Jamison 1873 -
...... 2 Robert Jamison 1875 -
.... +Kathleen Esdale
.... 3 Robert Wallace Jamison 1900 -
.... 3 Isabel Ingram Jamison 1905 -
.... 3 Rachael Wallace Jamison 1907 -
.... 3 Laura Christina Loiuse Jamison 1909 -
...... 2 Isabella Edith Jamison 1877 - 1891
...... 2 James Reid Jamison 1880 - 1887
...... 2 Lavetina Louise Jamison 1884 -
...... 2 James Albert Jamison 1888 - 1889

Robert Jamison was a plumber and gas fitter in High Street, Ballymoney. He married Rachael Wallace and had eight known children. Several of the children died young of tuberculosis.

His son Robert worked with his father in the business, married Kathleen Esdale from Scotland and a family of four. They were members of 1st Ballymoney Presbyterian Church.

NEIL

GRAVE no. 259

?
lieth the body of
John Neil who
departed this life
18 day of ?
?

STIRLING

Erected
by
John Stirling
of Ballygabbin in memory
of his son John who departed
this life 18th March 1849
aged 42 years

John was the son of John Stirling (see grave 262).

STIRLING

GRAVE no. 261

In memory of
Eliza
wife of Alex Stirling Ballygobbin
who died 8 Feb 1855
Also
His two infant daughters Margt
and Anna aged respectively 5 years
and twenty years
The above named Alex Stirling
who died 2 Sept 1875
aged 65 years
Their son
John Hamilton Stirling B.A.
Sometime minister of Castlederg
Presbyterian Church
Died 18 Aug 1908 aged 58 years

1 William Moore
...... 2 Eliza Moore - 1855
.... +Alexander Stirling 1810 - 1875
.... 3 Margaret Stirling
.... 3 John Hamilton Stirling 1850 - 1908
.... 3 Anna Stirling

Eliza, daughter of William Moore of Inchinagh, married Alexander Stirling in 1846 in Trinity Presbyterian Church.

STIRLING

GRAVE no. 262

Erected by
Alex to the memory of his father
John Stirling late of Ballygobbin
who departed this life 29th May 1860
aged 85 years
Also
of his mother who died 27th Sept 1851
aged 77 years
and also
of his brother Hamilton
who died Jan 1851
Grace Ann Kelly
second wife of
Alexander Stirling
died 30th September 1908
aged 90 years

1 John Stirling 1775 - 1860
...... 2 Alexander Stirling 1810 - 1875
.... +Eliza Moore - 1855
.... 3 Margaret Stirling
.... 3 John Hamilton Stirling 1850 - 1908
.... 3 Anna Stirling
...... *2nd Wife of Alexander Stirling:
.... +Grace Ann Kelly 1818 - 1908
...... 2 John Stirling 1806 - 1849
.... 3 John Stirling
.... +Eliza Rachael McFadden 1840 -
.... 3 David John Stirling
.... +Matilda Picken 1834 -
.... 4 Jane Picken Stirling 1862 -
.... +Stewart Christie
.... 3 Anna Stirling - 1892
.... +Daniel Cooper - 1897
.... 4 William John Cooper - 1932
.... +Agnes Nevin 1865 - 1937
.... 4 Samuel Nevin Cooper - 1892
...... 2 Hamilton Stirling - 1854

John Stirling had at least three children.
His son Alexander married Eliza Moore who died in 1855 and then again to Grace Ann, daughter of Robert Kelly of Carracloughy, in 1858 in Roseyards Presbyterian Church.
Another son John married and had three known children. His son John married Elizabeth Rachael, eldest daughter of Rev. Joseph McFadden of Ballymoney, in 1860 in 1st Ballymoney Presbyterian Church. His son David John married Matilda, daughter of James and Jean (McCay) Picken of Taghey, in 1862 in St. James Presbyterian Church. His daughter Anna married Daniel, son of John Cooper of Bendooragh, in 1855 in Trinity Presbyterian Church.

UNREADABLE *GRAVE no. 263*

A small stone with no inscription

DIXON

GRAVE no. 264

Here
lieth the body
of John Dixon
late of Culduff
who departed
this life 25
Feb 1812
aged 65 years

1 John Dixon 1746 - 1812
...... 2 John Dixon
.... +Mary Patterson
.... 3 Mary Dixon 1820 - 1907
.... +John Speers 1800 - 1881
.... 3 Mary Dixon 1817 -
.... 3 Ester Dixon 1813 -
...... 2 Leslie Dixon
.... +Bess
.... 3 John Dixon
.... 3 Ann Dixon
.... 3 Margaret Dixon
.... 3 Sarah Ann Dixon

John Dixon possibly had two sons Leslie and John. In 1803, there were two John Dixons at Culduff. John junior married Mary, daughter of Henry and Rose Patterson (or Pattison) of Culduff.

BOYD

GRAVE no. 265

Here lieth the
body of John Boyd late
of Culbrim who departed
this life the 25 January
1809 aged 79 years
Also his mother in law
Mary Scot
who departed this life
The 24 of December
1808 aged 98 years

John Boyd was present in Culbrim in 1803. In 1817, there was only an Abraham present (see grave 85). In 1822, Samuel and Mary (Dinsmore) Boyd were present. He was possibly a nephew of John. Samuel was born in 1790 at Macfin.

HUTCHINSON

GRAVE no. 266

This a large walled enclosure with no headstones or information. It is reputed that it belonged to the Hutchinson family (see graves 140, 141, 142).

MCCAW

GRAVE no. 267

Erected
by
Jane McCaw Ballymoney
in memory of her father
Alexander McCaw
who died 9th June 1852 aged 64
Also her beloved and affectionate mother
Jane McCaw
who died 2nd October 1876 aged 58 years

Alexander McCaw was a farmer at Ballaghmore and married Jane Wilson in 1839. Alexander joined the Unitarian Church in Ballymoney in 1838. They had two daughters, Jane born in 1840 and Esther born in 1842. After Alexander died Jane and her daughters moved into Ballymoney and owned a grocer's shop in Church Street.

Their daughter Jane died in Ballymoney in 1916.

LESLIE

GRAVE no. 268

Underneath this stone are
deposited the mortal
Remains of Mary wife of
James Edmund Leslie Esq of
Leslie Hill who departed this
life on the first day of
February 1847
Also James Leslie Esqr.
J.P. D.L. Her husband
who departed on the 17th day of
April 1847
also
of Henry Leslie Esq. J.P.
Their second son
He died on the 5 day of Jul 1864
Also
of E.D. Leslie D.L.
Who died on the 27th day of
January 1904

1 James Leslie 1768 - 1847
.. +Mary Ann Cuppage 1768 - 1847
...... 2 James Edmund Leslie 1800 - 1881
.... +Sarah Sandford 1800 - 1864
    see grave 271
...... 2 Henry Leslie 1803 - 1864
.... +Harriet Ann Hammer - 1887
.... 3 Henry Hammer Leslie 1853 -
.... 3 Mary Emily Leslie
.... 3 Helen Leslie
.... 3 Constance Harriett Leslie - 1885
.... 3 Edith Leslie
...... 2 Francis Seymour Leslie 1805 - 1881
...... 2 John Charles William Leslie 1808 - 1877
...... 2 Bartholew George Leslie 1812 - 1815

    James Leslie of Leslie Hill, married Mary, daughter of Adam Cuppage of Dunacloney, in 1795 and had five known children.
    Their son Henry married Harriet Ann Hammer of Holbrook Hall, Suffolk in 1849 and lived at Seaport House, Portballintrae. He died at Leslie Hill. They had five children.

LESLIE

GRAVE no. 269

Underneath are deposited the remains of James Leslie Esqr. Of Leslie Hill J.P. Who departed this life 1st April 1796

There is no photograph available for this grave.

James Leslie was the son of Rev. Peter and Jane (Dopping) Leslie of Ahoghill, and brother of Re. Edmund Leslie, Vicar of Dunluce, who married Jane McNaughton of Benvarden in 1735 in Dublin. He was High Sheriff of Co. Antrim in 1759.

Edmund had four sons, Peter who died in London, Bartholomew who died in India in 1790 and Edmund who also died in India in 1793 and James (see grave 268).

The Leslie family originally lived in a castle at Prospect about a mile from Ballymoney town. The castle was demolished about 1766, when the present "Leslie Hill" house was built.

There was a William Leslie at Cloughorr who married Mary Leslie about 1688. They had three daughters, Sarah, Margaret and Elizabeth. Sarah Leslie married John Corry, M.P., and had children Martha, Leslie, Sarah, Mary and Elizabeth. Leslie Corry died in 1741. Martha married her cousin Edmund Leslie M.P. and changed his name to Corry. He died in 1764.

The youngest daughter of John Corry married Archibald Hamilton and then James Leslie. This James Leslie, son of Peter, and nephew of Edmund inherited the Leslie Hill estates.

He had no family so his nephew James, son of Edmund, then inherited Leslie Hill.

```
1 Peter Leslie
.. +Jane Dopping
...... 2 James Leslie - 1796
.......... +Sarah Fleming
.......... *2nd Wife of James Leslie:
.......... +Elizabeth Corry 1715 - 1791
...... 2 Edmund Leslie 1735 -
.......... +Jane McNaughton
............... 3 James Leslie 1768 - 1847
................... +Mary Ann Cuppage 1768 - 1847
............... 3 Peter Leslie
............... 3 Bartolomew Leslie - 1790
............... 3 Edmund Leslie - 1793
...... *2nd Wife of Edmund Leslie:
.......... +Eleanor Portis
_____

1 Henry Leslie
...... 2 William Leslie - 1698
.......... +Mary Leslie - 1701
............... 3 Sarah Leslie
................... +John Corry
...................... 4 Martha Corry
.......................... +Edmund Leslie - 1764
...................... 4 Sarah Corry
.......................... +Galbraith Lowry
...................... 4 Mary Corry
.......................... +Margetson Armour
...................... 4 Leslie Corry - 1741
...................... 4 Elizabeth Corry 1715 - 1791
.......................... +Archibald Hamilton - 1753
............................... 5 Archibald Hamilton 1754 - 1774
.......................... *2nd Husband of Elizabeth Corry:
.......................... +James Leslie - 1796
```

LESLIE

GRAVE no. 270

Underneath this stone are
deposited the remains of
Sarah
wife of James Edmund Leslie Esq.
Of Leslie Hill
who departed this life on the
20th day of December 1861
Also of
James Edmund Leslie Esq., J.P. D.L.
who died on the
17th day of January 1881

Sarah Sandford was born in Edinburgh and married James Edmund, son of James Leslie Hill, in 1823. They had a family of eleven.

LESLIE

GRAVE no. 271

Near to this was laid to rest
the body of
Edmund Douglas Leslie, D.L.
Late Lt Col. (Hon.Col.)
4th Battn Royal Irish Rifles
eldest surviving son of
James Edmund and Sarah Leslie
of Leslie Hill
He was born on the 22nd Sept 1828
and died on the 27th January 1904

"The memory of the just is blessed"
Proverbs 10.7

1 James Edmund Leslie 1800 - 1881
.. +Sarah Sandford 1800 - 1864
...... 2 James Sandford Leslie 1824 - 1829
...... 2 Henry Erskine Leslie 1825 - 1829
...... 2 Edmund Douglas Leslie 1828 - 1904
...... 2 Daniel Sandford Leslie 1830 - 1830
...... 2 Seymour Montague Leslie 1835 - 1891
.... +Louisa Graham - 1869
.... 3 Sarah Harriet Penelope Leslie 1867 - 1957
.... 3 James Graham Leslie 1868 - 1949
.... +Grace Brodie
   *2nd Wife of Seymour Montague Leslie:
.... +Sarah A. 1842 -
.... 3 Edmund V. Leslie 1880 -
...... 2 Francis McNaughton Leslie 1838 - 1909
...... 2 Erskine Douglas Leslie 1839 - 1839
...... 2 Frances Mary Leslie
.... +Andrew George Gilmore
...... 2 Mary Wilhemina Leslie
...... 2 Sarah Agnes Leslie
.... +Herbert Bruce Sandford
...... 2 Jane Elizabeth Leslie

James Edmund, eldest son of James and Mary Ann (Cuppage) Leslie of Leslie Hill, married Sarah Sandford of Edinburgh in 1823. He was High Sheriff for Co. Antrim in 1854.

Five of their sons died young. Edmund Douglas was their third son and a bachelor. He inherited Leslie Hill Estate.

Their fifth son Seymour Montague married Louisa Graham of Berkshire in 1866 and had two children. She died in 1869 and he was married again to Sarah Alice Vincent in 1878 by whom he had another son and daughter. He worked in London. His eldest son James Graham married Grace Brodie in 1901.

LESLIE

GRAVE no. 271a

In remembrance
of
Col. E. D. Leslie
of Leslie Hill
who died on the 27th January 1904

His brother, sisters and nephew
have erected these
stones and restored the adjacent
family memorials
Easter 1904

See graves 268, 269, 270, 271

KNOX

GRAVE no. 272

Erected
to the memory of
Hugh Knox Secon
who departed ths life Jan 1859
aged 64 years

1 Hugh Knox 1795 - 1859
.. +Agnes Ramsay
...... 2 Margaret Knox 1820 - 1863
...... 2 James Knox 1822 - 1916
.... +Matilda Cochrane
.... 3 Matilda Knox 1861 -
.... 3 Hugh Knox 1864 - 1868
.... 3 John Knox 1866 -
.... +Jane Boyd 1871 -
.... 4 James Boyd Knox 1898 -
.... +Ieria H. ? 1901 - 1985
.... 4 Minnie Brown Knox 1900 -
.... +John Stuart
.... 4 Jeannie Knox 1902 - 1968
.... 3 Nancy Knox 1868 -
.... 3 Samuel Knox 1874 -
.... 3 Thomas Greer Knox 1876 -
...... 2 Nancy Knox 1823 -
...... 2 Alexander Knox 1827 -
...... 2 Hugh Knox 1827 -
...... 2 John Knox 1830 -
...... 2 Jane Knox 1835 - 1885

Hugh, son of James and Elizabeth Knox of Secon, married Agnes Ramsay of Newbuildings in 1st Ballymoney Presbyterian Church.

Their son James married Matilda, daughter of Samuel and Matilda (Martin) Cochrane, in 1861 in 1st Ballymoney Presbyterian Church. James was a woollen draper in Main Street. They are buried in Knock Road Cemetery.

WALLACE

GRAVE no. 273

Here lyeth the B
ody of Thoma
s Wallace
who died Decem
ber the 1 1768 ag
ed ? ? years

This is probably the father or uncle of James Wallace of Booton (see grave 274) and possibily related to the Wallace family of Newbuildings.

WALLACE

GRAVE no. 274

Erected by
the executors of the late
Thomas Wallace of Bootan
17th August 1877 aged 80 years
? his brother
? Wallace
? aged 68 years
? Wallace
? August 1857 aged 66 years

1 James Wallace
.. +Agnes
...... 2 Abigail Wallace 1784 - 1832
.... +John Pinkerton 1766 - 1824
              see grave 57
...... 2 John Wallace 1787 - 1859
.... +Fanny McAlister
.... 3 Alexander Wallace 1818 -
.... 3 John Wallace 1823 -
.... 3 William Wallace 1825 -
.... 3 Thomas Wallace 1826 -
.... 3 Fanny Wallace 1828 -
.... 3 Samuel Wallace 1830 -
.... 3 Robert Park Wallace 1832 -
.... 3 William Wallace 1834 -
.... 3 Robert Wallace 1837 -
...... 2 Mary Wallace 1790 -
.... +Samuel Dunn
.... 3 Nancy Dunn 1811 -
.... 3 Mary Dunn 1814 -
.... 3 Sarah Dunn 1816 -
.... 3 Jean Dunn 1818 -
.... 3 Abigail Dunn 1820 -
...... 2 James Wallace 1791 - 1857
...... 2 Thomas Wallace 1797 - 1877
...... 2 Jean Wallace 1799 -
...... 2 Sarah Wallace 1800 -
...... 2 Agnes Wallace 1801 -
.... +Richard Taggart
.... 3 John Taggart 1817 -
.... 3 Robert Taggart 1822 -
.... 3 James Taggart 1825 -
.... +Mary Ann Thompson 1829 -
.... 3 Thomas Taggart 1827 -
.... 3 Nancy Taggart 1830 -
.... +James Thompson

Thomas Wallace was a farmer and the son of James and Agnes Wallace of Booton. He made a will, naming his nephews and nieces which confirmed some of the relationships.

His eldest sister Abigail married John Pinkerton of Secon (see grave 57), his sister Mary married Samuel Dunn of Booton and his youngest sister Agnes married Richard, son of John and Martha Taggart of Forthtown. His eldest brother John married Fanny McAlister.

YOUNG

GRAVE no. 275

Here lieth
the body of
Mary Young
who departed
this departed
this life 8 of Jan
1821 aged 14 years

1 Adam Young
.. +Elizabeth Campbell
...... 2 James Young 1810 -
...... 2 Mary Young 1806 - 1821
...... 2 Elizabeth Young
...... 2 Samuel Young
...... 2 Margaret Young 1820 -
...... 2 William Young 1821 -

This is possibly the daughter of Adam and Elizabeth (Campbell) Young. Elizabeth was possibly the daughter of Samuel Campbell of Ballymoney.

MURPHEY

GRAVE no. 276

Sacred
to the memory of
James Murphey late
of Ballymoney who departed
this life 7 Nov 1846
Aged 84 years
Also his wife Isabella
who departed this life the
26th May 1846 aged 82 years

These are possibly the parents of Clarke Murphy (see grave 28).

CROZIER   GRAVE no. 277

Erected
to the memory of
William Crozier
late of Ballymoney
who died the 25th Feby 1853
Aged 53 years

William Crozier was a police sergeant in Ballymoney when he married Mary Osborne in 1827 in 1st Ballymoney Presbyterian Church. In 1846, he was a spirit merchant in Charles Street. His widow continued the business after his death.

HENRY

GRAVE no. 278

Erected
to the memory of
Susannah Henry
the beloved wife of
Alexander Henry
of Ballymoney
who departed this life
Novr 14th 1854 aged 37 years
Also the above
Alexander Henry
who departed this life on Friday
November 21st 1863 aged 53 years

1 Alexander Henry 1810 - 1863
.. +Susanna Archibald 1817 - 1854
...... 2 Jane Henry 1844 -
...... 2 Elizabeth Henry 1846 -
.... +John Biggart
.... 3 John Henry Biggart 1875 -
.... 3 Sarah Biggart 1876 -
.... 3 Robert Biggart
...... 2 John Henry 1847 -
...... 2 Ann Henry 1849 -
.... +James Best
.... 3 Sarah Best
...... 2 Alexander Henry 1850 -
...... 2 Nancy Henry 1848 -
...... 2 Susannah Henry 1853 -
.... +William Campbell
.... 3 Mary Jane Campbell
.... 3 Robert Campbell
.... 3 Catherine Campbell
.... +William John Pinkerton
...... 2 Sarah Henry 1854 -

    Alexander Henry was the son of John and Jane (Robinson) Henry of Bravellan and was a spirit dealer in Main Street, Ballymoney. He married Susannah Archibald.
    Ann married James Best in 1875 in 1st Ballymoney and for a time occupied the Royal Hotel, Ballymoney. After her husbands death Ann sold her business interests.
    Susannah married William Campbell, a prosperous farmer in Vow and their daughter Catherine married William John Pinkerton of Maddyduff in 1899 in Ballymoney Reformed Presbyterian Church.

MCCOOK

GRAVE no. 279

Sacred
to the memory of
Mrs Jane McCook
who departed this life 5th Sep 1825
aged 75 years
This tablet is raised by her son
John McCook
As a tribute of affection
to the best of mothers

Martha A M Hart. Her father
John Hart
19th August 1911 aged 71 years

Jane McCook owned a calico shop in Main Street, Ballymoney. Martha Hart, a child died in Coleraine in 1904. Her father John also died in Coleraine.

KNOX GRAVE no. 280

Here lieth the remains of Nancy Knox wife of Robert Knox of Curry siskan who departed this life 16 Oct 1829 aged 33 years

Robert, son of William and Margaret Knox, married Nancy, daughter of Robert and Agnes (Sharpe) Dick of Garry in 1st Ballymoney Presbyterian Church in 1822 (see grave 281).

KNOX

GRAVE no. 281

Sacred to the memory
of William Knox
late of Currysisken
who departed this
life the 19th day of
December 1819 aged
72 years
Also Margaret his
wife who died the
15th May 1825 aged
72 years

1 William Knox 1747 - 1819
.. +Margaret 1753 - 1825
...... 2 Margaret Knox 1794 -
.... +Andrew Wright 1781 - 1857
.... 3 John Wright
...... 2 Robert Knox 1796 -
.... +Mary Peacock - 1868
.... 3 William John Knox 1841 - 1888
...... *1st Wife of Robert Knox:
.... +Nancy MacAfee 1849 - 1921
.... 3 Elizabeth Knox 1843 -
.... +Nancy Dick 1796 - 1829
...... 2 William Knox 1798 -
...... 2 Andrew Knox 1800 -
.... +Mary MacAfee 1810 -
.... 3 William Knox 1821 - 1874
.... +Isabella McKay
.... 3 Robert Knox 1822 - 1863
.... 3 Margaret Knox 1825 - 1898
.... +Joseph Boyd 1817 - 1898
.... 3 Mary Ann Knox 1827 - 1907
.... +Andrew Wright 1817 - 1872
.... 3 Andrew Wright Knox 1829 -
.... 3 Andrew Knox 1832 -
.... 3 John Leslie Knox 1834 -
.... +Jane Moody 1840 -
.... 3 James Knox 1836 -
.... +Eliza Jane Boyd

William, son of Robert Knox, was a farmer at Currysisken and married Margaret. They had at least four children.

Their daughter Margaret married Andrew, son of Joseph and Mary (Curry) Wright in 1825.

Their eldest son Robert married Nancy, daughter of Robert and Agnes (Sharpe) Dick of Garry in 1822 in 1st Ballymoney Presbyterian Church (see grave 280). He married secondly to Mary Peacock and they had two children.

Their youngest son Andrew married Mary, daughter of Robert and Mary Ann MacAfee of Currysisken in 1821 in 1st Ballymoney Presbyterian Church.

TAYLOR

GRAVE no. 282

Sacred to
the memory of
Isaac Taylor
who departed
this life the 28 of
June 1817 aged
72 years
This stone was
erected here by
James Thompson
in gratitude for
faithful service
for 20 years in
their family

Isaac Taylor probably came from Ballinamoney, as there were other Isaac Taylors from that area.

HILL

GRAVE no. 283

Here
lyeth the bo
dy of Adam Hill
who departed
this life March
the 4th 1776 aged
66 years

There was a baptism recorded in 1st Ballymoney Presbyterian Church in 1750 of a William, son of Adam Hill. There was an Adam Hill present in 1740 and 1766.

In 1803, Adam and William Hill were living at Kirkhills. Adam had daughters Margaret (1803) and Ann (1805) baptised in 1st Ballymoney. William married Nancy and had children John (1808) and Jane (1810).

BORLAND

GRAVE no. 284

To the memory of
William Borland Snr
late of Landhead who
departed this life
The 1st day of December 1801
in the 54th year of his age
Also John Borland the son of
the above William Borland
who departed this life the 2nd
day of ? 1817 aged 20 years
Also Rachael Borland wife to the
above William Borland who
Departed this life the 14th
? ? 1819 aged ?

1 William Borland 1747 – 1801
 +Rachael -1819
...... 2 William Borland
.... +Alice McElderry 1780 -
.... 3 Robert Borland 1812 -
.... 3 Rachael Borland 1814 -
.... 3 Sarah Borland 1816 -
.... 3 Jean Borland 1819 -
.... 3 William Borland 1821 -
...... 2 Robert Borland 1780 -
.... +Jean Cochrane
.... 3 Rachael Borland 1814 -
.... 3 William Borland 1816 -
.... 3 John Borland 1820 -
.... 3 Elizabeth Borland 1822 -
.... 3 Charlotte Borland 1824 -
.... 3 William Borland 1827 -
...... 2 John Borland 1797 - 1817
...... 2 Alexander Borland
.... +Charlotte Neill
.... 3 Thomas Borland 1824 -
.... 3 William Borland 1827 -

William Borland had four known children. His son William married Alice, eldest daughter of Robert and Sally (Lyle) McElderry of Leitrim.
Robert married Jean Cochrane and Alexander married Charlotte Neill.

RICHART

GRAVE no. 285

Memento Mori
Here lays the
body of Will
iam Richart
who depart
ed this life
Jun the 3 1739
and aged 33
years 1741

Fergus and John Richard (as it is now spelt) were present in Kirkhills in 1666, James and William in the area in 1766 and the family were in the townlands of Ballyrobin, Cummingstown, Greenville and Kirkhills in 1803.

THOMSON

GRAVE no. 286

Sacred to the memory of
Adam Thomson
of Ballymoney Merchant who
Died the 3rd day of March 1817
aged 60 years
He was distinguished through life
for industry and integrity which
gained him the esteem of the
Worthy and endeared him to
His family and friends
Render immune his virtues and
you will meet in like Reward of a
Respected life and a Happy death
Here also lie the remains of his
daughter Ann who died the 10
Jan 1796 aged 9 months
Also his son Samuel who died
11th October 1796 aged 7 years 10 months

In the next grave lie the remains
of Agnes relict of the above
Adam Thomson who departed
this life on the 17th January 1821
in her 68th year. A sincere Christian

THOMSON

GRAVE no. 286

Adam was a merchant in Main Street.

Their son David was a farmer at Greenshields and their son Robert a farmer at Islandmore, Kilraughts.

Their son Benjamin was a boot and shoemaker in Church Street. His son James Ross became a respected surgeon in Ballymoney. His son Adam, a merchant, married Anne, daughter of Thomas and Elizabeth (Nevin) McElderry of Ballymoney in 1858 in Trinity Presbyterian Church. Their first daughter Roseanna died young and their second daughter Rose Anna married Archibald, son of Robert McCurdy of Lismorluss, Bushmills in 1848 in St. James Presbyterian Church.

Their son Adam, a physician in Ballymoney, married, firstly, Elizabeth Rogers in 1823 in 1st Ballymoney and had a daughter Letitia and secondly Sarah Gault of Kilrea in 1836 in St. James Presbyterian Church. Their son William George became a doctor.

Their daughter Jane married James, son of John and Ann Cramsie (see grave 371).

Their son James married Alicia Greene (see grave 286a).

```
1 Adam Thomson 1757 - 1817
.. +Agnes 1752 - 1821
...... 2 David Thomson 1777 - 1823
.......... +Elizabeth 1780 - 1841
...... 2 Robert Thomson 1778 - 1868
...... 2 Benjamin Thomson 1780 - 1838
.......... +Rose 1786 - 1861
.............. 3 James Ross Thomson 1816 - 1901
.............. 3 Rose Anna Thomson 1820 - 1825
.............. 3 Adam Thomson 1822 - 1900
.................. +Anne McElderry 1833 - 1928
.............. 3 Roseanna Thomson 1826 - 1854
.................. +Archibald McCurdy 1807 - 1885
.............. 3 David McCurdy Thomson 1830 - 1856
...... 2 Adam Thomson 1784 - 1864
.......... +Elizabeth Rogers 1808 - 1834
.............. 3 Letitia Marshall Thomson 1829 - 1879
...... *2nd Wife of Adam Thomson:
.......... +Sarah Gault 1813 -
.............. 3 Roseann Ross Thomson
.............. 3 William George M. Thomson 1840 -
.............. 3 Adam Thomson 1847 - 1861
.............. 3 Robert Henry Thomson 1854 -
...... 2 Jane Thomson 1785 - 1850
.......... +James Cramsie 1786 - 1855
            see grave 371
...... 2 Samuel Thomson 1789 - 1796
...... 2 Ann Thomson 1795 - 1796
...... 2 James Thomson 1798 - 1866
.......... +Alicia Greene 1800 - 1868
            see grave 286a
```

THOMPSON

GRAVE no. 286a

James Thompson Esquire
died 22nd January 1866 Aged 67 years
Underneath this tablet is also deposited
the mortal remains of his relict
Alicia Thompson
Aged 65 years
who departed this life on the 25th day of April
in the year of our lord 1868

    James was the son of Adam and Agnes Thomson, merchant of Ballymoney. He married Alicia Greene, probably the daughter of Rev. Dean Greene, rector of St. Patrick's Church, Ballymoney, in 1832 in St. Patrick's. They didn't seem to have any family.
    James took over the ownership of Balnamore Mills around 1836 from the Bryan family. He had previously been the first manager of the Belfast Bank in Ballymoney. The mills did not do well under his management and the Bryan family took over the mills again. He died at Balnamore.

CALDWELL

GRAVE no. 287

This stone was e rected by William Caldwell to the memory of Jane his former wife who was here in terred on the 17th of Augt 1773 aged 39 years and two of his children

William Caldwell had sons George and Joseph baptised in 1754 and 1755 in 1st Ballymoney Presbyterian Church.

CALDWELL

GRAVE no. 288

Here lieth
the body of
Mary Caldwell
wife to John Caldwell
of Corysisken
who departed this
life May the 21 in the
year of our Lord
1796 aged 71 years
Also the above named
John Caldwell
who departed this
life 8th June 1799
aged 85 years

John Caldwell had sons John, Adam and James baptised in 1753, 1754 and 1759 in 1st Ballymoney Presbyterian Church.

BIGGART

GRAVE no. 289

Sacred to the memory
of John Biggart
Late of Cabrough
who departed this life
the 5th of May 1823
Aged 52 years

1 John Biggart 1771 - 1823
.. +Mary ?
...... 2 William Biggart 1790 -
.... +Hannah Hopkins
.... 3 Ellen Biggart 1814 -
.... +William White 1793 -
.... 3 Solomon Biggart 1816 - 1818
.... 3 Solomon Biggart 1818 -
.... 3 Jean Biggart 1822 -
.... 3 William Biggart 1826 - 1911
.... +Nancy 1829 - 1910
.... 3 Margaret Biggart 1824 -
.... +James McAuley 1823 -
.... 3 Ann Biggart 1829 -
.... 3 Hanna Biggart 1831 -
.... 3 Peggy Biggart 1834 -
.... 3 John Biggart 1836 -
.... 3 Hanna Biggart 1840 -
...... 2 John Biggart
...... 2 Sarah Biggart 1807 -
.... +Alexander Dripps
.... 3 John Dripps 1836 -

The Biggart Family were farmers in Cabra from at least the early 1700s. There were also Biggart families at Bendooragh, Artigoran, Currysisken and Druckendult. The Biggarts are all buried in the same area in the old churchyard but there seemed to be several headstones missing.

Ellen Biggart married William, son of John and Mary White of Artigoran.

Margaret Biggart married James, son of Alexander and Margaret (Falkoner) McAuley of Cloint in 1858 in 1st Ballymoney Presbyterian Church.

Sarah Biggart married Alexander Dripps also of Cabra.

BIGGART

GRAVE no. 290

Erected in memory of
Solomon Biggart
of Cabra
who departed this life on the 1
of Feb 1818 aged 2 years

Solomon was the son of William and Hannah (Hopkins) Biggart of Cabra. He was named after his maternal grandfather Solomon Hopkins, also a farmer at Cabra. Another son was named Solomon later in 1818 which was common practice at this time.

BIGGART

GRAVE no. 291

In
loving memory of
William H. Biggart
of Cabra
Born 1st October 1870
Died 22nd December 1903
Also his mother Nancy Biggart
Died 5th April 1908
aged 72 years
Also his father William Biggart
Died 13th August 1911
aged 84 years

1 William Biggart 1790 -
.. +Hannah Hopkins 1796 - 1873
...... 2 Ellen Biggart 1814 -
.... +William White 1793 - 1883
.... 3 John White 1834 - 1912
.... +Jane Biggart 1830 -
.... 3 William White 1836 -
.... 3 Robert White 1837 -
.... 3 Hannah White 1839 -
.... +James Curry
.... 3 Solomon White 1841 -
.... 3 Jane White 1842 -
.... +William White 1840 -
.... 3 Marshall White 1847 -
.... +Mary Curry
.... 3 James Moore White
...... 2 Solomon Biggart 1816 - 1818
...... 2 Solomon Biggart 1818 -
...... 2 Jean Biggart 1822 -
...... 2 William Biggart 1826 - 1911
.... +Nancy McIlroy 1829 - 1910
.... 3 William H. Biggart 1870 - 1903
...... 2 Margaret Biggart 1824 -
.... +James McAuley 1823 -
...... 2 Ann Biggart 1829 -
...... 2 Hanna Biggart 1831 -
...... 2 Peggy Biggart 1834 -
...... 2 John Biggart 1836 -
...... 2 Hanna Biggart 1840 -

William Biggart was born at Cabra, son of William and Hannah (Hopkins) Biggart, and died at Inchadohill. He was a farmer. He married Nancy, daughter of Thomas McIlroy of Glasgort, Agivey, in Moneydig Presbyterian Church in 1869.

GRIFFITH

GRAVE no. 292

Benjamin Griffith
of Ballymoney died on the
5 of April 1824 aged 76 years
His wife Margaret Griffith
Died on the 3 of April 1809
aged 33 years
Also
Their son James Griffith
Died on the 22 of May 1827
aged 23 years

1 Benjamin Griffith 1747 - 1824
.. +Margaret ? 1776 - 1809
...... 2 Alexander Griffith 1798 -
...... 2 Margaret Griffith 1799 - 1864
.... +James Ussher 1811 - 1874
...... 2 John Griffith 1802 -
.... +Miss McKeown
...... 2 James Griffith 1804 -

Benjamin Griffith was a book and leather seller in Main Street, Ballymoney. His daughter Margaret married Rev. James Ussher, Presbyterian Minister of St. James Church Ballymoney, in 1840 in Carncullagh Presbyterian Church, Dervock.

FYNES

GRAVE no. 293

FYNES

1 James Fines 1802 - 1873
...... 2 William Fines 1826 - 1894
.... +Elizabeth Chestnutt 1822 - 1900
.... 3 Thomas Fines 1854 - 1926
.... +Jane McCoubrey 1855 - 1925
.... 4 Bessie Matilda Fines 1875 -
.... 4 William Fines 1877 - 1879
.... 4 Thomas Fines 1880 - 1924
.... +Rachael Stewart 1885 - 1962
.... 4 Mary Jane Fines 1882 - 1893
.... 4 James Fines 1883 - 1909
.... 4 John Fines 1886 - 1929
.... +Mary ?
.... 4 Hugh Fines 1889 - 1910
.... 4 Isobel McAlonan Fines 1892 - 1925
.... 3 James Fines 1857 - 1935
.... +Mary Knipe 1867 - 1952
.... 4 William Fines 1888 - 1911
.... 4 James Fines 1890 -
.... 4 Robert Chestnutt Fines 1893 -
.... 4 Thomas Fines 1895 - 1895
.... 4 Edward Fines 1897 -
.... 4 David Fines 1902 - 1913
.... 4 George Fines 1908 - 1970
.... 4 Hugh Fines 1910 -
.... 4 Andrew C. Fines 1913 - 1977
...... 2 John Fines 1820 - 1900
.... +Jane 1822 - 1897
.... 3 William Fines 1846 -
.... 3 Robert Fines 1849 -
.... 3 John Fines 1852 -
.... 3 Thomas Fines 1854 -
.... 3 Margaret Jane Fines 1857 -
.... 3 David Fines 1862 -
.... 3 Mary Fines 1865 -
.... 3 Thomas Fines 1865 - 1886
...... 2 James Fines 1827 -
...... 2 Catherine Fines 1829 - 1880
...... 2 Margaret Fines 1833 -

This family also was spelled Fines. They were members of St. Patrick's Parish Church. James Fines, a car man, had five known children and died in Meetinghouse Street in 1873.

His eldest son William married Elizabeth, daughter of Robert Chestnutt in 1850 in Ballymoney Registry Office and they lived at 21, Castle Street.

Their eldest son Thomas was a pork dealer and married Jane, eldest daughter of James and Eliza Jane (Purdy) McCoubrey in 1874 in St. Patrick's Parish Church.

Their son James, a cooper and then a pork dealer, married Mary, daughter of David Knipe of Balnacree in 1887, also at St. Patrick's.

KNOX

GRAVE no. 294

In memory of
William Knox
who died 21 May 1855
aged 42 years
Also of his son James
who died 15 June 1867
aged 14 years
His wife Elizabeth
Died 8th October 1900
Their daughter Mary
who died 13 Nov 1911 aged 65 years
Their daughter Jane
Died 16th December 1931 aged 79 years

1 John Knox 1769 - 1866
.. +Mary 1767 - 1861
...... 2 Jane Knox
.... +David Smith
...... 2 John Knox
.... +Mary Peacock
.... 3 Robert Knox
...... 2 Elizabeth Knox 1802 - 1891
.... +Samuel Peacock 1798 - 1875
...... 2 William Knox 1813 - 1855
.... +Elizabeth Gamble 1819 - 1900
.... 3 Mary Knox 1846 - 1911
.... 3 James Knox 1848 - 1867
.... 3 Ellen Knox 1849 -
.... 3 Jane Knox 1852 - 1931
.... 3 John Knox 1854

William, son of John and Mary Knox of Islandmore, Kilraughts, married Elizabeth, daughter of William Gamble in 1845 in 1st Ballymoney Presbyterian Church. Elizabeth may have been a daughter of William, son of Alexander and Catherine Gamble, but no marriage or children could be found in church records.

They had five children. After her husband's death, Elizabeth became a postmistress at Drumart. Elizabeth and her daughter Mary died at Drumart. Her daughter Jane died in Ballymoney.

William's sister Jane married David Smith, farmer of Islandmore in 1845. His brother John married Mary, daughter of Thomas and Ann (Richard) Peacock of Roseyards in 1838 in Armoy Presbyterian Church and his sister Elizabeth married Samuel Peacock, Mary's brother.

GAMBLE

GRAVE no. 295

Sacred
to the memory of
Thomas Gamble
late of Ballymoney who
departed this life the 14th of
December 1829 aged 44 years
Also John Gamble who
departed this life the 27th of
July 1830 aged 37 years
Joseph Gamble
Died 12th April 1853 aged 76 years
William Gamble
Died 30th October 1866 aged 82 years

1 Alexander Gamble 1762 - 1798
.. +Catherine Maclure 1760 - 1845
...... 2 Joseph Gamble 1781 - 1858
...... 2 William Gamble 1783 - 1866
...... 2 Thomas Gamble 1785 - 1829
...... 2 Alexander Gamble 1790 - 1863
.... +Martha McIlreavy 1797 - 1874
             see grave 296
...... 2 John Gamble 1793 - 1830
...... 2 Adam Gamble 1795 -
.... +Catherine McCahon
.... 3 Alexander Gamble 1821 -
.... 3 Catherine Gamble 1821 -
.... 3 Thomas Gamble 1823 -
...... 2 Samuel Gamble 1797 -
.... +Martha Culbertson 1798 - 1822

Alexander and Catherine (McClure) Gamble had a family of seven. Their son Alexander married Martha McIlreavy (see grave 296).

Their son Adam married Catherine McCahon and had three children in Ballymoney.

Their son Samuel married Martha, daughter of James Culbertson of Ballywattick in 1821 in 1st Ballymoney Presbyterian Church.

GAMBLE

GRAVE no. 296

Erected
to the memory of
Alexander Gamble of Ballymoney
who departed this life the 23rd May 1863
aged 72 years
Martha McIlrevy, his wife who departed
this life 11th January 1874 aged 76 years
Alexander Gamble, their son who departed
this life at Coleraine
13th December 1853 aged 33 years
Martha Gamble, their daughter
Born 10 September 1830 died 7th October 1883
William John Gamble, Ballymoney
Died 12th December 1916 aged 81 years
James Gamble
Died 20th April 1919 aged 80 years

1 Alexander Gamble 1790 - 1863
.. +Martha McIlreavy 1797 - 1874
...... 2 Alexander Gamble 1820 - 1853
...... 2 John Gamble 1822 -
...... 2 William Gamble 1823 -
...... 2 Samuel Gamble 1827 - 1916
.... +Elizabeth Given 1819 - 1882
...... 2 Martha Gamble 1830 - 1883
...... 2 Robert Gamble 1833 -
...... 2 William John Gamble 1835 - 1916
...... 2 James Gamble 1837 - 1919

    Alexander, son of Alexander and Catherine (McClure) Gamble married Martha, daughter of John and Hannah (Quigg) McIlreavy in 1819 in 1st Ballymoney Presbyterian Church.
    Their only child who was recorded as getting married was Samuel who married Elizabeth, daughter of John and Mary (Miller) Givin (see grave 240).

GAMBLE

GRAVE no. 297

In memory
of
Alexander Gamble
of Ballymoney
an insurgent of "98
Who was executed and buried
in Ballymoney Market Square
on 25th June 1798
aged 35 years
Raised and re-interred here
on 14th September 1883
Catherine Maclure
His wife
Died 14th February 1845
aged 84 years
They rose in dark and evil days
to right their native land

An inhabitant of Ballymoney, a soap worker called Alexander Gamble had been in Ballymena on the 8th June at the time of the 1798 troubles in Ireland, and although he was not a leader, he was arrested on his return and condemned to be executed. It is said that he was offered a reprieve, provided that he would disclose the names and identities of his comrades. He refused to be be an informer and consequently was hanged, after being kept in custody for a fortnight. His execution, along with another man called Caulfield, took place from the tower of the Market House at the Ballymoney Diamond, both bodies being buried in Main Street immediately at the foot of the tower.

In 1882, when excavations were being made in the Ballymoney streets, the remains of two coffined bodies were unearthed at the tower a few feet below the street. Samuel and William J. Gamble, grandsons of Alexander, and sons of Alexander junior, were informed and took possession of their grandfather's body. It was re-interred in the Old Churchyard and a tomb erected (see graves 295).

MCILREVY

GRAVE no. 298

Sacred
to the memory of John
McIlrevy late of Booton
who departed this life
April 10th 1849 aged 87

1 John McIlreavy 1761 - 1849
.. +Hannah Quigg
...... 2 Martha McIlreavy 1797 - 1874
.... +Alexander Gamble 1790 - 1863
...... 2 John McIlreavy 1798 - 1861
.... +Christina
...... 2 Hannah McIlreavy 1801 -
.... +Daniel Simpson 1799 -
...... 2 Ann McIlreavy 1802 -
...... 2 James McIlreavy 1804 -
...... 2 Henry McIlreavy 1806 -
...... 2 Jean Moore McIlreavy 1808 -
...... 2 Robert McIlreavy 1810 -
...... 2 Agnes McIlreavy 1812 -
...... 2 Daniel McIlreavy 1814 - 1872
.... +Catherine Getty 1816 - 1881
...... 2 Rachael McIlreavy 1818 -

John and Hannah (Quigg) McIlrevy was alabourer at Heagles and Bootown and had a large family.

His eldest daughter Martha married Alexander, son of Alexander and Catherine (McClure) Gamble in 1819 in 1st Ballymoney Presbyterian Church (see grave 297).

Another daughter Hannah married Daniel, son of Samuel and Mary Ann Simpson of Forthtown, in 1825 in 1st Ballymoney.

His youngest son Daniel married Catherine, daughter of John and Mary Ann Getty of Ballywattick, in 1835 in 1st Ballymoney. They emigrated to Brooklyn, New York about 1848.

MCBRIDE

GRAVE no. 299

Erected by
James McBride of
Ballymoney in
memory of his father
Archey McBride
who departed this life
21st of November 1841
aged 26 years
The above James McBride
departed this life on the
21st of February 1865
aged 29 years

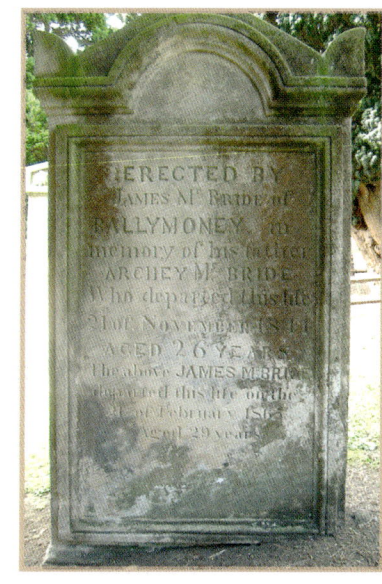

1 James McBride
.. +Agnes Kennedy
...... 2 Mary McBride
...... 2 Ann McBride 1802 -
...... 2 Bess McBride 1804 -
...... 2 John McBride 1806 -
...... 2 Robert James McBride
...... 2 Mary Ann McBride
...... 2 Martha McBride
...... 2 Archibald McBride 1815 -
.... +Harriet Davison
.... 3 James McBride 1835 - 1865
.... 3 Nancy Ann McBride 1836 -
.... 3 Mary Ann McBride 1839 -
...... 2 Jane McBride 1817 -
...... 2 Rachael McBride 1821 -

Archibald McBride was the son of James and Agnes (Kennedy) McBride of Polintamney. He married Harriet Davison and had three children, James, Nancy Ann and Mary Ann, all baptized in 1st Ballymoney Presbyterian Church.

PICKEN

GRAVE no. 300

Sacred to the memory of
James Picken Taughey
who departed this life 19th
December 1854
aged 62 years
? ? ? ?

1 James Picken 1792- 1854
.. +Jean McCay 1794 - 1866
...... 2 William Picken 1817 -
.... +Jean Moore 1819 - 1891
...... 2 Mary Ann Picken 1819 -
.... +William McKay
.... 3 Sarah J. McKay 1848 -
.... +Robert John Blakely 1834 -
.... 3 Mary Field McKay
.... +Henry Connolly
.... 3 Robert John McKay
.... +Mary Johnston
...... 2 Jane Picken 1821 -
.... +Samuel Chestnutt 1815 - 1905
.... 3 William Chestnutt
.... +Sarah Hanna 1860 -
.... 3 Samuel Chestnutt 1858 - 1907
.... +Elizabeth McLaughlin 1865 - 1931
.... 3 Alexander Chestnutt - 1946
.... +Letitia Blair - 1953
.... 3 Lizzie Chestnutt
.... +James Crawford
...... 2 James Picken 1823 - 1913
...... 2 Maria Picken 1826 -
...... 2 Elizabeth Picken 1831 -
.... +Samuel Dougherty
...... 2 Matilda Picken 1834 -
.... +David John Stirling
.... 3 Jane Picken Stirling 1862 -
.... +Stewart Christie
...... 2 Martha Picken 1834 -
...... 2 Nancy Picken 1838 -
.... +William John Barr

James, son of William Picken of Taghey married Jean McCay (or McKay) about 1815.

Their eldest son William married Jean, daughter of John and Letitia (Watt) Moore of Drumaheglis in 1841 in 1st Ballymoney Presbyterian Church.

Their eldest daughter Mary Ann married William, son of Daniel McKay of Bellisle in 1846 in 1st Ballymoney.

Their daughter Jane married Samuel, son of John Chestnut of Ballygan in 1st Ballymoney.

Their daughter Elizabeth married Samuel, son of John Dougherty of Ballywattick, in 1861 in 1st Ballymoney.

Matilda married David John, daughter of John Stirling of Ballygabbin in 1862 in St. James Presbyterian Church.

Their youngest daughter Nancy married William John, son of James Barr of Ballygan in 1869 in St. James.

MCINTYRE

GRAVE no. 301

Erected by
Jane McIntyre
to the memory of her father
James McIntyre
who died 11th February 1864
Aged 70 years
Also her sister Mary
who died 11th December 1876
aged 52 years

Nothing is known about this family.

RAMSAY

GRAVE no. 302

Memento Mori
To the memory of
Adam Ramsay late
of Dunnyverny who
departed this life
the 26th day of April
1786 aged 49 years
Also his son John
who departed the 2nd
of Jany 1783 aged 22

The Ramsay family were no longer at Dunaverney in 1803, though Thomas, John and James were at Kirkhills and John and William at Culramoney.

RAMSAY

GRAVE no. 303

Erected
in memory of
James Ramsay
of Culramoney
Who died 18th July 1876
Aged 71 years
Also of his sister Martha
Who died 15th April 1882
Aged 82 years
and of his sister Mary
Who died 26th Aug 1888

1 William Ramsay
.. +Jane - 1855
...... 2 Henry Ramsay
...... 2 Hugh Ramsay - 1871
.... +Mary Tweed - 1881
.... 3 William James Ramsay 1850 - 1905
.... +Sarah Boyd Thomson 1870 - 1929
.... 4 William James Ramsay 1900 - 1981
.... +Mary Wallace 1902 - 1994
.... 4 Hugh Ramsay 1904 - 1977
.... +Evelyn Elizabeth Hazlett 1907 - 1985
.... 3 Mary Jane Ramsay - 1907
.... +William Robinson 1846 - 1930
.... 3 James Ramsay
...... 2 Margaret Ramsay
.... +William Ferguson 1801 - 1884
...... 2 Thomas Ramsay 1786 - 1864
...... 2 Martha Ramsay 1800 - 1882
...... 2 James Ramsay 1805 - 1876
...... 2 Mary Ramsay 1806 - 1888

James was a son of William and Jane Ramsey of Culramoney. His brother Hugh, married Mary, daughter of Robert Tweed of Ballyboyland in 1848 in Carncullagh Presbyterian Church.

Their eldest son William James married Sarah Boyd, daughter of William and Marianne (Boyd) Thomson of Dunaverney in 1893 in Trinity Presbyterian Church.

There is still a Ramsay family living at Culramoney.

HANNAH

GRAVE no. 304

Here lies
Martha Hannah
Who died 26 May 1867
aged 89 years
Also her grandson
James Hannah
Who died 16th Octr 1863
aged 19 years

It is not known where this family were from. The main Hannah (or Hanna) families were from Clintyfinnan, Drumaheglis (see grave 383) or Secon.

RAMSAY

GRAVE no. 305

Sacred
to the memory
of William Ramsay
of Cullermoney
whose ashes mingle
with those of three children
Thomas Jenny and John
who died at years of maturity
with those of his wife
Jane Ramsay

1 William Ramsay
.. +Jane - 1855
...... 2 Henry Ramsay
...... 2 Hugh Ramsay - 1871
.... +Mary Tweed - 1881
     ..... 2 Margaret Ramsay
.... +William Ferguson 1801 - 1884
...... 2 Thomas Ramsay 1786 - 1864
...... 2 Martha Ramsay 1800 - 1882
...... 2 James Ramsay 1805 - 1876
...... 2 Mary Ramsay 1806 - 1888

William and John Ramsay were present in Cullermoney in 1803. William and Jane Ramsay had six known children (see grave 303).

GALBREATH   GRAVE no. 306

Here lieth the body of
Hector Galbreath
Late of
Drunkendult
who departed this
life the 4th day of
May 1778 aged 67
years.   His wife
Sarah
aged 58 years

```
1 Hector Galbraith 1711 - 1778
.. +Sarah
...... 2 John Galbraith 1740 - 1821
.......... +Letitia Marshall 1760 -
............... 3 Elizabeth Galbraith 1780 -
................... +Robert Taylor 1780 -
....................... 4 John Taylor 1811 -
........................... +Ellen Hay 1815 -
....................... 4 Rachael Taylor 1813 -
........................... +Alexander Cubitt
....................... 4 Samuel Taylor 1815 -
........................... +Elizabeth Warnock
....................... 4 Bess Taylor 1817 -
....................... 4 Robert Taylor 1820 -
........................... +Catherine Warnock
....................... 4 Sally Jean Taylor 1823 -
....................... 4 William Taylor 1825 -
............... 3 Sarah Galbraith 1785 -
................... +William McAnaul
............... 3 Nancy Galbraith 1787 -
................... +Major Scott 1790 - 1869
....................... 4 John Scott
........................... +Ellen Laughlin
....................... 4 Elizabeth Scott
........................... +William Orr
............... 3 Jane Galbraith 1789 - 1863
................... +George Washington Thompson 1787 - 1840
                    see grave 81
...... 2 Hector Galbraith 1763 - 1827
...... 2 Mary Galbraith
.......... +Benjamin Thompson
...... 2 James Galbraith
...... 2 George Galbraith
...... 2 Sarah Galbraith 1756 -
```

Hector and Sarah Galbraith (the usual spelling) had six known children.

Their son John married Letitia Marshall and had four daughters. Elizabeth married Robert, son of Samuel Taylor of Inchinagh. Sarah married William McAnaul of Dunluce in 1826 in 1st Ballymoney Presbyterian Church. Nancy married Major Scott of Mostragee in 1819 in Roseyards Presbyterian Church. Their daughter Jane married George Washington, son of William and Letitia Thompson of Greenshields and they emigrated to Illinois.

Their son Hector emigrated to Bucks, Pennsylvania.

ADAMS

GRAVE no. 307

Erected
to the memory of the late
John Adams of Ballymoney
who died on the 8 day of
February 1818 aged 57 Rachel
his wife died on the 10 day of
April 1836 aged 77
Samuel Adams son of the
above died 22nd Oct. 1830
aged 30.
John Adams died 7th Novr 1850 aged 55
Elizabeth Adams died 27th December 1866
aged 70. Adam B. Adams died 21st August 1872
aged 75. Wm Adams died 2nd May 1876 aged 72

Also the following members
of the family of
Wm Adams of Ballymoney
James died 27th January
1848 aged 3 years Charles
died 28th July 1853
aged 6 years. John died
17th June 1857, aged 20 years
Samuel, died 15th October 1863
aged 22 years

John Adams, a butcher in Ballymoney married Rachael, daughter of Adam and Rose Blair. Their eldest son Adam, married Bess, daughter of John and Elizabeth (Bateson) Robinson of Culduff and had no known children.

Their youngest son William married Catherine Cubitt of Ganaby and was a pork merchant.

1 John Adams 1761 - 1818
.. +Rachael Blair 1759 - 1836
...... 2 Elizabeth Adams 1796 - 1867
...... 2 Adam Blair Adams 1797 - 1872
.... +Bess Robinson
...... 2 John Adams 1795 - 1850
...... 2 Samuel Adams 1800 - 1830
...... 2 William Adams 1803 - 1876
.... +Catherine Cubitt 1812 - 1893
.... 3 John Adams 1837 - 1857
.... 3 Adam Adams 1839 -
.... 3 Samuel Adams 1841 - 1863
.... 3 James Adams 1844 - 1848
.... 3 Charles Adams 1846 - 1853
.... 3 Thomas Adams 1850 - 1877
.... 3 Charles Adams 1854 -
.... 3 Elizabeth Adams 1858 -
.... +John Henderson
.... 3 Jane Adams
.... +James Cooper 1838 -
.... 4 Margaret Jane Cooper 1866 -
.... 4 Samuel Adams Cooper 1869 -
.... 4 James Rankin Cooper 1871 -
.... 4 Catherine Cubitt Cooper 1873 -
.... 4 Elizabeth Janetta Cooper 1877 -
.... 3 Alexander Kerr Adams 1843 -

HUTCHINSON — GRAVE no. 308

Underneath lieth
The body of Mary Hut
chinson who departed
this life Nov 1774 aged
72 years also Alice
Dobbin who departed
this life the 9 day of
Feb 1802 aged 59 years

TEMPLETON

GRAVE no. 309

Here lieth the bo
dy of Adam Templeton who departed this life
March the ? Aged
78 1772 Also his wife ? Who departed this life
October 21 176?

In 1669, an Adam Templeton was present in Bellisle, near Dervock. There was a baptism of an Adam in 1753 to an Adam in 1st Ballymoney Presbyterian Church. There were no Adam Templetons found in the Ballymoney in 1740. In 1803 there were two, one in Derrykeighan and one in Cuppindale and in 1825 there is a John senior and Adam in Cuppindale. An Adam of Cuppindale left a will with probate in 1814.

BLACK

GRAVE no. 310

Underneath lieth the
Body of John Black
late of Glenstall
aged 61 years
Also of Thom^S Black
his son aged 25 years
And were both here
interred on the 5th
Day of April 1767
Mary Black relict of
the sd John Black d
eparted this life the
18 day of April in the
year of our lord 1795
aged 86 years
George Black son of
the sd John and Mary
Black departed this
life the 18 day of March
in the year of our lord
1809 aged 76 years

1 John Black 1706 - 1767
.. +Mary 1709 - 1795
...... 2 George Black 1733 - 1809
...... 2 Thomas Black 1742 - 1767
...... 2 Henry Black 1753 -

In 1766, a John Black was present in Glenstall, in 1803, there was a George and in 1825 there was a John. A baptism of Henry was recorded in 1753 in 1st Ballymoney Presbyterian Church, son of a Mr. John Black. They were a wealthy family.

UNREADABLE   *GRAVE no. 311*

Overturned and broken

MITCHELL   GRAVE no. 312

In memory
of
John Mitchell
Ballymoney
Died 13th May 1883
Aged 72 years
Also his beloved wife
Margaret
Died 31st May 1867
Aged 54 years
Also their son John
Died 21st Sept 1866
Aged 28 years

Erected by their son James

1 John Mitchell 1811 - 1883
.. +Margaret Haggarty 1812 - 1867
...... 2 Sarah Mitchell 1832 -
...... 2 John McCullough Mitchell 1834 - 1866
...... 2 Sarah Jane Mitchell 1836 -
...... 2 Nancy Mitchell 1839 -
...... 2 James Mitchell 1841 -
.... +Elizabeth McGlade
...... 2 Robert Mitchell 1847 -

    John Mitchell was a grocer in Main Street, Ballymoney. He was possibly the son of Samuel and Martha Mitchell, publican in Main Street.
    John married Margaret, daughter of William and Jean (McCay) Haggarty of Secon. When his wife Mary died in Balnamore, he was a weaver.
    Their son James married Elizabeth, daughter of Philip McGlade of Balnamore in 1865 in Drumreagh Presbyterian Church.
    There is also another grave erected to this family which is now broken and lying flat (see grave 336).

CAMERON

GRAVE no. 313

In memory
of
Archibald Cameron
of Ballymoney
Died 11 October 1860 aged 53 years
Rachael his beloved wife
Died 30 July 1857 aged 43 years
His daughter Hannah Jane
Died 25 October 1856 aged 18 years
His son James
Died at Arcachon, France
18th July 1870 aged 21 years
His son Daniel
Died at Parramatta, Australia
30th July 1889 aged 53 years
His son John Leslie
Died 23rd June 1891 aged 51 years

1 Archibald Cameron 1807 - 1860
.. +Rachael Leslie 1814 - 1857
...... 2 Daniel Cameron 1836 - 1889
...... 2 Hannah Jane Cameron 1838 - 1856
...... 2 John Leslie Cameron 1840 - 1891
...... 2 Sally Ann Cameron 1843 - 1856
...... 2 James Cameron 1849 - 1870

Archibald was the son of Daniel and Grace (Scott) Cameron of Church Street, Ballymoney (see grave 374). He married Rachael Leslie in 1835 in 1st Ballymoney Presbyterian Church and was a carpenter, though was later an architect.

Their eldest son Daniel emigrated to Australia, died in Parramatta and is buried in Waverley Cemetery, Sydney. Their eldest daughter Hannah Jane died of consumption. Their second son John Leslie was a merchant in Ballymoney and died in Portstewart. None of their children married.

GAMBLE

GRAVE no. 314

Sacred
to the memory of Robert Gamble of Ballymoney who departed this life the 13th January 1824 aged 62 years
Also his wife Jane Gamble who died 7th February 1855 aged 97 years

1 James Gamble
.. +Agnes ? - 1785
...... 2 Robert Gamble 1752 - 1824
.... +Jean Patton 1758 - 1855
.... 3 Nancy Gamble 1778 -
.... +? Kennedy
.... 3 John Gamble 1779 -
.... 3 Sarah Gamble 1782 - 1856
.... 3 Margaret Gamble 1784 - 1856
.... 3 James Gamble 1786 - 1836
.... 3 Martha Gamble 1788 - 1822
.... 3 Mary Gamble 1791 -
.... +Archibald Carson 1796 -
.... 4 James Carson 1829 -
.... +Mary Gamble
.... 4 Jane Carson 1828 -
.... +William McCracken
.... 4 Andrew Carson 1832 -
.... 4 Margaret Carson 1831 -
.... 3 Robert Gamble 1793 - 1816
.... 3 Cochrane Gamble 1796 - 1836
.... 3 Jean Gamble 1798 -
...... 2 James Gamble 1755 -

Robert was the eldest son of James and Agnes Gamble of Ballymoney. James Gamble was an Innkeeper in Main Street, Ballymoney in 1767. In 1786, Robert was an Innkeeper and James a merchant. Robert married Jean Patton in 1752. None of their sons married (see graves 315, 317).

Their daughter Mary married Archibald Carson, son of Andrew and Agnes (Stevenson) of Artiferral in 1826 in 1st Ballymoney Presbyterian Church. Their children were born in Ballymoney.

GAMBLE

GRAVE no. 315

Cochran Gamble
Died
24th September 1836
aged
40 years

Cochran Gamble was the son of Robert and Jean (Patton) Gamble of Ballymoney. He was a bachelor. He died in Englishtown, Co. Londonderry (see grave 314).

GAMBLE

GRAVE no. 316

In memory of
James Gamble, Polintamney
Died 24th Jan 1880 aged 61 years
Martha Adams Gamble
His beloved wife
Born 14th Dec 1826
Died at Drumskea 5th Dec 1919
Their children
2 sons who died in infancy
Archibald Gamble
Born 17th Aug 1861, died 13th Dec. 1863
John Gray Gamble
Born Jan 1869, died 31st Oct 1888
Thomas Gamble, born 17th Aug 1850
Died at Claughey 7th May 1894
Jane Gamble Barr
Born 7th March 1847
Died 13th April 1906
Samuel Gamble
Died 12th September 1930
Also his wife Mary Jane
Died 25th March 1969

1 James Gamble 1819 - 1880
.. +Martha Adams 1826 - 1919
...... 2 Jenny Gamble 1846 -
...... 2 James Gamble 1848 -
...... 2 Thomas Gamble 1850 - 1894
.... +Elizabeth Dempsey - 1935
.   see grave 318
...... 2 Jane Gamble 1851 -
.... +Robert Cochrane
...... 2 Samuel Gamble 1855 - 1930
.... +Annie Taylor 1866 - 1905
.... 3 Mary Ann Gamble 1897 -
.... 3 Martha Jane Gamble 1898 - 1960
.... +Samuel Getty 1865 - 1938
.... 3 Annie Gamble 1903 -
...... *2nd Wife of Samuel Gamble:
.... +Mary Stewart (or Ross) 1871 - 1908
.... 3 James Gamble 1907 -
...... *3rd Wife of Samuel Gamble:
.... +Mary Dunlop
.... 3 Samuel Gamble 1918 -
.... 3 Sarah Young Gamble 1916 -
.... 3 Elizabeth Gamble 1911 -
...... 2 Sarah Gamble 1857 -
.... +William C. Gray
...... 2 Martha Anne Gamble 1859 -
.... +William Anderson Mann McGregor 1868 -
.... 3 Euphemia Mann McGregor
.... 3 Martha Gamble McGregor
.... 3 James Gamble McGregor 1898 - 1986
.... 3 William McGregor
.... 3 Alexander McGregor
...... 2 Archibald Gamble 1861 - 1863
...... 2 Mary Gamble 1864 -
...... 2 Elizabeth Gamble 1867 -
.... +John Stevens
.... 3 James Gamble Stevens 1903 -
.... 3 John Archibald Stevens 1896 -
...... 2 John Gray Gamble 1869 - 1869

GAMBLE

GRAVE no. 316

James, son of James and Jean Gamble of Polintamney, married Martha, daughter of Archibald and Sarah (Gray) Adams of Claughey in 1846 in 1st Ballymoney Church.

Their daughter Jane married Robert Cochrane, a widower, of Carragh, Co. Londonderry in 1884 in 1st Ballymoney.

Their son Samuel married three times. Firstly he married Annie, daughter of Joseph and Mary Ann (Kennedy) Taylor of Carneatly in 1894. He then married a widow, Mary Ross nee Stewart, in 1905 and finally Mary, daughter of William John Dunlop of Moneycannon in 1909, all in 1st Ballymoney.

GAMBLE

GRAVE no. 317

James Gamble
Died
9th September 1836
aged
50 years

James was the son of Robert and Jean (Patton) Gamble of Ballymoney. He was born on 25th July 1836 and died intestate on 9th September 1836 in Ballymoney (see graves 314, 315, 383).

GAMBLE

GRAVE no. 318

In
loving memory
of
Thomas Gamble
Claughey
Died 7th May 1894
His wife Elizabeth
Died 20th March 1935
their daughter Martha
Died 22nd March 1895

1 Thomas Gamble 1850 - 1894
.. +Elizabeth Dempsey - 1935
...... 2 Ellen Dempster Gamble 1883 -
...... 2 Martha Gamble 1883 - 1895
...... 2 Thomas Gamble 1886 -
...... 2 James Gamble 1889 -
.... +Maggie Logan
.... 3 Thomas Gamble 1924 -
.... 3 Jane Robina Huey Gamble 1934 -
...... 2 Annie Dempsey Gamble 1890 -
.... +Adam Taylor Elliott

Thomas was the son of James and Martha (Adams) Gamble of Polintamney. He married Elizabeth, daughter of John Dempsey of Millquarter, in 1883 in 1st Ballymoney Presbyterian Church. He was a farmer.

Their son James married Maggie, daughter of William Logan of Leck in 1923 in Garryduff Presbyterian Church.

Their daughter Annie married Adam Taylor, son of James Taylor and Matilda (Gaston) Elliott of Smallquarter, in 1871 in Ballyweaney Presbyterian Church.

TWEED

GRAVE no. 319

In
loving memory
of James Tweed Eden
who died 4th January 1900
aged 84 years
His wife Nancy Kane
Died 27th June 1886
aged 67 years
Also their daughter Maggie
Died 29th November 1921
aged 75 years
Their daughter Mary
Died 1st May 1926 aged 75 years
Their son William
Died 31st January 1931
aged 75 years
Their son Samuel
Died 20th May 1935

1 James Tweed 1815 - 1900
.. +Nancy Kane 1819 - 1886
...... 2 Maggie Tweed 1846 - 1921
...... 2 Mary Tweed 1850 - 1926
...... 2 William Tweed 1855 - 1931
...... 2 Samuel Tweed - 1935

It is not known where James Tweed was born or who his parents were. He married Nancy Kane before 1845 and he was a farmer. He had four known children, none of whom married. James and Nancy died at Eden, Maggie and William in Ballymoney and Mary at Drumahiskey.

MCDUFFEE

GRAVE no. 320

Sacred to the memory
of Malcolm McDuffee
late of Moore Lodge of which
place He acted as a fai
thful servant upwards of
Forty years: He departed
this life Novem 6th 1803 in
the 74th year of his age
This stone was erec
ted by one who was
long aquainted wi
th his worth and
integrity

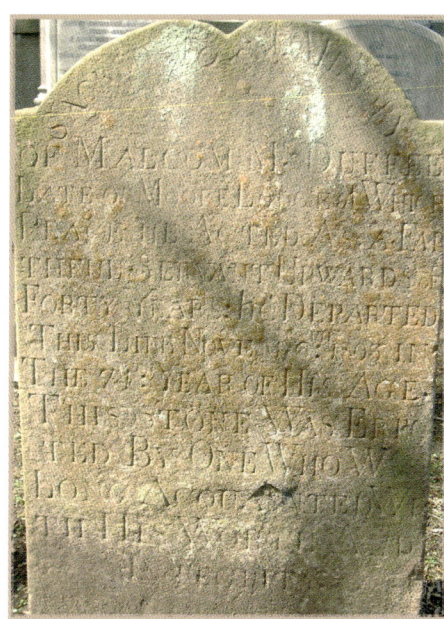

RAINEY

GRAVE no. 321

Erected
by
Catherine McMaster
Ballymoney
In memory of her parents
John Rainey
Bendooragh
Died 15 August 1879
aged 79 years
And his wife Mary
Died 12th April 1871
aged 70 years

1 John Rainey 1805 - 1879
.. +Mary Walker 1801 - 1871
...... 2 Ann Rainey 1814 -
.... +John McMaster 1814 -
.... 3 William John McMaster 1849 -
.... +Rosy Brown
...... 2 Jane Rainey
.... +John Given
...... 2 Mary Rainey
.... +James Hay 1830 -
.... 3 Sarah Hay 1854 -
.... 3 Mary Hay 1855 -
.... 3 Margaret Jane Hay 1859 -
.... 3 Nancy Hay 1863 -
...... 2 Sally Rainey 1831 - 1872
.... +Andrew Falloon 1820 - 1886
.... 3 Mary Jane Falloon 1859 -
.... 3 Sarah Ann Falloon 1865 -
.... 3 Annie Falloon 1867 -
.... 3 Andrew Falloon 1869 -
...... 2 John Rainey 1833 -
...... 2 Nancy Rainey 1835 -
...... 2 James Rainey 1837 -
.... +Nancy Dunlop 1846 -
...... 2 William Rainey 1842 -
.... +Margaret Jane Love
.... 3 Matilda Rainey 1876 -
.... 3 Margaret Jane Rainey 1878 -
...... 2 James Rainey 1845 -
...... 2 Catherine Rainey 1839 - 1923
.... +James McMaster 1829 - 1913

John Rainey was the son of John and Mary Rainey of Eden. He married Mary Walker of Inchinagh in 1826 in 1st Ballymoney Presbyterian Church. Their daughter Catherine was born at Topp and married James, son of James and Matilda (McDowell) McMaster of Cabra in 1826 in 1st Ballymoney (see grave 144).

MCLAUGHLIN

GRAVE no. 322

Memento
Mori Here lyeth
The body of Dan
iel McLaughlin
who departed th
is life April the
27th 1794 aged 37
years

There was a McLaughlin family lived at Newbuildings. This Daniel is possibly a brother of Thomas who had children Andrew (1803), Mary (1807) and Daniel (1810).

O'TOY

GRAVE no. 323

Here
Lieth the
Body of
Hugh O'Toy late
of Ballygobin
who departed
this life the 12th
May 1801 in the 79
year of his age

The O'Toy family were from Ballygobbin and members of the Established Church. In 1766, there was a William present in the Ballymoney area. In 1803, there were Alexander, Cornelius and Mary present in Ballygobbin and John, Cornelius and Mary present in 1824.

James Stirling of Ballygobbin married Sally O'Toy in 1818 and William Toy of Moneydig married Nancy Stirling of Ballygobbin in 1840 both in 1st Ballymoney Presbyterian Church.

There was a baptism of Hugh in 1808 to Patrick and Elizabeth O'Toy in St. Patrick's Parish Church.

Burials were recorded for Alexander in 1812 aged 49, William in 1815 aged 49, Mary in 1835 aged 74, Nancy in 1836 aged 60 and Widow O'Toy in 1839 aged 63 all in St. Patrick's Parish Church.

HEMPHILL

GRAVE no. 324

Here lyeth
the body of
Matthew Hemphi
ll who died the
19th September
1802 aged 75 years

In 1740, there were three Hemphills recorded in the area, Martha, James and James and in 1766 just a J. Hemphill. By 1803, Hugh, James, Matthew, Matthew, Robert, Samuel, Samuel and Widow Hemphill were living at Culbrim. In 1825, Hugh, James, Robert and Samuel were present.

HEMPHILL

GRAVE no. 325

Here lieth
the body of
Margaret Hemphill
wife to James Hemp
hill of Colbrim who
Died the 2nd June
1815 aged 59 years

In 1817, in Culbrim there was a James Hemphill, widower, with children John, Samuel, Mary and Margaret. At Culderry, William and Jennet (McFee) Hemphill and a daughter Margaret. They later had Robert born in 1824 and Jean in 1827.

Burials recorded were Widow Hemphill in 1815 aged 84, Nancy in 1820 aged 12 and James in 1823 aged 60.

WALLACE

GRAVE no. 326

Here lieth the Body
of Matthew Wallace
Who died 11th   ?
  1772 aged   ?

GORDON

GRAVE no. 327

In memory
of
Joseph Gordon
Died October 20 1815 aged 68
Mary Gordon
Died April 20 1823 aged 64
Elizabeth Gordon
Died January 15 1852 aged 64
Mary Gordon
Died February 1854 aged 67

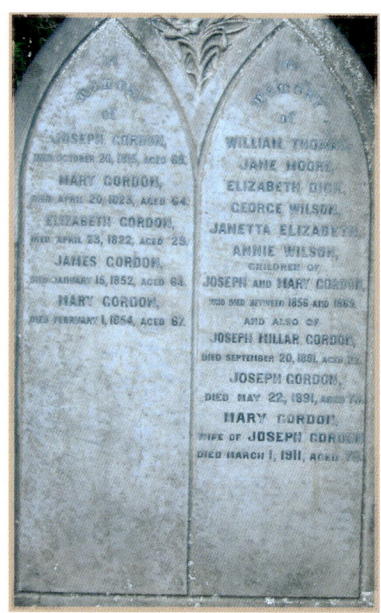

1 Joseph Gordon 1747 - 1815
.. +Mary Miller 1759 - 1823
...... 2 Mary Gordon 1785 - 1854
...... 2 James Gordon 1786 - 1852
.... +Elizabeth Dick 1793 - 1822
.... 3 Joseph Gordon 1821 - 1891
.... +Mary Sharpe 1832 - 1911
.... 4 James Andrew Gordon 1854 - 1907
.... +Ellen Miller
.... 4 Jane Moore Gordon 1856 - 1863
.... 4 William Thomas Gordon 1856 - 1856
.... 4 William Sharpe Gordon 1857 -
.... +Annie Masterson
.... 4 Joseph Miller Gordon 1858 - 1881
.... 4 Elizabeth Dick Gordon 1860 - 1863
.... 4 Mary Matilda Gordon 1862 -
.... +William Masterton 1861 - 1911
.... 4 John Sharpe Gordon 1863 - 1927
.... +Kathleen McCutcheon 1881 - 1971
.... 4 George Wilson Gordon 1865 - 1869
.... 4 Janetta Elizabeth Gordon 1867 - 1867
.... 4 Annie Wilson Gordon 1869 - 1869
.... 4 Florence Wilhemina Gordon 1872 -
.... +George Woods
.... 4 Robert Alexander Gordon 1874 - 1921
...... 2 Ann Gordon 1788 -
.... +James Wilson
...... 2 Thomas Gordon 1790 -

GORDON

GRAVE no. 327

In memory
of
William Thomas
Jane Moore
Elizabeth Dick
George Wilson
Janetta Elizabeth
Annie Wilson
children of
Joseph and Mary Gordon
who died between 1856 and 1869
and also of
Joseph Millar Gordon
Died September 1881 aged 22
Joseph Gordon
Died May 22 1891 aged 70
Mary Gordon
wife of Joseph Gordon
Died March 1 1911 aged 79

Joseph Gordon, a watchmaker, married Mary Miller of Ballymoney and had four known children. Their son James married Nancy, daughter of Robert and (Sharpe) Dick of Garry in 1819 in 1st Ballymoney Presbyterian Church.

They had a son Joseph who married Mary, daughter of Andrew and Jane (Moore) Sharpe of Moyarget, Ballycastle in 1853 in Ramoan Presbyterian Church, Ballycastle. He was also a watchmaker in Ballymoney.

COCHRANE

GRAVE no. 328

In memory
of
John Cochrane
Drumart
who died 2nd Jany 1884
aged 85 years
and his wife Matilda
who died 1st April 1887
aged 66 years

1 John Cochrane 1818 - 1884
.. +Matilda Liken 1820 - 1887
...... 2 John Cochrane 1840 - 1910
.... +Mary Annie Cochrane 1836 - 1921
.... 3 John Cochrane 1871 -
.... 3 Matilda Liken Cochrane 1873 - 1888
.... 3 Samuel Alexander Cochrane 1875 -
.... 3 Samuel Cochrane 1877 - 1949
...... 2 Samuel Cochrane
.... +Eliza Jane Camac 1840 -
...... 2 Annie Cochrane
.... +Charles Carson
...... 2 Jane Matilda Cochrane 1851 -
...... 2 Margaret Cochrane
.... +Robert Crawford
.... 3 Matilda Liken Crawford 1891 -
.... 3 Jane Peoples Crawford 1902 -

John Cochrane married Matilda Liken and was a farmer at Drumart.

Their son John married Mary Annie, daughter of Samuel and Matilda (Martin) Cochrane of Drumskea, in 1870 in 1st Ballymoney Presbyterian Church.

Their son John married Eliza Jane, daughter of Thomas and Eliza (Smyth) Camac, in 1865 in 1st Ballymoney. He was Presbyterian Minister at Clogherny, Co. Tyrone and died in U.S.A.

Their daughter Anne married Charles Carson, a farmer of Carnroe Co. Derry, in 1882 in Trinity Presbyterian Church.

NICKLESON

GRAVE no. 329

Here lieth
the body of
William Nickleson
late of Ballymoney
who departed this
life 23rd July 1812
aged 57 years

This name is sometimes shortened to Nickle. There was a baptism recorded in 1st Ballymoney Presbyterian Church in March 1756 of a William Nickle, son of John Nickle. William Nickle of Main Street had a son Daniel and a daughter Sarah Jane baptised in 1st Ballymoney Presbyterian Church in 1801 and 1804. William Nickle was present in 1803.

In 1824, a Mary Nickle was a publican in Main Street.

SNODGRASS

GRAVE no. 330

Erected
to the memory of
Sarah Snodgrass
wife of Robert Snodgrass
of Ballymoney
who departed this life the 26
day of February 1845 aged 56
Also their daughter
Mary Jane
who died March 15 1847 aged 16

1 Robert Snodgrass 1790 - 1870
.. +Sarah 1788-1845
...... 2 Mary Jane Snodgrass 1832 - 1849
...... 2 Elizabeth Snodgrass 1834- 1895
.... +Kennedy McIntyre - 1908
.... 3 Robert John McIntyre 1859 -
.... 3 Sarah Jane McIntyre 1860 - 1885
.... 3 Samuel Kennedy McIntyre 1863 - 1905
.... +Sara G. Linton
.... 3 Elizabeth Annetta McIntyre 1864 -
.... +William James Chambers
...... 2 Hannah Snodgrass
.... +Patrick McKinney
...... 2 William John Snodgrass 1823-1874

Robert Snodgrass was a grocer and clothes dealer in Main Street. He had four known children.
His daughter Hannah married Patrick McKinney in 1862.
Their son William John was a school master and a bachelor. He died in the workhouse.
His daughter Elizabeth married Kennedy McIntyre in 1859 in Coleraine. He was a pawnbroker. Their son Samuel Kennedy was a teacher and married Sara Linton of Bellaghy in 1892 in St. James Presbyterian Church. His daughter Elizabeth married William James Chambers, a teacher in Bushmills in 1885 in 1st Ballymoney.

HENDERSON

GRAVE no. 331

Erected
by
Matthew Henderson
in memory of his wife
Catherine
who died 20th Dec 1882
aged 65 years
Also their children
Bella died 1st Nov 1840
James died 20th Aug 1846
Margaret died 28th Apr 1861
Matilda died 12th Jany 1880
James died 9th Feby 1883
Mary died 14th Feby 1883
Daniel died 6th Dec 1884
Matthew Henderson
died Feby 27th 1893

1 James Henderson
.. +Isabella
...... 2 Martha Henderson
.... +David Getty
...... 2 Matthew Henderson 1812 - 1894
.... +Catherine Henderson 1817 - 1882
.... 3 Margaret Henderson 1835 - 1861
.... 3 Sibella Henderson 1839 - 1840
.... 3 Sibella Henderson 1841 -
.... 3 Matilda Henderson 1844 - 1880
.... 3 Daniel Henderson 1845 - 1884
.... 3 Mary Henderson 1850 - 1883
.... 3 James Henderson - 1846
.... 3 James Henderson 1848 - 1883
...... 2 William Henderson
.... +Martha Tomb 1801 - 1838
...... 2 John Henderson
.... +Mary Getty
...... 2 James Henderson 1805 - 1822

Matthew, son of James and Isabella Henderson of Topp married Catherine, daughter of Daniel and Margaret (Longmoor) Henderson in 1835 in 1st Ballymoney Presbyterian Church.
Matthew was a farmer and bridewell keeper and lived in Main Street. None of their children were known to have married.

LONGMOOR

GRAVE no. 332

Here lieth
the remains of
Thomas Longmoor
who departed this
life the life 7th of Feby
1807 aged 74 years

Thomas Longmoor, a whitesmith in Ballymoney, had a son William and a daughter Margaret who married Daniel Henderson.

Margaret and Daniel had a daughter Catherine who married Matthew Henderson of Topp (see grave 331).

POLLOCK

GRAVE no. 333

Erected
to the memory of
Nancy
who died 10th April 1826
Aged 50 years
Also her husband
James Pollock
late of Ballymoney
who died 12th Feby 1858
Aged 77 years

James and Nancy (or Ann) Pollock had four known children, Hugh, James and John Patrick and Ann. James was a shoemaker in Main Street in 1810.

Unfortunately, there were a lot of Pollocks named James living in Ballymoney in the 19th century so it is difficult to work out the various relationships.

POLLOCK

GRAVE no. 334

John Pollock
departed this life
Nov the 22nd 1774
aged 14 months

This is possibly a brother of James Pollock (see grave 333).

MACDONALD

GRAVE no. 335

In affectionate remembrance of
James MacDonald
who died October 13th 1871
Aged 64 years
Also
Mary Ann MacDonald
wife of the above
who died July 16th 1879
Aged 74 years
Also Mary their daughter
who died 15th May 1860
Aged 26 years

1 James McDonald 1807 - 1871
.. +Mary Ann Culbertson 1805 - 1879
...... 2 Margaret McDonald 1829 -
...... 2 Mary McDonald 1834 - 1860
...... 2 Nancy McDonald 1836 -
...... 2 Robert McDonald 1844 -
.... +Fanny Colvan 1845 -
.... 3 Thomas Colvin McDonald 1866 -
.... +Esther ?
.... 3 Alice McDonald 1867 -
.... 3 Mary Ann McDonald 1869 -
.... 3 Maggie McDonald 1873 -
.... 3 James McDonald 1875 -
.... 3 Elizabeth McDonald 1880 -
.... +David McIlhernon 1870 -
.... 3 Kate McDonald 1875 -
.... +Edward Hall
...... 2 Jane McDonald 1848 -
...... 2 Hugh McDonald 1851 -
...... 2 John McDonald 1832 -

    James, son of John and Mary MacDonald (or McDonald) of Artigoran, married Mary Ann, daughter of Robert and Mary (Wright) Culbertson in 1829 in 1st Ballymoney Presbyterian Church. He was a blacksmith.
    Their son Robert married Fanny, daughter of Thomas Colvan of Macfin in 1866 in St. Patrick's Parish Church. He was also a blacksmith.

MITCHELL

GRAVE no. 336

Erected
To the memory of
Margaret
beloved wife of John
Ballinamore who dep ?
the 31st May 1867
Also their son John
21st Sept 1866 aged ?

1 William Haggarty
.. +Jean McCay
...... 2 Jean Haggarty 1800 -
.... +John Brown 1804 -
.... 3 Jean Brown 1822 -
.... +James Culbertson
           see grave
.... 3 John Brown 1824 -
.... 3 Ebby Brown 1827 -
.... 3 Mary Brown 1829 -
.... +John Doherty 1824 - 1890
.... 3 Jenny Brown 1832 -
.... 3 James Brown 1835 -
...... 2 Alexander Haggarty 1802 -
...... 2 Robert Haggarty 1807 -
...... 2 Margaret Haggarty 1812 - 1867
.... +John Mitchell 1811 - 1883
           see grave 312
...... 2 Ibby Eliza Haggarty 1814 -
.... +William John Brown
...... 2 Hugh Haggarty 1819 -
...... 2 Mary Haggarty 1822 -

    This gravestone which is broken and lying flat has some of the same information as grave 312. Their son James obviously erected a better newer one after his father's death.
    Margaret, daughter of William and Jean (McCay) Haggerty married John Mitchell and had at least six children, Sarah, John McCullough, Sarah Jane, Nancy, James and Robert, all born at Ballygan.
    Margaret's eldest sister Jean married John, eldest son of James and Mary Brown of Ballywattick in 1821 in 1st Ballymoney Presbyterian Church. Another sister Ibby Eliza married William John Brown of Damhead in 1842 also in 1st Ballymoney.

ROBINSON

GRAVE no. 337

Erected
to the memory of
John Robinson Newbuildings
who departed this life 20th Jany 1862
aged 72 years
Also his son
William
who departed this life 9th June 1863
Aged 32 years
Also his beloved wife
Jane Robinson
died 28th February 1864 aged 72 years
James Robinson
died 5th June 1888 aged 59 years
John Robinson
died 5th July 1888 aged 61 years

1 John Robinson 1790 - 1862
.. +Jane McLester 1792 - 1874
...... 2 John Robinson 1826 - 1888
.... +Elizabeth Bacon
.... 3 Jane Robinson
.... +Samuel McVicker
.... 3 Elizabeth Robinson
.... +Hugh Lamont
.... 3 James Robinson 1878 -
.... 3 John Robinson 1880 -
.... 3 William Robinson 1882 -
.... 3 Robert Robinson 1884 -
.... 3 Alexander Robinson 1886 -
...... 2 James Robinson 1829 - 1888
...... 2 William Robinson 1831 - 1863
...... 2 Elizabeth Robinson 1835 - 1897
.... +Alexander McIlhatton 1819 - 1903
.... 3 Jane McIlhatton 1858 - 1935
.... +John Moore 1851 - 1911
.... 3 Mary McIlhatton 1859 -
.... 3 Alexander McIlhatton 1862 -
.... 3 William McIlhatton 1873 - 1931
.... +Margaret Hamilton 1883 - 1937
.... 3 James McIlhatton - 1915
.... 3 Sarah A. McIlhatton
...... 2 Sarah Ann Robinson 1841 - 1868
.... +James Baird 1831 - 1875
.... see grave 191

John, son of John and Elizabeth (Bateson) Robinson of Newbuildings married Jane McLester of Finvoy in 1825 in 1st Ballymoney Presbyterian Church.

Their eldest son John married Elizabeth, daughter of John Bacon of Newbuildings, in 1874 in 1st Ballymoney. Their other two sons were bachelors.

Their eldest daughter Elizabeth married Alexander, son of Alexander McIlhatton of Kilymoyangie, Kilraughts, in 1857 in 1st Ballymoney.

Their younger daughter Sarah Anne married James, son of James Baird of Ballymoney, in 1861 in 1st Ballymoney. He was a spirit merchant in Ballymoney.

CURRY

GRAVE no. 338

Sacred
to the memory
John Curry
who departed this life
the 23rd April 1839
Aged 50 years
Also his sister
Elizabeth Curry
who died 20th May 1870
Aged 78 years
And his sister
Martha Galloway
who died 1st December 1877
Aged 78 years

1 Elizabeth 1764 - 1846
.. +Mr Curry
...... 2 John Curry 1789 - 1839
...... 2 Elizabeth Curry 1792 - 1870
*2nd Husband of Elizabeth:
.. +Neal Galloway 1762 - 1858
...... 2 Martha Galloway 1799 - 1877
...... 2 Charles Galloway 1807 - 1887
.... +Sally Ann Cameron 1809 - 1841
...... *2nd Wife of Charles Galloway:
.... +Jane Leslie 1817 - 1888

There was a Jack Curry present in Ballymoney in 1803 according to Miller's list living in Gate end (Castle Street). He was Presbyterian. He doesn't appear in any other records.

His sister Elizabeth was living with Neal and Elizabeth Galloway in 1817 and their children Martha and Charles. There is a possibility that Elizabeth, wife of Neal, had previously been married and had children John and Elizabeth.

GALLOWAY

GRAVE no. 339

Elizabeth Galloway
died 25th February 1846
aged 81 years
Neal Galloway
died 28th May 1858
aged 96 years
Charles Galloway
died 23rd Sepr 1878
also his wife Jane Leslie
died 9th February 1888
aged 70 years

```
1 Neal Galloway 1762 - 1858
.. +Elizabeth 1764 - 1846
...... 2 Martha Galloway 1799 - 1877
...... 2 Charles Galloway 1807 - 1887
.......... +Sally Ann Cameron 1809 - 1841
...... *2nd Wife of Charles Galloway:
.......... +Jane Leslie 1817 - 1888
............... 3 Hannah Galloway 1842 -
............... 3 George Knox Galloway 1844 -
............... +Bessie Knox 1851 –
............... *2nd Wife of George Knox Galloway:
............... +Mary U. ? 1841 -
............... 3 Charles Galloway 1846 -
............... 3 David Galloway 1849 -
............... 3 Jane Galloway 1850 -
............... 3 Martha Galloway 1852 -
............... +William Leslie
............... 3 Nancy Galloway 1853 -
............... 3 William Knox Galloway 1858 -
............... 3 Rachael Galloway 1858 -
............... 3 Robert Knox Galloway 1860 -
```

Neal and Elizabeth Galloway had three known children and were living in Ballymoney in 1817. In 1824, they were living at Leaney. Neal was probably a brother of James (see grave 12).

His son Charles, a grain merchant, married Sally Ann, daughter of Daniel and Grace Cameron, who died young (see grave 391). He remarried Jane Leslie in 1841 in 1st Ballymoney Presbyterian Church and had a large family. In 1859, the family were living at Ballycormick.

Their eldest son George Knox, a grocer, married Bessie, daughter of Robert and Margaret (MacAfee) Knox of Springfield in 1871 in 1st Ballymoney and emigrated to Philadelphia. Their only other child known to have married was Martha, who married William, a farmer and son of Henry Leslie of Coleraine, in 1875. The rest of the family seem to have moved from the area.

BOYD

GRAVE no. 340

Interred here
Joseph Boyd late of Ballymoney
who died Feb 6th 1838 aged 77 years
Also Ann his wife who died June
1st 1825 aged 63 years
This small token of regard
was erected to their memory
by Elizabeth their daughter

Joseph and Ann Boyd had a family of four, Elizabeth, Joseph, Mary and Jean. Joseph was a calf butcher in Miller's list in Meetinghouse Lane.
Their son Joseph possibly married Nancy Martin of Millquarter in 1824 in 1st Ballymoney Presbyterian Church.

The Old Church Tower

MEGAW

GRAVE no. 341

Sarah Megaw
of Killyrammer
who died 1st Dec 1863
Aged 64 years
David John Megaw
died 12th Nov 1861 aged 73
Their son David
17th Feb 1868 aged 27
and their daughters
Rosanna
died 12th April 1899 aged 75
Elizabeth
died 11th June 1909 aged 71
Sarah Megaw
died 23rd October 1926 aged 85

1 David John Megaw 1794 - 1867
.. +Sarah Borland 1799 - 1863
...... 2 Sophia Megaw 1826 - 1899
.... +James McMaster 1819 - 1866
.... 3 James McMaster 1851 - 1933
.... +Lizzie Cameron Staveley 1852 - 1882
.... *2nd Wife of James McMaster:
.... +Lily Kirk - 1924
.... 3 David John McMaster 1853 - 1922
.... +Jane Moore Knox 1853 - 1942
.... 3 Mary M. McMaster 1855 -
.... 3 [2] Sarah McMaster 1857 - 1904
.... +[1] David John Megaw Robinson 1867 -
.... 3 May McMaster 1857 -
.... 3 Jane McMaster 1861 -
...... 2 Jane Megaw 1828 - 1908
.... +Robert John Huey - 1906
.... 3 David John Huey - 1940
.... 3 Letitia Huey - 1942
.... 3 James Huey - 1942
.... 3 Sophia Megaw Huey 1877 - 1947
...... 2 John Megaw 1830 - 1913
.... +Ellen Dick 1834 - 1925
.... 3 Isabella Megaw 1876 - 1943
.... +John Wallace 1867 - 1949
.... 3 Robert Dick Megaw 1868 - 1947
.... +Annie McElderry 1874 - 1968
.... 3 David Megaw 1869 - 1927
.... +Annie Lyle McElderry 1887 - 1979
.... 3 William James Megaw 1871 - 1945
.... +Ada Elizabeth Pinkerton 1874 - 1954

MEGAW   GRAVE no. 341

David John, son of John and Rose (Reynolds) Megaw of Killyrammer married Sarah Borland of Ballyboyland.

Their eldest daughter Sophia, married James, son of James and Mary McMaster of Topp in 1850 in Kilraughts Presbyterian Church.

Their daughter Jane married Robert John, son of David Huey in 1859 in 1st Kilraughts presbyterian Chruch.

Their son John married Ellen, daughter of Robert and Isabella (Wallace) Dick, in 1864 in Roseyards Presbyterian Church.

Their fourth daughter Margaret married Samuel, son of Samuel and Mary (Young) Robinson of Culcrum in 1860 in Ballyweaney Presbyterian Church.

William James married Anna Maria, daughter of Archibald and Sarah Anne (Stirling) Moore of Ballymoney in 1873.

.... 3 John Wallace Dick Megaw 1874 - 1958
.... +Helen Esmee Ward
.... 3 Sarah Megaw 1866 -
.... +Samuel Matthews
...... 2 James Megaw 1832 -
...... 2 Rosanna Megaw 1833 - 1899
...... 2 Margaret Megaw 1834 - 1895
.... +Samuel Robinson 1827 - 1910
.... 3 Mary Robinson 1862 -
.... +Robert Park
.... 3 Annie Adams Robinson 1863 -
.... +Thomas Gregg
.... 3 Samuel Robinson 1865 - 1958
.... +Mary Elizabeth Parkhill 1866 -
.... 3 Sarah Robinson 1870 - 1870
.... 3 James Kelly Robinson 1871 -
.... 3 Sarah Megaw Robinson 1874 - 1882
.... 3 William Moore M. Robinson 1876 -
.... +Mary Wallace Huey
.... 3 [1] David John Megaw Robinson 1867 -
.... +[2] Sarah McMaster 1857 - 1904
.... *2nd Wife of [1] David John Megaw Robinson:
.... +Annie Mairs
...... 2 William James Megaw 1836 - 1924
.... +Anna Maria Moore 1852 - 1934
...... 2 Elizabeth Megaw 1837 - 1909
...... 2 David Megaw 1840 - 1868
...... 2 Sarah Megaw 1843 - 1926

FREEMAN

GRAVE no. 342

In memory of Catherine wife of
John Freeman Ballymoney
who died 30th July 1879
aged 64 years
John Freeman
died 2nd March 1896
Aged 82 years

Engraved over the inscription
T Hargy

1 John Freeman 1824 - 1906
.. +Catherine Kilpatrick 1815 - 1879
...... 2 Susan Freeman 1855 - 1902
.... +Francis Hargy 1849 - 1918
.... 3 James Hargy
.... +Eveline Ewing
.... 3 John Hargy 1877 -
.... +Margaret Forbes 1877 -
.... 3 Joseph Hargy 1878 - 1912
.... +Isabella McMullan 1884 -
.... 3 Catherine Hargy 1880 -
.... +William Moggie
.... 3 Nancy Hargy 1882 -
.... +James Pattison or Patterson
.... 3 Susannah Hargy 1884 -
.... 3 Thomas Hargy 1886 -
.... +Mary Berryman
.... 3 Alice Hargy 1887 - 1968
.... +Robert John Colgan 1881 - 1922
.... 3 Francis Hargy 1891 -
.... 3 Hessie Hargy 1894 -
.... 3 Mary Hargy 1896 -
.... +Andrew Hogg 1898 -
...... 2 Eliza Freeman 1846 -
...... 2 James Freeman
...... 2 Daniel Freeman
...... 2 Sarah Jane Freeman 1850 - 1917
.... +William Campbell 1833 – 1915
         see grave 242
*2nd Wife of John Freeman:
.. +Sarah Curry

John, son of James and Margaret Freeman of Ballymoney, married Catherine Kilpatrick who died in 1879. He then married Sarah, daughter of Samuel Curry of Ballyboyland and widow of John Cameron, in 1891 in Trinity Presbyterian Church.

His daughter Susan married Francis, son of Neil and Nancy (Anderson) Hargy (see grave 378) in 1877 in Trinity. Francis was a painter in Ballymoney and his sons went into business with him.

Another daughter Sarah Jane married William, son of Samuel and Jean (McAlister) Campbell of Ballymoney in 1871 in Trinity.

MCCANN

GRAVE no. 343

Erected
in memory of
Robert McCann Secon
who died 2nd Feby 1871
Aged 84 years
Also his wife
Catherine
who died 3rd April 1874
Aged 80 years
Also his son John who died the
24th March 1883 aged 60 years

1 Robert McCann 1790 - 1871
.. +Catherine Gibson 1794 - 1874
...... 2 Jennet McCann 1816 -
...... 2 Sarah McCann 1817 -
...... 2 Mary McCann 1819 -
.... +John Johnston
...... 2 John McCann 1822 - 1883
.... +Matilda Stockman
...... 2 William McCann 1824 -
...... 2 Jenny McCann 1825 -
...... 2 Robert McCann 1830 -

Robert McCann of Ballygan married Catherine, daughter of John Gibson of Ballygan. They both died in Secon. He was a butcher.

Their daughter Mary married John Johnston, a servant in Newhill, Ballymoney, in 1865 in Trinity Presbyterian Church.

Their son John, a farmer in Secon, married Matilda, daughter of Hugh Stockman, also a farmer in Secon, in 1876 in 1st Ballymoney.

CREEK

GRAVE no. 344

Here lyeth ?
? the remains of
William Creek who
died the ? December
1787 aged 65 years
Also three of his
children
Likewise
? ? ?
Relict of said
William Creek
Who departed this
life Oct 11 ?
aged ? years

1 Edward Creek
...... 2 William Creek 1722 - 1787
.... +Catherine Black
.... 3 Edward Creek 1750 -
.... 3 William Creek 1752 -
.... 3 Mary Creek 1755 -
.... +Mr Reynolds
.... *2nd Husband of Mary Creek:
.... +James Gamble 1755 - 1792
.... 3 Ann Creek 1759 - 1817
.... 3 Elizabeth Creek 1761 -
.... 3 Catherine Creek 1763 -
.... +Mr. Byrne
.... 3 David Creek 1765 - 1816
.... 3 Charles Creek 1767 -
...... 2 David Creek

The name on this grave is unclear but it is most probably Creek. I found details of this family in a box of old legal documents in PRONI.

Edward Creek, a yeoman, took out a lease in Ballymoney in 1726. He was a tenant in the map of Ballymoney in 1734.

In 1766, Margaret (possibly Edward's widow) and William, his son were present. William's name was found on leases in 1762 in Mill Lane, 1765 in Main Street and 1776 in Piper Row. Baptisms were recorded for four of his children in 1st Ballymoney Presbyterian Church in the mid 1700s.

He died in Ballymoney and left a will with probate in 1788. He was a merchant in Main Street. He married Catherine Black and had eight known children. His daughter Mary was a widow of a Reynolds in 1797 and later married James Gamble also a merchant in Ballymoney. Another daughter married a Byrne. His sons David and Charles moved to Belfast.

LOVE

GRAVE no. 345

Sacred
to the memory of
Ephraim Love
of Taughey
who departed this life the
22nd May 1853 aged 54 years
Also his son William
who departed this life the
21st April 1857 aged 17 years

1 Ephraim Love - 1813
...... 2 Ephraim Love 1799 - 1853
.... +Margaret McMullan
.... 3 Ephraim Love 1830 - 1898
.... 3 Jenny Love 1832 -
.... 3 Elizabeth Love 1834 - 1900
.... +Daniel Henry 1820 - 1899
.... 3 Robert Love 1836 - 1913
.... 3 Mary Anne Love 1838 - 1914
.... 3 William Love 1840 - 1857
.... 3 Matthew Love 1843 -
...... 2 Elizabeth Love 1801 -
...... 2 James Love 1804 - 1875
.... +Sarah Murdock
.... 3 Ephraim Love 1832 -
...... 2 Robert Love 1804 -

Ephraim Love of Taghey died in 1813 and had at least four children. His son, James married Sarah Murdock and had a son Ephraim in 1832.

His oldest son Ephraim married Margaret McMullan in 1829 in 1st Ballymoney Presbyterian Church. They had a family of six but only their daughter Elizabeth married. She married Daniel, son of Matthew and Catherine (Lilley) Henry of Drumahiskey in 1856 in 1st Ballymoney.

LOVE

GRAVE no. 346

Erected by
Robert Love of Taughey
To the memory of his wife
Martha who departed this
life April the 26th 1834
aged 49 years
Robert Love,
Taughey
Died 21st January 1881
aged 72 years

1 Robert Love 1788 - 1861
.. +Martha Culbert 1784 - 1834
...... 2 Matthew Love 1804 -
...... 2 Thomas Love 1805 - 1864
.... +Margaret Leslie 1805 - 1883
...... 2 Robert Love 1808 - 1881
.... +Mary Ann Boyd
.... 3 Robert Love 1853 -
.... +Mary Wright 1851 -
.... 3 Nancy Love 1855 -
.... 3 Joseph Boyd Love 1857 -
.... 3 Ephraim Love 1858 -
.... 3 Martha Love 1862 -
.... 3 Mary Ann Love 1864 -
...... 2 Ephraim Love 1810 -
...... 2 Sarah Jane Love 1815 - 1881
.... +Samuel Small 1815 - 1870
...... 2 Matilda Love 1819 - 1841
.... +John McCandless
...... 2 James Love 1821 -
...... 2 Nancy Love 1824 -

Robert was possibly a brother of Ephraim. He married Martha Culbert and had eight children.

Their son Thomas married Margaret Leslie in 1835 in 1st Ballymoney Presbyterian Church. They were farmers at Artigoran (see grave 347).

Their son Robert married Mary Ann, daughter of Joseph Boyd of Strone, Dervock in 1851 in Roseyards Presbyterian Church and stayed at Taghey on the farm.

Their daughter Sarah Jane married Samuel, son of William and Rose Ann (Craith) Small of Ballywattick in 1843 in 1st Ballymoney (see grave 210).

Their daughter Nancy married Henry Johnston, Baronial surveyor in Ballymoney (see grave 16).

Their youngest daughter married John McCandless of Coleraine (see grave 346a).

MCCANDLESS

GRAVE no. 346a

Erected by
John McCandless
Coleraine
To the memory of his wife
Matilda who departed
this life the 31st May 1841
aged 22 years

Matilda, daughter of Robert and Martha (Culbert) Love of Taghey married John McCandless of Coleraine in 1839 in 1st Ballymoney Presbyterian Church (see grave 346).

LOVE

GRAVE no. 347

In memory of
Thomas Love
Died 17th Sepr 1864
aged 49 years
Also his wife
Margaret
Died 6th August 1883
Aged 78 years
and their children
Ephraim
Died 17th December 1863
Aged 19 years
Matilda C.
Died 17th April 1866
Aged 17 years
Robert died 5th Sept. 1868
Aged 26 years
Thomas
Died 5th August 1869
Aged 19 years
and Margaret W.
Died 7th Jany 1870
aged 24 years
Erected by J.L.Love of Artigoran

1 Thomas Love 1805 - 1864
.. +Margaret Leslie 1805 - 1883
...... 2 Robert Love 1842 - 1868
...... 2 Ephraim Love 1844 - 1863
...... 2 Matilda Culbert Love 1848 - 1866
...... 2 Thomas Love 1850 - 1869
...... 2 John Leslie Love 1853 -
...... 2 Margaret W. Love 1855 - 1870

Thomas, son of Robert and Martha (Culbert) Love was born at Taghey, but was a farmer at Artigoran after his marriage to Matilda Leslie, in 1837 in 1st Ballymoney Presbyterian Church. None of their children married.

CAMAC

GRAVE no. 348

In
loving memory of
Ellen
the beloved wife of
Rev. John Camac
Knowhead, Derry
who died 1st May 1908
Aged 75 years
Rev. John Camac
died in his 84th year
and his niece
Ellen Wallace Camac
wife of
Thomas Nevin Camac J.P.
died 23rd June 1946
Also the above named
Thomas Nevin Camac J.P.
died 6th Jan 1951

1 David Camac 1841 - 1916
.. +Matilda Magee Wales 1841 - 1933
...... 2 Thomas Nevin Camac 1868 - 1951
.... +Ellen Wallace 1862 - 1946
.... 3 Ellen Camac 1902 -
...... 2 Adam Wales Camac 1870 - 1936
.... +Eleanor Maria Gibbs
...... 2 Elizabeth Smyth Camac 1872 - 1959
...... 2 Matilda Magee Camac 1874 - 1949
.... +Israel Martin
...... 2 Ellen Camac 1876 - 1968
.... +James Colhoun 1867 - 1946
.... 3 Robert Eric Camac Colhoun 1908 -
.... +Ivy Acheson 1913 -
...... 2 John Camac 1878 - 1952
.... +Lilian Jane Pratt - 1964
...... 2 Jane Wales Camac 1880 - 1881
...... 2 Mary McClure Camac 1882 -
.... +James Greer
...... *2nd Husband of Mary McClure Camac:
.... +Thomas Torrens
...... 2 James Gamble Camac 1885 - 1951
.... +Maude Ashley 1888 -
.... 3 Kenneth Ashley Camac
.... 3 David Nevin Camac

Rev. John, son of Thomas and Eliza (Smyth) Camac, married Ellen, daughter of Richard and Mary Ann (Boyle) Wallace of Leitrim in 1857 in 1st Ballymoney Presbyterian Church. They had no children. He was minister of Knowehead Presbyterian Church, Muff, Donegal from 1857 to 1899. He retired and died in Eglinton Terrace, Portrush (see grave 349).

Thomas Nevin, eldest son of David and Matilda Magee (Wales) Camac of Coole, Derrykeighan, married Ellen Wallace, daughter of James and Nancy (Smyth) Wallace of Leitrim in 1901 in Bushvale Presbyterian Church. They had one daughter Ellen.

Nancy Smyth of Strone, Dervock was the niece of Thomas Nevin Camac's grandmother Eliza Smyth.

CAMAC

GRAVE no. 349

In
memory of
Thomas Camac, Garry
died 20th April 1885
Aged 81
His wife Eliza
died 3rd June 1893
Aged 92
and his mother Nancy
died 24th Jany 1849
Aged 83
David Camac, Coole
died 17th February 1933
Aged 75 years
and his wife Matilda Wales
died 17th February 1933
Aged 91 years
and their daughter
Elizabeth Smith Camac
died 23rd July 1969, aged 86 years

1 Thomas Camac 1803 - 1885
.. +Eliza Smyth 1801 - 1893
...... 2 Agnes Camac 1829 -
.... +George Campbell
...... 2 Jane Camac 1831 - 1912
.... +Peter Gamble Camac 1825 - 1912
.... 3 James Gamble Camac 1850 - 1916
.... +Ellen F. McKeown
.... 3 Matilda Camac 1851 -
.... 3 Jane Camac 1853 - 1854
.... 3 Mary Matilda Camac 1855 - 1933
.... +Robert John Roulston
.... 3 Thomas Camac 1856 -
.... 3 Eliza Anne Camac 1857 - 1878
.... 3 Isabella Camac 1859 - 1886
.... +James Laughlin Nevin 1854 - 1942
.... 3 Jane Rowan Camac 1861 - 1866
.... 3 Thomas Camac 1863 - 1937
.... 3 Mary Camac 1865 -
.... 3 Thomas Camac 1866 - 1937
.... 3 William Toland Camac 1867 - 1868
.... 3 Agnes Nevin Camac 1869 - 1946
.... +Robert Craig Millar - 1941
.... 3 Jane Rowan Camac 1871 - 1873
...... 2 John Camac 1833 - 1917
.... +Ellen Wallace 1830 - 1908
...... 2 William Camac 1835 - 1846
...... 2 James Camac 1838 - 1922
.... +Eliza Ann McKeown 1840 - 1911
.... 3 Eliza Smyth Camac 1863 - 1947
.... 3 Jane Stewart Camac 1864 - 1876

CAMAC

GRAVE no. 349

Thomas, son of John and Nancy (Nevin) Camac married Eliza, daughter of William and Jenny Smyth of Strone, Dervock in 1828 in Carncullagh Presbyterian Church.

Their eldest daughter Agnes married George Campbell of Sligo in 1857. Their second daughter Jane married her cousin Dr. Peter Gamble Camac of Drumart and Derrykeighan.

Their son James married Eliza, Ann, daughter of John McKeown of Clunties, in 1862 Toberdoney (or Toberkeigh) Presbyterian Church. He was a Rate Collector in Portrush and is buried in Billy Parish Churchyard near Bushmills.

Their youngest daughter Eliza Jane married Rev. Samuel, son of John and Matilda (Liken) Cochrane of Drumart, in 1865 in 1st Ballymoney Presbyterian Church. He was minister of Clogherny, Co Tyrone and died in U.S.A.

.... 3 Thomas Camac 1866 - 1895
.... 3 John Ferguson Camac 1868 -
.... 3 Mary Ellen Camac 1871 - 1893
.... +Samuel George Clark
.... 3 Samuel Joseph Camac 1875 - 1925
.... 3 Jane Stewart Camac 1877 - 1963
.... 3 James Camac 1879 - 1964
...... 2 Eliza Jane Camac 1840 -
.... +Samuel Cochrane 1848 -
...... 2 David Camac 1841 - 1916
.... +Matilda Magee Wales 1841 - 1933
................see grave 348
...... 2 William Camac 1846 -

GETTY

GRAVE no. 350

In
loving memory
of
Archibald Getty
Coldagh
died 7th December 1905
aged 65 years
Also his daughter
Minnie Getty
died 15th June 1892
aged 2 years
And his wife
Sarah Getty
died 14th September 1930
aged 72 years
Also their daughter
Annie Lily Getty
died 31st October 1939
aged 58 years

1 Patrick Getty 1780 - 1877
.. +Elizabeth Lynn 1811 - 1861
...... 2 Archibald Getty 1845 - 1905
.... +Sarah Dunlop 1853 - 1930
.... 3 Lillie Annie Getty 1880 - 1939
.... 3 Elizabeth Patterson Getty 1882 - 1933
.... +William John Donaghy 1876 - 1953
.... 4 Lizzie Donaghy 1910 -
.... 4 Mary Margretta Donaghy 1911 - 1994
.... +Arthur A. L. McKinley 1909 - 1979
.... 4 Sarah Donaghy 1913 - 1974
.... 4 James Donaghy 1915 - 1977
.... 4 Jane Donaghy 1918 - 2005
.... +John McCracken 1905 - 1985
.... 3 Sarah Getty 1885 - 1978
.... +James Donaghy Hart 1880 - 1975
.... 4 John Alexander Hart 1917 -
.... 4 Mary Jane Hart 1914 -
.... +Harold Burnside Holmes 1901 - 1979
.... 4 Archibald Getty Hart 1922 -
.... +Ellen Bolton Torrens 1933 - 1972
.... 3 Alexander Getty 1888 - 1949
.... 3 Maggie Getty 1890 - 1892
.... 3 Margaret Getty 1893 - 1977
.... 3 James Getty 1895 -
...... 2 Eliza Getty 1840 -
...... 2 Hannah Getty 1846 -
...... 2 James Getty 1853 -

Patrick Getty, a farmer, was the son of Archibald and Ann Getty of Coldagh. They had four children, nothing of which is known about the other three.

Patrick married Elizabeth Lynn in 1836 in 1st Ballymoney Presbyterian Church. Their son Archibald married Sarah, daughter of Alexander and Sarah (Patterson) Dunlop of Drumlee, Finvoy in 1879 in Finvoy Presbyterian Church.

Archibald and Sarah had seven children. Their daughter Elizabeth Patterson married William John, youngest son of James and Eliza Jane (Percy) Donaghy of Mostragee in 1909 in Drumreagh Presbyterian Church. Their daughter of Sarah married James Donaghy, son of Robert and Mary Jane (Donaghy) Hart.

CAMAC

GRAVE no. 351

Erected
to the memory of
William Camac
late of Garry
who died on the 17th November 1827
aged 59 years
Also his daughter
Rose
who died on the 15th April 1843
Also his wife
Jane
who died on the 30th August 1852
aged 66 years

1 William Camac 1768 - 1827
.. +Jane Caldwell 1786 - 1852
...... 2 James Moore Camac 1807 - 1823
...... 2 Rose Camac 1811 - 1843
...... 2 Robert Camac 1812 - 1887
.... +Mary Jane Adams 1817 - 1901
..............see grave 190
...... 2 David Camac 1815 - 1850
...... 2 Mary Jean Camac 1821 -
...... 2 Jane Camac 1823 -
.... +Thomas Moore Stuart 1818 - 1900
.... 3 Mary Moore Stuart 1849 - 1876
.... 3 John Stuart 1851 -
.... 3 William Camac Stuart 1853 -
.... 3 William Camac Stuart 1854 -
.... 3 David Stuart 1857 - 1924
.... +Jane Knox Turner 1852 - 1909
.... 3 Rose Stuart 1859 -
.... 3 Robert Camac Stuart 1862 - 1924
.... +Jane Nevin Moore
.... 3 Thomas Stuart 1867 -
.... +Martha Stewart 1880 -
...... 2 William John Camac 1826 - 1893

William Camac, son of William, was a farmer at Garry and married Jane Caldwell.

Their son Robert married Mary Jane, daughter of John and Mary Adams of Fernalizery and Ballyboyland (see grave 190).

Their daughter Jane married Thomas Moore, son of Thomas and Mary (Moore) Stuart of Landhead, in 1809 in 1st Ballymoney Presbyterian Church.

COMOCK

GRAVE no. 351a

Here lyeth the body of John Comock who departed Jany 26th 1707 aged 46.   Also Jean Hacket his wife who departed December the 16th 1726 aged 70. Also John Comock there grandson who died Jan the 16th 1738 aged 14 years

John Comock (Camac) was the great grandson of George, the first Camac in the area. He married Jean Hacket. The Hacket family lived at Drumaheglis.

ESDALE
GRAVE no. 352

In loving memory of
John Esdale
and his sisters
Mary Ann, Margaret and Jane
Esdale

1 James Esdale 1810 - 1891
.. +Mary Ann Lyons 1823 - 1913
...... 2 John Esdale 1848 - 1931
...... 2 James Esdale 1852 -
...... 2 Jane Esdale 1854 -
...... 2 Mary Ann Esdale 1857 - 1908
...... 2 Margaret Esdale 1864 - 1916
...... 2 William Esdale 1865 -

James Esdale, a labourer, married Mary Ann Lyons and had six children. The youngest four were born at Ballywindland. James, Mary Ann and their daughters Mary Ann and Margaret died at Balnamore. John was a retired mill manager and died at Portstewart.

STEWART

GRAVE no. 353

Let the living remember they are to die.
Here lyeth the body of Thos Stewart who departed this life Febr 16th 1760 aged ?5 years. Also his dowghter in law Jenet Stewart who departed this life Jwly 15th 1770 aged 43 years also seven of her children

MCGARRY

GRAVE no. 354

McGARRY

1 David McGarry
.. +Sarah Keers
...... 2 Matthew McGarry 1821 - 1892
.... +Nancy Farrell 1829 - 1889
.... 3 Sarah McGarry 1844 -
.... 3 James McGarry
.... 3 David McGarry
.... 3 William McGarry
.... 3 Jane McGarry 1857 -
.... 3 William John McGarry 1863 -
...... 2 Matilda McGarry 1822 -
.... +John Wallace
.... 3 Nancy Wallace 1847 -
.... 3 John Wallace 1851 -
...... 2 Esther McGarry 1824 -
.... +Wilson McAfee
.... 3 David McAfee
.... +Mary McCracken
.... 4 Mary Knox McAfee 1904 - 1956
.... +Robert Joseph Moore
.... 3 William McAfee 1845 -
.... 3 Wilson McAfee 1857 -
.... 3 John Alexander McAfee 1858 -
.... 3 Matilda McAfee 1859 -
.... +William Murphy
.... 3 Mary Jane McAfee 1860 -

According to the Interment book 1882-1932, there were four McGarrys buried in the Old Churchyard. I am assuming that these are all the same family buried in this grave.

David and Sarah (Keers) McGarry had three children. He was a weaver in Ballymoney in 1837 and attended St. James Presbyterian Church. The name was often spelled Magarry.

Matthew married Nancy Farrell of Ballymoney in 1843 in St. James and had at least six children. He lived in Milltown for a time, though seems to have died in Ballymoney.

MOORE

GRAVE no. 355

To the memory
of
Mary Moore
wife of William Brown
late of Culermoney
who died Feb 26 1856
aged 64 years

William Brown, a farmer at Culramoney, was living with his sisters Jean, Agnes and Jenny in 1817. He married Mary, daughter of James and Margaret (Killough) Moore of Fernalizery in 1822 in 1st Ballymoney Presbyterian Church.

BROWN

GRAVE no. 356

Sacred to the memory of James Brown of Lisnamuck who departed this life on the 8th day of Decr 1831 aged 89 years. Also his wife Rose Brown who departed this life the 28th January 1834 aged 85 years

BROWN

GRAVE no. 357

Here lieth the
Body of Elisabeth
Brown who departed
this life the 15 of De
cember 1807 aged 26

This Elisabeth is possibly related to the Brown families in graves 355 and 356.

BOYD

GRAVE no. 358

Sacred
to the memory of
David Boyd
late of Carnany who
departed this life
Sep 6th 1816 aged 76

1 David Boyd 1740 - 1816
...... 2 Thomas Boyd
.... +Charity Laverty
.... 3 Ann Ralston Boyd 1805 -
.... 3 Thomas Boyd 1809 -
.... 3 David Boyd 1811 -
.... 3 James Boyd 1813 -
.... 3 Alexander Boyd 1815 -
.... 3 Samuel Boyd 1817 -
.... 3 Elizabeth Alexandra Boyd 1818 -
...... 2 John Boyd - 1817
.... 3 James Boyd 1809 -

David Boyd of Carnany had two known sons, Thomas and John. Thomas married Charity, daughter of John Laverty of Druckendult. Her sister was possibly Margaret who married Hugh McLaughlin of Carnany (see grave 360).

GIVEN GRAVE no. 359

Erected by
James Given of Ballymoney
of the members of his family
interred in this ground

Left Side — His father Samuel
Died 7th Oct 1835 aged 77 years
His mother Elizabeth
Died Aug 1847 aged 88 years
his brother
Alexander M Given
died 17th Dec 1820 aged 22 years

Right Side — James Given Ballymoney
Died 28th July 1866
Aged 65 years
His sons James Huey Given
Died 21st Sep 1858 aged 17 years
John Reynolds Given
Died 22nd Apr 1859 aged 10 years
Samuel Given
Died 28th Jany 1860 aged 8 years
His wife
Martha Given
Died 20th Jan 1866
Aged 58 years

1 Samuel Given 1758 - 1835
.. +Elizabeth 1759 - 1847
...... 2 John Given 1791 - 1842
.... +Mary Miller 1792 - 1862
.... 3 Jane Given 1817 - 1851
.... 3 William Given 1818 - 1827
.... 3 Elizabeth Given 1819 - 1882
.... +Samuel Gamble 1827 - 1916
.... 3 Alexander Marshall Given 1821 - 1845
.... 3 James Given 1823 - 1870
.... 3 Samuel Given 1826 - 1844
...... 2 Alexander M. Given 1798 - 1820
...... 2 James Given 1800 - 1860
.... +Matilda Huey 1807 - 1866
.... 3 Martha Given 1839 - 1901
.... +William John Cameron 1827 - 1893
.... 4 Grace Scott Cameron 1859 - 1877
.... 3 James Huey Given 1841 - 1858
.... 3 John Given 1844 -
.... 3 John Reynolds Given 1848 - 1859
.... 3 Samuel Given 1851 - 1860
.... 3 Mary Given 1846 - 1917
.... +James Tweed 1847 - 1917
.... 4 William Tweed 1877 - 1927
.... +Mary Moody Knox 1871 - 1912
.... *2nd Wife of William Tweed:
.... +Catherine Orr - 1925

GIVEN

GRAVE no. 359

Samuel and Elizabeth Given came to Ballymoney some time around 1810. Their son Alexander was a bachelor.

Their eldest son John married Mary, daughter of Samuel Miller of Ballymoney in 1815 in St. Patrick's Parish Church. Only their daughter Elizabeth married (see grave 240).

Their youngest son James, a merchant in Ballymoney, married Matilda Huey. Only their two daughters married. Martha married William John, son of Daniel and Grace (Scott) Cameron in 1857 (see grave 375). Mary married James, second son of William and Barabara (McClure) Tweed of Culduff in 1870 in 1st Ballymoney Presbyterian Church. They had one son William.

MCLAUGHLIN

GRAVE no. 360

Sacred
to the memory of
Hugh McLaughlin of Carnaney
who died ? ? March 1856
aged ? ? years
And ? ? Margaret
who ? ? er 1856
Erected
by their son James Alexander
of Philadelphia U.S.

Hugh and Margaret (Laverty) McLaughlin were farmers at Carnany. Their daughter Jean married James McGlaughlin of Eden in 1820 in 1st Ballymoney Church. Their son John married Ann Miller, daughter of John Williamson of Carnany. Their second daughter Mary married Robert, son of John and Elizabeth (Bateson) of Newbuildings in 1827 in 1st Ballymoney. Rachael married David, son of John and Rose Robinson of Newhill in 1832 in 1st Ballymoney.

Their son James Alexander married Mary, daughter of William and Margaret (Orr) Hay of Ballybrakes in 1837 in 1st Ballymoney. They emigrated to Philadelphia.

```
1 Hugh McLaughlin - 1856
.. +Margaret Laverty - 1856
...... 2 Hugh McLaughlin 1805 -
...... 2 Jean McLaughlin 1807 -
.......... +James McGlaughlin
...... 2 John McLaughlin 1808 -
.......... +Ann Miller Williamson 1805 -
............... 3 Hugh McLaughlin 1825 -
............... 3 Margaret Jane McLaughlin
.................. +William Henning
...... 2 Mary McLaughlin 1811 -
.......... +Robert Robinson 1797 - 1883
............... see graves 361, 362
...... 2 Rachael McLaughlin 1813 -
.......... +David Robinson 1807 -
............... 3 Peggy Jane Robinson 1833 -
............... 3 Nancy Robinson 1838 -
............... 3 Sally Jane Robinson 1838 -
............... 3 Hugh Robinson 1840 -
.................. +Mary Smith
............... 3 Mary Robinson 1843 -
............... 3 Rachael Robinson 1845 -
............... 3 Elizabeth Robinson 1848 -
............... 3 Mary Robinson 1849 -
............... 3 Hanna Robinson 1850 -
............... 3 Martha Robinson 1855 -
...... 2 James Alexander McLaughlin 1815 -
.......... +Mary Hay 1814 -
............... 3 Margaret McLaughlin 1838 -
............... 3 Anne Orr McLaughlin 1839 -
............... 3 John McLaughlin 1843 -
............... 3 Matilda McLaughlin 1845 -
............... 3 Bessie McLaughlin 1848 -
.................. +? Henning
............... 3 Mary Hay McLaughlin 1850 -
............... 3 William McLaughlin 1853 -
...... 2 John Alexander McLaughlin 1820 -
```

ROBINSON

GRAVE no. 361

Erected
in loving memory of
William Robinson
Newbuildings
who died 17th Novr 1917
aged 78 years
Also his wife Ellen
who died 11th May 1926
aged 76 years

1 William Robinson 1843 -
.. +Ellen Rice 1850 -
...... 2 Robert Robinson 1887 - 1949
.... +Mary Tweed 1893 - 1948
.... 3 James McClure Robinson 1935 - 1982
.... 3 David Tweed Robinson
.... +Marie Elizabeth Quail
...... 2 William Robinson 1889 -
.... +Minnie Warnock
...... 2 Alexander Robinson 1891 - 1895

    William, son of Robert and Mary (McLaughlin) Robinson, married Ellen, daughter of Dennis and Anne (Lusk) Rice of Pharos, Loughguile in 1886 in Carncullagh Presbyterian Church.
    Their son Robert married Mary, daughter of David and Mollie (McClure) Tweed of Culduff in 1919 in 1st Kilraughts Presbyterian Church.
    Their second son William married Minnie, daughter of William and Rachael (Pinkerton) Warnock of Newbuildings in 1931 in Ballymoney Reformed Presbyterian Church.
    Their youngest son Alexander died young.

ROBINSON

GRAVE no. 362

Erected
by
John Robinson
in
memory of his son
Robert
who died Augst 23 1864
aged 2 years

1 John Robinson 1832 - 1912
.. +Mary Jane Connell 1832 - 1898
...... 2 Robert Robinson 1862 - 1864
...... 2 Maria C. Robinson - 1921
...... 2 Margaret Robinson
.... +James Alexander Kinnear
...... 2 Mary Jane Robinson 1864 - 1909
...... 2 Robert Robinson 1867 -
.... +Helen ? 1878 -
.... 3 Margaret Robinson 1922 -

Robert was the son of John and Mary Jane (Connell) Robinson, of Church Street, Ballymoney.

His father John, farmer at Newbuildings, was the son of Robert and Mary (McLaughlin) Robinson (see graves 360, 361).

His sister Margaret married James Alexander Kinnear in 1901 in 1st Ballymoney Presbyterian Church and lived in Dublin.

His brother Robert emigrated to Denver, Colorado and married Helen.

RENEY

GRAVE no. 363

Erected
to the memory of the late
William Reney of Eden
who departed this life Septr 28
1848 aged 36 years
Also his son John who died
11th Octr 1857 aged 20 years
and two infant children

1 John Rainey
.. +Mary
...... 2 James Rainey 1798 -
.... +Jean Graham
...... 2 Mary Rainey 1800 -
...... 2 Margaret Rainey 1801 -
.... +Hugh Graham
...... 2 Andrew Rainey 1803 -
...... 2 Neal Rainey 1808 -
.... +Rachael Dinsmore Hay 1817 -
...... 2 John Rainey 1805 - 1879
.... +Mary Walker 1801 - 1871
...... 2 Alexander Rainey 1810 -
.... +Elizabeth Graham
...... 2 William Rainey 1812 - 1848
.... +Margaret McDowell
...... 2 Henry Rainey 1816 -
...... 2 Sarah Rainey 1803 -
.... +Edward Hay 1806 -
...... 2 Ann Rainey 1814 -
.... +John McMaster 1814 -

The modern spelling of Reney is Rainey. John and Mary had a family of eleven.
  Their son William married Margaret McDowell of Cabra in 1834 in 1st Ballymoney Church.
  Their son James married Jean, daughter of John and Jean Graham of Drumreagh and his sister Margaret married Hugh, Jean's brother.
  Neal married Rachael Dinsmore, daughter of James and Margaret (Dinsmore) Hay of Drumskea, in 1839 in 1st Ballymoney and his sister Sarah married Rachael's brother Edward in 1828. John married Mary, daughter of James Walker of Drumskea, in 1826 in 1st Ballymoney. Alexander married Elizabeth Graham of Drumreagh in 1833 in 1st Ballymoney. His youngest sister married John, son of James and Mary (Falloon) McMaster of Cabra in 1848.

ROBINSON

GRAVE no. 364

Left side
In loving memory of
Sarah Sinclair
wife of
Henry Robinson
who died
1st December 1923
aged 71 years

Front
In loving memory of
Henry Robinson
who died at
Newbuildings
12th February 1909
in his 59th year
In sure and certain hope
of a glorious resurrection

Right side Mary Robinson
daughter of
Henry Robinson
who died
14th Feb 1965
aged 74 years

1 Henry Robinson 1788 - 1856
.. +Jane Warnock
...... 2 Elizabeth Robinson 1827 -
...... 2 John Robinson 1829 -
...... 2 Margaret Robinson 1832 - 1916
.... +Thomas Stuart 1820 - 1886
...... 2 Mary Robinson 1832 -
.... +Moore Stuart 1826 - 1903
...... 2 James Robinson 1835 -
.... +Jane Cunningham
...... 2 Jane Robinson 1837 - 1877
.... +William Tweed 1821 - 1882
...... 2 Rose Robinson 1839 -
.... +Robert Smith
...... 2 Anne Robinson 1841 -
...... 2 Catherine Robinson 1841 - 1873
.... +Stewart McClure
...... 2 Henry Robinson 1845 - 1905
.... +Sarah Sinclair 1852 - 1923
.... 3 Jane Robinson 1886 - 1944
.... 3 Mary Kirkpatrick Robinson 1890 - 1965
...... 2 John Robinson 1848 -

Henry, son of Henry and Jane (Warnock) Robinson of Newbuildings, married Sarah, daughter of James and Sarah (Kirkpatrick) Sinclair (see grave 73) of Druckendult in 1884 in 1st Ballymoney Presbyterian Church. They had two daughters who did not marry.

Henry and Jane had eleven children. Their daughter Margaret married Thomas, son of Archibald and Elizabeth (Scott) Stuart of Glennylough in 1856 in 1st Ballymoney. Their daughter Mary married Moore, son of Thomas and Mary (Moore) Stuart of Landhead in 1852 in 1st Ballymoney. James married Jane, daughter of William Cunningham of Glennylough in 1859 in 1st Kilraughts. Jane married William, son of William and Mary (Robinson) Tweed of Culduff in 1863 in 1st Ballymoney. Rose married Robert Smith of Drumdollagh in 1866 in 1st Ballymoney. Catherine married Stewart, son of William McClure of Craigatempin in 1861 in 1st Ballymoney.

ROBINSON

GRAVE no. 365

This
Stone was erected by
James Robinson in memory
of his father
Robert Robinson
late of Culduff who departed
this life the 3rd of June 1822
aged 76 years

1 James Robinson 1697 - 1769
.. +Margaret 1715 - 1777
...... 2 William Robinson 1746 - 1829
.... +Mary McPeake
...... 2 James Robinson
...... 2 Robert Robinson 1746 - 1822
.... 3 James Robinson
...... 2 Henry Robinson
...... 2 Jane Robinson
.... +Mr Knox
...... 2 Margaret Robinson
...... 2 John Robinson
————-+Elizabeth Bateson

Robert was the son of James and Margaret Robinson of Culduff (see grave 364). Nothing more is known.

ROBINSON

GRAVE no. 366

Here lyeth the body
of James Robinson
who departed this
Life the 16th of March
1769 aged 68 years
Also
Margaret his wife
who departed this
life the 25th of March
1777 aged 59 years
Also
Their son Wm Robinson
late of Newbuildings who
Departed this life the 22nd of
Febry 1822 in the 82nd year of
his age
Died at Culduff 16th Oct
1871 Neal Robinson
Surgeon in the Royal Navy
in the 84th year of his age
Also his wife Hester
and his two sons Wm and Neal

ROBINSON

GRAVE no. 366

According to the history of the Robinson family, four brothers named James, John, William and Robert, came from Scotland and settled in the townlands of Culduff and Newbuildings South, in the Parish of Ballymoney. The other three brothers left and James stayed at Newbuildings where his family prospered. James was made a J.P. For the County of Antrim. In his will he left his farm at Culduff to his eldest son William and his farms at Newbuildings to his sons John and Henry.

His son William married Mary, daughter of James McPeake, and brother of Neal McPeake Esq., solicitor. Their son Neal married Ester Robinson and was a medical doctor in the Royal Navy.

Their daughter Hester married Samuel Taylor, a butcher and publican in Main Street, and one of their sons William was a distinguished doctor in Ballymoney. His portrait was in Ballymoney Town Hall.

His sons James and Henry emigrated.

His son John (or Jack) was an important man in the area. He refused to join the Rebels or the United Irishmen in the 1798 rebellion. He married Elizabeth Bateson and had eight children. Their son Henry married Jane Warnock of Carnately (see grave 364). Robert married Mary McLaughlin of Carnany (see graves 360, 361, 362). Mary married William Tweed of Culduff in 1820 in 1st Ballymoney Presbyterian Church. John married Jane McLester of Finvoy in 1825 in 1st Ballymoney. James married Rose Robinson. William married Jane Neill, Jane married John Henry of Bravellan and Bess married Adam, son of John and Rachael (Blair) Adams of Main Street, Ballymoney.

```
1 James Robinson 1697 - 1769
.. +Margaret 1715 - 1777
...... 2 William Robinson 1746 - 1829
.......... +Mary McPeake
................ 3 Neal Robinson
.................... +Ester Robinson
................ 3 Hester Robinson 1764 - 1864
.................... +Samuel Taylor - 1845
.................... 3 Margaret Robinson
...... 2 James Robinson
...... 2 Robert Robinson 1746 - 1822
................ 3 James Robinson
...... 2 Henry Robinson
...... 2 Jane Robinson
.......... +Mr Knox
...... 2 Margaret Robinson
...... 2 John Robinson
.......... +Elizabeth Bateson
................ 3 Henry Robinson 1788 - 1856
.................... +Jane Warnock
................ 3 Robert Robinson 1797 - 1883
.................... +Mary McLaughlin 1811 -
................ 3 Mary Robinson 1786 -
.................... +William Tweed
................ 3 Bess Robinson 1784 -
.................... +Adam Blair Adams 1797 - 1872
................ 3 John Robinson 1790 - 1862
.................... +Jane McLester 1792 - 1874
................ 3 James Robinson
.................... +Rose Robinson 1783 - 1865
................ 3 William Robinson - 1875
.................... +Jane Neill
................ 3 Jane Robinson
.................... +John Henry
```

HENRY

GRAVE no. 367

Memento mori
Here were interred
the remains of
James Henry of Bravallin
who died about the year 1717
and Elizabeth his wife who
died the 13 of Novr 1737 far
advanced in years
Also James Henry Junr & William
his brother the former of whom
died in 1728 or 29 of a wound he
received in a duel & the latter In 1750
both in the prime of life
most sincerely & deservedly
lamented by all their relatives
& acquaintances

1 James Henry - 1717
.. +Elizabeth ? - 1737
...... 2 John Alexander Henry 1700 - 1773
.... +Margaret Johnston 1723 - 1802
.... 3 Johnston Henry 1754 - 1794
.... 3 Alexander Henry 1755 - 1810
.... +Mary ?
.... 3 Jane Henry
.... +Archibald Stuart 1746 -
.... 4 Charles Edward Stuart 1782 -
.... 4 Alexander Stuart 1784 -
.... 4 Archibald Stuart 1786 -
.... 4 Elizabeth Stuart 1788 - 1845
.... +Robert Loughead 1787 - 1844
.... 4 Margaret Stuart 1790 -
.... +Daniel Henry McCay - 1847
.... 4 Frances Stuart 1792 - 1863
.... +Hugh Hall
.... 4 Jane Stuart 1793 -
.... +Dr. Beatty
.... 3 James Henry
.... 3 Elizabeth Henry
.... 3 Frances Henry
...... 2 Alexander Henry 1706 - 1787
.... +Mary Boyd 1712 - 1784
...... 2 James Henry 1699 - 1728
...... 2 William Henry - 1730

James Henry was a wealthy landowner in Bravellan outside Ballymoney and was married to Elizabeth. He had four known sons, two of whom died young.

Another son John Alexander married Margaret Johnston in 1751 and lived at Cloverhill near Stranocum. Their daughter Jane married Archibald, son of Rev. Irwin Stuart, Vicar of Ballywillium, and Elizabeth McDaniel, in 1781 and had a family of seven. None of their sons married.

Their son Alexander married Mary Boyd (see grave 367a).

HENRY

GRAVE no. 367a

Here lyeth the remains of
Mary Henry alias Boyd
who departed this life on
the 21st day of July Anno
Domini 1784 aged about 72
years during warm long
cries of time she marvelled?
Fulfilled all the respective
duties incumbent on her in
every state and condition
of her progress through life
with the most exemplary
re ? tude and propriety of
deportment
Underneath this stone lieth the
body of Mary Boyd alis Henry
relict of Hugh Boyd of Mount Edwards
Esq. who departed this life
1 day of December 1831 aged 86
Every ? adored her exercising
faith in her redeemer and in the hope of a
blessed ? Blessed are the dead who die
in the Lord
Also Letitia Johnston her daughter who
died 28th Oct 1846 aged 73 years

1 Alexander Henry 1707 - 1787
.. +Mary Boyd 1712 - 1784
...... 2 William Henry 1746 - 1826
...... 2 Mary Henry 1745 - 1831
.... +Hugh Boyd 1737 - 1816
.... 3 Letitia Boyd 1773 - 1846
.... +Robert Johnston 1768 - 1851
.... 3 Mary Boyd - 1833

Alexander, son of James and Elizabeth Henry of Bravellan married Mary, daughter of Captain Hugh Boyd, and had two children William and Mary. William didn't marry so Mary inherited the lands at Bravellan.

Mary married Hugh, son of Samuel Boyd of Mount Edwards, and had two daughters. Their daughter Mary didn't marry and died in Charlotte Street, Ballymoney. Their daughter Letitia married Robert Johnston, a watchmaker from Ballymoney, in 1791, and had six children (see grave 367b).

HENRY   GRAVE no. 367b

In this sepulcure lyeth
the remains of Alexander Henry
Late of Bravellan who departed this life on
the morning of the 7th day of
May in the year of ourLord
1787 aged 81 years
A man in whom was so
?ile Also that of his son
William Henry
of Bravellan Esq
Obit 10 April ?
A man of it might
be truly said that for
integrity of principle more
than religion rectitude he
has left behind him a character
well worthy of imitation
Departed this life the 26th October
1830 Leonard Johnson in the
34 year of his age
departed on the 14th Sep 1847
Alex B Johnston in the 37 year of his age
Robert Johnston father of the
above Leonard and Alex B. Johnston
died 20 May 1851 aged 83 years

HENRY

GRAVE no. 367b

Alexander, son of James and Elizabeth Henry was granted a quarter land of Bravellan in 1737 from the Earl of Antrim.

Alexander and Mary (Boyd) Henry had two children. Their eldest son William didn't marry, although he was said to have three illegitimate children. When he died his sister Mary inherited Bravellan. Some of the lands were seized due to debts incurred by William. She married Robert Johnston, a clockmaker from Ballymoney and had six children. Leonard married Jane Boyd, but died young without issue. His widow lived in Dublin. Letitia died in infancy. Alexander, Samuel and William all died without family. Their daughter Sophia married William Hill in 1834 and had six children. Their other daughter Mary married Hugh, son of William Boyd, in 1848 in 1st Ballymoney Presbyterian Church. Hugh was a merchant in Ballymoney but had been living in Illinois. They had no children and Mary died in Portrush leaving the annuity from her share of Bravellan land to her nieces, daughters of her sister Sophia.

```
1 Alexander Henry 1707 - 1787
.. +Mary Boyd 1712 - 1784
...... 2 William Henry 1746 - 1826
...... 2 Mary Henry 1745 - 1831
.......... +Hugh Boyd 1737 - 1816
............... 3 Letitia Boyd 1773 - 1846
................... +Robert Johnston 1768 - 1851
....................... 4 Leonard Johnston 1796 - 1830
........................... +Jane Boyd - 1879
....................... 4 Letitia Boyd Johnston 1809 - 1809
....................... 4 Alexander Boyd Johnston 1810 - 1847
....................... 4 Samuel Boyd Johnston 1812 - 1846
....................... 4 Sophia Johnston 1814 -
........................... +William Hill - 1847
....................... 4 William Johnston 1817 - 1846
....................... 4 Mary Boyd Johnston - 1869
........................... +Hugh Boyd
............... 3 Mary Boyd - 1833
```

HAY

GRAVE no. 368

Here
Lieth the body of
James Hay
of Ballybrake who departed
this life 11th August 1825
Aged 88 years
Also Margaret the beloved
wife of William Hay who
departed this life 11th Octr
1845 aged 55 years

William Hay
died 13 May 1868 aged 86 years
His youngest daughter Elizabeth
died 23th September 1886 aged 63 years

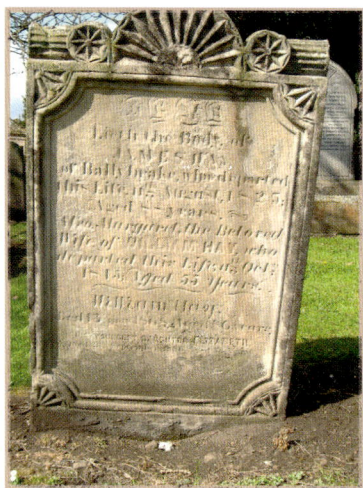

1 James Hay 1737 - 1825
.. +Mary
...... 2 William Hay 1782 - 1869
.... +Margaret Orr 1790 - 1845
.... 3 James Hay 1810 -
.... 3 Agnes Hay 1812 -
.... 3 Mary Hay 1814 -
.... +James Alexander McLaughlin 1815 -
.... 3 Robert Hay 1815 -
.... 3 Martha Hay 1820 -
.... 3 Bess Hay 1823 - 1886
.... 3 John Hay 1829 -
.... 3 William Hay 1829 -
.... 3 Edward Hay 1831 -
...... 2 Sarah Hay
...... 2 James Hay
...... 2 Margaret Hay
.... +James Millar
...... 2 Catherine Hay

William Hay was the son of James and Mary and was a farmer at Ballybrakes. He married Margaret Orr and had seven children. Only their daughter Mary is known to have married (see grave 360). Their son William was a surgeon.

There was also a Hay family living at Drumskea, who are thought to be related.

UNREADABLE

GRAVE no. 369

Here lyeth
?
?

KEASEY

GRAVE no. 370

Here lyeth
the body of
Dunkan Keasey
who was late of
Taughey
He departed this life
the 21 of December 1808
Aged 80 years
Also his son
John Keasey who
departed this life
the 26 of May 1805
Aged 17 years

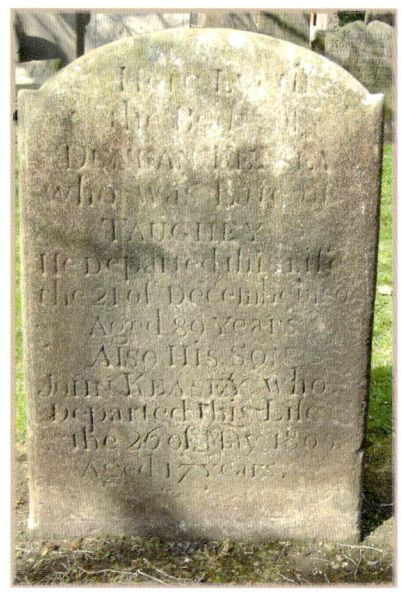

Duncan Keasey (or Casey) was a farmer in Taghey and Ballygobbin. He had possibly a son Daniel who was farming in Taghey and Ballygobbin in 1803 and 1825.

CRAMSIE   GRAVE no. 371

Sacred to the memory
of John Cramsie late of
Ballymoney who departed
this life the 20 Sepr 1819
Aged 79 years. Ann his wife
who died the 14th June 1821
Aged 81 years
Also three of their children
James, Jane and Margaret

1 John Cramsie 1740 – 1819
. +Ann 1737 – 1821
...... 2 Jane Cramsie
...... 2 Margaret Cramsie
...... 2 Anne Cramsie 1778 - 1850
.... +James Moore 1769 - 1834
.... 3 Margaret Moore 1806 - 1894
.... +James Cairns 1809 - 1870
.... 3 Archibald Moore 1809 - 1877
.... +Sarah A. P. Stirling 1817 - 1894
.... 3 James Moore 1811 - 1884
.... +Eliza Gunning 1812 - 1895
.... 3 John Moore 1813 - 1891
.... +Hannah Edwards 1819 -
.... 3 Hugh Moore 1817 - 1860
.... +Susan Moore 1817 - 1852
.... 3 Elizabeth Moore 1817 -
.... +James Wilson
...... 2 James Cramsie 1786 - 1855
.... +Jane Thomson 1785 - 1850
.... 3 Adam T. Cramsie 1815 - 1843
.... 3 James Cramsie 1818 - 1873
.... +Eliza Murray 1820 - 1896
.... 3 John Cramsie 1820 -
.... 3 William Sinclair Cramsie 1823

    The Cramsie family were originally Roman Catholics but became Quakers at the beginning of the 18th Century. Because of this they moved in 1709 to Ballymoney, which had at that time a flourishing and numerous Society of Friends. The story goes that the family had been living at Ballycramsey, Co Donegal, with the implication that Ballycramsey was named after them. Patrick Cramsie's wife Miss Moore is said to have been a great heiress.

    Their son John married Ann and had at least four children he was a merchant in Ballymoney. Anne married James, son of Archibald and Margaret (Moore) Moore of Kilraughts. James married Jane, daughter of Adam and Agnes Thomson of Ballymoney in 1814 in St. Patrick's Parish Church.

    John's brother James married a Miss Todd and lived at Coldagh. This branch still lives at O'Harabrook.

CAMERON

GRAVE no. 372

Erected
by
Angus Cameron of
Portrush to the memory of his daughter
Martha who died 30th May 1849
Aged 16 years
Also his wife Rachael
who died 17 October 1872
aged 69 years
And the above
Angus Cameron
who died 19th October 1882
John Cameron
who died 4th April 1888 aged 56 years

1 Angus Cameron 1793 - 1882
.. +Rachael Burns - 1872
...... 2 Sarah Cameron 1827 - 1866
...... 2 John Cameron 1831 - 1888
...... 2 Martha Cameron 1833 - 1849
...... 2 Alexander Cameron 1839 - 1902
...... 2 Jane Cameron 1841 - 1913

Angus, son of Archibald and Martha Cameron of Ballymoney, married Rachael Burns. He was a farmer at Meadow Parks, Portrush and none of his children seem to have married.

CAMERON

GRAVE no. 373

Here lieth the body
of Daniel Cameron
Ballymoney
died 27th September 1767
aged 48
His wife Sarah
died 20th August 1778
aged 76 years
Their son Archibald
died 17th July 1821
aged 69 years
His wife Martha
died 17th July 1827
aged 71 years
Their son Alexander
died 7th January 1826
aged 36 years
Their son Daniel
died 17th April 1850
aged 68 years
His wife Grace
died 28th July 1860
aged 73 years

1 Daniel Cameron 1719 - 1767
.. +Sarah 1722 - 1778
...... 2 Archibald Cameron 1752 - 1821
.... +Martha 1756 - 1827
.... 3 Daniel Cameron 1782 - 1850
.... +Grace Scott 1787 - 1860
.... 3 Sarah Cameron 1784 - 1866
.... +Robert Caldwell 1786 - 1862
.... 3 Alexander Cameron 1789 - 1826
.... 3 Martha Cameron 1791 - 1871
.... +Alexander Erskine 1782 - 1865
.... 3 Angus Cameron 1793 - 1882
.... +Rachael Burns - 1872
.... 3 John Cameron 1792 -
.... +Esther Mitchell
...... 2 Eleanor Cameron 1753 -

Daniel and Malcolm Cameron left Scotland after a rebellion and came to Ballymoney as carpenters (see grave 8).

Daniel married Sarah and his son Archibald married Martha. Archibald had six known children. Daniel, a carpenter in Church Street, married Grace Scott (see grave 374).

Sarah, a dressmaker, married Robert Caldwell, a shoemaker of, Church Street and had six children.

Martha married Alexander Erskine, a farmer of Dunaverney in 1825 in 1st Ballymoney Presbyterian Church (see grave 237).

Angus married Rachael Burns (see grave 372).

John married Esther, daughter of William Mitchell and sister of James of Ballymoney, in 1823 in 1st Ballymoney.

CAMERON

GRAVE no. 374

Erected
In memory of the following
members of the family of the
Late Daniel Cameron
Ballymoney
Alexander Cameron
died in America in 1853
aged 36 years
Daniel
died 15th June 1850
aged 27 years
Alicia
died 9th January 1854
aged 22 years
Grace
died 28th July 1859
aged 30 years
Elizabeth Orr
died 29th April 1862
aged 43
years
Mary-Jane
died 11th April 1863
aged 41 years
James
died 18th January 1890
aged 77 years

CAMERON

GRAVE no. 374

Daniel, eldest son of Archibald and Martha Cameron, married Grace Scott of Ballymoney, had a family of thirteen and lived in Church Street.

Their eldest son Archibald married Rachael Leslie in 1835 in 1st Ballymoney Presbyterian Church (see grave 313).

Their daughter Sally Ann was the first wife of Charles Galloway and married in 1835 in 1st Ballymoney (see grave 391).

Their son James was a carpenter and bachelor. He died in Market Street Ballymoney.

Their daughter Ellen married James Cameron, a distant cousin, in 1836 in 1st Ballymoney (see grave 8).

Their daughter Matilda married William Young in 1836 in 1st Ballymoney (see grave 393).

Their daughter Elizana married James John Orr, son of William and Mary (Mitchell) Orr in 1842 in 1st Ballymoney (see grave 51).

Their daughter Agnes Thompson married Joseph Park Mitchell, a solicitor, in 1852 in 1st Ballymoney. After her husband's death she ran her own business and then moved to Dublin where she died (see grave 256).

Their son William John married Martha Given in 1857 in 1st Ballymoney and had one daughter (see grave 375).

```
1 Daniel Cameron 1782 - 1850
.. +Grace Scott 1787 - 1860
...... 2 Archibald Cameron 1807 - 1860
.......... +Rachael Leslie 1814 - 1857
...... 2 Sally Ann Cameron 1809 - 1841
.......... +Charles Galloway 1807 - 1887
...... 2 James Cameron 1811 – 1890
...... 2 Ellen Cameron 1812 - 1850
.......... +James Cameron 1808 - 1886
...... 2 Alexander Cameron 1814 - 1850
...... 2 Matilda Cameron 1817 - 1867
.......... +William Young 1812 – 1880
...... 2 Elizana Cameron 1820 - 1862
.......... +James John Orr 1819 -
...... 2 Mary Jane Cameron 1820 - 1863
...... 2 Daniel Cameron 1823 - 1850
...... 2 Agnes Thompson Cameron 1825 - 1879
.......... +Joseph Park Mitchell 1826 - 1858
...... 2 William John Cameron 1827 – 1893
.......... +Martha Given 1839 - 1901
...... 2 Grace Cameron 1829 - 1859
...... 2 Alicia Moore Cameron 1831 - 1854
```

CAMERON

GRAVE no. 375

In memory of
Grace Scott Cameron
Ballymoney
only child of
William John Cameron
and Martha Given his wife
born 12th May 1859
Died 8th December 1877
Also above named
William John Cameron
Died 8th November 1893
aged 66 years
Also
in memory of
Martha Given Cameron
his widow
Died 18th October 1901, aged 62 years

1 William John Cameron 1827 - 1893
.. +Martha Given 1839 - 1901
...... 2 Grace Scott Cameron 1859 - 1877

William John, youngest son of Daniel and Grace (Scott) Cameron married Martha, eldest daughter of James and Matilda (Huey) Given of Ballymoney in 1857 in 1st Ballymoney Presbyterian Church. He was a grain and potato merchant and lived in Church Street. They only had one daughter who committed suicide aged 18 years.

Martha left money in her will to 1st Ballymoney Presbyterian Church.

ORR

GRAVE no. 376

In
memory
of
William Orr of Ladeside
who died 6th February 1851 aged 65 years
His wife Jane Boyd
Died 29th July 1860 aged 73 years
Their daughter
Martha Orr wife of John Young L.L.D.
Their sons Robert Orr and
Daniel Orr in America
Also William John Orr
Ladeside Ballymoney
who died 5th Feby 1900 aged 80 years

1 William Orr 1785 - 1851
.. +Jane Boyd 1787 - 1860
...... 2 Martha Orr 1813 -
.... +John Young
...... 2 Robert Orr 1815 -
...... 2 Daniel Orr 1817 -
...... 2 William John Orr 1820 - 1900

William and Jane (Boyd) Orr had family of Martha, Robert, Daniel and William John.

Martha married Rev. John, son of Robert and Mary Young, in 1837 in St. James Presbyterian Church. He was born in Ballylough, Kilraughts and went to U.S.A. as a baptist pastor. He became a Unitarian and then studied law, himself a distinguishing barrister in Indianapolis. In 1860, he helped Lincoln with his Presidential campaign and in 1861 returned to Belfast as the American consul for the Port of Belfast. He served as consul to 1866, returned to U.S.A. and died in Indiana.

William John Orr was a bachelor and died at Bravellan. He was a grandson of Robert Orr and partners from Main Street, Ballymoney.

FALOON

GRAVE no. 377

Erected
by
James Faloon
of Ballymoney
In memory of his father
James Faloon
Late of Inchinaugh
And also his mother
Margaret
And his sister Sarah
The above James Faloon
Died 30th Oct 1888 aged 78 years

1 James Falloon
.. +Margaret
...... 2 Sarah Falloon 1807 -
...... 2 Jean Falloon 1809 -
...... 2 James Falloon 1810 - 1888
...... 2 Robert Falloon 1812 -

James and Margaret Faloon had four children baptized in 1st Ballymoney Presbyterian Church. James died before 1817. James junior died at Cemetery House in Ballymoney and was a workhouse porter.

James senior had a brother Samuel who lived at Inchinagh until about 1820 when he moved to Cabra.

HARGY

GRAVE no. 378

The
HARGY'S
Burying ground

1 Neil Hargy 1811 - 1888
.. +Nancy Anderson
...... 2 James Hargy 1835 -
.... +Jane Adams 1840 -
...... 2 Jane Hargy 1837 - 1886
.... +Henry Douthart
.... 3 Nancy Douthart 1859 -
.... +Neal Hardie
.... 3 Ellen Jane Douthart 1861 -
.... 3 Alice Jane Douthart 1863 -
.... 3 James Douthart 1866 -
.... +Sarah Jane Brolly
.... 3 Francis Henry Douthart 1871 -
.... +Annie J. Colgan
.... 3 Mariah Douthart 1873 -
.... 3 Margaret Moore Douthart 1877 -
.... 3 Rosetta Douthart 1880 -
...... 2 Daniel Hargy 1838 -
...... 2 Nancy Hargy 1840 -
...... 2 Francis Hargy 1849 - 1918
.... +Susan Freeman 1855 - 1902
.... see grave 342

Neil Hargy was working in Milltown when he married Nancy Anderson, also of Milltown, in 1834 in 1st Ballymoney Presbyterian Church.

Their eldest son James married Jane, daughter of John and Margaret Adams, of Ballymoney in 1867 in St. Patrick's Parish Church.

Their eldest daughter Jane married Henry, son of Stephen Douthart of Bravellan in 1859 in St. Patrick's. They lived in Meetinghouse Street, then Meetinghouse Lane in Ballymoney.

Their youngest son Francis married Susan, daughter of John and John and Catherine (Kilpatrick) Freeman (see grave 342).

CLEMENTS

GRAVE no. 379

Erected by
J. Clements
In memory of his
sister Annie
who died 9th May
1907

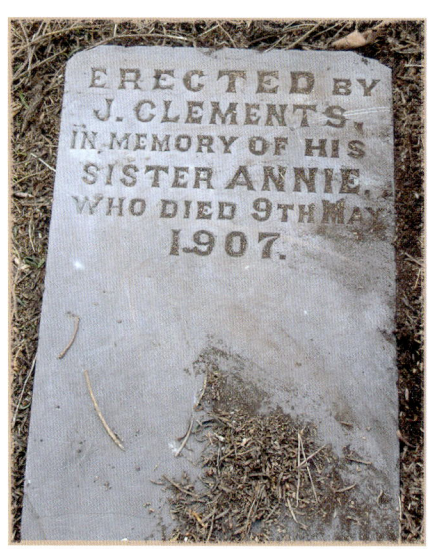

1 James Clements 1830 - 1900
.. +Mary 1829 - 1883
...... 2 Mary Clements
.... +James McCaughern
...... 2 Annie Clements 1859 - 1907
...... 2 Martha Clements 1862 -
...... 2 James Clements 1865 -
.... +Elizabeth Devine 1864 -
.... 3 Mary Clements 1888 -
.... 3 John Clements 1889 -
.... 3 James Clements 1891 -
...... 2 Andrew Clements 1867 -

Annie Clements lived in Balnamore, but died in Ballymoney workhouse aged 48 years. It is possible that her parents were James and Mary Clements of Balnamore. James was a flax dresser, died in 1900 and was buried in the Old Graveyard. Her mother Mary died in 1883 aged 54 at Currysisken.

HARRISON

GRAVE no. 380

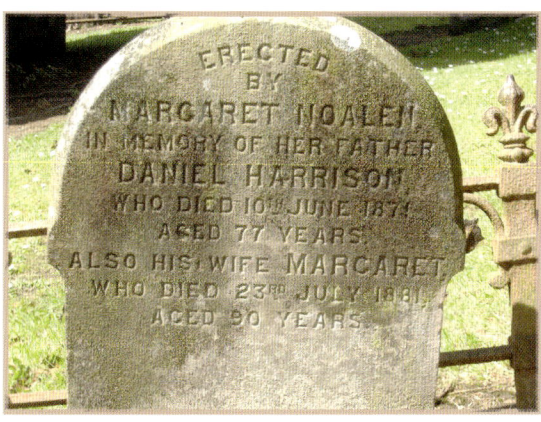

Erected
by
Margaret Noalen
In memory of her father
Daniel Harrison
who died 10th June 1871
aged 77 years
Also his wife Margaret
who died 23rd April 1881
aged 90 years

1 Daniel Harrison 1794 - 1871
.. +Margaret 1791 - 1881
...... 2 Margaret Harrison 1825 - 1897
.... +John Noalen
.... 3 Sarah Noalen 1870 - 1887
.... 3 Daniel Noalen 1866 -
.... +Hannah McAuley 1875 -
.... 4 Sarah Noalen 1894 -
.... 4 John Noalen 1898 -
.... 4 Margaret Noalen 1900 -

Daniel Harrison was a pedlar and lived in Castle Street, Ballymoney. His daughter Margaret doesn't appear to have married in Ballymoney. It seems that she was a widow when she returned. Her son Daniel married Hannah, daughter of William McAuley, and they too lived in Castle Street.

SMILEY

GRAVE no. 381

Erected
to
the memory of
Hugh Smiley Balnamore
who died 22nd March 1872
aged 75 years
Also his wife Agnes Smiley
who died the 29th June 1878
aged 78 years

The only marriage found of a Hugh and Agnes Smiley was in Trinity Presbyterian Church in 1856. Hugh, son of John Smiley, and a farmer at Balnamore married Nancy, daughter of Charles Cunning, also a farmer at Balnamore.

SMILEY

GRAVE no. 382

Erected
by
James Smiley
in
Loving remembrance of
His daughter Christina
who died 28th August 1874
Aged 25 years
Also Jannie
who died 26th October 1884
aged 76 years
James Smiley
Died 2nd Nov 1894 aged 82

James Smiley was a builder and died in Belfast. Christina was a schoolmistress at Balnamore at the time of her death.

The only Smiley families recorded in 1803 were James and William in Kilymoyangie, Kilraughts and Andrew, Hugh, John, John and Samuel in Legacurry, Kilraughts. In 1825, in the Ballymoney area were two and Samuel at Claughey.

HANNAH

GRAVE no. 383

Sacred
to the memory of
Samuel Hannah
late of Drumaheigles
who departed this life
2nd June 1844 aged 66
Also his sister
Elizabeth Hannah
who died 13th Dec 1857
aged 78

Samuel Hannah was living at Drumaheglis in 1817 with his sisters Ann and Elizabeth. In 1803, Widow, Samuel and Hugh were present.

BROWN

GRAVE no. 384

Erected
to the memory of
James Brown
of Ballywattick
who departed this life
on the 16 day of November 1860
aged 86 years

1 James Brown 1774 - 1860
.. +Mary
...... 2 John Brown 1804 -
.... +Jean Haggarty 1800 -
.... 3 Jean Brown 1822 -
.... +James Culbertson
.... 3 John Brown 1824 -
.... 3 Ebby Brown 1827 -
.... 3 Mary Brown 1829 -
.... +John Doherty 1824 - 1890
.... 3 Jenny Brown 1832 -
.... 3 James Brown 1835 -
...... 2 James Brown 1806 -
...... 2 Hugh Brown 1809 -
...... 2 Robert Brown 1812 -
...... 2 Isabella Brown 1815 -
.... +Alexander Culbertson 1801 -
.... 3 Robert Culbertson 1839 -
...... 2 Thomas Brown 1818 -
.... +Mary Reynolds

James and Mary Brown were farmers at Ballywattick and had a family of five.
John married Jean, daughter of William and Jean Haggarty of Secon and had six children.
Isabella married Alexander, son of Alexander and Martha (Dinsmore) Culbertson junior, of Ballywattick in 1838 in 1st Ballymoney Presbyterian Church.
Thomas married Mary, daughter of John Reynolds of Culduff in 1853 in St. James Presbyterian Church.

CULBERTSON

GRAVE no. 385

In
loving memory
of
Hugh Culbertson
of Artigoran
who died 16th April 1883
Aged 71 years
Also his wife Margaret
who died 27th Dec 1896
Aged 80 years
Also their son William John
Died 19th January 1929

1 Hugh Culbertson 1811 - 1883
.. +Margaret Montgomery 1816 - 1896
...... 2 Robert Culbertson 1845 - 1883
.... +Jane Getty
...... 2 William John Culbertson 1848 - 1929
...... 2 James Culbertson 1850 -
...... 2 Mary Culbertson 1852 -
...... 2 William Culbertson 1854 -
...... 2 Andrew Culbertson 1856 -
...... 2 Nancy Culbertson 1858 -
.... +? Ellis

Hugh was the son of Robert and Mary (Wright) Culbertson of Artigoran. He married Margaret, daughter of Robert Montgomery, a leather cutter of Main Street, Ballymoney in 1844 in 1st Ballymoney Presbyterian Church.

Their eldest son Robert, a gardener, married Jane, daughter of Samuel and Jane (Lilley) Getty of Drumaheglis, in 1868 in Drumreagh Presbyterian Church. They emigrated to U.S.A.

Their son William John was a a bachelor and died at Artigoran.

GAMBLE

GRAVE no. 386

Sacred
to the memory of
Martha Gamble
wife of Samuel Gamble
of Ballymoney who
departed this life 28
January 1822 aged 23

1 James Culbertson 1760 - 1810
...... 2 Hannah Culbertson 1792 - 1868
.... +John Flanagan
.... 3 Samuel Flanagan 1825 - 1838
...... 2 Martha Culbertson 1798 - 1822
.... +Samuel Gamble 1797 -
...... 2 Hugh Culbertson 1800 -

Samuel, son of Alexander and Catherine (McClure) Gamble married Martha, daughter of James Culbertson of Ballywattick in 1821 in 1st Ballymoney Presbyterian Church. Her sister Hannah married John Flanigan of Prospect (see grave 2). She also had a brother Hugh.

CULBERTSON

GRAVE no. 387

Underneath Lie
The mortal remains
of James Culbertson
late of Ballymoney
who departed this
life the 28 day of May
1810 aged 46 years
Also
four of his children
William Young
Trench
Died 13th February 1867
aged 71 years
His wife
Jane Culbertson
Died 19th June 1853
aged 61 years
His daughter
Martha
Died 28th Feby 1864
Mary Jordan
wife of James Culbertson
and great grandmother of
Robert Adams, Ballymoney
died 1818
Aged 42 years

1 James Culbertson 1754 - 1810
.. +Mary Jordan 1776 - 1818
...... 2 Jane Culbertson 1792 - 1853
.... +William Young 1796 - 1867
.... 3 Mary Young 1828 - 1896
.... +David Adams 1818 – 1877
see graves 59, 60
.... 3 Robert Young 1831 -
.... 3 Jane Young 1832 -
.... 3 Jane Young 1834 -
.... 3 Martha Young 1836 - 1864
...... 2 James Culbertson 1807 - 1809

James Culbertson was a publican in Ballymoney and married Mary Jordan, daughter of James and Jane (Anderson) Jordan of Main Street, Ballymoney. Their daughter Jane married William Young, son of William and Ann Young of Trench, in 1828 in 1st Ballymoney Presbyterian Church.

Their eldest daughter Mary married David, son of Archibald and Mary (Kennedy) Adams of Claughy, in 1852 in 1st Ballymoney Presbyterian Church.

Their son Robert married Elizabeth, daughter of Moore and Martha (Erskine) Stuart of Carnany. Robert was a watchmaker in Church Street, Ballymoney.

MCELROY

GRAVE no. 388

McElroy

1 Samuel Craig McElroy - 1914
.. +Marianne Jordan 1839 - 1899
...... 2 Samuel C. McElroy 1860 - 1901
.... +Martha Cochrane 1878 -
...... 2 Robert McElroy 1862 - 1864
...... 2 dau McElroy 1863 -
...... 2 Jane Hopkins McElroy 1865 - 1869
...... 2 Marianne McElroy 1866 -
.... +W. Bradshaw
...... 2 dau McElroy 1868 -
...... 2 Emma McElroy 1870 -
.... +William Manson Nevin 1871 - 1943
.... 3 Robert Nevin 1900 -
.... 3 Samuel Craig Nevin 1896 - 1972
.... 3 William Alexander Nevin 1905 -
.... 3 Thomas Harold Nevin 1907 - 1910
.... 3 Marion Jordan Nevin 1910 -

Samuel Craig, son of Daniel McIlroy, and grandson of Alick McIlroy, married Marianne Jordan, youngest daughter of Robert and Jane (Hopkins) Jordan of Main Street, Ballymoney in 1859 in Trinity Presbyterian Church and had seven children. Samuel was a printer and editor of Ballymoney Free Press.

Their eldest son Samuel Craig married Martha, daughter of Robert and Catherine Jane (Morrison) Cochrane of Carnbore in 1902 in Bushvale Presbyterian Church. He was an auctioneer and died in Belfast.

Their daughter Marianne emigrated to Australia.

Their daughter Emma married William Manson, son of Rev. Robert and Kathleen (Manson) Nevin in 1894 and emigrated to South Africa.

NO GRAVESTONE FOUND

GRAVE no. 389

UNKNOWN

GRAVE no. 390

?
?
?
who departed
this life May 10
1798 aged 62 years.

This gravestone is broken and has the upper portion missing. It is at present sitting propped up against the wall. No more is known

GALLOWAY

GRAVE no. 391

Erected
by Charles Galloway
to the memory of his wife
Sally Ann who departed this life
10th March 1841 aged 31 years
And their son George
aged 5 months

1 Charles Galloway 1807 - 1887
.. +Sally Ann Cameron 1809 - 1841
...... 2 Elizabeth Galloway 1837 - 1846
...... 2 Grace Anna Galloway 1838 -
...... 2 George Galloway 1841 - 1841
*2nd Wife of Charles Galloway:
.. +Jane Leslie 1817 - 1888

Charles Galloway was the son of Neal and Elizabeth Galloway. He married Sally Ann, daughter of Daniel and Grace (Scott) Cameron of Church Street, Ballymoney in 1835 in 1st Ballymoney Presbyterian Church. They had three children, two of whom died young and Grace Anna, who emigrated to Australia. Sally Ann died shortly after the birth of her youngest child George. Charles was married again in December 1841 to Rachael Leslie in 1st Ballymoney (see grave 339). He was a grain merchant in Ballymoney.

YOUNG

GRAVE no. 392

Here lieth the remains of
Robert Young
late of Ballymoney who
departed this life 8th Nov. 1843
aged 66 years
Also
Two of his sons Robert died
May 1849 aged 29 years
and John who died
9th June 1843 aged 16 years

1 Robert Young 1777 - 1843
.. +Mary Bateson 1789 - 1862
...... 2 William Young 1812 - 1880
.... +Matilda Cameron 1817 - 1867
          see grave 393
...... 2 Mary Ann Young 1814 - 1902
.... +John Small 1810 – 1882
          see grave 68
...... 2 Jane Young 1816 - 1816
...... 2 Eliza Young 1818 - 1820
...... 2 Robert Young 1820 - 1849
...... 2 Isabella Young 1823 - 1849
...... 2 John Young 1827 - 1843

    Robert Young was born in Ballydivity between Dervock and Bushmills, son of William, a blacksmith. His family are buried in Billy Churchyard.
    Robert married Mary Bateson, daughter of William and Jenny Bateson. William was dead before 1800 and Jenny owned and ran a delph shop in Piper Row, Ballymoney. She had two other daughters Elizabeth, who married James Thomson of Dunaverney (see grave 116) and Jean.
    Robert was a blacksmith and died in Charlotte Street (previously called Piper Row), Ballymoney.

YOUNG GRAVE no. 393

Here lieth the remains of
Isabella Young
who departed this day 19th
May 1849 aged 26 years
Two of her sisters also Eliza and Jane
aged 2 years and 6 years
Also the remains of
their mother Mary Young
wife of Robert Young
late of Ballymoney
She departed this life
the 6th June
1862 aged 73 years

1 William Young 1733 - 1783
...... 2 Robert Young 1777 - 1843
.... +Mary Bateson 1789 - 1862
.... 3 William Young 1812 - 1880
.... +Matilda Cameron 1817 - 1867
.... 3 Mary Ann Young 1814 - 1902
.... +John Small 1810 - 1882
.... 3 Jane Young 1816 - 1816
.... 3 Eliza Young 1818 - 1820
.... 3 Robert Young 1820 - 1849
.... 3 Isabella Young 1823 - 1849
.... 3 John Young 1827 - 1843

These are the rest of the family who were buried in grave 392. Robert and Mary Young are the great great great great grandparents of the author.

YOUNG

GRAVE no. 394

Underneath lies Matilda
Beloved wife of William Young,
Ballymoney
She died 10 Mar 1867 aged 50 years
and
Beside her lies her dear son William Young
a medical student
He died in Belfast 8th February 1867
aged 22 years
Also their son Daniel Young
Died 30th September 1872
aged 25 years
The above named William Young
Died 30th March 1880
aged 68 years
Also their son John
Died 12th May 1888 aged 38 years
Their son James
Died 2nd March 1906 aged 53 years
Their daughter Matilda
Died 12 March 1907 aged 64 years
their daughter Grace
Died 9th November 1922
aged 83 years

1 William Young 1812 - 1880
.. +Matilda Cameron 1817 - 1867
...... 2 Robert Young 1838 - 1916
.... +Anne Jane Moon 1836 - 1914
.... 3 Robert Steele Young 1868 -
.... 3 Matilda Cameron Young 1869 -
.... +William Keers 1869 - 1943
.... 3 Margaret Moore Young 1871 -
.... 3 William Young 1872 -
.... 3 John Moon Young 1875 - 1904
.... +Lottie McKee
.... 3 James Young 1879 - 1943
.... +Mary Wilson Smyth 1878 - 1944
...... 2 Grace Young 1839 - 1922
...... 2 James Young 1840 - 1906
...... 2 Mary Ann Young 1841 - 1906
.... +Joseph Beare 1840 - 1905
.... 3 William Beare 1866 - 1907
.... +Mary Speers - 1899
.... 3 Matilda Beare 1868 -
.... 3 Elizabeth Beare 1869 -
.... +William Campbell 1867 -
.... 3 Robert Beare 1871 -
.... 3 Thomas James Beare 1873 - 1941
.... +Frances Jane Thompson - 1941
.... 3 George Beare 1875 - 1956
.... +Ellen Orr Doole 1870 -
.... *2nd Wife of George Beare:
.... +Ann A. Anderson 1888 -
.... 3 Mary Jane Beare 1877 -
.... 3 David Beare 1879 - 1930

YOUNG

GRAVE no. 394

On side at top
Jane Bateson
died 31st March 1844
aged 82 years

On side at bottom
Alexander McCook
died 26th July 1789
aged 56 years

.... 3 Isabella Beare 1880 - 1973
.... 3 John Henry Beare 1882 -
.... +Margaret Thorburn 1881 -
.... 3 Samuel Bateson Beare 1883 - 1967
.... +Isabel Victoria Williams 1883 -
.... 3 Ellen Beare 1884 - 1885
.... 3 Female Beare 1885 -
...... 2 Matilda Young 1843 - 1907
...... 2 William Young 1845 - 1867
...... 2 Daniel Young 1847 - 1872
...... 2 John Young 1851 - 1888
...... 2 David Young 1855 -

William Young was the eldest son of Robert and Mary (Bateson) Young of Ballymoney. He married Matilda Cameron who was born in Church Street, Ballymoney, daughter of Daniel and Grace (Scott) Cameron, in 1836 in 1st Ballymoney Presbyterian Church. William became a builder and was in business with his Cameron cousins.

He had a family of nine with three of his sons dying young. Nothing is know of the youngest David. The two oldest sons were in business together and established the well known firm of R. & J. Young. Grace and Matilda were spinsters and lived in Church Street, Ballymoney. Matilda was a seamstress.

Their son Robert married Anne Jane, daughter of William Moon in 1867 in Garryduff Presbyterian Church. They are buried in Knock Road Cemetery.

The only daughter to marry was Mary Ann, who married Joseph, son of Robert and Elizabeth (Cavan) Beare of Culnady, Maghera in 1864 in 1st Ballymoney Presbyterian Church. He was a linen draper in Ballymoney for a time. He was a cousin of Rev. Thomas Beare, minister of Drumreagh Presbyterian Church.

They had a family of thirteen and emigrated to Delaware, York Co., Ontario where they both died.

Jane Bateson was the wife of William Bateson of Ballymoney and mother of Mary, Elizabeth and Jean. She was possibly the daughter of Alexander McCook, merchant of Ballymoney who died in 1789.

MCILHAIR

GRAVE no. 395

In loving memory of
Daniel McIlhair
who died 7 Nov. 1964 aged
80 years
Also his wife
Mary
Died 17th February 1960
aged 88 years

1 John McIlhair
.. +Eliza Smyth
...... 2 Jean McIlhair
.... +John McAuley
.... 3 Samuel McAuley 1870 -
.... 3 Mary Jane McAuley 1878 -
.... 3 Joseph McAuley 1878 -
.... 3 James McAuley 1879 -
...... 2 John McIlhair 1835 -
...... 2 Catherine McIlhair 1848 - 1896
...... 2 Joseph McIlhair 1851 - 1932
.... +Margaret ? 1854 -
.... 3 Daniel Redmond McIlhair 1884 - 1964
.... +Mary Willis 1871 - 1960
.... 4 Margaret McIlhair 1915 -
.... 4 Joseph John McIlhair 1917 - 1986
.... +Elizabeth Ruby Pinkerton 1916 -
.... 4 Annie Mary McIlhair 1918 -
.... +Robert White
.... 4 Jean Elizabeth McIlhair 1921 -
.... +Robert Harkness 1917 -
.... 4 Kathleen Helen McIlhair 1924 -
.... 3 Annie Josephine McIlhair 1886 -
.... +Robert White
.... 3 Lizzie McIlhair 1888 -
.... 3 William John McIlhair 1878 - 1920
...... 2 Margaret McIlhair 1855 -
.... +William Winlock 1855 -

Daniel Redmond McIlhair was a son of Joseph and Margaret McIlhair of Ballygobbin. He married Mary (known as Minnie) Willis in 1914 in Trinity Presbyterian Church, Ballymoney. She was the daughter of James Charles and Mary (Kirkpatrick) Willis, farmer of Claughy.

Joseph and Margaret had at least three other children, Annie Josephine who married Robert White of Cabra in 1914 in St. James Presbyterian Church, Lizzie and William John who died in Belfast.

SHANNON

GRAVE no. 396

William Shannon
Died 22nd Feby 1856 aged 45 years
Mary Orr Shannon
His daughter died 27th Decr 1865
aged 18 years
Also his infant child
Samson Shannon
Lies here
Margaret Jane Shannon
wife of Robert Melville
Died 24th November 1874
Aged 34 years
And William Shannon junr
Died on the 24 Sept 1877
Aged 33 years

1 William Shannon 1810 - 1856
.. +Margaret Pattison 1807 - 1891
...... 2 Margaret Jane Shannon 1840 - 1874
.... +Robert Melville - 1886
...... 2 William Shannon 1844 - 1877
...... 2 Samson Shannon 1846 - Infant
...... 2 Mary Orr Shannon 1846 - 1865

William Shannon, a cooper in Ballymoney, married Margaret Pattison in 1839. They had children Margaret Jane, William, Mary Orr and Samson. They attended St. James Presbyterian Church where they had married.

Their eldest daughter Margaret Jane married Robert, son of George Melville, a miller from Drumaheglis, in 1861 in St. James Presbyterian Church. Robert Melville remarried in 1875 in 1st Ballymoney Presbyterian Church Elizabeth, daughter of Robert and Mary (McLauglin) Robinson of Newbuildings. They had one son George. Robert died in 1886 at Drumaheglis and is buried in Knock Road Cemetery, Ballymoney.

UNREADABLE   *GRAVE no. 397*

MCDONALD

GRAVE no. 398

In memory of Annie McDonald
Died 25th Aug 1875
Aged 22 years
Jane McDonald
Died 9th February 1890
Aged 27 years

1 Hugh McDonald 1816 - 1890
.. +Annie McGregor 1825 - 1891
...... 2 Thomas McDonald 1849 -
...... 2 Martha McDonald 1850 -
.... +John Henry
.... 3 Martha Henry 1887 -
.... 3 John Henry 1889 -
.... 3 Thomas Hugh Henry 1894 -
.... 3 Jane Henry 1895 -
...... 2 Ann McDonald 1852 -
...... 2 Mary McDonald 1854 -
.... +John Hill
...... 2 Anne McDonald 1856 - 1879
...... 2 Sarah McDonald 1856 - 1912
.... +James Kane 1855 - 1925
.... 3 Sara Kane 1892 - 1968
.... 3 Elizabeth Kane 1893 - 1895
.... 3 Jane Kane 1896 -
.... 3 Elizabeth Kane 1903 -
...... 2 Elizabeth McDonald 1860 - 1926
...... 2 Jane McDonald 1862 - 1890

Annie and Jane were daughters of Hugh and Annie (McGregor) McDonald, a small farmer at Newhill, Ballymoney.
Their eldest daughter Martha married John, son of Patrick Henry, in 1887 in Benvarden Presbyterian Church.
Their daughter Mary married John, son of John and Jane Hill of Kirkhills in 1877 in 1st Ballymoney Presbyterian Church.
Their daughter Sarah married James, son of William and Isabella Kane in 1891 in St. Patrick's Parish Church. They are buried in the Parish Churchyard.

LESLIE

GRAVE no. 399

Thomas Leslie
Balnamore
1913

.1 John Leslie - 1889
...... 2 Mary Ann Leslie 1835 -
.... +John Moody 1835 -
.... 3 John Moody 1857 - 1931
.... +Mary Hogg 1862 - 1929
.... 3 Mary Jane Moody 1860 - 1917
.... +William Hogg 1857 - 1922
.... 3 James Moody 1862 -
.... +Margaret Lynch
.... 3 Margaret Annie Moody 1865 -
.... 3 Martha Moody 1868 -
.... 3 Ellen Moody 1870 -
.... 3 Thomas Moody 1874 -
...... 2 Ellen Leslie 1847 - 1921
.... +Moore Taylor McCurdy 1825 - 1906
...... 2 Thomas Leslie 1845 - 1917
.... +Sarah Clements 1846 - 1913

    Thomas, a widow and flax dresser of Balnamore, son of John Leslie, married Sarah, daughter of Thomas Clements, a tailor of Balnamore, in St. Patrick's Parish Church, Ballymoney in 1889. Thomas died in Balnamore in 1917 and his wife in 1913.
    He had a sister Mary Ann who married John Moody of Balnamore in St. James Presbyterian Church, Ballymoney in 1856 and had a family of seven.
    Another sister Ellen married Moore Taylor McCurdy (see grave 106).

UNREADABLE

GRAVE no. 400

CHESTNUT

GRAVE no. 401

To the memory of
John Chestnut of Ballyg
an who departed this
life Feb 9th 1818 aged 44

1 John Chestnut 1774 - 1818
.......+ Elizabeth 1778 - 1804
...... 2 Samuel Chestnut 1815 - 1905
.... +Jane Picken 1821 -
.... 3 William Chestnut
.... +Sarah Hanna 1860 -
.... 3 Samuel Chestnut 1858 - 1907
.... +Elizabeth McLaughlin 1865 - 1931
.... 4 Samuel Chestnut 1894 -
.... 4 Jane Picken Chestnut 1896 - 1985
.... +James Willis 1881 - 1956
.... 4 James John Chestnut 1901 -
.... 3 Alexander Chestnut - 1946
.... +Letitia Blair - 1953
.... 4 Sarah Jane Chestnut 1894 -
.... 4 John Chestnut 1896 -
.... 4 William James Chestnut 1899 - 1978
.... 4 Alexander Chestnut 1901 - 1989
.... 4 Samuel Chestnut 1904 -
.... 4 Annie Chestnut 1908 -
.... 4 Mary Chestnut 1913 -
.... 3 Lizzie Chestnut
.... +James Crawford
...... 2 Elizabeth Chestnut 1810 - 1893

    John and Elizabeth Chestnut had at least two children Elizabeth and Samuel. Samuel married Jane, daughter of James and Jean (McCay) Picken of Taghey, in 1847 in 1st Ballymoney Presbyterian Church and had four children.
    Their son William married Sarah, daughter of David and Jane (Sayers) Hanna of Secon in 1889 in St. James Presbyterian Church.
    Their son Samuel married Elizabeth, daughter of Daniel McLaughlin of Ballaghmore in 1892 in St. James.
    Their son Alexander married Letitia, daughter of John Blair of Killans in 1892 in Trinity Presbyterian Church and was a a farmer at Cross.
    Their only daughter Lizzie married James, son of Hugh Crawford of Culduff, in 1892 in Trinity.

COCHRAN

GRAVE no. 402

Erected by
James Cochran

In memory of his
father Hugh Cochran
who departed this life
March 26th 1799
Aged 55 years

There were two James Cochrans present in the 1803 census, one in Ballybrakes and the other at Garry. There were no James Cochrans present in 1825.

WHITE

GRAVE no. 403

WHITE

Shall be satisfied when
aware
in his likeness

No more information

HOWARD

GRAVE no. 404

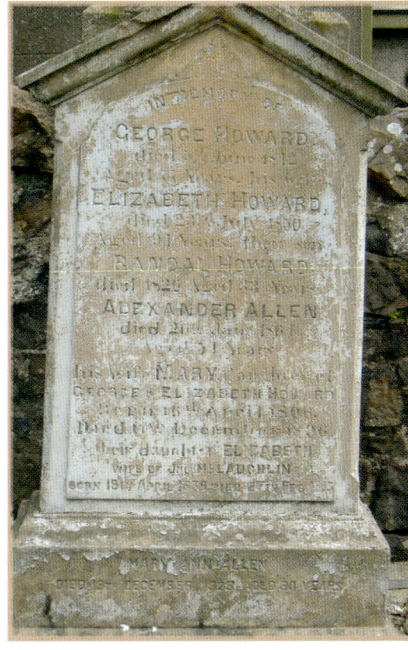

In Memory of
George Howard
died 3rd June 1812
Aged 77 years. His wife
Elizabeth Howard
died 23 July 1830
Aged 91 years. Their son
Randal Howard
died 1826 aged 33 years
Alexander Allen
died 26th Jan 1864
Aged 54 years
His wife Mary daughter of
George and Elizabeth Howard
Born 16th April 1806
died 11th December 1896
their daughter Elizabeth
wife of John McLaughlin
Born 19th April 1838 Died 27th Feb 1913
Mary Ann Allen
Died 19th December 1928 aged 80 years

1 George Howard 1735 - 1812
.. +Elizabeth 1739 - 1830
...... 2 Mary Howard 1806 - 1896
.... +Alexander Allen 1809 - 1864
.... 3 Elizabeth Allen 1838 - 1913
.... +John McLaughlin 1838 - 1921
.... 3 Mary Ann Allen 1848 - 1928
...... 2 Randal Howard 1793 - 1826

Nothing is known about the Howard family. They don't appear in any local records. Alexander Allen was a soldier and then a shopkeeper. He died in Castle Street.

Their daughter Elizabeth married John, son of Edward McLaughlin, in 1851 in Ballymoney Registry Office. They both died in Coleraine.

FORBES

GRAVE no. 405

FORBES

No more details

1 James Forbes
.. +Elizabeth McKillop 1837 - 1907
...... 2 Matilda Forbes
.... +John Darragh
...... 2 Joseph Forbes 1860 - 1927
.... +Elizabeth McComb
.... 3 Rachael Forbes 1888 - 1956
.... +Willian Drain - 1956
.... 4 Joseph Forbes Drain 1914 - 1914
.... 4 Alexander Drain 1915 -
.... +Evelyn McComb
.... 4 Elizabeth Forbes Drain 1918 -
.... 4 Rachael Drain 1920 -
.... 4 Joseph Forbes Drain 1921 -
.... 4 Margaret Drain 1923 -
.... +James McKay
.... 4 Dorothy Drain 1926 -
.... +Hedley Oliver Gardiner
.... 4 Tillie Drain 1927 - 1928
.... 4 William Drain 1927 -
.... +Agnes Fynes
.... 4 Birdie Drain 1929 -
.... 3 Elizabeth Forbes 1886 -
.... 3 Samuel Forbes 1890 - 1895
...... 2 Samuel Forbes 1869 - 1879
...... 2 Elizabeth Forbes 1871 -
.... +Hugh Ramsey

    James, son of John Forbes a labourer, married Elizabeth, son of Samuel McKillop of Druckendult in 1853 in Trinity Presbyterian Church.
    Their son Joseph married Elizabeth, daughter of James McComb of Portrush in 1879 in Trinity. He was a butcher in High Street, Ballymoney. Their only son died young. Their other daughter Rachael married William, son of Alexander Drain, a fisherman from Portrush, in 1906 in Trinity. The Drain family took over the business.

MCMICHAEL

GRAVE no. 406

Erected to the memory of
Charles McMicheal
late of Ballymoney
who departed this life
on the 17th February 1844
Aged 39 years

Charles McMichael married Rachael, daughter of Charles Devenney in 1824 in 1st Ballymoney Presbyterian Church and had four known children, James, Henry, Margaret (b.1833) and Charles (b.1837). They lived at Charlotte Street.

There were McMichael families also living in Drumreagh and Bendooragh in the early 19th century.

THOMSON

GRAVE no. 407

Erected
In memory of
Mary Ann Thomson
wife of John Thomson
of Ballygobbin
She died on the 14th day of
March 1847 aged 58 years
Here is also interred
Her husband John Thomson
who died on the 10th day of April
1856 aged 69 years

1 John Thomson 1786 - 1856
.. +Mary Ann Small 1788 - 1847
...... 2 James Thomson 1815 - 1895
.... +Catherine Neill
...... 2 Hugh Thomson 1818 - 1895
.... +Anna Small
...... 2 John Thomson 1821 -
.... +Olivia McAlister 1827 - 1850
...... 2 Rose Ann Thomson 1829 - 1873
.... +James Pinkerton 1829 -
.... 3 John Thomson Pinkerton 1857 -
.... 3 Mary Ann Pinkerton 1862 -
.... 3 Mary Jane Pinkerton 1867 -

    John, son of Hugh and Rose Thomson of Ballygobbin, married Mary Ann, daughter of James Small.
    Their son James married Catherine, daughter of James and Susan (Dinsmore) Neill of Druckendult in 1844 in 1st Ballymoney Presbyterian Church.
    Their son Hugh married Anna, daughter of James Small of Kilmoyle in 1875 in 1st Ballymoney.
    Their daughter Rose Ann married James, son of Samuel and Jean (McCrellis) Pinkerton in 1859 in 1st Ballymoney.

THOMSON

GRAVE no. 408

Erected
In memory of
Olivia
The beloved wife of
John Thomson, of Ballymoney
She died on the 9th of Decr 1850
aged 25 years

Olivia, daughter of Samuel McAlister, a clerk of Ballycastle, married John, son of John and Mary Ann (Small) Thomson of Ballygobbin in June 1850 in Ballycastle Presbyterian Church (see grave 407). John was a merchant in Ballymoney.

BECKETT

GRAVE no. 409

In loving memory
of
Catherine S. Beckett

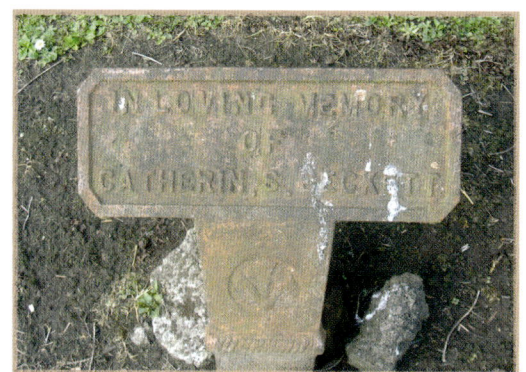

1 Henry Beckett 1872 - 1947
.. +Catherine Sterritt 1873 - 1917
...... 2 William Sterritt Beckett 1897 - 1969
.... +Ethel Sinclair Nevin 1902 - 1965
...... 2 Annie Sterritt Beckett 1900 -
.... +Hugh Meehan 1900 -
...... 2 Henry Sterritt Beckett 1902 - 1902
...... 2 Kathleen Elizabeth Beckett 1904 -
.... +Christopher Cody
...... 2 Robert Graham Beckett 1905 - 1906

Catherine, daughter of William Sterritt, a farmer, married Henry, son of Oliver and Mary (Kelly) Beckett of Balnamore, in 1896 in St. Patrick's Parish Church. Henry was a flax dresser at Balnamore at the time of his marriage. They lived in Balnamore and this is where Catherine died.

BECKETT

GRAVE no. 410

Sarah Beckett
died 28th November 1911

1. James Beckett 1867 -
. +Sarah
...... 2 Sarah Beckett 1887 - 1911
...... 2 Mary Beckett 1889 -
...... 2 Margaret Beckett 1889 -
...... 2 Robert Beckett 1892 -
...... 2 Alexander Beckett 1894 -

Sarah was the daughter of James and Sarah Beckett of Balnamore. She was born on 6th March 1887 in Balnamore and was baptized on 24th April 1887 at St. Patrick's Parish Church, Ballymoney.

HUSTON

GRAVE no. 411

Here lieth
the body
of Jane Huston
wife of William Mc?
? ? who died April
1756 aged 76 years

DUNLOP

GRAVE no. 412

Here lies
Margaret Dunlop
who died 17th Febr 1863
Aged 68 years
Also her son
David
who died 1849 aged 18 years

Nothing can be found on this family. There was an Alexander Dunlop in Main Street Ballymoney who was a boot and shoe seller in 1824, a grocer in 1846 and a grocer and leather seller in 1856.

In 1824, there were Dunlop families at Claughey, Drumskea and Kirkhills.

GETTY

GRAVE no. 413

Here lieth
Interred the body
of David Getty
Late of Kirkmoyle
who departed this life
the 8 Feb 1813 aged
64 years

1 James Getty 1709 - 1784
.. +Hannah - 1766
...... 2 James Getty - 1837
.... +Margaret McKeown
...... 2 John Getty 1747 - 1825
.... +Mary Moore 1748 - 1801
...... 2 David Getty 1749 - 1813
.... +Mary Taggart 1747 - 1825
...... 2 Andrew Getty 1755 - 1814
.... +Jane

David Getty was a son of James and Hannah Getty of Kirkmoyle. He married Mary Taggart and they had no known children (see graves 81, 82, 83).

MCKEAG

GRAVE no. 414

Here lieth the remains
of Mary McKeag
wife of Andw McKeag
of Ballywindeland
who departed this life
27th April 1811 aged 28
years
Also Ann McKeag
Their child departed
this life 26th April 1811
Aged 2 years

Mary married Andrew, son of Benjamin and Martha (Currry) McKeag (or McKeague) of Ballywindland (see graves 44, 415).

MCKEAG

GRAVE no. 415

Erected
to the memory of
Andrew McKeag
late of Ballywindland
Who died 1st April 1854
Aged 77 years
Also
Mary Ann McKeag
Who died 28th August 1864
Aged 76 years
Benjamin McKeag
Died 16th January 1898
Aged 87 years

1 Benjamin McKeague
.. +Martha Curry
...... 2 John McKeague 1789 - 1839
.... +Mary White 1799 - 1861
.... 3 Andrew McKeague 1833 - 1916
.... +Jane MacAfee 1829 - 1913
see grave 44
...... 2 Andrew McKeague 1776 - 1854
.... +Mary ? 1783 - 1811
.... 3 Ann McKeague 1808 - 1811
.... 3 Benjamin McKeague 1810 - 1898
...... 2 Mary Ann McKeague 1788 - 1864
...... 2 Benjamin McKeague
.... +Agnes Steen

Andrew was the son of Benjamin and Martha (Curry) McKeag (also spelt McKeague). He was a farmer at Ballywindland, married Mary and had two children. Their son Benjamin was a saddler in Ballymoney.

CULBERT

GRAVE no. 416

to the memory of
Alex Culbert of
Bllymoney who ?
The 5th Feby 17? aged
? years. Also Catrine
Culbert his wife who
died on the 10 Oct 1825
Aged 84 years

Alex Culbert was a tanner to James Moore. He was married to Katie and had three sons. Nathaniel married Mary, daughter of William Gerrow of Newhill. Alexander married Agnes McLaughlin and Francis married Jean, daughter of Robert and Martha (Small) Fullerton of Ballygabbin in 1825 in 1st Ballymoney Presbyterian Church.

1 Alex Culbert
.. +Katie ? 1744 - 1828
...... 2 Nathaniel Culbert
.... +Mary Gerrow
.... 3 Catherine Culbert 1812 -
.... 3 Eliza Culbert 1814 -
.... 3 Rose Culbert 1816 -
.... +William Forbis
.... 3 Alexander Culbert 1817 -
.... 3 John Culbert 1818 -
.... 3 William Culbert 1821 -
.... 3 Mary Jean Culbert 1826 -
.... 3 Martha Culbert 1829 -
.... 3 Sally Ann Culbert 1831 -
...... 2 Alexander Culbert 1785 - 1865
.... +Agnes McLaughlin
.... 3 Robert Culbert 1819 -
.... +Ellen McMaster 1824 -
.... 3 Roseann Culbert 1821 -
.... 3 Catherine Culbert 1832 -
.... 3 Alexander Culbert 1834 -
.... 3 Mary Culbert 1837 -
.... 3 Nancy Culbert
.... +William Picken 1825 -
...... 2 Francis Culbert 1788 -
.... +Jean Fullerton
.... 3 Matilda Culbert 1826
.... 3 Catherine Culbert 1828 -

DRAIN

GRAVE no. 417

In
Loving memory
of
Jane Drain
who died 8th Sep. 1884
aged 53
and of her brothers
William
Died 10th Dec. 1892, aged 48
Robert
Died 24th Sep. 1893, aged 66
Hugh
Died 28th Aug. 1899 aged 64
and her sister
Mary
wife of James McKeague
Died 15th June 1913 aged 70

1 Hugh Drain 1783 - 1853
.. +Anne Wilson 1800 - 1823
.... 2 Rebecca Drain 1820 -
.... 2 William Drain 1823 -
*2nd Wife of Hugh Drain:
.. +Nancy Donaghy 1808 - 1868
.... 2 Robert Drain 1827 - 1893
.... 2 John Drain 1829 -
.... 2 Jane Drain 1831 - 1884
.... 2 Martha Drain 1833 - 1848
.... 2 Joseph Drain 1841 -
.... 2 Hugh Drain 1835 - 1899
.... 2 Mary Drain 1842 - 1913
.... +James McKeag 1853 - 1933
.... 2 William Drain 1844 - 1892
.... 2 Henry McCay Drain 1849 -
.... +Jane Stewart 1848 -
.... 3 Robert Drain 1871 -
.... 3 Hugh Drain 1875 -
.... 3 Isabella Drain 1878 -
.... 3 Agnes Drain 1880 -

This is the family of Hugh and Nancy (Donaghy) Drain of Meetinghouse Lane who married in 1827 in St. Patrick's Parish Church (see grave 1).

Their daughters Jane and Martha also died at Meetinghouse Lane. Robert, Hugh, Mary and William all died at Roddenfoot. Robert was a bachelor and a farmer and proprietor of houses. Hugh was a blacksmith and William was also a farmer.

Mary married James, a blacksmith, and son of Robert and Mary (McKay) McKeag of Newbuildings in 1894 in St. Patrick's.

CAMAC

GRAVE no. 418

CAMAC
1610

Gravestone set into the wall

This is the oldest grave found. The Camac name was also spelt Cummock, Cammack, Comoc. This is thought to be of the first Camac to arrive in the Ballymoney area from England. A George Camac is thought to have come to the area, married a Mary, had three sons and died in 1610.

The name is thought to have originated in Sussex. Three brothers are said to have come to N. Ireland, one settling in Co. Down and the two others in the Ballymoney area. They seem to have always been in Garry, a townland about 5 miles north east of Ballymoney since they arrived. A Camac family is still living in Garry (see graves 190, 348, 349, 351).

DICK

GRAVE no. 419

In Memory of
Robert Dick of Garry
who died 20 February 1860
aged 72 years
and his wife Isabella
who died 13th April 1876
John Dick
died 24th December 1895
Robert Dick M.D., F.R.C.S.E.
Surgeon Major Army Medical Service
Born 1st June 1831 Died 14th Oct 1913

1 Robert Dick 1787 - 1860
.. +Isabella Wallace - 1876
...... 2 Nancy Dick 1826 - 1914
.... +Robert Pinkerton 1818 - 1903
.... 3 Isabella Pinkerton 1852 - 1937
.... +John Pinkerton 1845 - 1908
.... 3 Robert Dick Pinkerton 1853 - 1934
.... +Elizabeth Leese Magill 1860 - 1946
.... 3 Elizabeth Pinkerton 1855 - 1944
.... +John McKay 1831 - 1917
.... 3 Marianne Pinkerton 1857 - 1955
.... +John Hamill 1852 - 1927
.... 3 John Wallace Pinkerton 1858 - 1882
.... 3 Ellen Sharpe Pinkerton 1863 - 1937
.... +John Pinkerton 1840 - 1955
.... 3 Agnes Pinkerton 1866 - 1907
.... +Hugh Parry 1866 - 1938
.... 3 James Pinkerton
.... +May Paul
...... 2 Margaret Dick 1831 -
...... 2 Robert Dick 1831 - 1913
...... 2 John Dick 1829 - 1895
.... +Isabella McFadden 1842 - 1908
.... 3 Robert Dick 1879 - 1928
.... +Mary McRobert 1885 - 1964
...... 2 Ellen Dick 1834 - 1925
.... +John Megaw 1830 - 1913
................see grave 341
...... 2 William Moore Dick 1837 -
...... 2 Isabella Dick 1838 -
.... +Hugh Caldwell
.... 3 Thomas Reid Caldwell
.... 3 Isa Caldwell
.... 3 Robert Dick Caldwell
...... 2 Matilda Dick 1840 -

Robert Dick married Isabella, daughter of John and Ellen (Richard) Wallace of Kirkhills in 1824 in 1st Ballymoney Presbyterian Church.

Their eldest daughter Nanay, married Robert, son of John and Abigail (Wallace) Pinkerton of Secon, in 1851 in the Unitarian Church of Ballymoney.

Their son John married Isabella, daughter of Rev. Joseph and Mary (Hill) McFadden. Rex McFadden was Minister of

Their daughter Ellen married John, son of David John and Sarah (Borland) Megaw of Killyrammer in 1864 in Roseyards Presbyterian Church.

DICK GRAVE no. 420

To the memory of
Robert Dick late
of Garry
who departed this life
11th Sep 1818 aged 81 years
Agnes his wife died
28th July 1814 aged 58 years
Also their daughter Jean
departed 25th July 1795 aged 13 years
Rests the body of
Samuel Dick late of
Ballymoney, merchant
son to the above mentioned Robert
and Agnes Dick. He departed
this life 3rd day of June 1821
aged 26 years
Lamented by all who
knew him
Andrew Dick, eldest son of the
above Robert Dick died 23rd Aug
1848 aged 63 years

1 Robert Dick 1737 - 1818
.. +Agnes Sharpe 1756 - 1814
...... 2 Jean Dick 1782 - 1795
...... 2 Andrew Dick 1786 - 1848
...... 2 Robert Dick 1787 - 1860
.... +Isabella Wallace - 1876
...............see grave 419
...... 2 Elizabeth Dick 1793 - 1822
.... +James Gordon 1786 - 1852
.... 3 Joseph Gordon 1821 - 1891
.... +Mary Sharpe 1832 - 1911
...... 2 Samuel Dick 1795 - 1821
.... +Margaret 1798 -
.... 3 Samuel Dick 1820 -
...... 2 Rose Dick 1797 -
.... +William Bullick
.... 3 Thomas Alexander Bullick
...... 2 Ellen Dick
.... +Thompson
...... 2 Nancy Dick 1796 - 1829
.... +Robert Knox 1796 -

The Dick family were farmers at Garry from the 17th century. Robert, son of Andrew married Agnes Sharpe, possibly of Moyarget about 1780.

Their daughter Elizabeth married James Gordon, a Ballymoney watchmaker (see grave 327). Their son Samuel was a merchant in Ballymoney, married Margaret and had a son Samuel. Their daughter Ellen married a Thompson of Booton. Their daughter Nancy was the first wife of Robert Knox of Currysisken.

WILSON

GRAVE no. 421

To the memory of
Margaret wife of John Wilson
of Ballymoney
who died 17th June 1855
Aged 69 years

There was a John Wilson who was a boot and shoemaker in Main Street in 1824. There was also a John Wilson who was a provision merchant in Townhead Street in 1846.

There was a marriage recorded in St. Patrick's Parish Church of John Wilson and Margaret Gardner, both from the Parish of Loughgill, in 1816. John and Margaret had children, John (b.1816), (Flora b.1818), (John b.1821) and Alexander (b. 1825). None of these children were born in Ballymoney.

There also was a family of a William and Mary Wilson present in 1817 in Ballymoney, who had children John, James, David and William.

O'HARA

GRAVE no. 422

Sacred
to the memory of
several members of the
O'Harabrook
family

1 Henry O'Hara 1758 - 1823
.. +Sophia - 1857
...... 2 Charles O'Hara 1798 - 1873
.... +Margaret Innes 1800 - 1884
.... 3 Arthur O'Hara 1828 - 1866
.... 3 William O'Hara 1830 - 1859
.... 3 Anne O'Hara 1833 - 1869
.... +William Thomas Latham 1812 - 1882
.... 4 Margaret Florinda Latham 1867 - 1868
.... 3 James O'Hara 1835 - 1870
.... 3 Ellen Sophia O'Hara 1840 -
.... +William Armstrong
...... 2 James O'Hara 1800 - 1893
...... 2 Henry Robert O'Hara 1799 - 1854

There are also three graves to the O' Hara family in St. Patrick's churchyard. When the O'Hara line died out, the Cramsie family took over the estate. There is also a small, private burying ground in O'Harabrook called Lamb's Fold where members of the O'Hara, Cramsie and Moore families are buried.

Henry and Sophia had at least three sons. Charles lived at O'Harabrook, Rev. James was Rector of Coleraine and Henry Robert died at Coleraine Rectory from the effects of typhus fever.

None of Charles' sons married. His daughter Anne married Dr. William T. Latham of Charlotte Street in 1866 in St. Patrick's and she and her only child died young. His daughter Ellen Sophia married Rev. William Armstrong, Vicar of Newtoncrumlin in 1865 in St. Patrick's.

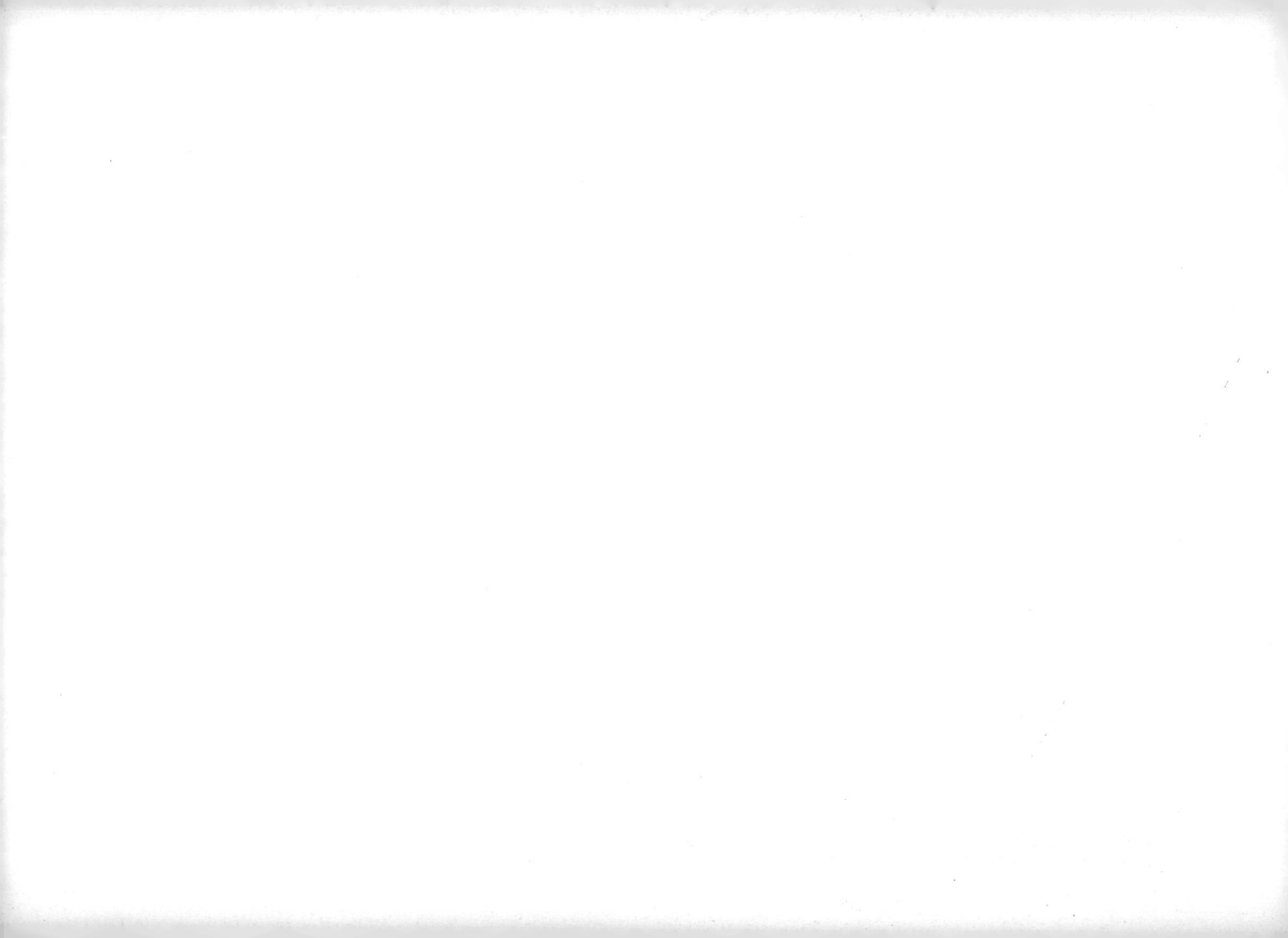

Gravestone name index

Please note, the numbers in the following index refer to grave numbers rather than page numbers.

Adair: 50, 114
Adams: 59, 60, 62, 80, 98, 130, 173, 183, 190, 215, 222, 236, 237, 307, 316, 318, 351, 366, 378, 387
Agnew: 241
Allen: 404
Anderson: 52, 79, 229, 230, 342, 378, 387
Andrews: 243
Archibald: 41, 278
Arthur: 134, 143
Atkinson: 242
Bacon: 337
Baird: 191, 337
Bamford: 148
Barr: 300, 316
Bateson: 68, 307, 337, 360, 392, 394
Beare: 394
Beckett: 21, 22, 183,184, 185, 409, 410,
Beers: 231
Bell: 123, 124, 133, 247
Bennett: 51
Best: 278
Biggart: 278, 289, 290, 291
Bingham: 120, 149
Black: 152, 310, 344
Blair (Blaire): 98, 98a, 102, 132, 133, 137, 232, 307, 366, 401
Borland: 179, 284, 341, 419
Boyce: 82
Boyd: 23, 44, 56, 78, 79, 85, 93, 99, 100, 103, 104, 105, 110, 116, 149, 151, 160, 179, 185, 213, 230, 243, 247, 248, 265, 303, 340, 346, 358, 367, 367a, 367b, 376
Boyle: 109, 193, 195, 348
Brewster: 101, 102
Brodie: 271
Brown: 79, 146, 167, 169,173, 179, 215, 222, 255, 336, 356, 356, 357, 384
Burns: 372, 373
Burnside: 23, 57, 100, 110, 116, 120, 149
Burriss: 146
Byrne: 344
Calderwood: 159, 218, 287
Caldwell: 190, 227, 287, 288, 351, 373
Camac: 190, 328, 348, 349, 351, 351a, 418
Cameron: 6, 7, 8, 9, 51, 222, 227, 236, 237, 256, 313, 339, 342, 359, 372, 373, 374, 375, 391, 394
Campbell: 53, 179, 194, 211, 214, 227, 242, 275, 278, 342, 349
Carson: 94, 236, 314, 328
Cassidy: 30, 31, 200, 201
Catherwood: 159
Caulfield: 297
Cavan: 394
Chambers: 330
Cherry: 78, 79
Chestnut: 293, 300, 401
Christy: 168, 185
Clements: 379, 399
Cochrane (Cochran): 58, 79, 244, 272, 284, 316, 328, 349, 388, 402
Colvan: 335
Comock: 351a
Conn: 222
Connell: 362
Connelly: 186

Connor: 189
Cooper: 6, 75, 80, 82, 11, 107, 173, 174, 268
Corkidale: 48
Corry: 269
Craig: 11, 133, 190
Craith: 208, 210, 346
Cramsie: 225, 226, 286, 371
Crawford: 238, 401
Creek: 344
Crilly: 103, 104
Cristy: 57
Cromie: 234
Crozier: 277
Cubitt: 307
Culbert: 16, 63, 210, 346, 347, 416
Culbertson: 2, 102, 160, 169, 229, 255, 335, 385, 386, 387
Cunning: 381
Cunningham: 25, 364
Cuppage: 268, 271
Curry: 6, 44, 96, 101, 107, 158, 160, 179, 198, 199, 281, 338, 342, 414, 415
Darcus: 207
Davison: 299
Dempster: 318
Devenney: 406
Dick: 57, 280, 281, 327, 341, 419, 420
Dickey: 196
Dickson (Dixon): 8, 264
Dinsmore (Dinsmoor): 23, 94, 97, 98, 101, 102, 107, 181, 208, 265, 405, 407
Dobbin: 61, 308
Doherty (Dogherty) (Dougherty): 25, 246, 255, 300

Donaghy: 168, 350, 417
Dorrans: 177
Douglas (Douglass): 10, 82, 204
Douthart: 186, 378
Drain: 1, 176, 405, 417
Dripps: 289
Dunlop: 25, 196, 316, 350, 412
Dunn: 274
Dunne: 100
Eason: 35
Edwards: 61
Esdale: 3, 258
Elder: 257
Elliott: 318
Erskine: 6, 59, 68, 98, 236, 237, 238, 373, 387
Esdale: 3, 352
Faloon (Falloon): 377
Ferguson: 69, 127
Ferrier: 75
Flanagan (Flanigan): 2, 3, 386
Fleming: 167
Forbes: 405
Forde: 142
Forsythe: 79, 141, 179
Foster: 236
Freeman: 214, 242, 342, 378
Fullerton: 73, 107, 155, 173, 246, 416
Fulton: 35
Fynes (Fines): 293
Galbreath (Galbraith): 87, 306
Galloway: 12, 313, 338, 339, 374, 391
Galt: 18, 77

Gault: 286
Gamble: 76, 240, 294, 295, 296, 297, 298, 314, 315, 316, 317, 318, 344, 386
Gardiner (Gardner): 149, 421
Gaston: 318
Gelston: 141
Gerrow: 63, 416
Getty: 11, 63, 80, 81, 82, 107, 111, 169, 174, 228, 236, 238, 298, 350, 385, 413
Gibson: 343
Gilmour (Gilmore): 58, 200, 222, 238, 249, 250
Given (Givin): 62, 109, 147, 239, 240, 298, 359, 374, 375
Glass: 98, 132, 133
Glen: 109
Gordon: 67, 78, 128, 327, 420
Graham: 271
Gray: 6, 60, 316
Greene: 286, 286a
Greer: 139, 200
Griffith: 292
Hacket: 14, 361a
Haggarty: 255, 312, 336
Hale: 190
Halliday: 4
Haltridge: 188, 189
Hamill: 57, 61, 94, 152, 192, 228, 238
Hamilton: 56, 212, 222, 223, 224, 225, 226, 249, 250, 251
Hammer: 268
Hanna (Hannah): 217, 257, 304, 383, 401
Hargy: 342, 378
Harkness: 11
Harpour: 126

Harrison: 380
Hart: 57, 58, 168, 279, 350
Haughey: 48
Hay: 187, 360, 368
Hayes: 64, 66, 67
Hemphill: 324, 325
Henderson: 331, 332
Henery: 31
Henry: 4, 5,32, 278, 345, 366, 367, 367a, 367b, 398
Heywood: 135
Hill: 79, 283, 367b, 398, 419
Hodges: 11
Holmes: 171
Hopkin (Hopkins): 17, 37, 107, 143, 230, 289, 290, 291, 388
Howard: 94, 404
Huey: 14, 15, 215, 341, 359, 375
Hunter: 45, 46, 48, 49, 56, 99, 100, 107, 108, 177, 179, 225, 235
Huston:
Hutchinson: 140, 141, 142, 266, 308
Jameson: 68, 136
Jamison: 111, 136, 152, 210, 258
Jellie: 79
Johnson: 14, 16, 30, 31, 50, 59, 98, 101, 115, 229, 343, 346, 367, 367a, 367b
Jordan: 37, 210, 229, 230, 387, 388
Judges: 26
Junk: 185
Kane: 319, 398
Keasey (Casey): 370
Keers: 63, 160
Kelly: 27, 210, 229, 262, 409

Kennedy: 5, 14, 40, 131, 185, 206, 299, 316, 387
Kidd: 155, 156
Killen: 8
Killough: 215, 216, 355
Kilpatrick: 51, 242, 342, 378
Kinnear: 249, 251, 334, 362
Kirkpatrick: 60, 73, 395
Knipe: 293
Knox: 56, 78, 93, 94, 100, 105, 128, 152, 153, 195, 210, 237, 272, 280, 281, 294, 339, 420
Kyle: 178
Lamont: 14, 39, 98, 160, 190, 200, 234, 257
Laverty: 28, 358, 360
Lecky: 140, 141, 142
Leslie: 58, 128, 198, 199, 268, 269, 270, 271, 271a, 313, 339, 346, 347, 374, 391, 399
Liken: 328, 349
Lilley: 7, 9, 345, 385
Linton: 330
Logan: 318
Long: 131, 186
Longmoor: 331, 332
Loughead: 222
Loughridge: 200
Love: 16, 19, 157, 179, 210, 345, 346, 346a, 347
Lowry: 200
Lusk: 117, 361
Lyle: 51, 65, 78, 114, 128, 152, 167, 284
Lynch: 107, 108
Lynn: 350
Lyons: 14, 58, 160, 198, 199, 257, 313, 352

Macafee (McAfee) (McFee) (McAffee): 44, 51, 56, 64, 67, 93, 94, 100, 105, 128, 149, 152, 153, 158, 281, 325, 339
Macgill: 202
Mackey: 202
MacManus; 137
Mallett: 14, 15, 16
Manson: 388
Marshall: 87, 145, 306
Martin: 53, 117, 129, 169, 211, 272, 328
Matchett: 9
Matthews: 78, 172, 227
McAleese: 11
McAlister: 149, 211, 214, 227, 242, 274, 342, 408
McAlonan: 86
McAnaul: 306
McAula: 167, 192
McAuley: 110, 289
McAyeale: 73, 246
McBride: 145a, 238, 299
McCandless: 346, 346a
McCann: 343
McCaughan: 11
McCaw: 246, 267
McCay: 115, 262, 300, 312, 336, 401
McCeuity: 47
McClelland: 245
McClure: 79, 296, 297, 298, 359, 361, 364, 386
McCollum: 55
McComb: 405
McConaghie: 190
McCook: 173, 279, 394
McCoubrey: 245

McCrellis: 58, 83, 84, 198, 407
McCullough: 217
McCurdy: 6, 106, 110, 119, 157, 217, 222, 223, 224, 250, 286, 399
McCutchion: 220, 221
McDaniel: 367
McDermott (McDermot): 41, 42, 43
McDonald (MacDonald): 335, 398
MacDougall: 133
McDowell: 219, 245, 321
McDuffe (McDuffee): 154, 93, 320
McElderry: 65, 119, 284, 286
McElroy: 37, 230, 388
McElvery: 228
McFadden: 262, 419
McFarland: 39, 187, 245
McGarry: 354
McGlade: 312
McGregor: 149
McHenry: 19
McHugh: 40
McIlfatrick: 120
McIlhair: 395
McIlhargy: 6
McIlhatton: 337
McIlhernon: 131, 134
McIlhose: 102
McIlrevy (McIlreavy): 61, 101, 296, 298
McIntyre: 250, 301, 330
McIlroy: 68, 249, 291
McKay: 57, 120, 300, 417
McKeag (McKeague): 44, 94, 96, 103, 182, 207, 414, 415, 417
McKeesock: 176

McKeown: 59, 61, 192, 217, 229, 349
McKighan: 13
McKillop: 405
McKinlay (McKinlai): 24, 65
McKinney: 330
McLaughlin: 152, 322, 358, 360, 361, 362, 366, 396, 401, 404, 416
McLean: 58
McLeesh: 208
McLester: 191, 366
McMaster: 6, 32, 144, 165, 166, 236, 321, 341
McMichael: 28, 147, 406
McMullan: 84, 345
McNaughton: 207, 269
McNaul: 115
McPeake: 366
McQuillan: 188, 189
Megaw: 341, 419
Melville: 396
Michael: 4
Millar (Miller): 109, 147, 177, 239, 296, 327, 359
Miskelly: 26
Mitchell: 50, 51, 94, 98, 146, 232, 256, 312, 336, 373, 374
Montgomery: 385
Moody; 399
Moon: 9, 394
Moore: 23, 57, 82, 103, 109, 110, 111, 120, 149, 165, 179, 198, 203, 204, 205, 212, 215, 216, 217, 222, 226, 232, 237, 261, 300, 327, 341, 351, 355, 364, 371
Morrison: 4, 19, 21, 60, 219, 388
Moss: 128
Mullans: 41
Munnis: 50, 114

Murdock: 212, 223, 224, 249, 250, 251, 345
Murray: 191
Murphy (Murphey): 28, 69, 276
Murtagh: 21
Neil (Neal)(Neill): 65, 75, 99, 109, 111, 150, 180, 181, 253, 254, 259, 284, 366, 407
Neillie: 189
Nelson: 30
Nevin: 58, 65, 75, 76, 111, 119, 127, 165, 222, 286, 349, 388
Nickleson: 329
Ogilvy: 120, 137
O'Hara: 422
O'Neill: 137
Orr: 6, 46, 50, 51, 52, 94, 98, 114, 174, 360, 368, 374, 376
O'Toy (Toy): 323
Oulton: 226
Overend: 257
Park: 146, 168, 256
Patrick: 65, 111
Patterson: 156, 243, 264, 350
Pattison: 214, 227, 264, 396
Patton: 7, 14, 148, 314, 315, 317
Peacock: 100, 281, 294
Percy: 350
Perry: 199, 230
Picken: 31, 115, 169, 262, 300, 401
Pinkerton: 56, 57, 58, 100, 107, 198, 225, 274, 278, 361, 407, 419
Pollock: 48, 333
Poole: 169
Prince: 100
Purdy: 245, 293

Quigg: 168, 296, 298
Rainey: 21, 22, 183, 187, 321
Ramsay: 272, 302, 303, 305
Rankin: 179
Reney: 363
Reynolds: 175, 341, 344
Rice: 117, 361
Richard: 285, 294, 419
Richart: 285
Robinson: 3, 6, 73, 74, 174, 191, 237, 278, 307, 337, 341, 360, 361, 362, 364, 365, 366, 396
Rodgers: 78
Rosborough: 212, 249, 250, 251
Ross: 30, 31, 200, 316
Rowan: 50, 135, 137, 138
Sandford: 177, 270, 271
Sayers: 257, 401
Scott (Scot): 9, 51, 165, 166, 256, 265, 306, 313, 359, 364, 373, 374, 375, 391, 394
Shanks: 219
Shannon: 396
Sharpe: 57, 280, 281, 327, 420
Shaw: 107, 115
Sherrard: 196
Shields: 219
Shiels: 6
Simpson: 148, 236, 246, 298
Sinclair: 73, 74, 364
Sinclaire: 141
Sloss: 148
Small: 30, 63, 68, 69, 70, 82, 99, 101, 200, 201, 208, 209, 210, 211, 212, 213, 214, 236, 249, 250, 346, 405, 406, 416

Smiley: 5, 381, 382
Smith: 66, 67, 196, 197, 294, 364
Smoll: 200
Smylie: 145a
Smyrell: 67
Smyth: 68, 191, 197, 236, 328, 348, 349
Snodgrass: 330
Speers: 8, 150
Spence: 38, 160
Stafford: 234
Stavely: 222
Steele: 80
Steen: 7, 44, 100, 257
Sterritt: 409
Stevenson: 150, 314
Stewart: 7, 29, 87, 127, 131, 134, 135, 138, 143, 157, 173, 178, 25, 226, 230, 236, 316, 353
Stirling: 75, 160, 168, 260, 261, 262, 300, 323, 341
Stockman: 343
Stuart: 59, 148, 237, 351, 364, 367, 387
Sutton: 238
Swan: 75
Taggart: 11, 173, 230, 252, 274
Taylor: 22, 167, 178, 231, 234, 282, 306, 316, 366
Templeton (Tampleton): 19, 120, 121, 122, 125, 149, 211, 214, 309
Thompson (Thomson): 44, 58, 76, 87, 90, 100, 117, 118, 119, 149, 183, 282, 286, 286a, 303, 306, 371, 392, 407, 408, 420
Thorburn: 222
Todd: 122, 208, 209, 371
Toland (Trolland): 257

Tonner: 150
Townsend: 242
Turner: 237
Twaddle: 19, 257
Tweed: 131, 134, 303, 319, 359, 361, 364
Tylor: 20
Unreadale: 36, 54, 89, 91, 95, 162, 164, 233, 259, 263, 311, 369, 389, 390, 397, 400
Wales: 109, 348, 349
Walker: 117, 321
Wallace: 9, 57, 72, 73, 149, 179, 192, 238, 258, 273, 274, 326, 341, 348, 419
Warburton: 140, 141
Warnock: 73, 178, 237, 361, 364, 366
Watson: 128
Watt: 111, 204, 300
Webb: 238
Weir: 71
White: 14, 28, 50, 103, 112, 113, 114, 115, 148, 155, 204, 215, 216, 289, 395, 403
Williamson: 360
Willis: 395
Wilson (Willson): 6, 107, 128, 135, 137, 155, 156, 173, 204, 246, 267, 421
Wood: 141
Woodside: 68, 127
Workman: 94
Wright: 38, 96, 158, 160, 161, 169, 170, 198, 199, 281, 335, 385
Wylie (Wiley): 6, 163, 173, 174, 236, 237
Young: 57, 59, 60, 68, 69, 229, 275, 341, 392, 363, 374, 376, 387, 392, 393, 394

Number Index

1. Drain, R
2. Flanigan of Prospect
3. Flanagan of Prospect
4. Henry of Leaney
5. Kennedy of Laney
6. Wiley of Dunaverney
7. Lilley of Ballymoney
8. Cameron of Ballymoney
9. Cameron of Ballymoney
10. Douglass of Balnacree
11. Craig of Islandboy
12. Galloway, James of Ballymoney
13. McKighan
14. Mallett of Ballygan
15. Mallett of Ballygan
16. Johnston, Mallett of Ballymoney
17. Hopkin
18. Galt
19. Morrison of Secon
20. Tylor
21. Rainey, of Ballymoney; Murtagh
22. Beckett of Ballycormick
23. Boyd, Robert of Macfin
24. McKinlai
25. Dunlop
26. Miskelly, John of Ballindreen
27. Kelly of Ballymoney
28. Murphy of Ballymoney
29. Stewart, John
30. Cassidy of Ballymoney; Nelson of Ohio
31. Ross of Ballymoney
32. Henry of Drumahiskey
33. Henry, John and James
34. Henry, Matthew
35. Fulton of Ballymoney
36. Unreadable
37. Hopkins, William of Ballymoney
38. Spence of Currysisken
39. McFarland of Landhead
40. McHugh, Patrick; Kennedy of Ballymoney
41. McDermott of Cullermoney
42. McDermott, Clarke of Cullermoney
43. McDermott, William of Cullermoney
44. McKeague, Andrew; Macafee of Ballywindland
45. Hunter, Adam of Ballinagarry
46. Hunter
47. McCeuity of Ballymoney
48. Hunter, Thomas of Gortnee
49. Hunter, William
50. Orr of Ballymoney
51. Orr, William of Ballymoney
52. Anderson, Orr of Ballymoney
53. Martin
54. Unreadable
55. McCollum
56. Pinkerton of Knowhead
57. Pinkerton of Secon
58. Pinkerton, James of Coleraine
59. Adams of Ballymoney
60. Adams of Claughey
61. Getty
62. Given, Robert of Booton

63. Gerrow of Ballymoney
64. McAfee, Robert
65. McElderry of Leitrim and Ballymoney
66. Hayes, Caroline of Newbuildings
67. Hayes of Newbuildings
68. Small of Kirkhills
69. Small, John of Churchills(Kirkhills)
70. Small, Jane of Churchills(Kirkhills)
71. Wallace; Loudon, Weir; of Newbuildings
72. Wallace of Newbuildings
73. Sinclair; McAyeal of Druckendult
74. Sinclair of Druckendult
75. Nevin of Claughey
76. Nevin of Claughey
77. Galt of Ballymoney
78. Boyd, James of Fortown
79. Boyd, John of Fortown
80. Getty of Kirkmoyle and Heagles
81. Getty of Kirkmoyle
82. Getty of Kirkmoyle
83. McCrelis of Kirkmoyle
84. McMullan, McCrellis of Kirkmoyle
85. Boyd of Culbrim(Coolebreene)
86. McAlonan, Archibald of Ballymoney
87. Thompson of Greenshields
88. Thompson, Mary
89. poss Thompson- unreadable
90. Thompson
91. poss Thompson-unreadable
92. Thompson, Nancy
93. MacAfee of Currysisken
94. MacAfee of Currysisken
95. Unreadable
96. Curry, Andrew
97. Dinsmore of Ballywattick
98. Johnson of Ballymoney
98a. Blaire of Ballymoney
99. Dinsmore of Ballywattick
100. McAfee
101. Dinsmore of Ballywattick
102. Dinsmore of Ballywattick
103. Boyd, Elizabeth of Ballywindland
104. Boyd, Thomas of Ballywindland
105. Boyd, Robert of Ballywindlind
106. McCurdy, Moore
107. Hunter of Secon
108. Hunter of Ballywattick
109. Moore of Dunluce
110. Moore of Dunluce and Cloney
111. Moore of Dunluce
112. White of Coleraine and Coolebreene
113. White of Artigoran
114. White
115. White of Currysisken
116. Thomson of Dunaverney
117. Walker of Ballymoney
118. Thompson of Greenshields and Islandmore
119. Thompson of Ballymoney
120. Templeton of Moneycannon
121. Templeton
122. Todd, Hugh of Ballygan
123. Bell of Prospect

124. Bell of Prospect
125. Templeton
126. Harpour, James of Drumafivey
127. Ferguson of Cluntyfinnan
128. McAfee of Ballymoney
129. Martin of Ballinamoney
130. Adams, Martin of Ballymoney
131. Tweed of Pleasure Step
132. Glass of Ballymoney
133. Glass of Ballymoney
134. Stewart of Loughabin
135. Rowan of Garry and Bellisle
136. Jamison of Druckendult
137. Rowan
138. Rowan of Mullans; Stewart of Garry
139. Greer of Turner's Grove
140. Lecky of Ballymoney
141. Hutchinson of Ballymoney
142. Hutchinson of Ballymoney
143. Stewart of Cabra
144. McMaster of Ballymoney
145a. Marshall, Rev
145b. Smylie, Rev
146. Park, Rev. of Ballymoney
147. Miller of Ballymoney
148. Patton, Bamford of Cuppindale
149. Burnside of Macfinn
150. Speers of Ballymoney
151. Boyd of Culramoney
152. MacAfee
153. McAfee of Bootown
154. McDuffee
155. Wilson of Tullaghgore
156. Kidd of Tullaghgore
157. McCurdy; Stewart
158. Wright of Culbrim
159. Calderwood
160. Wright of Culbrim
161. Wright, Andrew of Culbrim
162. Unreadable
163. Wylie of Artigoran
164. Unreadable
165. McMaster
166. McMaster
167. Brown; Taylor; Lyle
168. Hart of Culderry; Cristy
169. Getty of Taghey
170. Wright, Rev John of Donegore
171. Holmes of Ballymoney
172. Matthews of Craigatempin
173. Cooper of Kilmoyle; McCook
174. Cooper and Getty of Kilmoyle
175. Reynolds of Ballymoney
176. McKeesock of Ballymoney
177. Dorrans; Millar; Sandford of Ballymoney
178. Taylor
179. Forsythe of Forttown; Brown; Wallace
180. Neill, William of Druckendult
181. Neill of Druckendult
182. McKeag, Rev. Patrick
183. Beckett
184. Beckett, Philip of Lislagan

185. Beckett of Drumart
186. Long of Ballymoney
187. Hay of Ballymoney
188. Haltridge; McQuillan of Ballymoney
189. Haltridge of Ballymoney
190. Camac of Garry
191. Baird of Ballymoney
192. Hamill, Daniel of Heagles
193. Boyle, Thomas of Topp
194. Campbell of Topp
195. Boyle of Cubbindale
196. Smith of Bendooragh
197. Smyth, Marey
198. Lyons of Heagles; Leslie
199. Lyons of Drumaheglis
200. Smoll (Small) of Ballymoney
201. Cassidy of Garryduff
202. Magill; Mackey
203. Moore of Drumaheglis
204. Douglas; Moore of Drumaheglis
205. Moore of Burnquarter
206. Kennedy, J
207. Darcus of Ballybrakes
208. Small, Joseph of Ballywattick
209. Small, John of Ballywattick
210. Small, William of Ballymoney and Ballywattick
211. Small of Kilmoyle
212. Rosborough of Ballymoney
213. Small of Kilmoyle
214. Campbell of Ballymoney
215. Adams; Moore of Fernalisery
216. White of Ballymoney
217. Moore, David of Ballyboyland
218. Calderwood
219. Shields; Morrison
220. McCutcheon
221. McCutcheon
222. Hamilton; McCurdy of Ballymoney
223. McCurdy
224. Hamilton, James of Moneygobbin
225. Hamilton, Alexander and Hugh
226. Hamilton of Moneygobbin; Stewart
227. Campbell
228. Hamill, Neal of Ballywattick
229. Johnston; Jordan; Kelly of Ballymoney
230. Boyd; Hopkins; Jordan; Stewart of Ballymoney
231. Beers of Ballymoney
232. Mitchell, Thomas of Ballymoney
233. Unreadable
234. Ferguson; Stafford of Drumskea
235. Hunter of Ballymoney, late Bushmills
236. Erskine, Adam of Dunaverney
237. Erskine; Stuart of Dunaverney
238. Erskine of Dunaverney
239. Given of Ballymoney
240. Gamble and Given of Ballymoney
241. Agnew, Niven
242. Campbell
243. Andrews; Boyd; Patterson
244. Cochran, William of Ballygan
245. McDowell of Ballymoney
246. McAyeale, Mary of Tullaghgore

247. Boyd of Ballymoney
248. Boyd of Ballymoney
249. Hamilton; Gilmore of Ballymoney
250. Hamilton of Ballymoney; Kinnear
251. Hamilton of Ballymoney
252. Taggart, Jenny
253. Neill, John
254. Neill, Thomas
255. Doherty
256. Mitchell of Ballymoney
257. Toland of Secon; Elder
258. Jamison of Ballymoney
259. Unreadable
260. Stirling of Ballygobbin
261. Stirling of Ballygobbin
262. Stirling of Ballygobbin; Kelly
263. Unreadable
264. Dixon of Culduff
265. Boyd of Culbrim; Scot
266. Hutchinson
267. McCaw of Ballymoney
268. Leslie of Prospect and Leslie Hill
269. Leslie, Jas
270. Leslie, James Edmund
271. Leslie, Col E.D.
271a. Leslie, Col E.D.
272. Knox, Hugh of Secon
273. Wallace of Booton
274. Wallace, Thomas of Booton
275. Young, Mary
276. Murphy, James of Ballymoney
277. Crozier of Ballymoney
278. Henry, Alexander of Ballymoney
279. McCook; Hart
280. Knox, Robert of Currysiskin
281. Knox, William of Currysisken
282. Taylor, Isaac; Thompson
283. Hill, Adam
284. Borland of Landhead
285. Richart, William
286. Thompson of Ballymoney
286a. Thompson of Ballymoney
287. Caldwell
288. Caldwell of Currysisken
289. Biggart of Cabra
290. Biggart of Cabra
291. Biggart of Cabra
292. Griffith, Benjamin of Ballymoney
293. Fynes of Ballymoney
294. Knox, William
295. Gamble, Thomas of Ballymoney
296. Gamble, Alexander of Ballymoney; McIlrevy
297. Gamble; McClure of Ballymoney
298. McIlrevy of Booton
299. McBride of Ballymoney
300. Picken of Taughey
301. McIntyre
302. Ramsay, Adam of Dunaverney
303. Ramsay, James of Culramoney
304. Hannah, Matilda
305. Ramsay, William of Culramoney
306. Galbreath, Hector of Druckendult

307. Adams of Ballymoney
308. Hutchinson, Dobbin
309. Templeton
310. Black of Glenstall
311. Unreadable
312. Mitchell, John of Ballymoney
313. Cameron, Archibald of Ballymoney
314. Gamble, Robert of Ballymoney
315. Gamble, Cochran of Ballymoney
316. Gamble; Barr; Adams of Polintamney, Claughey
317. Gamble, James
318. Gamble, Thomas of Claughey
319. Tweed; Kane of Eden
320. McDuffee of Moore Lodge
321. Rainey; McMaster of Bendooragh
322. McLaughlin, Daniel
323. O'Toy, Hugh of Ballygobbin
324. Hemphill, Matthew
325. Hemphill, Margaret of Culbrim
326. Wallace, Matthew
327. Gordon of Ballymoney
328. Cochrane of Drumart
329. Nickleson of Ballymoney
330. Snodgrass of Ballymoney
331. Henderson of Topp
332. Longmoor of Ballymoney
333. Pollock of Ballymoney
334. Pollock
335. McDonald of Artigoran
336. Mitchell of Ballinamore
337. Robinson of Newbuildings
338. Galloway; Curry of Ballymoney
339. Galloway; Leslie of Ballymoney
340. Boyd of Ballymoney
341. Megaw of Killyrammer
342. Freeman; Hargy of Ballymoney
343. McCann of Secon
344. Creek of Ballymoney
345. Love, Ephraim of Taghey
346. Love, Robert of Taghey
346a. McCandless of Coleraine
347. Love, Thomas;
348. Camac of Garry
349. Camac of Garry; Wales
350. Getty of Coldagh
351. Camac of Garry
351a. Comoc of Garry
352. Esdale
353. Stewart
354. McGarry
355. Moore; Brown of Cullermoney
356. Brown, James of Lisnamuck
357. Brown, Elizabeth
358. Boyd, David of Carnany
359. Given of Ballymoney
360. McLaughlin, Hugh of Carnany
361. Robinson of Newbuildings
362. Robinson of Newbuildings
363. Reney, William of Eden
364. Robinson of Newbuildings; Sinclair
365. Robinson of Culduff
366. Robinson of Newbuildings and Culduff

367. Henry of Bravellan
367a. Henry of Bravellan; Boyd; Johnston
367b. Henry of Bravellan; Johnston
368. Hay of Ballybrake
369. Unreadable
370. Keasey of Taghey
371. Cramsie of Ballymoney
372. Cameron, Angus of Portrush
373. Cameron, Daniel of Ballymoney
374. Cameron, Daniel of Ballymoney
375. Cameron, William John of Ballymoney
376. Orr of Ladeside; Boyd; Young
377. Faloon, James of Ballymoney and Inchinagh
378. Hargy of Ballymoney
379. Clements
380. Harrison, Daniel; Noalen
381. Smiley, Hugh of Balnamore
382. Smiley of Balnamore
383. Hannah of Drumaheglis
384. Brown, James of Ballywattick
385. Culbertson of Artigoran
386. Gamble of Ballymoney
387. Culbertson of Ballymoney; Young of Trench
388. McElroy of Ballymoney
389. Vacant
390. No name
391. Galloway of Ballymoney
392. Young; Bateson; McCook of Ballymoney
393. Young of Ballymoney
394. Young of Ballymoney
395. McIlhair of Ballygobbin
396. Shannon of Ballymoney
397. Unreadable
398. McDonald
399. Leslie, Thomas of Balnamore
400. Unreadable
401. Chestnut, John of Ballygan
402. Cochrane, Hugh
403. White
404. Allen; Howard; McLaughlin
405. Forbes of Ballymoney
406. McMichael, Charles of Ballymoney
407. Thomson of Ballygobbin
408. Thomson, Olivia of Ballymoney
409. Beckett, Catherine of Balnamore
410. Beckett, Sarah of Balnamore
411. Huston
412. Dunlop
413. Getty, David of Kirkmoyle
414. McKeag, Andrew of Ballywindland
415. McKeag of Ballywindland
416. Culbert
417. Drain, McKeague of Ballymoney
418. Camac of Garry
419. Dick, Robert of Garry
420. Dick, of Garry
421. Wilson, Margaret
422. O'Hara